# RHETORIC FOR LEGAL WRITERS

## THE THEORY AND PRACTICE OF ANALYSIS AND PERSUASION

■ ■ ■

By

## Kristen Konrad Robbins–Tiscione

*Professor, Legal Research and Writing*
*Georgetown University Law Center*
*Washington, D.C.*

**AMERICAN CASEBOOK SERIES**®

**WEST**®

A Thomson Reuters business

Mat #40224781

© 2009 Thomson Reuters
    610 Opperman Drive
    St. Paul, MN 55123
    1–800–313–9378
Printed in the United States of America

**ISBN:** 978–0–314–15184–1

TEXT IS PRINTED ON 10% POST CONSUMER RECYCLED PAPER

*To Nick, who is everything.*

# PREFACE

The goal of this book, as more fully described in Chapter One, is to fuse rhetorical theory and the practice of legal writing. It is divided into two main sections. The first section focuses on rhetorical theory and its impact on legal argument from the time of ancient Greece to date. The second section focuses on practical applications of rhetorical theory to the specific task of learning to think and write like a practicing lawyer in the twenty-first century.

The book is intended for first-year law students, advanced legal writing students, law students interested in a seminar on rhetoric, and writing professors interested in introducing more substance into the teaching of writing. I have attempted to include in one volume the most important concepts a law student needs to learn to analyze and argue effectively. Recognizing that no one volume can hope to be exhaustive in its treatment of such a broad subject, I refer students to additional reading material throughout the book. The only subject I specifically did not attempt to include in the book is the mechanics of legal research, although I do discuss research from a conceptual point of view in Chapter Five. First year law students will benefit most by reading both the theoretical and practical chapters of the book, with an emphasis on the latter. Advanced legal writing and seminar students might be more interested in exploring the information and ideas raised in the theoretical chapters. Seminar paper topics could come from these chapters and cited source materials.

I do not profess to be an expert in either philosophy or rhetoric, nor do I think expertise in these areas is required to use this book. Although Chapters Two and Three trace the evolution of philosophy and its impact on rhetoric, the book is designed for legal writing students, not students in the Classics. Chapter Four discusses in detail the substance of classical rhetoric: invention, arrangement, and style. These beginning chapters provide the historical context law students need to understand why lawyers argue the way they do and what makes analysis sound and argument effective. Like good lawyers, good teachers should not be afraid to admit when they do not know something. Using the questions for consideration that appear throughout the book, student and teacher can learn together about the philosophy, history and ethics of legal argument.

The second half of the book uses the classical canons of rhetoric as a framework for discussing legal writing. Chapter Five explores in detail the process of inventing arguments based on reason: collecting information through research, synthesizing rules of law and learning to create deductive arguments that are logical. Chapter Six focuses on arguments based on emotion and the importance of learning to appeal to one's audience. Chapter Seven discusses the need to be ethical—credible and trustworthy—in one's writing in order to be persuasive. Chapter Eight focuses on the canon of arrangement in the context of legal memoranda and brief writing. Finally, Chapter Nine addresses style in legal writing, including the need to be clear and concise, adhere to legal writing conventions, to follow basic rules of grammar, usage, and punctuation, and to cite correctly to legal authority.

KRISTEN K. ROBBINS-TISCIONE

Professor, Legal Research and Writing

Georgetown University Law Center

Washington, D.C.

May 2009

# ACKNOWLEDGMENTS

One sabbatical, one research leave, and several summer writing grants helped make this book possible. I am grateful to **Dean Alexander Aleinikoff** for Georgetown University Law Center's financial support of my scholarship. I am also grateful to the following faculty and colleagues, whose advice and expertise proved invaluable:

*Noelle Adgerson,* Executive Assistant, Legal Research and Writing, Georgetown University Law Center

*Wayne Davis*, Philosophy Department Chair and Professor, Georgetown University

*Jennifer Locke Davitt,* Head of Faculty Services, Georgetown Law Library, Georgetown University Law Center

*Vicki Girard*, Professor, Legal Research and Writing, Georgetown University Law Center

*Dee Konrad,* Professor of English, Barat College

*Heather McCabe*, Associate Professor, Legal Research and Writing, Georgetown University Law Center

*Anna Selden*, Assistant Director, Office of Faculty Support and Campus Services, Georgetown University Law Center

*Louis Michael Seidman*, Carmack Waterhouse Professor of Constitutional Law, Georgetown University Law Center

*Robin West*, Frederick J. Haas Professor of Law and Philosophy, Georgetown University Law Center

I thank my tireless research assistants, **Amanda Rome, Gabriel Lerner (in memoriam), Margaret Engoren, Jonathan Ammons,** and **Rex Winter**, whose hard work and enthusiasm for the book helped sustain me. Finally, I thank my husband for his unflagging belief in me and my ability to complete this project.

*If ancient Greece and Rome are dust,*
*we are but wind to keep them aloft.*

# SUMMARY OF CONTENTS

*PRACTICAL APPLICATIONS OF RHETORICAL THEORY
TO LEGAL WRITING*

# TABLE OF CONTENTS

# RHETORIC FOR LEGAL WRITERS:

## THE THEORY AND PRACTICE OF ANALYSIS AND PERSUASION

# CHAPTER 1

## WHY RHETORIC AND WHY NOW . . . AGAIN?

■ ■ ■

*"For most lawyers, there is simply more going on in the creation of sound and convincing arguments than they can intuit in the pressure-filled context of law school and legal practice."*—George D. Gopen

Only a law student understands how it is possible to take a course in contracts and still not know how to draft one. Law schools think of themselves as preparing students to think like lawyers, not to practice law. A tax law student might read a series of judicial opinions and craft a theory about the goals of tax law and the relative success of the tax code in achieving those goals. However, classroom discussions are more likely to focus on the propriety of engineering social change through income taxation than on what forms an S corporation must file. In contrast, clinical courses—those that involve writing, advocacy, and student representation—do teach practical lawyering skills. Just as the core law school curriculum tends to ignore the practical implications of what it teaches, clinical courses tend to ignore the theory that informs them. To become a good legal writer, though, one must fuse the theory and practice of argument. Only then does a legal writer have depth—the ability to analyze an issue effectively using all available resources—as well as breadth—the ability to transfer her talent from one context to another.

Because most matriculating law students intend to practice law in some fashion, the question arises why law schools do not feel obliged to prepare their students for it. The answer is more complicated than you might think. First, law faculties as a whole tend to be comprised of scholars, not practitioners. Although most law teachers in the nineteenth century were practicing lawyers, a conscious choice was made at the turn of the twentieth century to switch to legal scholars instead. That decision was first made by Harvard Law School's Dean, Charles Langdell, and most schools quickly followed Harvard's lead. Langdell believed that law should be taught more like science than art, and he thought scholars were more qualified to teach it that way. The notion of law as science had its roots in the work of seventeenth century philosophers such as Francis Bacon and the revolutionary thinking they engendered. Bacon

1

and others had argued that knowledge is not acquired by reasoning logically, as had been assumed, but inductively. In Bacon's view, logic is useful but can only demonstrate the relationship between things that are already known. True knowledge, he argued, is acquired only through a systematic method of careful observation that leads from particular observations to more general conclusions. Bacon fundamentally altered man's view of the world, propelling him toward the Scientific Age and the industrialization of the Western world. Against this backdrop, the allure of a scientific method for teaching law students is easy to understand. Langdell's vision was that students would discover true principles of law by reading a series of cases and making general conclusions based on their systematic observations.

The major shift in legal pedagogy that followed also contributed to the modern law school's emphasis on legal theory. In conjunction with an inductive approach to teaching law, Langdell introduced the Socratic teaching method. Instead of asking students to recite the law found in treatises, he questioned them about the cases they had read for class and encouraged them to think for themselves—to articulate and critique the court's reasoning. At first, students were opposed to Langdell's method because he was not teaching them black letter law. Despite these complaints, Langdell convinced his students that his approach was worthwhile, and students gradually accepted it. Without questioning the assumption that "true" principles of law actually exist,[1] several law schools, including Columbia, Northwestern, Cornell, and Stanford, had switched to the case method by the mid–1890s.

The adoption of a truth-seeking, Socratic approach to legal education was monumental because it permanently changed the conception of law school as a trade school to law school as a philosophical endeavor. Langdell's successors soon realized that Langdell's method was better for teaching legal reasoning (*i.e.,* how to *think* like lawyers) than deducing true principles of law, but the Socratic method persisted. Although most legal scholars no longer believe that rules of law exist apart from their cultural, social, and political roots, traditional law faculties still function largely as truth finders in the classroom, urging students to participate meaningfully in a quest for the truth about law, with little regard for the students' ability to practice it. Although most law schools offer some form of clinical education, these courses emerged more in spite of than in furtherance of the traditional law school's mission. Clinics first appeared in the late 1960s in response to pressure from students and the practicing bar to provide pro bono legal services for their communities, not as the result of the schools' conviction that they were a necessary component of legal education. Soon thereafter, in the mid–1970s, legal writing programs emerged in response to the poor writing skills of incoming students and outside pressure from the bar to provide students with practical writing instruction.

Just as traditional law classes have failed to apply theory to practice,

---

1.    The assumption that true principles of law exist independent of those who frame them was not seriously questioned until the 1920s and 1930s. *See infra,* p. 83.

clinical courses—particularly legal research and writing—often fail to consult their theoretical underpinnings. As a novice teacher, I noticed myself teaching writing more as imitation than a skill grounded in argumentation theory. I told my students what to do—draft a legal memorandum, for example—and then sent them off to do it, but the look on some of their faces was nothing short of terrified. It was as if I had shown them a video clip of sky divers and then sent them up for their first jump with no instruction in between. That's when I knew I was not giving my students enough context to understand what they were doing or why they were doing it that way. My frustration with many good legal writing books is the same: they explain or show what a typical memorandum or brief should look like, but they often fail to explain why lawyers write the way they do or how to emulate them. The end result? Both teacher and students feel frustrated and discouraged.

Having identified the nature of my teaching problem, I was at a loss for the theory that explained what I knew intuitively but could not articulate. Like most lawyers, I had learned to write "on the job"; I got indirect feedback on my writing in the form of senior attorneys' revisions and took my cues from them as to what made for good legal writing. This approach may have been sufficient for drafting my own briefs, but it was wholly inadequate for teaching. Thus I began to research in earnest the subject of "good legal writing" and happily stumbled upon rhetoric, a discipline as complex and influential as philosophy that I knew absolutely nothing about. As soon as I found it, I knew it was the answer. The question was why didn't I know about it sooner?

As you will learn, rhetoric unites all practical aspects of lawyering. It is the study of persuasion, and Aristotle is credited with first articulating its principles in the fourth century BCE. As Aristotle conceived it, rhetoric involves the discovery, creation, arrangement, and presentation of all forms of argument, including legal argument. Aristotle considered rhetoric the intellectual equal and counterpart to philosophy, and he wrote books on both subjects. Aristotle believed that philosophy seeks universal truth, whereas rhetoric seeks to persuade. Attorneys marshal and present their best arguments to a jury as to why a defendant should or should not be considered liable. In the face of conflicting evidence and competing arguments, there is no right or true answer to this question, but rhetoric enables the jury to reach the "best truth" under the circumstances. Aristotle's teacher, Plato, criticized rhetoric because it cannot produce certain truth. Because rhetoric can be used to argue for evil as well as good outcomes, Plato distrusted it. Even then, rhetoric had a reputation for distorting truth, and it has struggled for respect ever since.

The primary reason lawyers know next to nothing about rhetoric is that by the 1900s, it had virtually disappeared from all levels of education in the United States. As you now know, it never made its way into legal education. At one time, rhetoric was taught alongside logic (what we now think of as philosophy), as a coherent discipline involving the creation, arrangement, and expression of arguments designed to persuade. During the Renaissance, the French humanist

Peter Ramus argued that to the extent rhetoric and philosophy overlapped, they should be separated into discrete disciplines. According to Ramus, the creation and arrangement of argument belonged to philosophy, and the style and delivery of argument belonged to rhetoric. "Ramism" had an enormous impact on education in England, Spain, France, and the New World. Harvard College modeled its curriculum on Ramus' views in 1636. The effect was to strip rhetoric of much of its intellectual substance; what remained was seen as the manipulation of language or speech-making. With no coherent discipline left, the teaching of these skills was distributed among English, Speech, and Communications departments.

Rhetoric is an intellectual endeavor that combines the creation, arrangement, and expression of ideas. A return to rhetoric as the counterpart of philosophy is invaluable for the modern legal writer. Just as the teaching of classical rhetoric combined theory and practice to teach persuasive argument, I have struggled to combine the theory and practice of legal writing in a way that is both unique and helpful. This book is the culmination of that struggle. My goal has always been to help students engage in sophisticated legal analysis and produce better legal writing. Good thinking begets good writing, and good thinking requires a conceptual understanding of the process in which one is engaged. In my view, the demand for better teaching in this field increases exponentially, as students come to law school with increasingly deficient research and writing skills, and the "pressure-filled" pace of legal practice approaches light speed.

The book is divided into two major sections: the first section (Chapters Two through Four) summarizes the history of rhetoric and rhetorical theory and its relationship to legal argument. It also describes how logic (as opposed to rhetoric) came to dominate university education during the Middle Ages, and the effect that shift in emphasis has had on modern legal education. Finally, it discusses the canons or substance of rhetoric itself (*i.e.*, the methodology of good legal argument). The second section (Chapters Five through Nine) examines each of the traditional canons of rhetoric as they relate to the legal writer's task to create, arrange, and write persuasive analysis and argument.

---

### QUESTIONS FOR CONSIDERATION

1. **Did it surprise you that law school is more theoretical than practical in its approach?**

2. **Did you know there is a distinct discipline called rhetoric devoted to the art of persuasion? Did you expect to learn about it in law school?**

3. **What do you expect to learn in a legal writing course? How do you think it will differ from any other writing course you have taken?**

4. What are the strengths and weaknesses in your writing? What aspect of your writing process needs work? Why?

5. How would you characterize the nature of your writing— scholarly, scientific, creative, etc.? To what extent do you think legal writing will differ?

# THE THEORETICAL UNDERPINNINGS
## OF LEGAL ARGUMENT

■ ■ ■

# CHAPTER 2

## A SHORT HISTORY OF RHETORIC

■ ■ ■

*"From Rome rhetoric, in education, in public activity, and in all forms of writing, spread through the world, its influence waning only in the nineteenth century."*—Brian Vickers

The word "rhetoric" has been used for centuries to mean so many things that its original meaning is lost in modern, everyday usage. Today, it can mean everything from the noble pursuit of good citizenship to manipulative or often empty, political speech. The root word comes from the Greek words *rhema*, which means "word," and *rhetor*, which means public speaker. The English word comes from the Greek phrase *rhetorike techne*, which translates into rhetorical art, and the French noun *rhetorique*.[1] Despite its varied connotations, rhetoric here refers to the art of persuasion through eloquent, inventive, and strategically organized discourse, both oral and written.

Rhetoric, or oratory as the ancients called it, emerged first in Sicily in 466 BCE. The citizens of Syracuse had revolted against a tyrant and attempted to recover land he had stolen from them. In response to the citizens' need to represent themselves in court, Corax of Syracuse taught them rhetoric. He may even have written a textbook on the subject.[2] Corax thus launched one of the most controversial and complex disciplines known to man. Great philosophers, rhetoricians, clerics, humanists, logicians, psychologists, linguists, and others have devoted lifelong careers to understanding the power of language and debating its rightful use in organized society. In conjunction, scholars have debated the ability of rhetoric to produce knowledge or truth with any level of certainty. The great philosopher Plato was the first to argue that rhetoric could produce only probable truth and, for that reason, was inferior to philosophy, the quest for universal truth. Although the question of rhetoric's value was first raised by Plato in the fourth century BCE, the debate that ensued is alive and well today.

---

1. EDWARD P.J. CORBETT & ROBERT J. CONNORS, CLASSICAL RHETORIC FOR THE MODERN STUDENT 15 (4th ed. 1999).

2. *See* THE OXFORD CLASSICAL DICTIONARY 388 (SIMON HORNBLOWER & ANTONY SPAWFORTH, eds., 3d ed. 1996). *See also* DANIEL FOGARTY, ROOTS FOR A NEW RHETORIC 9–10 (1959); BRIAN VICKERS, IN DEFENCE OF RHETORIC 6 (1988).

As you read about the history of rhetorical theory and the purposes for which rhetoric evolved, two things should become clear. First, it is fair to say that scholars who have practiced or studied law have made some of the greatest contributions to rhetorical theory. That alone makes rhetoric worthy of study for law students. Second, rhetoric developed specifically to teach advocacy, the mainstay of the legal profession. Although rhetoric examines persuasion in a variety of contexts, its focus has always been on judicial rhetoric (*i.e.*, legal argument). Because rhetoric is so broad a subject, an exhaustive history is neither possible nor desirable here. Instead, this chapter summarizes the history and evolution of rhetoric in relation to legal argument. The extent to which this rich history informs legal argument today cannot be overestimated.

# A. ANCIENT GREECE AND ROME
# (c. 466 BCE—50 CE)

Rhetoric first emerged as a discipline in ancient Greece, but not even the Greeks claimed to have invented it. Scholars like Corax believed that a talented man's natural ability to speak persuasively could be observed, articulated, and taught as an art form. In educating students of rhetoric, both the Greeks and Romans looked first to Homer, the great Greek poet, for examples of rhetorical skill. Homer's accounts of the Trojan War in the *Iliad* and the *Odyssey* were written c. 800 BCE, a good 300 years before Corax. The study of rhetoric thus emerged first in the fifth century BCE as a codification of the skills already honed by poets and orators alike, and this codification came about as the result of a massive legal dispute.

## 1. THE GREEKS

In the mid–400s, a Greek tyrant named Thrasybulus confiscated land from citizens living in and around Syracuse, an island town in modern day Sicily, Italy. In 466, they revolted against Thrasybulus and established a democracy. Many citizens then filed lawsuits claiming title to the land he had stolen. There was no direct evidence to support the citizens' claims, and they had to rely on circumstantial evidence. Corax recognized that the citizen plaintiffs needed help to persuade the jury, and he created a system of rules for arranging and arguing their cases. Corax's greatest contribution to the development of rhetoric is thought to be his outline for judicial argument: proem (introduction), narration (statement of facts), argument (both for and in anticipation of counter-arguments), and peroration (conclusion).[3] This basic pattern is used today in all forms of legal analysis and argument. Twenty-first century law students often encounter this pattern when writing their first objective legal memorandum that predicts the outcome of a hypothetical legal dispute.

There were no law schools, lawyers, or judges in ancient Greece. The parties

---

**3.**    *See* THE OXFORD CLASSICAL DICTIONARY, *supra* note 2, at 388; CORBETT & CONNORS, *supra* note 1, at 490.

argued their own cases. Since there were no government prosecutors, private citizens tried criminal cases too. A trial consisted of one or two speeches given by each of the parties. If a party did not feel qualified to prepare his own speech, he hired a logographer, a writer of courtroom speeches. He then memorized the speech and delivered it to a jury that could contain up to 500 men. Many handbooks, like the one Corax probably wrote, helped guide the Greek citizenry on how to win the jurors' favor.

There were also philosopher-teachers, known as sophists, who traveled among the Greek city-states. They taught rhetoric and other subjects to the sons of wealthy families and those who could afford their services. The early Greek sophists included Protagoras, Gorgias, Hippias, and Isocrates. "Sophos" translates into knowledge or expert, and a "sophist" was a respected teacher who imparted valuable knowledge. Because Greek society revolved around the spoken word and direct participation in civic affairs, sophists were thought to prepare their students to participate in politics and serve the common good. Philosophers like Plato, however, objected to the sophists because they could argue either side of a dispute without regard to its truth or rectitude. The sophists, on the other hand, were not troubled by a jury finding that was inconsistent with the facts because they believed the jury defined what was true and right. In combination with some sophists' questionable ethics in taking spurious cases, the sophists' success converted the word "sophist" from a compliment to an insult. Today, the dictionary defines a sophist as "a person who uses clever but false arguments."[4]

Rhetoric thus originated as a method of studying legal argument and developed into a profession devoted to writing courtroom speeches. Although criticized from the outset for enabling opportunism in the courtroom and disregarding justice and truth, rhetoric quickly expanded to new fields. Soon, rhetoric was championed as a tool to enhance the general welfare of the Greek polis through eloquent and persuasive political involvement, a necessary component of education, and a stepping stone to a leisurely life.

## a. GORGIAS (483–378 BCE)

Gorgias brought the art of rhetoric to mainland Greece. In 427 BCE, he moved from Sicily to Athens because Athens was the intellectual and financial center of Greece. *See Figure 1, p. 13.* Like many sophists, he taught rhetoric and gave public speeches to demonstrate his rhetorical skill, but he preferred the title rhetorician to sophist precisely because of its negative connotations. His elaborate speaking style appealed to Athenians, who found it both intellectual and aesthetically pleasing. However, the clever and ornate speech that appealed to Athenians also made it vulnerable to attack by Plato, who accused Gorgias of elevating form over substance in speechmaking. Plato also accused the sophists of appealing to the base pleasures of the Greek audience and ignoring what was true and good in favor of the audience's self-interest. Although there is some

---

4.   *See, e.g.,* THE OXFORD COMPACT ENGLISH DICTIONARY 1098 (Catherine Soanes ed., 2d ed. 2003).

indication that the sophists manipulated their audiences, the degree to which they were criticized in Greek culture was due primarily to Plato's disparagement of them.[5]

## b. ISOCRATES (436–338 BCE)

Isocrates is considered one of the "ten great Attic orators" of classical Greece and was known for his pure and simple writing style.[6] He is thought to have been a student of Socrates, Plato, and Gorgias. Although he was not a great public speaker himself, Isocrates began his career as a courtroom speechwriter, and he went on to write political speeches as well. Although his *Art of Rhetoric* is lost, about six courtroom speeches, fifteen political speeches, and nine letters survive. In c. 393, Isocrates founded the first permanent institution of higher learning in Athens, predating Plato's Academy by almost six years. He was the most influential and well-known teacher of oratory for almost fifty years. Isocrates died at the age of 98, supposedly having starved himself to death when the Macedonians invaded and occupied Athens in 338 BCE.

Known as a sophist, Isocrates too eschewed that title, comparing himself instead to the early sophists, who were "the best and most renowned orators [and] were responsible for the greatest goods in Athens."[7] In a letter entitled *Against the Sophists*, he questioned the value of his contemporaries' teachings because they charged so little for their services.[8] Unlike many of the sophists, who were sympathetic to the wealthy oligarchs, Isocrates was a great believer in democracy.[9] He devoted himself to teaching young Athenians to be good citizens through speechmaking and writing. "People improve and become worthier," he wrote, "if they are interested in speaking well, have a passion for being able to persuade their audience, and also desire advantage."[10]

---

5.    In Plato's dialogue, *Gorgias*, Socrates says, "Well then, Gorgias, I think there's a practice that's not craftlike, but one that a mind given to making hunches takes to, a mind that's bold and naturally clever at dealing with people. I call it flattery, basically." Plato, Complete Works ¶ 463b (John M. Cooper ed., 1997).

6.    The "ten Attic orators" describes a group of native Greek orators from the province of Attica in the fourth and fifth centuries. Their speeches were included in the Alexandrian canon, a list compiled by Aristophanes of Byzantium, the librarian of the Alexandrian Library, in roughly 195 BCE. The ten Attic orators were Aeschines, Demosthenes, Lysias, Hyperides, Isocrates, Lycurgus, Isaeus, Antiphon, Andocides, and Dinarchus. The Oxford Classical Dictionary, *supra* note 2, at 212.

7.    Isocrates, *Antidosis*, in 1 Isocrates 247, ¶ 231 (Michael Gagarin ed., David Mirhady & Yun Lee Too trans., 2000).

8.    *Against the Sophists*, in 1 Isocrates, *supra* note 7, at 62, ¶ 3.

9.    *Antidosis*, in 1 Isocrates, *supra* note 7, at 247–62, ¶¶ 231–315.

10.   *Id.* at 275.

# ANCIENT GREECE AND ROME

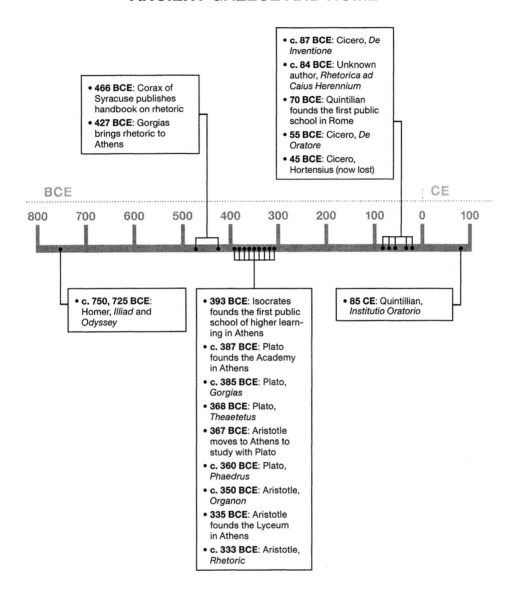

- **c. 87 BCE**: Cicero, *De Inventione*
- **c. 84 BCE**: Unknown author, *Rhetorica ad Caius Herennium*
- **70 BCE**: Quintilian founds the first public school in Rome
- **55 BCE**: Cicero, *De Oratore*
- **45 BCE**: Cicero, Hortensius (now lost)

- **466 BCE**: Corax of Syracuse publishes handbook on rhetoric
- **427 BCE**: Gorgias brings rhetoric to Athens

BCE                                                                    CE

800   700   600   500   400   300   200   100    0    100

- **c. 750, 725 BCE**: Homer, *Illiad* and *Odyssey*

- **393 BCE**: Isocrates founds the first public school of higher learning in Athens
- **c. 387 BCE**: Plato founds the Academy in Athens
- **c. 385 BCE**: Plato, *Gorgias*
- **368 BCE**: Plato, *Theaetetus*
- **367 BCE**: Aristotle moves to Athens to study with Plato
- **c. 360 BCE**: Plato, *Phaedrus*
- **c. 350 BCE**: Aristotle, *Organon*
- **335 BCE**: Aristotle founds the Lyceum in Athens
- **c. 333 BCE**: Aristotle, *Rhetoric*

- **85 CE**: Quintillian, *Institutio Oratorio*

## FIGURE 1

Isocrates agreed with Plato that rhetoric was often used to manipulate juries, and he criticized Corax and others who professed to fix in writing "the rules" of courtroom oratory:

They promised to teach lawcourt skills and picked out the most wretched of terms, which those opposing this education ought to have used, not those supporting it. Inasmuch as it was teachable, these terms belong to a subject that could be of no greater help for lawcourt speeches than for any others.[11]

As far as Isocrates was concerned, there are no fixed rules for the art of oratory, and anyone who professes to know them is not to be trusted.

Isocrates was the first to combine theory and practice in teaching oratory. Prior to Isocrates, students would read and analyze speeches, but they did not actually write or deliver their own speeches.[12] Isocrates recognized that in order for a student to be successful, he not only had to possess natural ability and learn the principles (as opposed to the rules) of effective speech, he had to practice, practice, and then practice some more. Isocrates said:

> In addition to having the requisite natural ability, the student must learn the forms of speeches and practice their uses. The teacher must go through these aspects as precisely as possible, so that nothing teachable is left out, but as for the rest, he must offer himself as a model, so that those who are molded by him and can imitate him will immediately appear more florid and graceful than others.[13]

Isocrates relied heavily on imitation and models as teaching tools. Using repetition and imitation of texts (such as Homer's *Iliad* or speeches that Isocrates wrote), he prepared students to handle a wide range of situations in public life.[14]

## c. PLATO (427–347 BCE)

Although Isocrates criticized the sophists for manipulating audiences, Plato was their greatest critic. Plato was born in Athens in the same year that Gorgias arrived. Plato studied with Socrates, a famous teacher of philosophy, as a young man and throughout Socrates' life. In c. 387, Plato opened his own school of philosophy, Plato's Academy, which survived for nine hundred years. Plato dedicated his life to discovering truth and rejecting what he considered to be the false rhetoric of his day, which he found embodied in the teachings of the sophists. According to Plato, oratory appealed to man's base desires and served the interests of politicians, whom he despised. Born to wealthy and influential parents, Plato was no proponent of democracy. Unlike Isocrates, Plato believed the public was ignorant and lacked self-control. What he perceived as the corruption of Greek society, he attributed to the weakness of the public.

Plato used the singular teaching method—the dialogue or "dialectic"—he had learned from Socrates. Plato believed that the only way to discover truth was to exchange ideas with another scholar. Oratory, on the other hand, was designed to persuade, not to discover truth. At best, it could produce opinion only (as in the verdict of a jury). Since Plato valued truth, not opinion, he thought oratory and its study were largely irrelevant. These views are well-documented

11. *Against the Sophists, in* 1 ISOCRATES, *supra* note 7, at 19–20.

12. *See* TAKIS POULAKOS, SPEAKING FOR THE POLIS 97–98 (1997) ("Isocrates ... contests the dominant trends in educational activities of his times: the emphasis on acquisition of knowledge over its use, mastery of a field of study over its practical application, expertise over experience.").

13. *Against the Sophists, in* 1 ISOCRATES, *supra* note 7, at 17–18.

14. *See* EKATERINA V. HASKINS, LOGOS AND POWER IN ISOCRATES AND ARISTOTLE 45–46 (2004).

in several of his dialogues, particularly *Gorgias*, *Phaedrus*, and *Theaetetus*.[15] In *Gorgias*, for example, Plato developed his idea that oratory is merely a form of flattery and not a substantive art.[16] In a dialogue between Socrates and Gorgias, Socrates states that oratory is an empty subject. To say the substance of oratory is persuasion is to say nothing because all subjects, such as arithmetic and astronomy, influence their audience through speech.[17] Gorgias replies that oratory is the kind of speech found in law courts and large gatherings and addresses the just and unjust.[18] Socrates disagrees because a skillful orator can convince an audience to believe in falsity and to act unjustly. As an example, Socrates cites an orator's ability to convince a jury to spare the life of a man whose crime warrants the death penalty.[19] In Socrates', and perhaps Plato's, view, rhetoric can provide only the illusion of justice.[20] Philosophy, on the other hand, seeks both truth and justice.[21]

Plato's disdain for rhetoric appears in *Phaedrus* as well, in which Socrates compares rhetoric to an evil and selfish form of love that serves only itself. Philosophy, on the other hand, is noble love because it seeks truth without regard to human manipulation.[22] Again, Socrates criticizes rhetoric because it enables the orator to argue either side of an argument. Since both sides of an argument cannot be right, truth is inevitably lost. With reference to courtroom oratory, Socrates tells Phaedrus:

> SOCRATES: What do adversaries do in the law courts? Don't they speak on opposite sides? What else can we call what they do?
>
> PHAEDRUS: That's it, exactly.
>
> SOCRATES: About what is just and what is unjust?
>
> PHAEDRUS: Yes.
>
> SOCRATES: And won't whoever does this artfully make the same thing appear to the same people sometimes just and sometimes, when he prefers, unjust?[23]

Plato was troubled not only by the orator's ability to argue in favor of opposing outcomes but also by his ability to argue on the basis of probability (*e.g.*, a preponderance of the evidence) instead of certainty. Socrates continues:

---

**15.** Plato's dialogues often featured his mentor, Socrates, and addressed major philosophical issues of concern to Plato such as morality, ethics, and virtue. *See, e.g.*, PLATO, COMPLETE WORKS, *supra* note 5.

**16.** Socrates states, "You've now heard what I say oratory is. It's the counterpart in the soul to pastry baking, its counterpart in the body." *Gorgias, in* PLATO, COMPLETE WORKS, *supra* note 5, at ¶ 465e.

**17.** *Id.* at ¶¶ 449d–450d.

**18.** *Id.* at ¶ 454b.

**19.** *Id.* at ¶¶ 481a-b.

**20.** *Id.* at ¶¶ 464b–465d.

**21.** *Id.* at ¶¶ 500b-e.

**22.** *Phaedrus in* PLATO, COMPLETE WORKS, *supra* note 5, at ¶¶ 237d–238c and 260a–261b.

**23.** *Id.* at ¶¶ 261c-d.

> [O]ne who intends to be an able rhetorician has no need to know the truth about the things that are just or good or yet about the people who are such either by nature or upbringing. No one in a lawcourt, you see, cares at all about the truth of such matters. They only care about what is convincing. This is called "the likely," and that is what a man who intends to speak according to art should concentrate on. Sometimes, in fact, whether you are prosecuting or defending a case, you must not even say what actually happened, if it was not likely to have happened—you must say something that is likely instead.[24]

This is the crux of Plato's problem with rhetoric. As a philosopher dedicated to discovering truth, he could not tolerate a process that did not purport to lead to certainty in a mathematical sense.

Nowhere is Plato's dislike of oratory more plain than in *Theaetetus,* in which Plato explored the nature of knowledge. Throughout the dialogue, Socrates tells Theaetetus that knowledge is something that ordinary men cannot perceive; it must be discerned by philosophers. In contrast, Socrates describes the life of an orator as a life spent "knocking about in law courts."[25] Orators are always in a hurry, he says, having to watch and worry about the clock, but a philosopher has no such time constraints. Because he has no jury or audience to convince, the philosopher is a free man.[26] Socrates goes on to say that because the courtroom orator works under such time pressure, his soul is

> small and warped. His early servitude prevents him from making a free, straight growth; it forces him into doing crooked things by imposing dangers and alarms upon a soul that is still tender. He cannot meet these by just and honest practice, and so resorts to lies and to the policy of repaying one wrong with another; thus he is constantly being bent and distorted, and in the end grows up to manhood with a mind that has no health in it, having now become—in his own eyes—a man of ability and wisdom. There is your practical man.[27]

Given Plato's influence on Western philosophical thought, is it any wonder that modern society is predisposed to dislike lawyers?[28]

## d. ARISTOTLE (384–322 BCE)

Aristotle was Plato's student, but he disagreed with Plato about the value of oratory. Aristotle was born in Macedonia and moved to Athens when he was seventeen years old to study at Plato's Academy. He studied at the Academy

---

**24.** *Id.* at ¶¶ 272d-e.

**25.** *Theatetus, in* PLATO, COMPLETE WORKS, *supra* note 5, at ¶ 172d.

**26.** *Id.* at ¶¶ 172d–173c.

**27.** *Id.* at ¶ 173a–b.

**28.** A generalized disdain for lawyers continued to permeate all Western culture, particularly great literature. *See, e.g.,* CHAUCER, *Prologue, in* CANTERBURY TALES, ll. 323–24 ("Nowhere a man so busy of his class, and yet he seemed much busier than he was."); WILLIAM SHAKESPEARE, THE SECOND PART OF KING HENRY VI act 4, sc. 2 ("The first thing we do, let's kill all the lawyers.").

for twenty years and began teaching oratory before Plato's death. Aristotle was not chosen to lead the Academy when Plato died in 347, and soon thereafter, he left Athens. In 342, he began teaching Alexander of Macedon, the son of Philip II, who became Alexander the Great.[29] Aristotle returned to Athens in 335 and established his own school of philosophy at the Lyceum, a gymnasium and garden with covered walkways that Aristotle was famous for pacing as he taught.[30] *See Figure 1, p. 13.* Aristotle devoted the rest of his life to studying, teaching and writing, and giving lectures both to selected students and the general public. In 323, when Alexander the Great died, Aristotle fled Athens to escape prosecution on charges of impiety. Aristotle died one year later on the island of Chalcis in Euboea at the age of 62.

In contrast to Plato, Aristotle believed in the value of "best truths" as well as certain truth. He devoted much of his career to observing and classifying all aspects of life, including human behavior. He wrote in the areas of logic, rhetoric, philosophy, ethics, astronomy, physics, biology, politics, and psychology. Some of his most famous works include *Organon* (c. 350) and *Rhetoric* (published c. 333). *Organon* is a collection of six separate works that explore the process of logical thinking as well as inventing argument.[31] Most important in the context of this book, *Organon* explores the nature of the syllogism, a formal type of deductive reasoning that often proceeds from general to specific conclusions.[32] Aristotle's teachings on the syllogism have had an immeasurable impact on the development of philosophical and rhetorical thought. *Rhetoric* is Aristotle's most definitive work on the subject of rhetoric and remains the most influential work ever written about it. A collection of lectures and teaching notes, *Rhetoric* discusses the force and value of rhetoric; the types of rhetoric, including judicial rhetoric; and the process by which a speaker best persuades the audience in a given circumstance.[33]

Aristotle defined rhetoric as the "faculty of discovering in the particular case what are the available means of persuasion. This is the function of no other art."[34] According to Aristotle, there are three basic ways to persuade:

> Of the means of persuasion supplied by the speech itself there are three kinds. The first kind reside in the character of the speaker; the second consist in producing a certain attitude in the hearer; the third appertain to

---

**29.** The Oxford Classical Dictionary, *supra* note 2, at 166.

**30.** *Id.* Aristotle's students were referred to as "the peripatetics," a Greek word meaning "walking up and down" (which Aristotle did as he taught). The Oxford Compact English Dictionary, *supra* note 4, at 840.

**31.** 1–2 Aristotle, The Organon, (Harold P. Cooke & Hugh Tredennick eds., 1960). The Organon includes Aristotle's *Categories, On Interpretation, Prior Analytics, Posterior Analytics, Topics,* and *On Sophistical Refutations.*

**32.** A common example of a syllogism is the following: Major premise: All men are mortal. Minor premise: Socrates is a man. Conclusion: Socrates is mortal. The syllogism and its relationship to legal argument are discussed in detail in ch. 5, *infra,* pp. 150–170.

**33.** *See infra,* ch. 4, at 100.

**34.** Aristotle, Rhetoric (c. 333), *reprinted in* The Rhetoric of Aristotle (Lane Cooper, trans., 1932).

the argument proper, in so far as it actually or seemingly demonstrates.[35] *See Figure 2, below*. He referred to these methods as appeals to *ethos* (the speaker's character), *pathos* (the audience's emotions), and *logos* (logic or reason). He criticized the sophists, not because they engaged in oratory, but because they relied too heavily on emotional appeals.[36]

| Artistic Appeals | Non-Artistic Appeals | Types of Rhetoric | Canons |
|---|---|---|---|
| • *Ethos*— appeal to speaker's character | • Witnesses<br><br>• Admissions under torture | • Deliberative (political)<br><br>• Forensic (judicial) | • Invention<br><br>• Arrangement<br><br>• Style |
| • *Pathos*— appeal to audience's emotions | • Written Contracts<br><br>• Oaths | • Epideictic (ceremonial) | • Memory<br><br>• Delivery |
| • *Logos*— appeal to logic or reason | | | |

### FIGURE 2

Echoing Plato's *Gorgias*,[37] Aristotle described rhetoric as "the counterpart of Dialectic."[38] He divided rhetoric into three types and articulated five stages or canons of the creative process. According to Aristotle, there are three types of rhetoric: deliberative (political), forensic (judicial), and epideictic (ceremonial).[39] The same process is used to create all three types: invention, arrangement, style, memory, and delivery. Aristotle defined *invention* as the process of "discovering" (creating) arguments that appeal to *ethos*, *pathos*, and *logos*.[40] These he called "artistic" as opposed to "inartistic" proofs, the latter being Aristotle's term for evidence.[41] The primary form of appeal to *logos* or logic is the syllogism. The second canon, *arrangement*, refers to the ordering of arguments, and Aristotle favored an introduction, statement of the issues, argument, and conclusion.[42] The next canon, *style*, refers to the nature of the writing, which Aristotle said

---

**35.** *Id.* at 8, ¶ 1356a.

**36.** *See id.* at bk. 1, chs. 1–2.

**37.** *See supra* note 16.

**38.** ARISTOTLE, *supra* note 34 at 1, ¶ 1354a.

**39.** *Id.* at 17, ¶ 1358b.

**40.** *See id.* at bk. 2, chs. 1–26, pp. 90–181.

**41.** *Id.* at 8, ¶ 1355b. The late eighteenth century epistemologists elevated witness testimony to artistic proof. *See infra*, pp. 51, 53, and 55.

**42.** *See* ARISTOTLE, *supra* note 34, at bk. 3, chs. 13–19, pp. 220–241.

should be appropriate to the purpose and audience of the speech.[43] Although Aristotle acknowledged the last two canons, *memory* and *delivery,* he devoted very little attention to either of them. Delivery was not seriously studied until the late eighteenth century.[44]

Aristotle valued rhetoric as a distinct discipline for the very reasons that Plato rejected it. In Aristotle's view, rhetoric serves justice because the clash of opposing views leads to truth, even if that truth is uncertain. Aristotle wrote:

> [T]he art of Rhetoric has its value. It is valuable, first, because truth and justice are by nature more powerful than their opposites; ... Thirdly, in Rhetoric, as in Dialectic, we should be able to argue on either side of a question; not with a view to putting both sides into practice—we must not advocate evil—but in order that no aspect of the case may escape us, and that if our opponent makes unfair use of the arguments, we may be able in turn to refute them.[45]

Although Aristotle was more interested in political rather than judicial rhetoric, he was fascinated by the nature of wrongdoing, the criminal mind, and the challenge of persuading a jury. Several chapters in *Rhetoric* explore these subjects.

Although Aristotle did not view the adversarial process as negatively as Plato did, he did express some concern about judges' ability to be objective. Aristotle thus advised the legislature[46] to anticipate in advance as many problematic situations as possible, in order to decrease the cases a judge would have to decide:

> [A] member ... of the court must decide present and individual cases, in which their personal likes and dislikes, and their private interests, are often involved, so that they cannot adequately survey the truth, but have their judgment clouded by their own pleasure or pain. On other points, then, we say the authority of the judge should be reduced as far as possible; but the decision whether a thing has or has not occurred, will or will not occur, is or is not so, must be left in the hands of those who judge, since for these matters the legislator cannot provide.[47]

Aristotle thus stressed that an orator should not "warp" a judge's opinion by appealing to his anger, jealousy, or compassion.[48]

---

**43.** *See id.* at bk. 3, chs. 1–12, pp. 182–219.

**44.** *See infra*, p. 58.

**45.** *Id.* at 6, ¶ 1355a.

**46.** In Athens, the legislature was called the Assembly and comprised of men who met in public to discuss matters of law and state.

**47.** *Id.* at 2–3, ¶ 1354b. See *infra*, p. 83, for a discussion about legal realism and the notion that judicial decisions are always subjective.

**48.** *Id.* at 2, ¶ 1354a.

## 2. THE ROMANS

The Romans were heavily influenced by the Greeks, and, as in so many things, they took Greek rhetorical theory and refined it. Unlike the Greeks, however, who were interested primarily in political speech, the Romans were interested primarily in legal argument. Most of the great Roman philosopher-orators were trained in rhetoric as well as law, and they emphasized the value of studying legal argument. Roman teachers of rhetoric were also different from their Greek predecessors in their practical approach to rhetoric and its usefulness in society. Both Cicero and Quintilian followed in Isocrates' footsteps, advocating the teaching and practice of rhetoric in the judicial and political arena. To these Romans, becoming an orator was a great achievement; to be an orator combined a mastery of philosophy, rhetoric, and the law with civic virtue.

### a. MARCUS TULLIUS CICERO (106–43 BCE)

Cicero is considered the greatest Roman orator. He was a successful lawyer and politician, and he wrote dozens of philosophical books and essays. Roughly sixty of his courtroom and political speeches survive today. He began his career in law, gaining notoriety through trying landmark cases and giving speeches. He was elected to each major office in the Republic, serving as a treasurer, judge, chief magistrate, and member of the Roman Senate. His works on rhetoric include *De Inventione*, *De Oratore*, and *Orator*.[49] *See Figure 1, p. 13.* Cicero single-handedly transformed the nature of public education in ancient Rome. In contrast to Isocrates, Cicero had a grand, eloquent style that served for hundreds of years as a model for students of rhetoric. As late as the nineteenth century, American lawyers and legislators were still emulating Cicero's style.

Cicero started his handbook on rhetoric, *De Inventione* (c. 87), when he was still a teenager. Although he intended to write about all five canons, he completed only the canon on invention, his primary interest. H.M. Hubbell, who translated it into English, stated, it "reads like a law book" because in ancient Rome, rhetoric "trained men entirely for speaking, and almost exclusively for speaking in the law court."[50] At the outset, Cicero defended rhetoric against Plato's criticisms:

> I find that many cities have been founded, that the flames of a multitude of wars have been extinguished, and that the strongest alliances and most sacred friendships have been formed not only by the use of reason but also more easily by the help of eloquence.... I have been led by reason itself to hold this opinion ... that wisdom without eloquence does too little for the good of states, but that eloquence without wisdom is generally highly disadvantageous and is never helpful.[51]

---

**49.** 2 CICERO, DE INVENTIONE (H.M. Hubbell trans., 1968) (c. 87 BCE); 3–4 CICERO, DE ORATORE, (E.W. Sutton trans., 1967) (c. 55 BCE); 5 CICERO, ORATOR (H.M. Hubbell trans., 1971) (c. 46 BCE).

**50.** CICERO, DE INVENTIONE, *supra* note 49, pp. xiii-xiv.

**51.** *Id.* at 3, bk. 1, ch. 1, ¶ 1.

In Cicero's opinion, orators were most qualified to lead the state because they could guide both the senate and the public.

Cicero's major contribution to rhetorical theory was the concept of "status," the "question ... from which the whole case arises."[52] Cicero described legal questions as questions of fact, definition, quality, or procedure. Understanding the nature of the question enables the orator to craft better arguments. Lawyers today conceive of the critical issues of a case in similar terms: questions of fact, law, mixed questions of law and fact, and procedure. Questions of fact involve the details—who, what, when, where, why, and how—of a given dispute. Fact questions are usually resolved by a jury who hears and observes all the evidence. Questions of law, on the other hand, involve questions of definition, that is, what the law is or means. These questions are usually reserved for the judge, who instructs the jury on the law and explains how to apply it to the facts. Mixed questions of fact and law involve both fact finding and the interpretation of law. Finally, each court has rules of procedure that prescribe the nature of cases to be tried there and the steps to take in prosecuting a case.

Written at roughly the same time as *De Inventione*, *Rhetorica ad Caius Herennium* (c. 84) was another popular handbook on rhetoric during Cicero's time. Until the seventeenth century, scholars believed Cicero had written it, but most scholars now agree that the author of *Rhetorica* is unknown. It too reflects the Romans' primary interest in judicial oratory.[53] *Rhetorica* is the oldest and most complete Latin book on rhetoric and was the first to discuss the canon relating to memory. *De Inventione* and *Rhetorica* were the two most popular books on rhetoric in the ancient world. Both continued to be influential in the Middle Ages and throughout the Renaissance.

Cicero believed that in order to be effective, an orator had to be well educated. For this reason, he transformed the study of rhetoric into the study of the liberal arts: grammar, rhetoric, logic, arithmetic, geometry, music, and astronomy.[54] The first three subjects, which relate to language, were considered prerequisites for studying the last four subjects, which relate to math and science.[55] Cicero expressed his devotion to a diverse education in *De Oratore* (c. 55), a dialogue between Crassus, a leading politician, and Antonius, a well-known public official. The subject of *De Oratore* is the nature of oratory, its value, and whether it is possible to teach it. Crassus, who represents Cicero's views, states that

no man can be an orator complete in all points of merit, who has not attained

---

**52.** *Id.* at 21, bk. 1, ch. 8, ¶ 10.

**53.** Author unknown, AD C. HERENNIUM (RHETORICA AD HERENNIUM) (Harry Caplan trans., 1954) (c. 84 BCE).

**54.** "Liberal arts" referred to the branches of knowledge available to "free" (*i.e.*, liberal) men as opposed to those who pursued an education to get jobs (*i.e.*, "not so free").

**55.** In the Middle Ages, the first three subjects were known as the *Trivium* and the last four as the *Quadrivium*. The combined study of theology and the liberal arts became known as Scholasticism during the Middle Ages. Medieval universities were later criticized for their Scholastic approach, which became synonymous with artificiality and closed-mindedness. *See infra*, pp. 38 and 43.

a knowledge of all important subjects and arts. For it is from knowledge that oratory must derive its beauty and fullness, and unless there is such knowledge, well-grasped and comprehended by the speaker, there must be something empty and almost childish in the utterance.[56]

Armed with knowledge, a man could develop the skills necessary to become a great orator and citizen.

Cicero thought of rhetoric as more than the art of persuasion; it could be used to prove something and to please an audience as well. Like Aristotle, Cicero taught the three basic modes of appeal. In *De Oratore*, Crassus states that one must rely on three things to persuade the audience: "the proof of our allegations, the winning of our hearers' favour, and the rousing of their feelings to whatever impulse our case may require."[57] Although Aristotle articulated these first, Cicero is credited with teaching them to his contemporaries because Aristotle's *Rhetoric* had been lost; it was not rediscovered until the Renaissance. As for style, Cicero said the best way to win an audience's favor was to adjust one's style to suit the needs of the audience. For proofs, an orator should use a plain style; for pleasing audiences, an orator should use a middle style; and for persuasion, he should use a grand style.[58] The orator who uses the grand style is

> magnificent, opulent, stately and ornate; he undoubtedly has the greatest power. This is the man whose brilliance and fluency have caused admiring nations to let eloquence attain the highest power in the state.... This eloquence has power to sway men's minds and move them in every possible way.[59]

In contrast to the Attic orators, Cicero favored the grand, "Asiatic" style, so called for its resemblance to the flowery style that had developed among the Greeks in Rome's province, Asia Minor. *See Figure 3, p. 23.*

---

**56.** CICERO, DE ORATORE, *supra* note 49 at 17, bk. 1, ch. 6, ¶ 20.

**57.** *Id.* at 281, bk. 2, ch. 27, ¶ 115.

**58.** CICERO, ORATOR, *supra* note 49, at 233, ch. 21, ¶ 69.

**59.** *Id.* at 238, ch. 28, ¶ 97.

Map base © copyright 2008. Ancient World Mapping Center
(www.unc.edu/awmc). Used by permission.

## FIGURE 3

## b. MARCUS FABIUS QUINTILIANUS (35–95 CE)

Quintilian was born more than 100 years after Cicero died but was heavily influenced by him. Born in Spain, Quintilian was the son of a Roman rhetorician, and his father sent him to Rome to be educated in rhetoric and the law. He founded the first public school in Rome and taught rhetoric and practiced law for twenty years. At the age of fifty, he wrote *Institutio Oratorio*, a twelve volume work on studying rhetoric throughout the course of one's life. He wrote more than any other Roman about courtroom technique, and *Oratorio* is a veritable encyclopedia of the Roman legal system.[60] In Book Three, Quintilian expanded on Cicero's idea of status. He agreed that the three major issues of a case involve questions of fact, definition, and quality and described them as "was it done, what was done, was it rightly done?"[61] To these issues of "logic," he added legal issues, which come in "inevitably more varieties, because there are many laws and they have various forms."[62] These legal issues resemble modern canons of statutory interpretation. As Quintilian explained, "[w]e rely on the letter of one [law], on the intention of another; others we harness to our cause, though we have no law really on our side; sometimes we compare one law with another,

---

**60.** VICKERS, *supra* note 2, at 38.

**61.** QUINTILIAN, INSTITUTIO ORATORIO bk. 3, ch. 11, ¶ 3, p. 159 (Donald A. Russell trans. & ed., 2001).

**62.** *Id.* at 93, bk. 3, ch. 6, ¶ 87.

sometimes we give different interpretations."[63]

In Book Twelve, Quintilian developed the concept of the perfect orator as a "good man skilled in speaking."[64] Embedded in that ideal is a broader view of *ethos*: the need for the speaker's *character*, not just his speech, to appeal to the audience. Unlike Aristotle and Cicero, Quintilian thought of *ethos* as more than the speaker's appeal at the time the speech was delivered. According to Quintilian, only a good man—free from vice, a lover of wisdom, a sincere believer in his cause, and a servant of the people—could appeal to *ethos*.[65] The fact that an orator had to be able to argue both sides of the same question did not detract from his goodness. "After all," Quintilian said, "the Academics argue both sides of a question, but live according to one side only."[66] As long as an orator believes in his cause, the audience will believe in him.

Quintilian even felt an orator was justified in lying (once in a while) or advocating for a bad cause as long as the orator's intentions were honorable.[67] With regard to arguing on behalf of a guilty defendant, he said:

> It is not useless to consider how one may on occasion speak for a falsehood or even for an injustice, if only because this enables us to detect and refute such things more easily, just as the person who knows what things are harmful will be better at applying remedies for them.... In fact, what virtue is revealed by its opposite, vice; equity is better understood by looking at its opposite; and in general most things are shown to be good by comparison with their contraries.[68]

An orator might even "cheat the judge of the truth" where the circumstances rightly required it. Suppose, for example, "a good general, someone without whom the state cannot defeat its enemies, is labouring under a manifestly true charge: will not the common good call our orator to his side?"[69]

---

### QUESTIONS FOR CONSIDERATION

1. **What is the difference between dialectical and rhetorical discourse? Why did Plato believe dialectic yields absolute truth but rhetoric cannot?**

2. **As a student of law and the legal process, what is your reaction to Plato's belief that judicial rhetoric distorts justice? Is it possible to discover truth by juxtaposing opposing arguments? Is it possible to come to "wrong" conclusions?**

---

63. *Id.* ¶¶ 87–88.
64. *Id.* at 197, bk. 12, ch. 1, ¶ 1.
65. *Id.* at 199–203, ¶¶ 3–10.
66. *Id.* at 215, ¶ 35.
67. *Id.* at 217, ¶¶ 36–37.
68. *Id.* at 215, ¶¶ 34–35.
69. *Id.* at 219, ¶ 43.

3. Is it necessary that rhetoric be an avenue to absolute truth for it to be valuable?

4. Does combining reason and eloquence, as Aristotle and Cicero advocated, adequately address Plato's concerns that rhetoric can be used to distort the truth? Does Quintilian's requirement that an orator be a good man address Plato's concern?

5. Can lying on behalf of a client be justified, as Quintilian suggests, by honorable intentions?

# B. EARLY CHRISTIANITY, THE MIDDLE AGES, AND THE RENAISSANCE (c. 50–1600 CE)

Western rhetoric from the first century CE through the Renaissance was influenced primarily by the decline of the Roman Empire and the birth of Christianity. As democracy and free speech disappeared in Rome, so did the need to train orators. What is now considered classical rhetoric survived, but scholars gradually shifted their attention from content to expression, focusing on matters of style, literary composition, and the management of day-to-day affairs. During the Middle Ages, growing populations moved out from urban centers, and the primary mode of communication became the written as opposed to spoken word. Oratory took on new forms, and by this time, the predominant subject of rhetoric was Christianity, not politics. Classical rhetoric continued to be used to train lawyers, particularly in Italy, but as questions of morality and politics became the province of Christian theology, the role of rhetoric became unclear. Although the Renaissance served briefly to regenerate interest in rhetoric as a worthy and independent discipline, it was short-lived. By the end of the sixteenth century, Plato's influence on rhetoric was as strong as ever.

## 1. THE SECOND SOPHISTIC (c. 60–230 CE)

Philostratus, a Greek historian, coined the phrase "second sophistic" to describe the revival of interest in the Greek sophists of the late fifth and fourth centuries BCE.[70] *See Figure 4, p. 28.* According to Philostratus, there were pure sophists and philosophical sophists. Pure sophists were teachers of rhetoric, who, like Isocrates, emphasized imitation and practice. Philosophical sophists, on the other hand, were career speechmakers. Some were also teachers, but their main function was to entertain audiences on political and cultural matters while demonstrating their rhetorical prowess. Their speeches helped stabilize the Roman Empire which was defending itself against attacks from the outside

---

**70.** George A. Kennedy, Classical Rhetoric & Its Christian & Secular Tradition from Ancient to Modern Times 47 (2d ed. 1999).

and religious movements from within, such as Christianity.[71]

Despite its revival, rhetoric did not play the political role it had in earlier times. The true democracy that had flourished in Greece was long gone. The Roman government had become an autocracy, and citizens were no longer free to speak their minds. The Roman emperors (the Caesars) punished political debate, which was monitored by a network of secret police,[72] and robbed the Roman Senate of its influence. The need to train citizens to be politically active thus decreased dramatically. Since only trained lawyers were then permitted to argue in the courtroom, the need to train legal advocates decreased as well.[73]

Even in the classroom, political speeches were to a large extent forbidden.[74] The pure sophists used classroom exercises, called *progymnasmata* and *declamatio* to teach rhetoric in a practical context. *Progymnasmata* (preparatory exercises) taught students the fundamentals for the preparation and performance of formal speeches. For example, an exercise might teach the student about the narrative form of prose by giving him an opportunity to retell a story in his own words, requiring that he include all relevant facts.[75] *Declamatio* (declamations or emphatic statements) were more advanced; they required students to prepare and deliver full speeches on imaginary political or legal issues.

Next came exercises in legal argument, known as *controversia*. These were considered the most difficult and were reserved for students preparing for legal careers.[76] The *controversia* posed hypothetical legal problems in the context of a particular client. The following example is typical:

> The law ordains that in the case of rape the woman may demand either the death of her seducer or marriage without dowry. A certain man raped two women in one night; one demanded his death, the other marriage.[77]

Who should prevail? In this example, students would be expected to analyze this problem on behalf of one or both of the women. They would then have to prepare a speech and submit it to the teacher for review. Having received feedback from the teacher on the written speech, the students would then deliver their speeches orally. The exercise often concluded with the teacher's commentary on the students' delivery and his own solution to the problem.

These ancient exercises are similar to the teaching methods used in legal education today. In class and on exams, twenty-first century law professors pose hypothetical problems that students must explore by offering alternative

---

**71.** *Id.* at 48.

**72.** JAMES J. MURPHY & RICHARD A. KATULA, A SYNOPTIC HISTORY OF CLASSICAL RHETORIC 230 (3d ed. 2003).

**73.** MURPHY & KATULA *supra* note 72, at 230–31.

**74.** JAMES J. MURPHY, RHETORIC IN THE MIDDLE AGES: A HISTORY OF RHETORICAL THEORY FROM SAINT AUGUSTINE TO THE RENAISSANCE 35 (2001).

**75.** *See generally* GIDEON O. BURTON, SILVA RHETORICAE, http://humanities.byu.edu/rhetoric/Silva.htm (last visited May 18, 2008).

**76.** MURPHY, *supra* note 74, at 38.

**77.** *Id.* at 40; KENNEDY, *supra* note 70, at 46.

arguments that address both sides of the legal issue. Legal writing classes, too, employ a method that teaches the interpretation and application of law in a given context. Like the sophists thousands of years before them, law professors today often then provide sample answers to the problems they pose. Who would think that law school in the twenty-first century could resemble legal training in the second?

Due to a shift in focus from content to expression, the second sophistic has been described as a period of "oratorical excess in which the subject matter became less important than the interest in safer matters like the externals of speech, especially style and delivery."[78] With the dual goal to educate and entertain, the philosophical sophists developed a manner and style of speaking designed to amaze their audience. They spoke at weddings, funerals, birthday parties, civic events, and festivals. Sometime during the first century CE, Longinus wrote the most famous treatise from this period entitled, *On the Sublime,* which captures the essence of the period:

> For grandeur produces ecstasy rather than persuasion in the hearer; and the combination of wonder and astonishment always proves superior to the merely persuasive and pleasant.[79]

Without necessarily intending to, the second sophists affirmed Plato's view that rhetoric is primarily form over substance.

---

**78.** Murphy & Katula, *supra* note 72, at 230.

**79.** Longinus, on Sublimity 1–2 (D.A. Russell trans., 1965).

## EARLY CHRISTIANITY AND THE EARLY MIDDLE AGES

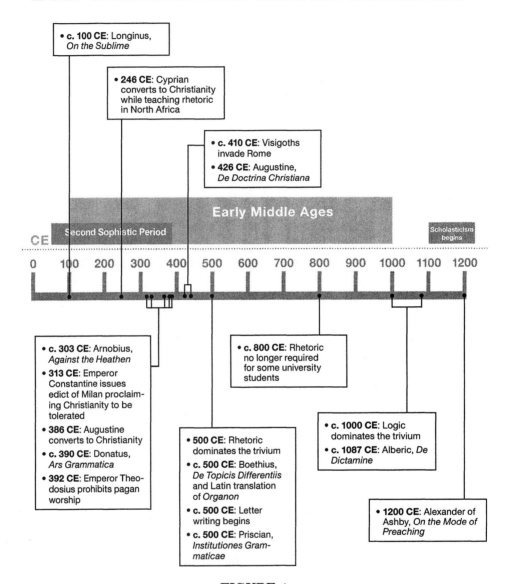

FIGURE 4

# 2. THE EARLY CHRISTIAN CHURCH
## (c. 150–400 CE)

The early Christians refused to worship the emperor of Rome, and the Roman government persecuted them for over 250 years. Despite the empire's effort to suppress it, Christianity grew steadily. Eventually, the empire lost its ability to resist Christianity's growth. In 313, the Emperor Constantine issued the Edict of Milan, which proclaimed that Christianity would be tolerated. By

392, Emperor Theodosius had prohibited pagan worship altogether. *See Figure 4, p. 28.* Many pagan temples were turned into churches, and the Church gained a stronghold in civic affairs.

As early Christians sought to defend and spread their faith, a Christian rhetoric emerged. The idea of a religious rhetoric was novel. Pagan priests had performed rituals, but they did not preach. In contrast, the New Testament directed Christians to teach about the life of Christ. The early Christians were opposed to classical rhetoric because of its pagan roots. Ironically, all eight of the great early Christians—the Latin Fathers of the Church—were trained in classical rhetoric.[80] Each wrestled with the problem of using rhetorical principles in their writing, and several of them severed their connection to their pagan past and focused only on the content of their writing without regard to stylistic considerations.

Cyprian, for example, was teaching rhetoric in northern Africa when he converted to Christianity in c. 246. In keeping with his new faith, he vowed never again to quote Roman poets or orators: "In courts of law, in public meetings, in political discussions, a full eloquence [rhetorical skill] may be the pride of vocal ambition, but in speaking of the Lord God, a pure simplicity of expression which is convincing depends upon the substance of the argument rather than the forcefulness of eloquences."[81] St. Jerome struggled with his appreciation for sophisticated (note the derivation of this word) speech and the conflicting Christian ethic that made it sinful to enjoy earthly pleasures. In translating the Old Testament into Latin, he avoided using rhetorical devices that would appeal more to rhetoricians than to the common man. He wrote, "We do not wish for the field of rhetorical eloquence, nor the snares of dialecticians, nor do we seek the subtleties of Aristotle, but the very words of Scripture must be set down."[82] Arnobius went so far as to denounce even the grammar of the classicists: "[H]ow is the truth of a statement diminished, if an error is made in number or case, in preposition, participle, or conjunction? Let that pomposity of style and strictly regulated diction be reserved for public assemblies, for lawsuits, for the forum and the courts of justice."[83]

The result of the struggle between classical rhetorical principles and Christian values was a new kind of rhetoric—preaching. Two popular but very different kinds of preaching developed: a plain, unadorned homily and a rhetorically rich panegyric sermon. Homily means "coming together" or conversation in Greek; the Latin equivalent is *sermo* or sermon.[84] "Homily" is still used today to describe

---

**80.** Tertullian, Cyprian, Arnobius, Lactantius, and Augustine were teachers of rhetoric; Ambrose, Hilary and Jerome had been trained in rhetorical schools. KENNEDY, *supra* note 70, at 167.

**81.** MURPHY, *supra* note 74, at 51. In this way, the early Christians eschewed the second sophists' ornate and clever speech as part of their rejection of classical rhetoric.

**82.** ST. JEROME, THE PERPETUAL VIRGINITY OF BLESSED MARY: AGAINST HELVIDIUS, (c. 383) http://www.cin.org/users/james/files/helvidiu.htm (last visited April 2, 2008).

**83.** ARNOBIUS, AGAINST THE HEATHEN, bk. 1, ¶ 59 (c. 303) http://www.newadvent.org/fathers/06311.htm (last visited Aug. 25, 2008).

**84.** *See* KENNEDY, *supra* note 70, at 156.

the point in a Christian service when a priest or minister interprets a passage from Scripture. Homilies were given to reinforce beliefs as much as to educate, and early preachings about Christ were marked by a simplicity uncharacteristic of their authors' classical training. Some homilies had no beginning or end and contained little or no repetition for emphasis. A panegyrical sermon on the other hand, employed sophistic devices such as figures of speech and parallelisms in its praise of Christ.[85] Chrysostom (347–407 CE) was well known for his panegyrical sermons and his homilies. Although he rejected a classical arrangement for his homilies, he used several rhetorical devices (apparently he could not resist). In this way, Chrysostom was characteristic of several Christian orators, who eschewed rhetoric in theory but not necessarily in practice.[86]

## St. Augustine (354–430 CE)

Augustine of Hippo converted to Christianity in 386 and became an early leader of the Church. *See Figure 4, p. 28.* His devotion to the power of rhetoric single-handedly resolved the Christians' problem with using rhetoric for theological purposes. Although Augustine had criticized the Asiatic style of the sophists, he came to believe that rhetoric provided the means for persuading men to lead a holy life. Like Plato, Augustine sought truth, but he did not believe truth could be discovered through dialectic. Instead, Augustine believed truth resided in Scripture and that rhetoric could enhance it.

Augustine was born in northern Africa, near Carthage, to a Christian mother and pagan father. *See Figure 3, p. 23.* He received a Christian education but struggled with his religious beliefs. Augustine studied rhetoric and planned to become a lawyer. He also taught rhetoric from 383–86. At the age of thirty-three, Augustine converted to Christianity and rejected law as a profession. In his famous autobiography, *Confessions*, Augustine recounted the process of his conversion, describing his rhetorical training as having

> had the objective of leading me to distinction as an advocate in the lawcourts, where one's reputation is high in proportion to one's success in deceiving people.... I wanted to distinguish myself as an orator for a damnable and conceited purpose, namely delight in human vanity.[87]

Augustine wrote that his life changed when he read Cicero's *Hortensius*, a work from 45 BCE that is now lost.[88] Augustine identified with Cicero's desire for wisdom but found the wisdom of Christianity missing in Cicero's work.[89] He was ordained as a priest in 391.

---

85. *See* GOLDEN, ET AL., THE RHETORIC OF WESTERN THOUGHT 60 (6th ed. 1997).

86. MURPHY, *supra* note 74 at 55–56; KENNEDY, *supra* note 70 at 165–66.

87. SAINT AUGUSTINE, CONFESSIONS 38, at bk. 3, ch. 3, ¶¶ 6–7 (Henry Chadwick trans., 1998).

88. *Id.* at 38–39. Cicero's *Hortensius* was a response to the Roman orator, Hortensius, who had argued that philosophy has no social value. Hortensius was the chief lawyer of the upper class Romans and often opposed Cicero, who prosecuted his clients for bribery and embezzlement.

89. KENNEDY, *supra* note 70, at 171.

In 396, Augustine began *De Doctrina Christiana*, a four-volume work, which sets forth principles for preaching Scripture.[90] Augustine believed that since much of the Bible is obscure and can be interpreted in different ways, one should be taught the meaning of Scripture as opposed to interpreting it oneself. A teacher of Scripture thus must have a thorough knowledge of the text and be able to convey that knowledge effectively.[91] The fourth volume, completed around 426, addresses Christian oratory and is heavily influenced by Cicero. Augustine states that wisdom without eloquence is of little benefit and eloquence without wisdom is useless.[92] Augustine advised Christians to preach the Word of God with a learned eloquence. According to Augustine, eloquence should move the audience to believe the correct interpretation of the Word. Augustine also argued that rhetoric was acceptable in preaching because it was "not produced by human labour, but poured from the divine mind with both wisdom and eloquence."[93] He urged Christians to look to the eloquent writings of Paul and the book of Amos, which include rhetorical methods such as climax, periodic sentences, and tropes.[94]

Like Aristotle and Cicero, Augustine was undaunted by the orator's ability to argue in favor of opposing points of view. According to Augustine, truth was derived from the Word of God, but even His Word needed the power of rhetoric behind it to stir the emotions and compete with false prophets:

> Since rhetoric is used to give conviction to both truth and falsehood, who could dare maintain that truth, which depends on us for its defence, should stand unarmed in the fight against falsehood? This would mean that those who are trying to give conviction to their falsehoods would know how to use an introduction to make their listeners favourable, interested, receptive, while we would not.[95]

Augustine was less concerned than Quintilian about the "goodness" of the orator; instead, he focused on rhetoric as a tool to spread the Good News. Like his Roman predecessors, Augustine emphasized *ethos*. For Augustine, however, the speaker's authority came from God.

---

90. This subject is known today as Homiletics.

91. *See* KENNEDY, *supra* note 70, at 176.

92. Augustine's words reflect Cicero's influence. In *De Inventione*, Cicero said, "[W]isdom without eloquence does too little for the good of states, but ... eloquence without wisdom is ... never helpful." *See* CICERO, DE INVENTIONE, *supra* note 49, at 3, bk. 1, ch. 1, ¶ 1.

93. ST. AUGUSTINE, DE DOCTRINA CHRISTIANA 223, bk. 4, ¶ 59 (R. P. H. Green ed. and trans., 1995).

94. KENNEDY, *supra* note 70, at 178.

95. SAINT AUGUSTINE, DE DOCTRINA CHRISTIANA, *supra* note 93, at 197, bk. 4, ¶ 4.

## THE HIGH MIDDLE AGES AND THE RENAISSANCE

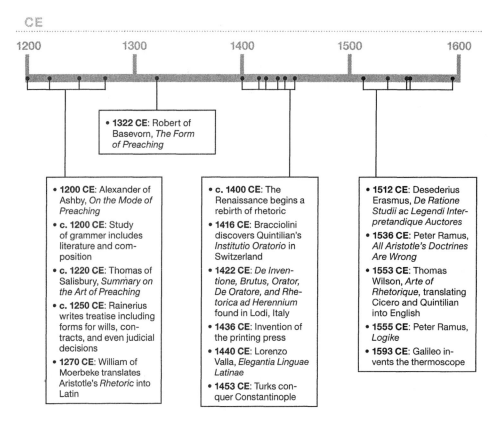

CE

| 1200 | 1300 | 1400 | 1500 | 1600 |

• **1322 CE**: Robert of Basevorn, *The Form of Preaching*

• **1200 CE**: Alexander of Ashby, *On the Mode of Preaching*
• **c. 1200 CE**: Study of grammer includes literature and composition
• **c. 1220 CE**: Thomas of Salisbury, *Summary on the Art of Preaching*
• **c. 1250 CE**: Rainerius writes treatise including forms for wills, contracts, and even judicial decisions
• **1270 CE**: William of Moerbeke translates Aristotle's *Rhetoric* into Latin

• **c. 1400 CE**: The Renaissance begins a rebirth of rhetoric
• **1416 CE**: Bracciolini discovers Quintilian's *Institutio Oratorio* in Switzerland
• **1422 CE**: *De Inventione, Brutus, Orator, De Oratore*, and *Rhetorica ad Herennium* found in Lodi, Italy
• **1436 CE**: Invention of the printing press
• **1440 CE**: Lorenzo Valla, *Elegantia Linguae Latinae*
• **1453 CE**: Turks conquer Constantinople

• **1512 CE**: Desederius Erasmus, *De Ratione Studii ac Legendi Interpretandique Auctores*
• **1536 CE**: Peter Ramus, *All Aristotle's Doctrines Are Wrong*
• **1553 CE**: Thomas Wilson, *Arte of Rhetorique*, translating Cicero and Quintilian into English
• **1555 CE**: Peter Ramus, *Logike*
• **1593 CE**: Galileo invents the thermoscope

FIGURE 5

## 3. MIDDLE AGES (c. 500–1400 CE)

As the Christian church usurped many of the functions of the Roman government, the focus of rhetoric shifted once again from secular argument to preaching. The shift was dramatic for several reasons. First, the variety of sources formerly available for inventing arguments was reduced to one source, Scripture, for the Christian orator. Second, classical rhetoricians had taught that audiences were persuaded by appeals to *logos*, *ethos*, and *pathos*, and, in the realm of *logos*, most proof was based on probability as opposed to certainty. In contrast, the early Christians focused almost exclusively on *ethos*, and the Word of God constituted unimpeachable proof. Finally, the majority of early Christians adopted an informal, unstructured preaching style that stood in contrast to the ornate style of the sophists. Despite Saint Augustine's advice to establish a rhetorical theory for preaching, the early Christians assumed that the message of Christ would speak for itself. A truly rhetorical form of preaching—

the "thematic" sermon—did not appear until 1200.[96]

The decline in rhetorical studies was also due to the declining need for rhetorical skills in the western secular world. By 410, the Visigoths—nomadic "barbarians" from Germany—had invaded Rome.[97] *See Figure 4, p. 28.* Various northern cultures invaded Italy repeatedly for the next forty-five years. As the western part of the Roman Empire fell, its culture crumbled. Many of the illiterate barbarian kings in the West wanted to learn Latin, and a working knowledge of Greek was lost. In the eastern part of the Empire, much of Roman culture survived. Spoken Greek survived in Byzantium until 1453, when the Turkish Ottomans conquered it. Until that time, rhetoric continued to be useful both in government and church-related matters. Despite the existence of a senate and law courts there, ceremonial oratory was the predominant form of rhetoric. It was used to strengthen loyalty to the government and the Christian Church.[98]

Although no longer dominant, classical rhetoric survived in part. Medieval scholars pursued discrete areas of interest, including logic, grammar, letter writing, and preaching.[99] Medieval letter writing is particularly interesting because it produced administrative orders, contracts, and "fill in the blank" legal documents. Although they arguably represent a low point in the inventiveness of legal writing, form documents proved to be tremendously efficient and influential. Form letters and contracts are still used today.

## a. THE DOMINANCE OF LOGIC OVER RHETORIC

Classical rhetorical works survived the Middle Ages, but they competed directly with the rhetorical work of medieval scholars and a rising interest in teaching logic. Because Aristotle's *Rhetoric* had yet to be translated into Latin, Cicero was the most influential classical author during the early Middle Ages. The two most cited works were *De Inventione* and *Rhetorica ad Herennium*, the latter of which was still thought to be by Cicero.[100] Aristotle's *Rhetoric* was virtually ignored in the West until 1270, when it was translated into Latin.[101] Some scholars believe that *Rhetoric* was then viewed more as a work on ethics and

---

**96.** *See infra* p. 37.

**97.** "Barbarian" comes from Greek and refers to the Greeks' perception that the northern Europeans' speech sounded like "barking." The term came to mean an uncivilized, illiterate, almost sub-human person.

**98.** KENNEDY, *supra*, note 70, at 193–95.

**99.** *See* MURPHY, *supra* note 74, at chs. 3–6.

**100.** During the fifteenth century, Lorenzo Valla, a Renaissance humanist, questioned the *Rhetorica's* authorship. In 1491, Raphael Regius divorced the piece from Cicero's name, and the true author is unknown to this day. *See* AD C. HERENNIUM (RHETORICA AD HERENNIUM), *supra* note 53, at viii-ix.

**101.** Aristotle's *Rhetoric* made its way back to the West via Al–Farabi, a ninth century Arab scholar who had written about Aristotle. Al–Farabi was translated into Latin by Hermannus Allemanus in 1240. Two Latin translations of *Rhetoric* were then made from the original: the first was very poorly regarded and may have been by Bartholomew of Messina, an Englishman, sometime before 1250. The second translation was made in 1270 by William of Moerbeke, another Englishman. *See* MURPHY, *supra* note 74, at 90–93.

political science than on persuasion,[102] and for that reason, Aristotle's influence did not reemerge until the Renaissance. Parts of *Organon*, Aristotle's essays on inventing arguments and logic, were far more popular.[103] Quintilian's *Institutio Oratoria* was popular for a short period of time in the mid-twelfth century, but its use was not widespread until the fifteenth century.[104]

Medieval scholars worked to preserve rhetorical tradition, but in some ways, they diminished it. Encyclopedists like Cassiodorus (480–575) catalogued classical authors for religious and secular study but devoted more space to dialectic than to rhetoric.[105] Although Cassiodorus included the basic principles of rhetoric, he discussed its use in the past without applying it to contemporary studies of Scripture or sermon-writing.[106] By the early 500s, Boethius—a Roman scholar and politician—had translated Aristotle's *Organon* into Latin and written a commentary on Cicero and his own book on logic. In his book, *De Topicis Differentiis*,[107] Boethius attempted to distinguish dialectic from rhetoric but failed to recognize that the study of rhetoric was more than just appeals to logic.[108]

Due, in part, to the writings of medieval scholars, logic achieved ascendency over rhetoric in academia. In the early Middle Ages, rhetoric dominated the *trivium* (*i.e.*, rhetoric, logic, and grammar). By the ninth and tenth centuries, however, some university students were not even required to take it. Logic was taught in conjunction with dialectic—Plato's process for the exchange of ideas that would lead to truth—and the terms became synonymous. By the eleventh century, logic had replaced rhetoric as the dominant subject of the *trivium*.[109] *See Figure 4, p. 28*. Medieval translations of Aristotle's *Organon* had become the standard texts for students of logic, not rhetoric.[110]

## b. GRAMMAR

Medieval grammar included poetic interpretation and the proper use of language. Children who attended school went first to "grammar school," where they learned the basics of language and became acquainted with poetry and prose. Grammar schools resembled the schools of ancient Rome, but these children were not being trained as orators. Grammar was seen as the first of many subjects essential to a good education:

---

102. *See* MURPHY, *supra* note 74, at 97–98.

103. *See id.* at 90–92.

104. *Id.* at 123–27, 360–61. Aristotle's Rhetoric did not appear in any form in English until the mid–1600s, when the philosopher, Thomas Hobbes, paraphrased its contents in English.

105. *See* MURPHY, *supra* note 74, at 64, 66.

106. KENNEDY, *supra* note 70, at 200–01.

107. BOETHIUS, DE TOPICIS DIFFERENTIIS (Eleonore Stump ed. & trans., 2004).

108. *See* KENNEDY, *supra* note 70, at 202.

109. MURPHY, *supra* note 74, at 97 n.27.

110. *See id.* at 104.

Grammar is the gateway of all other sciences, the most apt purgatrix of stammering speech, the helper of logic, the master of rhetoric, the interpreter of theology, the refreshment of medicine, and the most praiseworthy foundation of the *quadrivium*.[111]

At first, grammarians like Donatus (St. Jerome's teacher) and Priscian explored the parts of speech (*i.e.* nouns, verbs, adjectives, etc.), sentence structure, and figures of speech (*e.g.,* metaphor, simile, alliteration, etc.).[112] After 1200, the study of grammar expanded to include what we now consider linguistics, literary criticism, and composition. Boethius, for example, who translated much of Aristotle's *Organon* into Latin, was one of many grammarians interested in using logical methods to explain the structure of language.[113] Others, such as Thomas of Capua, studied rhythmic prose—a form of prose that focused on syllables and consonance of sounds.[114] *See Figure 5, p. 32.*

## c. LETTER WRITING

Letter writing did not appear until the Middle Ages. In the ancient world, messages were communicated orally, even if they were written down. A messenger usually had significant flexibility and often communicated just the general ideas of the message to the recipient. By the time Rome fell, however, messages were being read and responded to in writing.[115] Many subsequent kings were so poorly educated they could not compose coherent messages. For that reason, they relied on their servants not only to handwrite their messages but to compose them. As Cassiodorus, the encyclopedist said, the task fell to servants to "speak the king's words in the king's own presence."[116]

As the medieval feudal system developed and populations spread out, secular and church offices hired letter writers to handle important correspondence. At first, form letters were drafted to cover typical situations as efficiently as possible. These were similar to the boilerplate forms that lawyers use today for simple wills, contracts, and deeds.[117] In Italy, a separate doctrine on notation developed specifically for the construction of legal documents. "Notaries" were admitted to practice upon the recommendation of judges and lawyers.[118] A treatise by Rainerius from the mid-thirteenth century includes forms for wills, contracts,

---

111. *See id.* at 137–38 (quoting unknown author). *"Quadrivium"* here refers to the four-subject course of graduate study that often included arithmetic, geometry, astronomy, and music. *Id.* at 44.

112. *Id.* at 138–40. Donatus' textbook on the parts of speech, *Ars Minor,* is the single most successful book in the history of education. *See id.* at 139.

113. *See* The Oxford Classical Dictionary, *supra* note 2, at 247; Murphy, *supra* note 74, at 152–53.

114. Murphy, *supra* note 74, at 157.

115. *See id.* at 194–95.

116. *Id.* at 198.

117. *See, e.g.,* American Jurisprudence Legal Forms 2d; West's Legal Forms.

118. Today, a notary public serves a more limited function of attesting to the identity and oath of the individual signing an official document. Modern notaries are commissioned by state governments for a period of two or three years.

and even judicial decisions.[119]

By the eleventh century, form books could no longer address the myriad purposes for which they were needed. Alberic, a monk and teacher at the monastery in Monte Cassino, Italy, first articulated a theory of letter writing to meet this need. *See Figure 4, p. 28.* In two treatises written about 1087, he drew on classical rhetoric to develop an outline for a standard letter and an appropriate writing style. Inspired by Cicero's parts of a speech,[120] Alberic established five parts that resemble business correspondence today: greeting, introduction, narration of facts, argument or body, and conclusion. Alberic added the greeting because he thought it necessary to acknowledge from the outset both the purpose of the letter and the social relationship between the writer and the recipient. The function of the introduction was reminiscent of Cicero: to make the audience "attentive, docile, and well-disposed."[121] In describing the style of the writing, Alberic referred to the high, middle, and low styles with which his audience would have been familiar.[122]

## d. PREACHING

Although Christian preaching began with Christ, preaching in general dates back to Ezra, a Jewish scribe, in 400 BCE.[123] Surprisingly, a formal theory of preaching did not evolve until the Middle Ages, and it was derived from classical rhetoric. The early Christians adopted a simple and unadorned preaching style in an attempt to distance themselves from what they considered to be the immoral rhetoric of sophists and pagans. Homilies or sermons thus had no formal structure, with no real beginning or end. Preachers assumed that Scripture contained the power of God, so they focused on the content of their message instead of its composition or delivery. The first real theories on preaching composition did not appear until 800 years after Augustine had urged their development.

In 1200, an Englishman named Alexander of Ashby wrote the first real treatise on how to write sermons. *See Figure 5, p. 32.* Like Alberic, he relied heavily on Cicero. Alexander's *On the Mode of Preaching* began with the same reference to Cicero Alberic had made: "In every written work and speech what is needed first is the intention of the wise man that he should render his readers or hearers docile, well-disposed, and attentive."[124] Like Alberic, Alexander drew

---

**119.** MURPHY, *supra* note 74, at 265. At that time, judicial opinions were written by lawyers on behalf of the judges who read them out loud in court.

**120.** Alberic relied on Isidore of Seville (c. 579–636), a classical rhetorician who had reduced Cicero's six or seven parts of a typical oration to four: introduction, statement of issue, argument, and conclusion. *See* MURPHY, *supra* note 74, at 205. This schema recalls that of Corax, who divided legal argument into introduction, statement of facts, argument, and conclusion. *See supra* note 3.

**121.** MURPHY, *supra* note 74 at 205.

**122.** LES PERELMAN, *The Medieval Art of Letter–Writing: Rhetoric as Institutional Expression, in* TEXTUAL DYNAMICS OF THE PROFESSIONS 103 (Charles Bazerman and James Paradis, eds., 1991).

**123.** *See, e.g.*, JOSEPH BLENKINSOPP, EZRA-NEHEMIAH: A COMMENTARY 282–83 (1998).

**124.** MURPHY, *supra* note 74, at 312.

from Cicero in identifying the parts of a sermon as introduction, division, proof, and conclusion.[125] Division referred to the point at which the preacher explained the themes he intended to cover in the sermon. Although Cicero had always assumed that the argument was a separate part of any speech, Alexander suggested that sermons could be divided into parts, and each part should be followed by its argument or explanation before moving on to the next one.[126] This idea might have come from *Rhetorica ad Herennium*, which cautioned against "abandoning a chain of argument before it has been completed, and making an inappropriate transition to the next argument."[127] Modern legal writing is no stranger to this pattern of arrangement.[128]

Ten to twenty years later, Thomas of Salisbury developed a full-blown thematic sermon.[129] *See Figure 5, p. 32.* Thomas compared the duty of the preacher to the duty of the ancient rhetorician and acknowledged the need to persuade audiences about the Word of God. In comparing a sermon to a speech, Thomas stated the goal of the sermon was to persuade men to good conduct. As a result, "the doctrine of the orator is absolutely necessary to carry out the office of a preacher."[130] Thomas' sermon included an opening prayer, the introduction of the theme, the theme itself or a quotation from Scripture, the division or statement of the parts of the theme, the development of each of the themes or sub-themes, and a conclusion.[131] By the time of the Renaissance, several manuals on the art of preaching had been written, the most notable of which was written by Robert of Basevorn in 1322.[132]

# 4. THE RENAISSANCE (c. 1400–1600 CE)

In the early fifteenth century, an explosion of creativity in both the arts and sciences occurred in Europe, which distinguished this period from the "dark" Middle Ages. The Renaissance, as it is often called, signaled a return to the subjects of antiquity. Writing, painting, sculpting, architecture, science, and rhetoric experienced a rebirth.[133] As the works of Aristotle and Quintilian became available, Europeans renewed their interest in rhetoric and ancient texts.[134] Renaissance writers sought to emulate the rhetoric of Aristotle, Cicero, and Quintilian, and judicial and other forms of oratory improved. For a relatively brief period—about two centuries—the study and practice of rhetoric (then

---

125. *Id.* at 313.

126. *Id.* at 315.

127. RHETORICA AD HERENNIUM, *supra* ch. 2, note 53, at bk. 2, ch. 18, p. 107.

128. *See infra,* ch. 8.

129. *See* MURPHY, *supra* note 74, at 317–25.

130. *Id.* at 322.

131. *Id.* at 325.

132. *See id.* at 344–55 for the complete text of Basevorn's manual.

133. Dante, Raphael, Michelangelo, Palladio, and Da Vinci, are just a few examples of the artists working during this period.

134. *See* KENNEDY, *supra* note 70, at 227.

called "eloquence") was valued as it had been during the period of the Second Sophistic.[135] In countries where civic participation was permitted and valued, rhetoric became even more important as it took on a political purpose.

This renewed interest in classical subjects and forms was due, in large part, to the humanists. The humanists were teachers and scholars of the humanities: grammar, rhetoric, history, poetry, and philosophy. They translated classical texts into their own languages, commented on rhetorical theories, and taught rhetoric as a discipline equal to dialectic. They even aided in the rediscovery of notable classical works. Although Aristotle's *Rhetoric* had been translated into Latin in 1270, it did not become popular until the Renaissance. In 1416, Poggio Bracciolini, who had been secretary to Pope John XXIII, discovered a complete copy of Quintilian's *Institutio Oratoria* in the dungeon of a monastery in Switzerland. Quintilian had not been read with any real interest for nearly 600 years. In 1422, copies of Cicero's *De Inventione, Brutus, Orator*, and *De Oratore*, as well as *Rhetorica ad Herennium* were found in a cathedral in Lodi, Italy. The invention of the printing press in 1436 made it possible to reproduce and distribute these works throughout Europe.

## a. LORENZO VALLA (1407–1457 CE)

Lorenzo Valla, an Italian humanist, was instrumental in revitalizing rhetoric during the early Renaissance. Although criticized by the Church and pursued by the Inquisition for advocating "pagan eloquence," he was appointed apostolic secretary to Pope Nicholas V in 1448.[136] Valla was opposed to the "scholasticism" of the Middle Ages, which combined Aristotelian philosophy (*i.e.*, the use of logic to acquire knowledge) and the tenets of the Catholic church in a university setting.[137] Although rhetoric was viewed as a subset of dialectic (because it allowed for the expression but not the discovery of truth),[138] Valla argued that dialectic was a subset of rhetoric. The function of dialectic is to teach, but the duties of an orator are to teach, please, and persuade.[139] Furthermore, Valla said, dialectic is a form of confirmation and refutation:

> These are parts of invention; invention is one of the five parts of rhetoric. Logic is the use of syllogism. Does not the orator use the same? Certainly he does, and not only that, but also the enthymeme and the epicheireme, in addition to the induction.[140]

Valla also refuted the early Church's stance that discourse could not be written or spoken with eloquence. In his *Elegantiae linguae latinae* (The

---

**135.** *See supra*, at 25.

**136.** *See* WAYNE A. REBHORN, RENAISSANCE DEBATES ON RHETORIC 35 (2000).

**137.** Recall that by the ninth or tenth century, logic was the dominant subject of the *trivium*, and some students were not even required to take rhetoric. *See supra*, p. 34.

**138.** *See infra*, at 41, on Ramus.

**139.** *See* KENNEDY, *supra* note 70, at 242.

**140.** *Id.* Epicheireme refers to a more complicated pattern of reasoning than the enthymeme. *See infra* ch. 4, at 119.

Refinements of the Latin Language), Valla defended the use of eloquence against criticisms carried over from the early Christian Church and the Middle Ages. *See Figure 5, p. 32.* While conceding that Cicero could lead one too far from Christian philosophy, Valla argued that eloquence could be and was often used for good. He stressed that every important Christian figure, including the Apostles, used eloquent speech.[141] Valla wrote:

> One should not condemn the language of the pagans, nor grammar, nor rhetoric, nor dialectic, nor any of the other arts—note that the Apostles wrote in the Greek language—but rather, only dogmas, religions, and false opinions concerning the performance of virtuous actions by means of which we are supposed to ascend to heaven. All the other arts and sciences are matters indifferent in that you can use them for good or for ill.[142]

## b. DESEDERIUS ERASMUS (1469–1536 CE)

Desederius Erasmus was a classical scholar and Christian priest. In 1512, he wrote *De ratione studii ac legendi interpretandique auctores* (On the Method of Study) and *De Duplici copia verborum ac rerum* (Copia: Foundations of the Abundant Style). *See Figure 5, p. 32.* These textbooks set the standard for rhetorical studies in English grammar schools. In *Copia*, Erasmus wrote:

> [S]tyle is to thought as clothes are to the body. Just as dress and outward appearance can enhance or disfigure the beauty and dignity of the body, so words can enhance or disfigure thought. Accordingly a great mistake is made by those who consider that it makes no difference how anything is expressed, provided it can be understood somehow or other.... Our first concern should be to see that the garment is clean, that it fits, and that it is not wrongly made up. It would be a pity to have people put off by a spotty, dirty garment, when the underlying form is itself good.... Nearly as bad a sin is committed by those who mix the sordid with the elegant [or] disfigure their purple with patches.[143]

Erasmus later proposed a successful compromise to a serious debate among rhetoricians on the extent to which rhetoric should adhere to Ciceronian tradition. "Ciceronians," scholars of Cicero, had insisted that no Latin word be used in rhetoric that could not be found in the works of Cicero. They also advocated that Cicero's elaborate sentence structure be closely imitated. Erasmus proposed a compromise: a classical style that drew on a variety of ancient authors, in addition to Cicero. His proposal turned out to be very influential. A group of humanists, known as Figurists, went on to develop a specialized interest in

---

141. Here, Valla displayed the influence of Saint Augustine, who wrote that God's message was delivered to men in eloquent fashion and written down accordingly.

142. REBHORN, *supra* note 136, at 40.

143. DESEDERIUS ERASMUS, DE DUPLICI COPIA VERBORUM AC RERUM 306–07 (Craig R. Thompson ed., Univ. of Toronto 1978).

figures of speech.[144]

## c. THOMAS WILSON (1525–1581 CE)

In 1553, Thomas Wilson, an English humanist, wrote *The Art of Rhetoric*.[145] *See Figure 5, p. 32.* Wilson's *Rhetoric* translated much of the rhetoric of Cicero and Quintilian into English for the first time, but it was not a textbook. It was written for adults entering careers in public service, the law, or the Church.[146] In it, Wilson sought to teach classical rhetoric, including each of the five canons, and to impart Christian values. He defined rhetoric as

> an art to set forth by utterance of words matter at large, or as Cicero doth say, it is a learned, or rather an artificial, declaration of the mind in the handling of any cause called in contention, that may through reason largely be discussed.[147]

He believed orators were needed "to speak fully of all those questions which by law and man's ordinance are enacted and appointed for the use and profit of man," in contrast to geometry, for example, which "rather asketh a good square than a clean flowing tongue."[148] Drawing on Cicero, he viewed the orator's goal to teach, to please, and persuade, and his judicial oratory is Ciceronian, focusing on the nature of legal issues and how they should be resolved.

Wilson was unique because he used examples from classical and contemporary literature to illustrate his text. For instance, emphasizing that an orator must ensure that his audience will understand him, he wrote:

> For what man can be delighted, or yet be persuaded, with the only hearing of those things which he knoweth not what they mean.... Therefore, Favorinus the philosopher ... did hit a young man over the thumbs very handsomely for using overold and overstrange words. 'Sirrah,' quod he, 'when our old great ancestors and grandsires were alive, they spake plainly in their mother's tongue and used old language, such as was spoken then at the building of Rome. But you talk me such a Latin as though you spake with them even now ... and only because you would have no man understand what you say.'[149]

Speech, Wilson said, should be plain, appropriate, well-composed, and beautiful, and the orator has three styles of speech at his disposal: the high or mighty, the small, and the low.[150] Wilson recommended that to speak plainly, the orator should speak as much as possible in his own language and avoid affectations of a foreign tongue.[151]

---

144. KENNEDY, *supra*, note 70, at 239. *See, e.g.*, RICHARD SHERRY, A TREATISE OF SCHEMES AND TROPES (1550).

145. THOMAS WILSON, THE ART OF RHETORIC (Peter Medine ed., 1994).

146. KENNEDY, *supra* note 70, at 248.

147. WILSON, *supra* note 145, at 45.

148. *Id.*

149. *Id.* at 46–47.

150. *Id.* at 191, 195.

151. *Id.* at 189–91.

## d. PETER RAMUS (1515–1572 CE)

The fly in the ointment for the Renaissance of rhetoric appeared in the form of Peter Ramus, a French humanist and logician. Ramus earned his Master of Arts degree from the University of Paris in 1536, having written a thesis entitled, "All Aristotle's Doctrines Are Wrong." Ramus differed from the Italian humanists in that he had no interest in revitalizing secular rhetoric for courts and assemblies.[152] He was interested in teaching students to write in a clear and simple style, as opposed to the Asiatic style of Cicero. He thought the study of style was limited to figures of speech and grammar was the study of words and sentence structure. Ramus also simplified invention by isolating ten topics from which all arguments could be generated, thus contributing to a "neatness" of style. According to Ramus, one could use these topics, such as cause, effect, and subject, to create an argument about any potential subject.[153]

As a teacher of philosophy and rhetoric, Ramus was troubled by the doctrinal overlap between dialectic and rhetoric. He thought the canons of invention and arrangement should belong to the discipline of philosophy and style and delivery should belong to rhetoric.[154] In Ramus' view, the process of discovering argument was to be distinguished from the expression of argument, and rhetoric merely expressed what logic discovered. Ramus influenced teachers primarily in England, France, and Spain. "Ramism," as his views became known, appealed to the English Puritans because it advocated a plain style. The Puritans brought Ramism to America, and Harvard College, for example, modeled its curriculum on Ramist beliefs. Ramus' influence can be seen today in the modern American university curriculum. Logic, the canon of rhetoric that Aristotle called invention, continues to be taught as a course in philosophy. The canons that Ramus left to rhetoric—arrangement, style, and delivery—are divided among contemporary English, Communications, and Speech departments.

---

### QUESTIONS FOR CONSIDERATION

1. The history of rhetoric during this period suggests that as people's freedom to speak and ability to effect social change decline, so does their interest in means of persuasion. Is that necessarily true?

2. To what extent is modern political speech designed to stabilize society "defending itself against attacks from the outside and religious movements from within?" (see pages 25–26). How do modern politicians resemble the philosophical sophists of the first centuries?

---

152. KENNEDY, *supra* note 70, at 251.

153. *See* REBHORN, *supra* note 136, at 152–53.

154. *See* PETER RAMUS, LOGIKE 17 (1574).

3. *Controversia* were advanced exercises in Roman legal argument in which students of rhetoric composed speeches and submitted them for review. Students received feedback on their written speeches and then delivered them orally. The teacher then commented on the students' delivery and often gave his own solution to the problem. Would this be a good model for legal education?

4. Why was it necessary to assign logic exclusively to the discipline of philosophy? To what extent has the fracturing of rhetoric, which began in the Middle Ages, into grammar, literature, speech, and communications perpetuated rhetoric's bad name?

5. Do contemporary audiences necessarily have the same attitude toward rhetoric that contemporary speechmakers have? How does this affect people's attitudes about the legal profession? How will this affect the way you practice law?

# C. FROM EPISTEMOLOGY TO THE ELOCUTIONARY MOVEMENT (c. 1600–1900 CE)

Rhetoric during this period can best be understood in relation to the scientific advances, inventions, and literary achievements that occurred. In the early 1600s, Galileo was pursuing Copernicus' theory that the earth was not the center of the universe and rotated around the sun. This theory was considered heretical by the Roman Catholic Church because it challenged the idea that man was made in the image of God and superior to all things.[155] In 1593, Galileo invented the thermoscope (a precursor to the modern thermometer) and in 1609, he built the first telescope to observe the solar system. At the same time, poetry and literature flourished. Donne and Milton wrote in the seventeenth century, and Shakespeare's great tragedies—*Hamlet*, *Macbeth*, and *Othello*, to name a few—were first performed between 1600 and 1613. By the end of the eighteenth century, the novel was established as a new literary art form. Daniel Defoe, for example, wrote *Robinson Crusoe* in 1719, Jonathan Swift wrote *Gulliver's Travels* in 1726, and Henry Fielding wrote *Tom Jones* in 1749. By 1755, Samuel Johnson had published the first English language dictionary.

Against this backdrop of creativity, rhetoric was challenged and championed. *See Figure 6, p. 44.* In the seventeenth century, philosophers known as epistemologists questioned traditional views on how knowledge is acquired. Convinced that logic could not produce new knowledge, they explored

---

155. In 1600, Giordano Bruno, who suggested that space was infinite and earth was part of many solar systems, was tried before the Inquisition and burned at the stake for his "Copernican" beliefs. In 1633, Galileo was also tried and convicted. His life was spared, though, and he was sentenced to renounce his beliefs and house arrest until his death in 1642.

methodologies for learning based on sensory perceptions and personal experience. They too criticized the "scholasticism" of the Medieval university system.[156] Many also criticized rhetoric, as Plato did, because of its perceived inability to discover knowledge (i.e., truth) with any level of certainty. Others, like Francis Bacon and Giambattista Vico, defended and promoted rhetoric.

By the eighteenth century, many leading epistemologists were ordained ministers. They had a specific interest in rhetoric because they wanted to use it to prove the existence of God and defend the beliefs of the Christian church. A few notable rhetorical movements developed during the period. First to emerge in the early 1700s was neoclassicism, which insisted on a rigid adherence to ancient rhetorical models and clear, unambiguous writing.[157] In the middle of the eighteenth century, the Belle Lettres Movement emerged. Belletristic scholars were primarily interested in defining taste, beauty, and sublimity; they sought out these qualities in poetry, prose, oratory, history, and philosophy. Their study of all types of literature transformed rhetoric from the study of persuasive speech into the broader discipline of literary criticism, and that transformation forever changed rhetorical study in the western world. While the Belle Lettres Movement expanded the focus of rhetoric to include the study of all literary forms, the Elocutionary Movement of the late 1800s narrowed it to delivery. Elocutionists studied the physical manifestation of human emotion and developed rules of movement for effective public speaking. The elocutionists believed the quality of speech had deteriorated in general society. Consequently, they attempted to establish a universal pronunciation and punctuation for the English language.

---

**156.** *See supra* p. 38. Aristotle thought that objects are made up of their material substance and also their universal "form," such that a human being is not only a physical body but also the universal nature of a human, namely, a rational being. Aristotle thus believed that one could acquire knowledge of the universal nature of an object through reason. For instance, one might observe that all acorns turn into oak trees. Since (as Aristotle thought) the nature of an object is the final condition of that object, the form (or universal nature) of an acorn is an oak tree. Epistemologists took issue with Aristotle's reliance on universal form to describe the character of an object (which is called teleology) and with his method of describing qualities of an object. They particularly disagreed about the question of movement. Whereas Aristotle thought that an object moves from a state of potentiality (an acorn) to its end (an oak tree), epistemologists looked for scientific explanations for movement, like gravity. *See, e.g.,* The Oxford Classical Dictionary, *supra* note 2, at 167–68.

**157.** The idea that writing should be clear assumes that the writing process is not generative and simply reflects clear thinking. This attitude toward the writing process characterizes the formalist method of teaching writing, a method that is still used today from elementary to graduate school. Twentieth-century composition theorists would later challenge the idea that writing does not create knowledge. *See infra* ch. 3, pp. 78–82.

# THE SEVENTEENTH, EIGHTEENTH, AND EARLY NINETEENTH CENTURIES

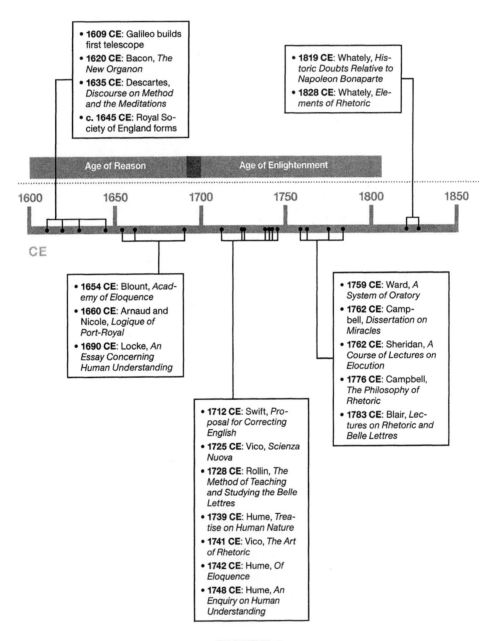

FIGURE 6

# 1. THE SEVENTEENTH CENTURY EPISTEMOLOGISTS

Inspired by the scientific advances of their day, the early epistemologists, including Bacon, Descartes, Locke, and Vico, studied the process of knowledge acquisition and its ultimate reliability. Like Plato, they struggled to understand what knowledge (truth) is and to develop a methodology for defining it. Potential sources of truth included the teachings of the Christian church (Catholicism as well as several Protestant faiths existed by this time), reason, and sensory perceptions of the world. For the most part, the early epistemologists were empiricists who believed that knowledge is acquired primarily through collecting and interpreting sensory data. They stood in stark contrast to Rene Descartes, a French philosopher who believed that some knowledge could be acquired through reason alone. The early epistemologists' struggle to articulate the process of acquiring knowledge had an enormous impact on rhetoric. The theories of just a few of the major epistemologists are included here; as you will read, their attitudes toward rhetoric varied widely.

## a. FRANCIS BACON (1561–1626 CE)

Francis Bacon, an Englishman, was the first great empiricist to reject reason as a major source of knowledge. *See Figure 6, p. 44.* He was also a successful lawyer and politician. At various times in his career, he served as Solicitor General, Attorney General, and ultimately, Lord Chancellor of England. In 1605, Bacon embarked on a plan, his so-called "Great Instauration," to develop a new philosophy about the acquisition of knowledge in all aspects of life. Bacon argued that scientists had relied too much on the logic of ancient philosophers: "[M]en have withdrawn themselves too much from the contemplation of nature and the observations of experience, and have tumbled up and down in their own reason and conceits."[158] Although Bacon did not complete his ambitious plan, he published the first of his intended series of works, *The New Organon*, in 1620. This work, titled to signify a departure from Aristotelian philosophy, detailed his method for a new kind of learning.

Bacon thought that knowledge is acquired by induction, a systematic method of careful observation that leads from particular observations to more general conclusions about the nature of things. Because the conclusions can still be false due to inadequate human perception,[159] they have to be tested. Bacon argued that Aristotelian logic demonstrates only the relationship between things *already* known. In *The New Organon*, Bacon wrote:

---

158. FRANCIS BACON, *Book 1 of the Advancement and Proficiency of Learning, in* SELECTED WRITINGS OF FRANCIS BACON 191 (Hugh C. Dick ed., 1955).

159. Bacon described faulty human perception in terms of four idols: the idol of the tribe (the inherent limitations of man like excessive emotions and inadequate sensory perception), the idol of the cave (the negative impact that an individual's personality and experiences has on one's ability to interpret sensory perceptions), the idol of the market place (the inadequacy of language among people), and the idol of the theater (the perpetuation of faulty thinking from generation to generation). *See* BACON, *Book 1 of the New Organon, id.* at 469–81.

Current logic is good for establishing and fixing errors (which are themselves based on common notions) rather than for inquiring into truth...

The syllogism consists of propositions, propositions consist of words, and words are counters for notions. Hence if the notions themselves ... are confused and abstracted from things without care, there is nothing sound in what is built on them. The only hope is true induction.[160]

Thus, Bacon rejected Aristotelianism[161] as well as the humanism of the Renaissance. Like Plato, Bacon wanted to distinguish the known from the unknown, but he disagreed with Plato that a contemplative life could actually *produce* knowledge. Nor did he think that reason could reveal fault in logic with regard to what was already known. Bacon's new philosophy was so revolutionary that in the mid–1640s, a group of philosophers formed the Royal Society of England, modeled on the French Society of Port–Royal, to discuss his ideas.[162]

Bacon's views threatened established beliefs about rhetoric as well. Having practiced law, Bacon knew the value of rhetoric, particularly in cases where reason alone was not convincing. Bacon said, "The duty and office of Rhetoric is *to apply Reason to Imagination* for the better moving of the will."[163] Bacon thought rhetorical arguments come from the *memory* of knowledge already acquired: Aristotle's topics[164] and the "commonplaces" one acquires throughout life. Commonplaces consist of popular notions of what is good and evil; typical arguments people used for and against a particular position; stock phrases already in use; and pithy statements to be "sprinkled where you will."[165] Thus, when people formulate arguments, they draw on their knowledge of the topics and commonplaces from their memory. That knowledge comes, in part, from their experience of the world (*e.g.*, a stock phrase that one hears, stores in memory, and then recalls to fit a particular occasion). Bacon even recommended that a person keep a journal of "commonplaces" observed in daily life.

As for style, Bacon preferred simplicity in writing. Like Ramus, Bacon criticized the ornate style of the Ciceronians.[166] He was particularly fond of Seneca the Younger, a Roman lawyer, philosopher, and playwright from the

---

**160.** *Id.*, aphorisms XII & XIV, at 463–64.

**161.** This term is used here to refer to Aristotle's philosophy as a whole and to distinguish it from that of Plato. *See supra* note 156 for an explanation of Aristotelian philosophy in relation to epistemology.

**162.** The Society of Port–Royal was formed in France in 1637 by a group of highly educated and religious men dedicated to prayer, study, and education. The Royal Society of London, the British counter-part to the Society of Port–Royal, still exists today. As opposed to the French Society, which was interested in literature and linguistics, the British Royal Society was and is primarily involved in scientific research.

**163.** SELECTED WRITINGS OF FRANCIS BACON, *supra* note 158, at 309.

**164.** Aristotle's "topics" were the types of argument an orator used to persuade. Aristotle thought of these as places an orator goes to find the appropriate arguments for a particular purpose. *See infra*, ch. 4, p. 105.

**165.** GOLDEN ET AL., *supra* note 85, at 88–89 (quoting 1 FRANCIS BACON, THE WORKS OF LORD BACON, 310 (1838)).

**166.** *See supra*, p. 41.

first century CE Seneca was well-known in seventeenth century England for his plain, direct style and *sententia*—brief pithy statements.[167] Accordingly, Bacon thought prose should be simple and functional. In Bacon's view, the Renaissance had focused too much on classical forms and not enough on substance. Bacon said:

> [M]en began to hunt more after words than matter; and more after the choiceness of the phrase, and the round and clean composition of the sentence, ... than after the weight of matter, worth of subject, soundness of argument, life of invention, or depth of judgment.[168]

Bacon's preference for simple prose mirrored the clarity of scientific certainty he was trying to achieve.[169]

Bacon's views on style had an immediate impact on his contemporaries. In 1599, John Hoskins, a lawyer and politician, published a handbook on writing that focused primarily on style. In *Directions for Speech and Style*, Hoskins urged brevity, perspicuity, wit, and propriety in letter writing,[170] and the handbook itself is written in a clear and matter-of-fact style. In 1654, Thomas Blount, also a lawyer, published *Academy of Eloquence*, another book on style, which became the most popular book on rhetoric for nearly thirty years. In the 1930s, Hoyt Hudson, a rhetoric professor from Princeton, discovered that Blount had plagiarized much of Hoskins' work. However, Blount added nearly 200 pages on commonplaces and form letters for everyday use. Blount's section on commonplaces was divided into situational categories so that a reader could easily find a phrase for a specific use. One commonplace for "Comparisons" reads: "My expression is but like a picture drawn with a [coal], wanting those lively colours which a more skilfull pen might give it."[171]

## b. RENE DESCARTES (1596–1650 CE)

Like Bacon, Rene Descartes had a law degree, but Descartes never practiced law. As a young man, he began studying mathematics and physics, which he loved for their certainty. Like Bacon, Descartes rejected logic as the means of acquiring knowledge because its "precepts are of avail rather in the communication of what we already know ... than in the investigation of the unknown."[172] He sought to develop a method for distinguishing "the true from the false, in order that [he]

---

167. Sententiae were intended to grab the reader's attention and often took the form of proverbs such as "to need no pleasure is itself a pleasure" or "no one is laughable who can laugh at himself." Not surprisingly, Cicero criticized Seneca's liberal, "undisciplined" use of sententiae.

168. SELECTED WRITINGS OF FRANCIS BACON, *supra* note 158, at 181.

169. *See* GOLDEN, ET AL., *supra* note 85, at 92.

170. JOHN HOSKINS, DIRECTIONS FOR SPEECH AND STYLE 4–8 (Hoyt H. Hudson ed., 1935).

171. THOMAS BLOUNT, THE ACADEMY OF ELOQUENCE 59 (R.C. Alston ed., Scolar Press Ltd. 1971) (1654).

172. RENE DESCARTES, DISCOURSE ON METHOD AND THE MEDITATIONS 20 (John Veitch trans., 1989). Part Four of *Discourse* contains Descartes' famous statement, "I think therefore I am," which served, in his mind, to establish the existence of the human mind as being separate from the body. *See id.* at 30.

might be able clearly to discriminate the right path in life, and proceed in it with confidence."[173] In 1635, Descartes published *Discourse On Method*, which set out the following steps for acquiring certain knowledge: 1) accept as true only those propositions that are absolutely free from doubt, 2) divide each inquiry into as many parts as possible, 3) move from simple to complex concepts, and 4) be thorough.[174] *See Figure 6, p. 44.* The method he articulated relied heavily on the power of reason to determine truth and control the imagination and became known as rationalism.

In *Discourse,* Descartes recounted the evolution of his intellectual interests. As a young man, he said, he thought that "eloquence" was a gift, like the ability to write poetry, but it was not a subject that taught any true knowledge.[175] He observed that those who have a natural talent for rhetoric are always the most persuasive, whether or not they are familiar with the rules of rhetoric. Like Plato, he thought rhetoric could lead only to probable truth, so he turned to subjects he found more satisfying. Descartes believed that humans had innate knowledge that could be trusted as certain. Motivated in part by his desire to prove the existence of God, Descartes claimed that the idea of God was innate in his mind. As Descartes said, without that knowledge, "I do not see that I can ever be certain of anything."[176]

Descartes' views heavily influenced the work of the Society of Port–Royal.[177] In 1660, French philosophers Arnaud and Nicole published *Logique of Port–Royal,*[178] which expanded on Descartes' views. According to Arnaud and Nicole, the primary pursuit in life was to gain truth with a mathematical certainty, and they too eschewed old-fashioned logic, appeals to emotion, and even Bacon's commonplaces. By declaring that the function of rhetoric is to communicate knowledge acquired by philosophers, Arnaud and Nicole further cemented the division between logic and rhetoric.[179]

## c. JOHN LOCKE (1632–1704 CE)

John Locke, an English empiricist, conceived of the mind as having two major faculties: the understanding (Locke's term for knowledge) and the will. Unlike

---

173. *Id.* at 15.

174. *Id.* at 21.

175. *Id.* at 14.

176. *Id.* at 87. Descartes assumed that any object that you can conceive of has a true and immutable nature. Even mathematical figures, which no one has ever seen, have indisputable properties. To discover these properties, one must only think of the object and use the faculty of reason. Similarly, Descartes argued that he could perceive a supreme being, and using his faculty of reason, he could not imagine such a being as anything but all-powerful and benevolent. God would not be perfect unless He existed, and if he were not benevolent, we would not be able to trust our perceptions at all. *See id.* at 86–97.

177. *See supra* note 162.

178. ANTOINE ARNAUD & PIERRE NICOLE, LOGIC, OR THE ART OF THINKING (Jill Vance Buroker ed., 1996).

179. *See, e.g., id.* at 16 and 181–82.

Descartes, Locke thought that people start out as blank slates. Knowledge comes from sensory perceptions that are stored in our memories as ideas. Ideas then become related to one another, and we associate them together in our minds. Locke agreed with Bacon and Descartes that logic relates only to knowledge already acquired. The syllogism, he said, is "the art of fencing with the little Knowledge we have, without making any addition to it."[180] Locke went even further in saying that syllogisms "are not the only nor the best way of reasoning, for the leading of those into truth who are willing to find it and desire to make the best use they may of their reason for the attainment of knowledge."[181]

Locke thought that ideas alone could not motivate action. To affect the faculty of the will, one had to rely on rhetoric. According to Locke, a person must be in a state of uneasiness, which he described as the absence of some good, before he will act. When a person is at ease, he is content without action. To stir a person to uneasiness required rhetoric—the arousal of emotion.[182] Although he recognized the power of rhetoric, Locke agreed with Plato that rhetoric is a "powerful instrument of error and deceit."[183] He even went so far as to argue that the sole purpose of eloquence and rhetoric was to "insinuate wrong *ideas*, move the passions, and thereby mislead the judgment."[184] In the end, though, Locke thought it hopeless to argue against the use of rhetoric, because "*[e]loquence*, like the fair Sex, has too prevailing beauties in it.... [a]nd it is vain to find fault with those Arts of Deceiving, wherein Men find pleasure to be Deceived."[185]

## d. GIAMBATTISTA VICO (1668–1744 CE)

Vico, an Italian rhetoric professor, was well versed in the classics and admired Plato, Tacitus,[186] and Cicero. He defined rhetoric as "the faculty of speaking appropriate to the purpose of persuading."[187] He shared the epistemologists' interest in knowledge, but he disagreed with Descartes that mathematical concepts were more certain than other man-made concepts. Vico believed that all knowledge was subjective, and therefore, reason based on probability can lead to truth just as much as mathematics can. Vico believed that logic alone prevented the development of new ideas. He thought one should study logic and philosophy only after having a command of rhetorical principles so rhetoric could be used to expand on what was already known.[188] His ideas aided in the development of the

---

180. JOHN LOCKE, AN ESSAY CONCERNING HUMAN UNDERSTANDING vol. 2, bk. IV, ch. xvii, p. 272 (John Yolton ed., 1964).

181. *Id.* at 265.

182. *Id.* at vol. 1, bk II, ch. xx, pp. 190–93.

183. *Id.* at vol. 2, bk. III, ch. x, p. 106.

184. *Id.* at 105.

185. *Id.* at 106.

186. Tacitus was a Roman orator and historian in the first century CE, who wrote in a grand Ciceronian style.

187. GIAMBATTISTA VICO, THE ART OF RHETORIC 5 (Giorgio A. Pinton & Arthur W. Shippee trans. and eds., 1996) (c. 1711–44).

188. *See* KENNEDY, *supra* note 70, at 272.

current scientific method based on hypotheses.

Vico later expanded his ideas on the importance of rhetoric in his 1725 book *New Science. See Figure 6, p. 44.* In this work, Vico argued that rhetoric was the key to understanding past cultures, including their ideas, customs, and modes of communication.[189] He then studied several cultures based on their rhetoric and other modes of communication. He believed that past and present cultures are cyclical in their progression of belief systems because they all start by believing in a form of mythology and later develop advanced philosophical systems.[190]

## 2. THE EIGHTEENTH CENTURY EPISTEMOLOGISTS

Christianity's intellectual stronghold weakened during the eighteenth century, and the interest in scientific knowledge and its acquisition intensified. Rationalism—a theory of knowledge based on the use of logic and reason—took root in Europe, while empiricism dominated in England. This general thirst for secular knowledge spurred the creation of many scientific societies, libraries, encyclopedias, and dictionaries.[191] David Hume, for example, explored the nature of sensory perception, taking issue with nearly all well-established philosophical ideas. His work has had an enormous impact on modern epistemological theory. Others, including George Campbell and Richard Whately, focused on psychology and science in studying man's relationship to God, the nature and function of human discourse, and the potential for persuasive argument in democratic and Christian societies.[192]

## a. DAVID HUME (1711–1776 CE)

Hume was a Scottish philosopher who approached politics, religion, epistemology, and a host of other philosophical subjects from a skeptical point of view. Although heavily influenced by Descartes, Hume was a staunch empiricist. He questioned both Descartes' reliance on reason and his belief in the existence of innate ideas. Hume was interested in Locke's work on the capacity of human understanding, and in 1739, he published *A Treatise of Human Nature.*[193] *See Figure 6, p. 44.* According to Hume, all mental perceptions are the product either of ideas or sensory impressions, such as seeing an object. All subsequent ideas about that object are "copied" from our impressions and can be traced back to our original external sensation of that object or internal feeling in response to it.[194]

---

**189.** THE NEW SCIENCE OF GIAMBATTISTA VICO 65, 75–76 (Thomas Goddard Bergin & Max Harold Fisch trans., 3d ed. 1984).

**190.** *See id.* at 104–06.

**191.** GOLDEN, ET AL., *supra* note 85, at 97.

**192.** Other eighteenth century English epistemologists include David Hartley, Henry Homes (Lord Kames), and Joseph Priestly.

**193.** DAVID HUME, A TREATISE OF HUMAN NATURE (David Fate Norton & Mary J. Norton eds., 2000).

**194.** *Id.* at pt. 1, § 1, p. 7.

The only difference between our ideas and impressions is one of degree.[195]

Like Locke, Hume believed that knowledge was acquired through experience and observation, but Hume doubted the reliability of human perception, particularly with regard to religion. These doubts translated into a direct attack on the reliability of inductive reasoning in *An Enquiry On Human Understanding*.[196] According to Hume, the problem with inductive reasoning, referred to then as "the scientific method," was that it was circular. If one billiard ball is moving toward another, and you want to predict what the balls will do, there is no way to prove your theory is right. Although each time you observe the balls hit you begin to form an idea of what will happen the next time, you can never be certain. Although we assume there is a connection between an observed pattern of behavior and future behavior, that connection can only be inferred.[197] Hume was particularly skeptical about Christians' claims of having witnessed miracles, and he found their testimony unsupportable: "[N]o testimony is sufficient to establish a miracle, unless the testimony be of such a kind, that its falsehood would be more miraculous, than the fact, which it endeavors to establish."[198]

Like Locke, Hume thought appeals to emotion were necessary to induce action. Hume said, "Eloquence, when at its highest pitch, leaves little room for reason or reflection; but addressing itself entirely to the fancy or the affections, captivates the willing hearers, and subdues their understanding."[199] In 1742, Hume published a collection of essays, including *Of Eloquence,* in which he bemoaned the quality of oratory in contemporary England and called for a return to inspired speech. With reference to the oratorical accomplishments of the ancient world, Hume said, "[I]f we be superior in philosophy, we are still, notwithstanding all our refinements, much inferior in eloquence."[200] Hume preferred Cicero's Asiatic style to the popular and simple style of the Attic orators. He urged the English orators of his day to focus more on "order and method" so as to make their point

> conspicuous to the hearers, who will be infinitely pleased to see the arguments rise naturally from one another, and will retain a more thorough persuasion, than can arise from the strongest reasons, which are thrown together in confusion.[201]

As a key figure in what became known as the Age of Enlightenment, Hume inspired

---

195. *Id.*

196. David Hume, An Enquiry Concerning Human Understanding (Tom L. Beauchamp ed., 2000).

197. *See id.* at § 4, pt. 1, ¶ 25, p. 29.

198. *Id.* at § 10, pt. 1, ¶ 91, pp. 115–16. Aristotle put oaths, witness testimony, and documents in the category of non-artistic proofs, a category he considered unimportant. Hume's interest in the reliability of witness testimony was new.

199. *Id.* at § 10, pt. 2, ¶ 93, p. 118.

200. 3 Philosophical Works of David Hume 164 (T.H. Green & T.H. Grose eds., 1964).

201. *Id.* at 174.

some of the greatest speeches of the American and French Revolutions.

## b. GEORGE CAMPBELL (1719–1796 CE)

Born in Aberdeen, Scotland, Campbell started his career as a law student in Edinburgh but quickly became interested in theology and philosophy. In 1748, Campbell was ordained as a Presbyterian minister and became a professor of divinity at Marischal College in Aberdeen. Influenced by Bacon, Locke, and Hume, Campbell used his observations of human nature to explain argument, poetry, and preaching. In doing so, he articulated general principles of rhetoric that could be used to teach it. In 1776, Campbell published *The Philosophy of Rhetoric*,[202] which combined the best theories of the classical and eighteenth century philosophers, rhetoricians, and scientists. *See Figure 6, p. 44.* Like Locke, Campbell believed that the mind had the faculties of understanding and will, but to these he added the faculties of imagination and the passions. According to Campbell, a speaker must engage the audience's imagination in order to stir its passions.[203] Although Campbell's rhetorical theory can be applied to all forms of rhetoric, he intended it to prepare Christians to defend their beliefs against attacks, such as Hume's attack on miracles.

Similar to Vico, Campbell defined rhetoric as " 'that art or talent by which the discourse is adapted to its end.' "[204] Campbell said that rhetoric had one of four goals: to enlighten understanding, to please the imagination, to move the passions, or to influence the will.[205] According to Campbell, truth could only be achieved through logic, but persuasion required logic grounded in truth. Rhetoric then sparked the imagination and passions and motivated the will:

> If the orator would prove successful, it is necessary that he engage in his service all these different powers of the mind, the imagination, the memory, and the passions. These are not the supplanters of reason, or even rivals in her sway; they are her handmaids, by whose ministry she is enabled to usher truth into the heart, and procure it there a favourable reception.[206]

In Campbell's view, the best way to persuade was to combine strong appeals to reason and powerful, emotional appeals to the passions.

Campbell explored in detail two of the five traditional canons of rhetoric: invention and style. Like Ramus and many epistemologists before him, Campbell viewed logic as a separate "art of thinking and reasoning."[207] Although rhetoric employed logic, the art of reasoning and the process of acquiring knowledge were not a part of rhetoric. With regard to logical appeals, Campbell said they should consist primarily of moral evidence, which could establish the existence

---

202. GEORGE CAMPBELL, PHILOSOPHY OF RHETORIC (1851).

203. *Id.* at 95–97, 99–103.

204. *Id.* at 1.

205. *Id.*

206. *Id.* at 94.

207. *Id.* at 56.

of a fact but not its certainty. Moral evidence consisted of experience, analogy, testimony, and calculations of chances, such as statistical probabilities.[208] In contrast to Hume, Campbell argued that credible witness testimony is the best form of evidence for proving the existence of a fact because it is based on personal observation and not conjecture.[209] In 1762, he wrote his *Dissertation on Miracles*, which argued, in direct response to Hume, that the Apostles' testimony was credible because it had yet to be disproved.[210]

Like his predecessors, Campbell examined the emotions likely to motivate action and added both humor and wit to the growing list.[211] With respect to ethical appeals, Campbell recognized that the audience must trust the speaker, a particular problem for lawyers because the audience knows

> that he must defend his client, and argue on the side on which he is retained. We know, also, that a trifling and accidental circumstance, which nowise affects the merits of the cause, such as a prior application from the adverse party, would probably have made him employ the same acuteness and display the same fervour on the opposite side of the question. This circumstance, though not considered as a fault in the character of the man, but a natural ... consequent of the office, cannot fail ... to make us shyer of yielding our assent.[212]

Campbell also observed that lawyers' explanations of the law could be so complicated that they "hath come to be distinguished by the name *chicane*, a species of reasoning too abstruse to command attention of any continuance even from the studious, and, consequently, not very favourable to the powers of rhetoric."[213]

Campbell's views on style were as influential as his views on knowledge and invention. Like Cicero and Bacon, Campbell admonished speakers to consider the audience when fashioning their speech. Generally, he advised that audiences respond best to arguments that can be understood (*i.e.*, clear), use lively language, are organized in such a way as to be memorable, and stir the emotions. He also advised speakers to know the characteristics of their particular audience, and he recognized that the more varied the individuals in the audience, the more difficult it is to be effective.[214] As between lawyers, politicians, and preachers, he thought it easiest for lawyers to anticipate their audience:

> The pleader has, in this respect, the simplest and the easiest task of all; the

---

**208.** *Id.* at 72.

**209.** *Id.* at 76–78.

**210.** *See generally* GEORGE CAMPBELL, A DISSERTATION ON MIRACLES (2007).

**211.** CAMPBELL, PHILOSOPHY OF RHETORIC, *supra* note 202, at 30–42.

**212.** *Id.* at 123.

**213.** *Id.* at 127. Chicane comes from French and means "to quibble"; Chaucer, who also studied law, associated the legal profession with trickery as early as the fourteenth century. *See supra*, at note 28.

**214.** He advised the speaker to consider his audience's "age, rank, fortune, education, [and] prejudices." CAMPBELL, *supra* note 202, at 124.

judges ... being commonly men of the same rank, of similar education, and not differing greatly in respect of studies or attainments. The difference in these respects is much more considerable when he addresses the jury.[215]

With respect to word choice, which he called usage, Campbell thought that words should be chosen that are reputable, national, and of present use. "Reputable" meant language that conforms to a standard to be measured against the language of authors of reputation, known for their knowledge and communicative skills. "National" meant language that was neither provincial nor foreign, and "of present use" meant language that was neither modern nor obsolete.[216]

## c. RICHARD WHATELY (1787–1863 CE)

Like Campbell, Richard Whately was an ordained minister (but in the Episcopal Church). He became the Archbishop of Dublin in 1831. He too studied law and theology and was interested in exploring rhetoric's ability to defend Christianity. In 1819, he published *Historic Doubts Relative to Napolean Bonaparte*, a satire intended to show that Hume's skeptical response to the testimony of miracles could be used to doubt even the existence of Napolean, who was known to be alive and living on the Italian isle of Elba. In 1828, Whately published *Elements of Rhetoric*,[217] which was the precursor to modern argumentation theory, and its core concepts are still relevant today. *See Figure 6, p. 44.* In *Elements*, Whately confined his inquiry exclusively to the rhetoric of argument—as opposed to poetry or literature—and addressed invention, style, and delivery.

Whately agreed with Campbell that rhetoric uses knowledge acquired outside the rhetorical process, but he criticized Campbell's view that logic invents arguments. "[H]is [Campbell's] great defect ... is his ignorance and utter misconception of the nature and object of Logic;... Rhetoric being in truth an off-shoot of Logic, that Rhetorician must labour under great disadvantages who is not only ill-acquainted with that system, but also utterly unconscious of his deficiency."[218] Whately believed that logic could verify arguments, but rhetoricians invented them: "The *finding* of suitable arguments to prove a given point, and the skilful *arrangement* of them, may be considered as the immediate and proper province of Rhetoric, and that alone."[219] According to Whately, the speaker must know in advance the propositions he intends to establish and then convey his proof in an effective manner. Whately divided argument into two types: *a priori* and signs. He described *a priori* arguments as those that proceed from cause to effect, or an argument that points to some evidence that normally leads to a certain effect, which is the alleged proposition.[220] In contrast, a sign

---

215. *Id.*

216. *Id.* at 164–74.

217. RICHARD WHATELY, ELEMENTS OF RHETORIC (Douglas Ehninger, ed. 1963).

218. *Id.* at 9.

219. *Id.* at 39.

220. *See id.* at 46–52.

does not proceed from cause to effect but from effect to condition. The evidence in an argument based on a sign is not the cause of the alleged proposition, but it is a symbol of it and infers a connection between the evidence and the result.[221]

To illustrate the difference between *a priori* arguments and signs, Whately used the example of a man charged with murder: Assume the proposition to be proved is that the defendant is guilty. The prosecutor might try to establish the defendant's guilt by arguing that the defendant hated the victim. If the defendant's guilt were assumed for the moment, the defendant's hatred of the victim could account for or explain the defendant's act, and the argument would thus be *a priori*. According to Whately, the more likely a cause is to produce a given effect, the stronger the argument based on that cause. In the above example, the argument is relatively weak because many people hate others but do not murder them.[222] On the other hand, if the prosecutor argued that the defendant was guilty based on the fact that the defendant was found with blood on his clothes, that would be a sign of guilt (*i.e.*, the defendant's clothes got bloody in the act of murdering his victim). Assuming for the moment that the defendant is guilty, the blood on the defendant's clothes would not prove that he committed the murder, but it would suggest a probability that he did.[223]

Whately argued that the most credible kind of sign-type arguments was witness testimony. Like Campbell, he was interested in developing a theory that would enable him to argue that God exists. He categorized testimony into three types and advised a speaker to use a combination of types to achieve the best results. First, "undesigned testimony" was testimony that was incidental to the existence of a fact, as opposed to a direct assertion of its existence.[224] For example, one might testify, "I called to wave hello to the defendant just as the traffic light changed to red." According to Whately, that kind of testimony was more effective in proving the light was red than a direct statement from the plaintiff that "the light was red." Second, "negative testimony" was the failure to contradict an alleged proposition, which tended to establish the existence of that proposition in the jury's mind.[225] For example, if the plaintiff argued that the light was red as the defendant entered the intersection, the defendant's failure to contradict the plaintiff's testimony helped convince the jury that the light was indeed red. As you will learn, only in criminal cases is the jury prohibited from drawing negative inferences from a defendant's silence. Third, Whately's "concurrent testimony" referred to the independent weight juries give to testimony from multiple, credible witnesses whose testimony is identical but who have not collaborated.[226] In Whately's view, the whole of this testimony was greater than the sum of its parts. For example, although most people have not

---

221. *See id.* at 53–54.

222. *See id.* at 46.

223. *See id.* at 47.

224. *Id.* at 63–64.

225. *Id.* at 66.

226. *Id.* at 66–68.

observed the movement of the planets, they believe that the planets move in orbit around the sun. This belief is not based on personal observation but on the agreement of a large number of competing and independent scientists.

Whately is best known for his work on presumptions and burdens of proof. He defined a presumption as "such a *pre-occupation* of the ground, as implies that it must stand good till some sufficient reason is adduced against it; in short, that the *Burden of proof* lies on the side of him who would dispute it."[227] Stated in modern terms, a presumption is the advantage given by the fact finder to an alleged proposition. If there is a presumption in favor of a proposition, then the opposing party has the burden of disproving it. To use Whately's example, a defendant charged with a crime is presumed innocent; therefore, the prosecution has the burden of disproving his innocence (*i.e.*, proving guilt). Even if it is highly probable that the defendant is guilty, he need not state a defense until a sufficient quantum of evidence suggests his guilt. Whately concluded that although there might be a presumption in favor of a given proposition, the presumption did not make proof of the proposition more likely, and the presumption could still be refuted.[228] Once a presumption was refuted, the burden of proof would shift to the party whose position the presumption initially favored to prove the existence of the alleged proposition.[229]

## 3. NEOCLASSICISM (c. 1700–1740 CE)

Alongside the epistemologists, the neoclassicists struggled to preserve the pre-eminence of the classics. Writers like Jonathan Swift, Alexander Pope, John Lawson, John Ward, and John Dryden worried that empirical science would replace traditional literary precepts. Influenced by the French Academy under the reign of Louis XIV,[230] they were devoted to classical forms and advocated the study and imitation of Aristotle, Cicero, and Quintilian. The intensity of the struggle that took place between the neoclassicists and the epistemologists was captured by Jonathan Swift in a wonderful story, *The Battle of the Books*.[231] In it, a battle takes place between ancient and modern philosophers and rhetoricians, each of whom is represented by a book in the stacks of St. James Library in London. The books begin to quarrel and then engage in a battle that leaves the book of Bacon wounded and Descartes dead.

Several rhetorical texts were written during this period, but due in part to the neoclassicists' endorsement of imitation, these texts did not do much more than reiterate the principles of classical rhetoric in the English vernacular. John

---

227. *Id.* at 112.

228. *Id.* at 124.

229. *Id.* at 124–25.

230. The French Academy was and is the official authority on the French language. Its primary function is to prepare and revise the French dictionary. The Academy is often criticized for its conservative attitude toward recognizing new words and grammatical developments.

231. JONATHAN SWIFT, THE BATTLE OF THE BOOKS (Sir Henry Craik ed., 1912).

Ward, for example, published a lecture series called *A System of Oratory*,[232] in which he examined the canons of rhetoric, focusing on style. *See Figure 6, p. 44.* Although used in American colleges and universities until the nineteenth century, it contributed little to the field of rhetoric.[233] The neoclassicists' work did, however, inspire a renewed interest in style. Like Hume, they criticized the quality of public speaking. Swift thought the state of spoken English at that time was deplorable:

> [I]ts daily Improvements are by no means in proportion to its daily Corruptions; that the Pretenders to polish and refine it, have chiefly multiplied Abuses and Absurdities; and, that in many Instances, it offends against every Part of Grammar.[234]

Today, journalists, authors, and lawyers aspire to the "elegant middle style" Dryden and writers like Swift employed.[235]

## 4. THE BELLE LETTRES MOVEMENT IN THE EIGHTEENTH CENTURY

The Belle Lettres Movement in the mid–1700s affected rhetoric in Europe and the United States although not much space is devoted to it here. Although belletristic scholars were well acquainted with the classics, their rhetorical interests lay primarily in literature and literary criticism. Influenced by the revival of Longinus' *On the Sublime*,[236] French and English scholars explored the concepts of taste, beauty, and sublimity. As Longinus had defined it, sublimity was the power to amaze, not the ability to persuade.[237] Scholars like Joseph Addison, John Baillie, Edmund Burke, and Charles Rollin analyzed whether good taste is innate or learned and what makes a work of art beautiful or sublime. The Belle Lettres Movement shifted the focus of rhetorical theory from persuasive speech to all forms of literature (*e.g.*, poetry, drama, oratory, history, and philosophy) and their aesthetic effect. Rollin, for example, published *The Method of Teaching and Studying the Belle Lettres*,[238] in which he analyzed eloquence in the courtroom as well as in Christian oratory.

### Hugh Blair (1718–1800 CE)

The most influential belletristic scholar was Hugh Blair, an ordained minister and Professor of Rhetoric and Belle Lettres at the University of Edinburgh. Blair and his fellow Scotsmen, Campbell and Lord Kames, were often referred to as

---

**232.** John Ward, I & II A System of Oratory (1759).

**233.** Golden, et al., *supra* note 85, at 75.

**234.** Jonathan Swift, A Proposal for Correcting English 8 (R.C. Alston ed., 1969).

**235.** *See* The Plain English Movement, *infra*, pp. 260–263.

**236.** *See* Longinus, *supra* note 79.

**237.** *See id.* at 1–2.

**238.** Charles Rollin, The Method of Teaching and Studying the Belles Lettres (A. Bettesworth and C. Hitch trans., 1734).

the Scottish triumvirate, and Edinburgh was referred to as the "Athens of the North." Blair had been lecturing at Edinburgh on rhetoric for twenty-four years when he published his *Lectures on Rhetoric and Belle Lettres*[239] in 1783. *See Figure 6, p. 44.* A collection of forty-seven essays, Blair's *Lectures* was designed for students with little training in the classics. More than half of *Lectures* deals with aspects of writing: taste, sublimity, beauty, and style. He defined taste as the "power of receiving pleasure from the beauties of nature and art,"[240] and he believed it could be improved through education and culture.[241] According to Blair, sublimity, which is derived from simplicity and conciseness, has an explosive effect, whereas beauty produces a less violent but long-lasting serenity.[242]

Blair defined rhetoric as "the art of speaking in such a manner as to attain the end for which we speak" or "the Art of Persuasion."[243] He acknowledged its reputation for being a "contemptible art," but he recognized its usefulness in society:

> Whenever a man speaks or writes, he is supposed, as a rational being, to have some end in view; either to inform, or to amuse, or to persuade, or, in some way or other, to act upon his fellow-creatures. He who speaks, or writes, in such a manner as to adapt all his words most effectually to that end, is the most eloquent man. Whatever then the subject be, there is room for eloquence; in history, or even in philosophy, as well as in orations.[244]

Blair's division of rhetoric into three types differed from Aristotle's: eloquence (his word for celebratory and deliberative rhetoric), judicial, and pulpit.[245] Blair stated that the goal of "speaking at the bar" is to persuade judges about "what is just and true," and therefore, lawyers must speak primarily to the faculty of understanding.[246] Blair thought a lawyer "would expose himself to ridicule by attempting that high vehement tone, which is only proper in speaking to a multitude."[247] Blair's *Lectures* was enormously popular. By 1835, fifty editions had been published, and it was used in English and American schools until the end of the nineteenth century.

# 5. ELOCUTIONARY MOVEMENT

The elocutionists studied delivery—the canon of rhetoric that Aristotle had ignored. Scholars like Thomas Sheridan, John Rice, John Walker, James Burgh, and Gilbert Austin justified their narrow focus on several grounds: the lack of a definitive work on the subject of delivery (which they called elocution); increasing

---

**239.** HUGH BLAIR, LECTURES ON RHETORIC AND BELLES LETTRES (1833).

**240.** *Id.* at 10.

**241.** *Id.* at 12.

**242.** *Id.* at 42, 51.

**243.** *Id.* at 314–15.

**244.** *Id.*

**245.** *See* GOLDEN, ET AL., *supra* note 85 at 80.

**246.** BLAIR, *supra* note 239, at 360.

**247.** *Id.* at 360–61.

opportunities for public speaking in English law, politics, and society; and the continued poor grammar and pronunciation of contemporary speech and writing. In *A Course of Lectures on Elocution*, Sheridan stated, "That a general inability to read, or speak, with propriety and grace in public, runs thro' the natives of the British dominions, is acknowledged; it shows itself in our senates and churches, on the bench and at the bar."[248] Sheridan established a series of detailed rules for the management of the voice, countenance, and gesture in speaking, such as emphasizing certain syllables. He also advised speakers to articulate and pronounce words correctly, to speak with emphasis and intonation, and use appropriate facial expression and gesture. Above all, a speaker needed to appear to believe his own argument: "[H]ow can we suppose it possible that he effect this, unless he delivers himself in the manner which is always used by persons who speak in earnest? How shall his words pass for truth, when they bear not its stamp?"[249]

In *Elements of Elocution*, published in 1781, John Walker stated that every emotion has "a particular attitude of the body, cast off the eye, and tone of the voice that particularly belongs to that passion."[250] *See Figure 6, p. 44.* For example, Walker said, "When any thing sublime, lofty, or heavenly is expressed, the eye and the right hand may be very properly elevated; and when anything low, inferior, or grovelling is referred to, the eye and hand may be directed downwards."[251] James Burgh also said that each internal emotion has a unique outward manifestation. "Persuasion," he said, is characterized by "the looks of moderate love. Its accents are soft, flattering, emphatical and articulate."[252] At the turn of the century, Gilbert Austin established a comprehensive system for effective voice and gesturing in public speaking. In *Chironomia*, Austin devoted two chapters to voice and fifteen chapters to gesture.[253] The book included drawings of gestures and diagrams for movements to make while gesturing.[254]

---

### QUESTIONS FOR CONSIDERATION

1. **Do you agree with the epistemologists that deductive thinking—logic—is incapable of producing knowledge or truth? How certain must knowledge be in order for it to be valuable? How does that affect your attitude towards legal argument?**

---

248. THOMAS SHERIDAN, A COURSE OF LECTURES ON ELOCUTION 1 (1762, reissued 1968).

249. *Id.* at 5.

250. 2 JOHN WALKER, ELEMENTS OF ELOCUTION 264 (R.C. Alston, ed., 1969).

251. *Id.* at 266.

252. GOLDEN, ET AL., *supra* note 85, at 132.

253. GILBERT AUSTIN, CHIRONOMIA (1805). "Chironomia" translates roughly into the study of hand gestures. The term dates back to a theatrical code of hand gestures used by Roman actors as far back as the first century CE. Both Cicero and Quintilian acknowledged this practice in their discussions of an orator's delivery, and both Sheridan and Walker were actors.

254. *Id.* at 1–3.

2. Think about what happens when you write a paper or take an essay exam. Do you think that any kind of knowledge is created in the process? What impact does your answer have on the value or role of rhetoric in society?

3. Society's interest in the classics has been cyclical, most notably occurring during the Second Sophistic period, the Renaissance, and Neoclassicism. Why do people return to the classics?

4. Why was the Belle Lettres movement so successful in transforming rhetoric into the study of literature? What does that say about society's belief in its power to effect change?

5. Why has there been such a high correlation between rhetorical theorists and lawyers? Is it just coincidence?

# CHAPTER 3

## CONTEMPORARY RHETORIC

■ ■ ■

*"Rhetoric is the art, practice, and study of human communication."*
*—Andrea Lunsford*

As Andrea Lunsford's definition of rhetoric indicates, the field of rhetoric now includes the study of all aspects of communication. James Kinneavy, a leading rhetorician, noted in 1971 that rhetoric had come to mean "the whole field of the uses of language."[1] Kinneavy is best known for his triangular representation of language as consisting of an encoder (the person who encodes a message), the signal that carries the message (language), the reality to which the message refers; and the decoder (the receiver of the message).[2]

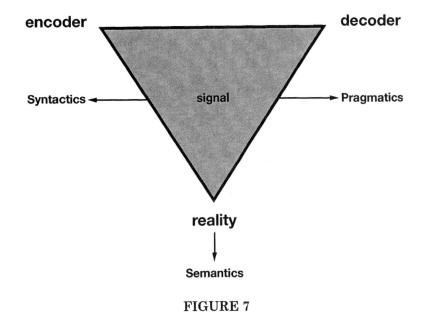

FIGURE 7

---

1.   JAMES L. KINNEAVY, A THEORY OF DISCOURSE 3 (1971).

2.   *Id.* at 19.

In *A Theory of Discourse*, Kinneavy explored the fields of study associated with each part of the communication triangle, known collectively as semiotics. The study of the signal (the message itself) he called syntactics or grammar. Syntactics includes the study of speech, sounds, word derivations, and the structure of language.[3] The study of the signal's meaning, both the words and the reality it represents, he called semantics.[4] Finally, the study of different types of texts, including fiction, non-fiction, poetry, argument, sermons, protests, and prayer, is called pragmatics.[5] Pragmatics generally describes the subject matter of a typical student's English classes from elementary school through college, whether devoted to reading literature or writing.

Each of these fields of rhetoric is relevant to the study of law. I.A. Richards, for example, was a well-known semanticist. In exploring the inadequacy of language to communicate meaning, he discussed the weakness of analogical reasoning. Since lawyers relying on common law use analogical reasoning, a familiarity with Richards' work is useful. Richard Weaver, a composition teacher and philosopher, argued that all discourse—dialectic and rhetoric—is persuasive discourse. He explored the ethics of persuasion, including legal argument. Kenneth Burke—considered to be the greatest rhetorician of the twentieth century—also believed that all forms of communication are persuasion. Weaver and Burke shed light on the meaning of "objective" legal analysis and the role it plays in the practice of law. Stephen Toulmin and Chaim Perelman, scholars of logic and rhetoric, articulated theories on informal logic that explain reasoning in everyday life in a way Aristotle's syllogism cannot. Of equal importance to law students is a familiarity with the composition theories that shaped them as writers and how these theories continue to influence their choices. Finally, every beginning law student should be familiar with the rhetoric of twentieth-century legal philosophers, who have had a profound impact on the legal academy and the practice of law. Understanding the influence of these philosophies on modern legal argument is essential to the legal writer.

# A. THE INADEQUACY OF LANGUAGE

I. A. Richards (1893–1979) defined rhetoric broadly as the "study of misunderstanding and its remedies."[6] He was particularly interested in how words acquire meaning and their inability to convey what people intend. Richards was an English-born literary critic, poet, teacher, and rhetorician. In the 1920s and 1930s, he taught in Peking as a visiting professor and at Harvard. He developed an interest in Basic English, a reduced version of the English language developed by C. K. Ogden in Cambridge, England. Ogden designed Basic English, comprised of just 850 words, to be a universal language that used

---

3.    *Id.* at 26.

4.    *Id.*

5.    *Id.* at 28.

6.    I.A. RICHARDS, THE PHILOSOPHY OF RHETORIC 3 (1936).

plain and simple terms.[7] Two of his most notable works are *The Meaning of Meaning*,[8] which he co-authored with Ogden, and *The Philosophy of Rhetoric*.[9]

Richards argued that language often leads to misunderstanding. Richards' view was reminiscent of Bacon's Idol of the Marketplace—the idea that language is often inadequate and leads to confusion.[10] Since words have no intrinsic meaning, they have only the meaning the listener attributes to them. Assume a friend tells you she is going on vacation with her family. Every family vacation you have ever been on has been a disaster, and the minute she says the word "vacation" you get a stomachache. To you, the word "vacation" means stress, arguments, lost tickets, and bad service. To your friend, "vacation" may mean something entirely different: relaxation, conversation, movies, and fun food. Richards would argue this example illustrates that the meaning we attach to words comes from past experiences. In this way, Richards said, words communicate our thoughts about things but not the things themselves.[11]

Thus "theory of abstraction" led Richards to conclude that language is primarily metaphoric. Since words mean different things to different people, we make comparisons to clarify meaning: "Thought is metaphoric, and proceeds by comparison, and the metaphors of language derive therefrom."[12] In *Romeo and Juliet*, for example, Romeo observes Juliet approach her bedroom window and cries, "But, soft! What light through yonder window breaks? It is the east, and Juliet is the sun."[13] Romeo compares Juliet (what Richards would call the tenor of the metaphor or the thing referred to) to the rising of the sun (what Richards would call the vehicle of the metaphor). The metaphor communicates Romeo's joy in seeing Juliet in a powerful and elegant way.

Legal argument too is metaphoric. Stare decisis requires that like cases be treated alike to ensure fairness and predictability. If the case before the court resembles a prior case in a number of significant ways, an advocate may convince the court to decide the case the same way. Because no two cases are identical, the most that metaphor can do is persuade the court to treat the two cases as though they were identical (*i.e.*, as if Juliet were the sun). Because the comparison

---

7. He criticized Campbell, for example, who advocated using the language of "those who have had a liberal education, and are therefore presumed to be best acquainted with men and things." *See* CAMPBELL, *supra* ch. 2, note 202, at 166. In Richards' view, words work well in combination; individual words cannot be taken out of context and held up as "the best" words for every occasion. RICHARDS, *supra* note 6, at 51–55.

8. I.A. RICHARDS & C. K. OGDEN, THE MEANING OF MEANING (1923).

9. RICHARDS, *supra* note 6.

10. *See* GOLDEN, ET AL, *supra* ch. 2, note 85, at 145–46. Bacon had said, "[T]he ill and unfit choice of words wonderfully obstructs the understanding ... words plainly force and overrule the understanding, and throw all into confusion, and lead men away into numberless empty controversies and idle fancies." FRANCIS BACON, *Idols of the Mind, in* RICHARD HUGHES & P. ALBERT DUHAMEL, RHETORIC: PRINCIPLES AND USAGE 361–62 (2d ed. 1967). *See also supra* ch. 2, note 159.

11. RICHARDS & OGDEN, THE MEANING OF MEANING, *supra* note 8, at 9.

12. RICHARDS, THE PHILOSOPHY OF RHETORIC, *supra* note 6, at 94.

13. WILLIAM SHAKESPEARE, ROMEO AND JULIET, act 2, sc. 2 (New Folger ed., Wash. Square Press 2004).

suggests only that the cases are sufficiently similar to be treated similarly, this form of reasoning is considered relatively weak. As Richards demonstrated, however, it continues to be a powerful form of reasoning in human interaction.

# B. THE ETHICS OF PERSUASION

Ethics is a natural part of rhetoric because one who seeks to persuade must make choices about what arguments to make, how to fashion them, what to emphasize, and what to leave out. These choices reflect the values of the speaker. Scholars like Karl Wallace, Chaim Perelman, Lucie Olbrechts–Tyteca, and Richard Weaver explored the ethical choices a speaker makes in crafting arguments.

## Richard Weaver (1910–1963)

Weaver was born in North Carolina and earned his English doctorate at Louisiana State University. He taught rhetoric and composition at Alabama Polytechnic Institute, Texas A & M University, and the University of Chicago, where he taught until his death in 1963. Weaver believed that all speech is persuasive speech, making the values and motives of the speaker worthy of study. According to Weaver, a rhetorician could be either noble or base:

> As rhetoric confronts us with choices involving values, the rhetorician is a preacher to us, noble if he tries to direct our passion toward noble ends and base if he uses our passion to confuse and degrade us.[14]

In drawing this distinction, Weaver relied directly on Plato's *Phaedrus*, in which Socrates described the three types of love as neutral, evil, and noble.[15] In a collection of essays,[16] Weaver interpreted Socrates' three types of love as a metaphor for three types of speech. Weaver said that the non-lover represents neutral speech, the noble lover represents moral speech, and the evil lover represents immoral speech.[17] Like noble lovers, who "endeavor by every means in their power to lead [their loved ones] to the likeness of the god whom they honor,"[18] noble rhetoricians attempt to inspire their audience to some moral end and do not twist the truth or intend to mislead listeners.

As part of his investigation of the moral speaker, Weaver ranked types of arguments from the most to least ethical. He identified four types: definition; relationships of similarity and dissimilarity; cause and effect; and testimony or authority. According to Weaver, definition is the most ethical type of argument because it attempts to capture the essence or truth about something.[19] He chose

---

14. RICHARD M. WEAVER, LANGUAGE IS SERMONIC 225 (Richard L. Johannesen, Rennard Strickland & Ralph T. Eubanks eds., 1970).

15. *See supra* ch. 2, at 15.

16. RICHARD WEAVER, THE ETHICS OF RHETORIC (1953).

17. WEAVER, LANGUAGE IS SERMONIC, *supra* note 14, at 60–61.

18. *Id.* at 69.

19. *Id.* at 212–13.

arguments based on relationships of similarity and dissimilarity next because analogy and metaphor "hint[] at an essence which cannot at the moment be produced."[20] Although analogy is a weak form of reasoning, Weaver recognized it as noble because it endeavors to find truth. Weaver ranked cause and effect third because one could argue cause and effect "without reference to principle or defined ideas,"[21] and it was thus subject to abuse by exaggerating or lying about an actual effect. He ranked testimony or authority last because it comes from an external source. Weaver warned that "an argument based on authority is [only] as good as the authority" itself.[22]

Late in his career, Weaver railed against the decline of rhetoric as an independent field of study and tried to restore its honor in the post-scientific age. He wrote:

> [I]n the not-so-distant Nineteenth Century, to be a professor of rhetoric, one had to be *somebody*. This was a teaching task that was thought to call for ample and varied resources, and it was recognized as addressing itself to the most important of all ends, the persuading of human beings to adopt right attitudes and act in response to them... [L]iterature was then viewed as a subject which practically anybody could teach... Today, I scarcely need point out, the situation has been exactly reversed.[23]

Weaver thought rhetoric had devolved from a course "dealing philosophically with the problems of expression to one which tries to bring below-par students up to the level of accepted usage."[24] He blamed the epistemologists, who had convinced society that "to think validly was to think scientifically"[25] and that logic alone was valuable. In Weaver's view, logic alone could not persuade—rhetoric was needed to appeal to emotion as well. Weaver saw nothing inherently wrong with emotional appeals because they have the power to move men toward noble ends. As long as a speaker does not exaggerate or emphasize the wrong point, persuasion is an ethical enterprise.

---

### QUESTIONS FOR CONSIDERATION

1. **Do you agree with Richards that words are inadequate to express meaning because their meaning is not fixed? What problems does this create for legal argument? What can be done to rectify the problem?**

2. **Why are metaphors and analogies so convincing, despite their inability to prove anything with certainty?**

---

20. *Id.* at 213.

21. *Id.* at 214.

22. *Id.* 216.

23. *Id.* at 201–02.

24. *Id.* at 203.

25. *Id.* at 204.

3. Would Richards' Basic English have resolved the inadequacy of language to convey meaning? Is Basic English any different from Campbell's recommendation that a writer only use the words or phrases of the "best" writers, which Richards criticized?

4. Do you think that a speech composed solely of Weaver's definitional arguments would be very successful? How does one strike a balance between more and less ethical arguments?

5. What would Weaver say about the morality of criminal attorneys, whose ethical code requires that they represent their clients zealously, whether or not they are guilty?

# C. PRACTICAL REASONING

Philosophers Stephen Toulmin and Chaim Perelman recognized that formal logic does not explain how people reason and resolve disputes in everyday life. Since judges, lawyers, politicians, and even philosophers do not reason syllogistically, they studied practical reasoning to formulate a generalized theory of argumentation. Their work is rooted in classical rhetoric, particularly Aristotelian rhetoric, and relies on legal argument as the ideal model for reasoning. Both Toulmin and Perelman believed that argument does more than convey ideas; it also creates them. In Kinneavy's terms, the ideas that argument creates take the form of a shared belief between encoder and decoder. Although they do not equate to absolute truth or knowledge, they represent probable truth or reasoned conclusions.

## 1. STEPHEN TOULMIN (b. 1922)

Stephen Toulmin is a professor of Anthropology and International Relations at the University of Southern California but is well-known as a philosopher and logician. Born in England in 1922, Toulmin studied physics and philosophy at the University of Cambridge. In 1949, while teaching at Oxford University, he became interested in epistemology, particularly logic, as the source of knowledge. Toulmin set out to determine what connection, if any, formal logic has to the way people assess the soundness, strength, and conclusiveness of arguments in everyday life. He relied heavily on the nature of legal disputes to explore how people reason. Just as lawyers make claims and defend them, Toulmin reasoned, people use a "rational process" to argue for and settle disputes.[26] In 1958, he published *Uses of Argument*, a series of essays, outlining this rational process.[27]

According to Toulmin, an argument "is like an organism. It has both a gross,

---

26. STEPHEN E. TOULMIN, THE USES OF ARGUMENT 1–2, 7 (updated ed. 2003).

27. *See id.*

anatomical structure and a finer, as-it-were physiological one."[28] An argument generally begins with evidence or data (D) that lead to a claim (C).[29] Assume your best friend, Jack, is starting law school next year, and you tell him that although the year will be rewarding, he should expect it to be difficult. Toulmin would sketch your argument as follows:

Jack is a first-year law student (D) → Jack is going to have a difficult year (C)

The data appears to support the claim, but to prove the legitimacy of the claim, you decide to include a warrant (W) to explain why the claim follows from the data (*e.g.,* The first year of law school is comprised of extraordinary amounts of work and stress):[30]

Jack is a first-year law student (D) → Jack is going to have a difficult year (C)

↓

Since the first year of law school is comprised of
extraordinary amounts of work and stress (W)

Toulmin explains that data function like questions of fact in the legal profession (*i.e.,* who did what, when, and where?), whereas warrants function like questions of law (*i.e.,* what is the law and how should it be applied to a particular circumstance?). In this example, the warrant or rule of law is based on your own experience as a first-year student and that of your classmates.

Warrants that are not absolute carry less force. Where the warrant is not absolute, one includes a qualifier (Q) indicating that it is only probably correct (*e.g.,* "is going to" v. "might have"). Just as "it is often necessary in the law-courts, not just to appeal to a given statute or common-law doctrine, but to discuss explicitly the extent to which this particular law fits the case under consideration,"[31] a person often needs to qualify his argument for it to be persuasive. The argument will be even more persuasive if it anticipates a rebuttal (R) or counter arguments that might defeat the claim (*e.g.,* Jack is a speed reader and impervious to stress):[32]

Jack is a first-year law student (D) → Jack is likely (Q) to have a difficult year (C)

             ↓                              ↓

Since the first year of law school is comprised of      Unless Jack is a speed reader
extraordinary amounts of work and stress (W)      and impervious to stress (R)

---

28. *Id.* at 87.

29. *Id.* at 90.

30. *See id.* at 91–93.

31. *Id.* at 93.

32. *See id.* at 93–94.

Finally, the warrant may not be convincing on its face, so you include a backing (B) for the warrant (*e.g.*, Law professors assign hundreds of pages of reading, and a student's grade is based on her performance on a single exam at the end of the semester):[33]

Jack is a first-year law student (D)   →   Jack is likely (Q) to have a difficult year (C)

↓                  ↓

Since the first year of law school is comprised of extraordinary amounts of work and stress (W)     Unless Jack is a speed reader and impervious to stress (R)

↓

Because law professors assign hundreds of pages
of reading, and a student's grade is based on her
performance on a single exam at the end of the semester (B)

Despite the commonality of the "rational process," Toulmin said the "logic" of arguments depends on the subject matter or "field" in which they are made.[34] The validity of arguments is "an intra-field, not an inter-field notion."[35] In Toulmin's view, an argument valid in one field might not be valid in another, and he urged formal logicians to "avoid condemning an ape for not being a man or a pig for not being a porcupine."[36]

## 2. CHAIM PERELMAN (1912–1984)

Chaim Perelman emigrated from Poland to Belgium in 1925. By 1938, he had earned his undergraduate, doctor of law, and doctor of philosophy degrees from the Universite Libre de Bruxelles (ULB). In that year, he was appointed a lecturer at the ULB in the Faculty of Philosophy and Letters. Early in his career, Perelman became interested in studying justice and philosophy. He observed that cases do not always yield predictable results and concluded this unpredictability was because judicial decisions involve value judgments. Since value judgments cannot be evaluated for correctness (*i.e.*, they are subjective), he concluded that judicial decisions are logically arbitrary.

Perelman and Lucie Olbrechts–Tyteca analyzed judicial, political, and philosophical rhetoric to identify the logic, if any, of value judgments. In 1958, they published *The New Rhetoric: A Treatise on Argumentation.*[37] They called their findings a "new rhetoric," signaling their re-discovery and revival of Aristotle, whose rhetoric was no longer being taught in Western education. According to

---

**33.** *Id.* at 95–96.

**34.** *See id.* at 14–15, 235–36.

**35.** *Id.* at 235.

**36.** *Id.* at 236.

**37.** CHAIM PERELMAN & LUCIE OLBRECHTS–TYTECA, THE NEW RHETORIC: A TREATISE ON ARGUMENTATION (1958).

Perelman and Olbrechts–Tyteca, all forms of reasoning involve rhetoric.[38] Even though philosophers seek a form of absolute truth, competing philosophies make it impossible to know which truth is the right one. Philosophers thus use rhetoric to persuade the universal audience about the best truth, not the "single truth," and they use rational but informal reasoning methods to do so.[39]

A speaker who seeks to persuade starts with a meeting of the minds (*i.e.*, a series of premises on which the speaker and audience theoretically agree). A meeting of the minds can be based on what is perceived by the speaker and audience to be true (*e.g.*, accepted facts and presumptions) or desirable (*i.e.*, based on value judgments).[40] A speaker then selects certain premises to emphasize and certain arguments to advance.[41] These choices make the speaker vulnerable to a claim of partiality, but the speaker's opponent is likely to present any relevant information the speaker left out. According to Perelman and Olbrechts–Tyteca, "A tendentious argument [advancing a definite point of view], deliberately put forward on behalf of a party it is one's interest or duty to favor, will have to be completed by the adverse argument in order to reach a balance in the appraisal of the known elements."[42] Finally, the speaker establishes a link between each element of his argument either by associating or dissociating ideas.[43]

## a. ARGUMENTS BY ASSOCIATION

There are three types of argument by association: quasi-logical arguments, arguments based on the structure of reality, and arguments that establish the structure of reality.[44]

### i) QUASI–LOGICAL ARGUMENTS

Quasi-logical arguments give the impression of being based on logic or mathematics and thus have the same psychological force.[45] According to Perelman, arguments "by division," for example, are quasi-logical: they draw their conclusion about the whole after reasoning about each part. "A lawyer, for example, tries to show that the accused, having acted out of neither jealousy, hate, nor cupidity, had no motive for murder."[46]

---

**38.** *See id.* at 45–47; *see also* CHAIM PERELMAN, THE NEW RHETORIC AND THE HUMANITIES 13–15 (1979).

**39.** *See* PERELMAN, THE NEW RHETORIC AND THE HUMANITIES, *supra* note 38, at 14.

**40.** *See* PERELMAN & OLBRECHTS–TYTECA, THE NEW RHETORIC, *supra* note 37, at 65–83; PERELMAN, THE NEW RHETORIC AND THE HUMANITIES, *supra* note 38, at 15–17.

**41.** *See* PERELMAN & OLBRECHTS–TYTECA, THE NEW RHETORIC, *supra* note 37, at 115–120; PEREL-MAN, THE NEW RHETORIC AND THE HUMANITIES, *supra* note 38, at 17–18.

**42.** PERELMAN & OLBRECHTS–TYTECA, THE NEW RHETORIC, *supra* note 37, at 119.

**43.** *Id.* at 190; PERELMAN, THE NEW RHETORIC AND THE HUMANITIES, *supra* note 38, at 118–19.

**44.** PERELMAN & OLBRECHTS–TYTECA, THE NEW RHETORIC, *supra* note 37, at 191.

**45.** *See id.* at 193–95. Perelman and Olbrechts–Tyteca cited as an example the rule of justice that "requires giving identical treatment to beings or situations of the same kind." *Id.* at 218.

**46.** CHAIM PERELMAN, THE REALM OF RHETORIC 50 (1982). *See also* PERELMAN & OLBRECHTS–TYTECA, THE NEW RHETORIC, *supra* note 37, at 234–42.

## ii) ARGUMENTS BASED ON THE STRUCTURE OF REALITY

There are two types of arguments based on the structure of reality that use accepted relationships between elements of reality to support a given argument: arguments of succession and arguments of co-existence.[47] Arguments of succession relate a phenomenon to its cause or effect, and arguments of co-existence rely primarily on the relationship between a person and his actions.[48] According to Perelman, arguments of succession occur often in the law. For example, when a person is found dead, several questions arise about the cause of death, and if someone is charged with that person's murder, the defendant's lawyer will argue that the defendant could not have *caused* the victim's death (*e.g.*, the defendant did not have motive, means, or opportunity).[49] In contrast, arguments of co-existence rely on the link between a person's essence and his outward manifestations, including his actions, modes of expression, emotional reactions, and judgments.[50] The relationship between how a person is perceived and how his actions are interpreted also plays a significant role in the law. For example, since people "are known only through their manifestations ..., our humanistic conception of right prevents us from punishing people preventively, before they have committed a crime."[51]

## iii) ARGUMENTS THAT ESTABLISH THE STRUCTURE OF REALITY

Arguments that establish the structure of reality are based on example or analogy. An argument based on example usually attempts to justify an action by relating it to a model that the audience already accepts as sound. Christ is used in the New Testament of the Bible, for example, as a model for human action.[52] In law, when a legal writer cites a case, she uses the case as an example to be followed in her client's case.[53] The other type of argument that establishes the structure of reality is based on analogy. According to Perelman, analogies demonstrate the resemblance of the relationship between elements: A is to B as C is to D.[54] Borrowing from Aristotle, Perelman used the following example: "For as the eyes of bats [C] are to the blaze of day [D], so is the reason in our soul [A] to the things which are by nature most evident of all [B]."[55] Perelman refers to the A and B of the analogy—the terms to which the conclusion relates—as the *theme*; the terms that serve to buttress the argument—C and D—are the

---

**47.**  *See* PERELMAN & OLBRECHTS–TYTECA, THE NEW RHETORIC, *supra* note 37, at 261–63.

**48.**  *See id.* at 262.

**49.**  *See* PERELMAN, THE REALM OF RHETORIC, *supra* note 46, at 81–82.

**50.**  PERELMAN & OLBRECHTS–TYTECA, THE NEW RHETORIC, *supra* note 37, at 293–96.

**51.**  PERELMAN, THE REALM OF RHETORIC, *supra* note 46, at 92.

**52.**  *See* PERELMAN, THE NEW RHETORIC AND THE HUMANITIES, *supra* note 38, at 22.

**53.**  *See* PERELMAN & OLBRECHTS–TYTECA, THE NEW RHETORIC, *supra* note 37, at 351.

**54.**  *Id.* at 372.

**55.**  *Id.* at 373. Perelman's example here would not be an argument in a formal logician's terms because it states an analogy but draws no conclusion from it.

*phoros.*[56] The theme and phoros need to be from different spheres or aspects of life for the analogy to be pure (*e.g.,* the response of a bat to sunlight as compared to the human response to what should seem obvious). Perelman would say that when a lawyer uses precedent to argue for the similar application of a rule of law, he argues by example because the two cases are taken from the same sphere or aspect of life.[57]

## b. ARGUMENTS BY DISSOCIATION

Whereas arguments by association link ideas to advance argument, dissociative arguments sever the link between ideas, generating "a profound change" in the way those ideas were formerly conceived.[58] Perelman's prototypical example of dissociation is the attempt to distinguish between that which is apparent and that which is real. For example, when one looks at an oar in water, it appears curved, but when it is out of the water, it appears straight. Because the oar cannot be both curved and straight, one uses the laws of nature to dissociate the apparent from the real.[59] Perelman notes that the process of reconciling conflicting claims is "carried on at every level of legal activity. It is pursued by the legislator, the legal theorist, and the judge."[60] In a case where competing rules of law appear to apply, both lawyer and judge must distinguish one of the rules to "restore coherence to the juridical system."[61]

Perelman and Olbrechts–Tyteca studied all forms of argumentative discourse, including philosophical debate. They recognized that even philosophers do not argue with the precision of mathematics; they must use rhetoric to convince their audience. Just as lawyers attempt to persuade juries, philosophers attempt to convince the "universal audience" about absolute truth.[62] Perelman has stated:

> After having sought, for centuries, to model philosophy on the sciences, and having considered each of its particularities as a sign of inferiority [to the certainty of science], perhaps the moment has come to consider that philosophy has many traits in common with law.[63]

Perelman believed that both law and philosophy rely on practical reasoning to persuade their audiences. "As soon as a communication tries to influence one or more persons, to orient their thinking, to excite or calm their emotions, to guide their actions, it belongs to the realm of rhetoric. Dialectic [philosophy], the technique of controversy, is included as one part of this larger realm."[64]

---

56. *Id.*

57. *Id.* at 374. *See infra* ch. 4, at 113.

58. PERELMAN, & OLBRECHTS-TYTECA, THE NEW RHETORIC, *supra* note 37, at 411–12.

59. *See id.* at 415–16.

60. *Id.* at 414.

61. *Id.*

62. *Id.* at 32.

63. CHAIM PERELMAN, JUSTICE, LAW, AND ARGUMENT 174 (1980).

64. PERELMAN, THE REALM OF RHETORIC, *supra* note 46, at 162.

---

*QUESTIONS FOR CONSIDERATION*

1. Does Toulmin's model of practical reasoning adequately describe the process of legal reasoning? To what extent can it help the legal writer create an effective argument?

2. Toulmin urged philosophers and rhetoricians to work together to evaluate the validity and strength of their arguments. What standards do you think lawyers use to judge the success or failure of their arguments?

3. Perelman said that competing philosophies make it impossible to know for sure which one is right. He also said that philosophers use rhetoric to persuade audiences about their version of truth.

4. Do you have the same confidence Perelman did that in the adversarial process a party's opponent is likely to present any relevant information the first party left out?

5. When audiences listen to arguments by example and analogy, on what basis do they decide if the argument is convincing?

---

# D. COMMUNICATION AS RHETORIC AND RHETORIC AS MOTIVE

Kenneth Burke (1897–1993) is considered the greatest rhetorician of the twentieth century.[65] Heavily influenced by the works of Aristotle, Marx, Freud, and Nietzsche, Burke was interested in human motivation and how people use language to create reality, a process he called dramatism. Burke's *A Grammar of Motives*[66] and *A Rhetoric of Motives*[67] form the bulk of his theory of rhetoric, which encompasses all of semiotics. Burke defined rhetoric as the study and use of persuasion, which seeks "to form attitudes or to induce actions in other human agents."[68] Because people can be persuaded to change their minds as well as to act, Burke said rhetoric seeks to affect attitudes as well as to induce action.[69]

In Burke's view, all action with a persuasive quality is rhetoric: "Wherever there is persuasion, there is rhetoric. And wherever there is 'meaning' there is 'persuasion.'"[70] Rhetoric can even be non-verbal. The presence and placement of medical equipment in a patient's examining room, for example, represent the advances of medical science and affect patient confidence.[71] Rhetoric can include

---

65. GOLDEN, ET AL., *supra* ch. 2, note 85, at 179.

66. KENNETH BURKE, A GRAMMAR OF MOTIVES (1945).

67. KENNETH BURKE, A RHETORIC OF MOTIVES (1950).

68. *Id.* at 41.

69. *Id.* at 50.

70. *Id.* at 172.

71. *See id.* at 171.

internal thought processes too: "A man can be his own audience, insofar as he, even in his secret thoughts, cultivates certain ideas or images for the effect he hopes they may have upon him."[72] In dreams, for example, a person's unconscious presents conflicting interests as the "*ego* with its *id* confronts the *super-ego* much as an orator would confront a somewhat alien audience, whose susceptibilities he must flatter as a necessary step towards persuasion."[73]

Burke believed a "generic divisiveness" exists among humans that is exacerbated by social class and communities.[74] As part of a " 'universal' rhetorical situation," people try to persuade each other through language.[75] Burke's term for persuasion is *identification* or the attempt to persuade one's audience by talking the audience's language through speech, gesture, tonality, order, image, attitude, and idea.[76] In Burke's view, classical rhetoric is one way of identifying with an audience.[77] To understand what motivates identification, Burke created the pentad, a five-pronged analysis.[78] For each rhetorical situation, there is the act (what is being done), the scene (the situation in which it occurs), the agent (the actor), the agency (the means used), and the purpose.[79] By looking at the relationship between the elements of the pentad, one begins to get a sense of a person's motivation.[80] For example, a criminal defense attorney might argue that a defendant is not guilty of first degree murder because the defendant acted in self-defense. By looking at the agent (the defendant) and the scene (the defendant being held against her will with a knife), the actor's motive becomes clear. Had the defendant been in a different situation (such as holding a gun to the victim's head), the defendant's motive and consequence would be different.

Burke's dramatist theory of rhetoric explains the motive behind what people say and do. By understanding motive, Burke believed the relationship between language and reality could be better understood. Burke's pentad and its goal of discovering motive inform legal writers who seek identification with their audience too. To be persuasive, the writer must ask herself, "What happened here? What is my goal? What is my role? Who is my audience? What methods and forms of persuasion are available to me?" These questions help anticipate the motives of one's opponent as well.

---

**72.** *Id.* at 38.

**73.** *Id.* at 37–38.

**74.** *Id.* at 146.

**75.** *Id.*

**76.** *Id.* at 55.

**77.** *Id.* at 56–58.

**78.** *See* BURKE, A GRAMMAR OF MOTIVES, *supra* note 66, at x.

**79.** *See id.*

**80.** *See id.* at x-xi.

# E. THEORIES OF COMPOSITION

By the end of the nineteenth century, rhetoric was no longer taught in European or American universities. All that remained of classical rhetoric in higher education were the canons of style and delivery. English departments converted the study of style into the study of literature and composition. Traditionally, even today, "[o]ne set of teachers is appointed to teach us how to read, while a second set tries to teach us how to write."[81] The development of writing as a separate subject led to several theories on the nature of writing and how best to teach it. Each theory focuses on the same four elements of the writing process: writer, reality, reader, and language.[82] According to James Berlin, in 1982, four major theories had dominated writing instruction in the United States: Neo–Aristotelianism or Classicism, Positivism or Current–Traditionalism, Neo–Platonism or Expressivism, and New Rhetoric.[83] By 1988, he had divided New Rhetoric into Cognitive and Social–Epistemic Rhetoric.[84] According to Berlin, each theory teaches the same process of writing, prewriting, writing, and rewriting, but they do not teach the same *process*.[85] As you read about them, try to understand what Berlin meant by that statement.

# 1. NEO–ARISTOTELIANISM OR CLASSICISM

The critical feature of neo-Aristotelianism or classicism is the assumption that reality "can thus be known and communicated, with language serving as the unproblematic medium of discourse."[86] Once a writer invents her arguments, via logic or reason, she engages in the relatively simple task of putting them down in writing. Unlike Plato, Aristotle considered invention a part of rhetoric, but even Aristotle assumed that once an orator's arguments were invented, there were words "out there" to communicate his meaning. As late as the 1960s and 1970s, Edward Corbett, Richard Hughes, and Albert Duhamel wrote textbooks on composition rooted in neo-Aristotelianism.[87] Neo–Aristotelianism is noteworthy for its theoretical differences from current-traditionalism, not for

---

**81.** JAMES J. MURPHY, *Rhetorical History as a Guide to the Salvation of American Reading and Writing: A Plea for Curricular Courage*, THE RHETORICAL TRADITION AND MODERN WRITING 3 (James J. Murphy ed., 1982).

**82.** James A. Berlin, *Contemporary Composition: The Major Pedagogical Theories, reprinted in* THE WRITING TEACHER'S SOURCEBOOK 9 (Gary Tate, Edward P.J. Corbett & Nancy Myers eds., 3d ed. 1994). Note the similarity to Kinneavy's communication triangle: encoder of a message, the reality to which the message refers, the decoder or receiver of the message, and the signal that actually carries the message. *See supra* at 61.

**83.** Berlin, *Contemporary Composition, supra* note 82, at 10.

**84.** *See* James Berlin, *Rhetoric and Ideology in the Writing Class, reprinted in* THE WRITING TEACHERS' SOURCEBOOK 9 (Edward P.J. Corbett, Nancy Myers & Gary Tate eds., 4th ed. 2000).

**85.** *See* Berlin, *Contemporary Composition, supra* note 82, at 21.

**86.** *Id.* at 11.

**87.** *See, e.g.,* EDWARD P.J. CORBETT, CLASSICAL RHETORIC FOR THE MODERN STUDENT (1971) and RICHARD HUGHES AND ALBERT DUHAMEL, PRINCIPLES OF RHETORIC (1967).

its large following.[88]

## 2. CURRENT–TRADITIONALISM

By the 1980s, current-traditionalism dominated writing instruction in the United States and affects all of us as writers. With its emphasis on the end-product as opposed to the writing process, current-traditionalism teaches the canons of arrangement and style.[89] Like neo-Aristotelianism, current-traditionalism assumes that arguments are invented as a function of some process other than the act of writing.[90] This assumption stems from the work of Bacon, Locke, Campbell, Blair, and Whately, who rejected Aristotle's deductive logic as the source of knowledge or truth in favor of scientific or inductive methods of discovery.[91] A writer takes knowledge or truth acquired through the scientific method (or genius) and then arranges it in such a way as to appeal to her audience.[92] Because current-traditionalism assumes the meaning of writing is fixed, it pays little attention to audience concerns.[93]

In the nineteenth century, current-traditionalists divided writing into four basic types: description, narration, exposition, and argument.[94] Alexander Bain, a prominent rhetorician, defined description as the representation of "an object of some degree of complexity," narration as reporting on a "stream of events;" exposition as writing "in the form of what is called the Sciences;" and argument as "the influencing of men's conduct and belief by spoken or by written address."[95] The focus on arrangement led writing teachers to stress large-scale organization, paragraph structure, and sentence construction.[96] The five-paragraph essay, with which nearly all U.S.-trained writers are familiar, followed soon thereafter.[97] Although these writing types were convenient to teach, they fell into disfavor

---

**88.** Berlin, *Contemporary Composition, supra* note 82, at 12–13.

**89.** *See, e.g.,* RICHARD YOUNG, PARADIGMS AND PROBLEMS: SOME NEEDED RESEARCH IN RHETORICAL INVENTION, RESEARCH ON COMPOSING: POINTS OF VIEW OF DEPARTURE 31 (Charles R. Cooper & Lee Odell eds., 1978).

**90.** *See* Berlin, *Contemporary Composition, supra* note 82, at 13.

**91.** *See supra* ch. 2, at 45, 49, 52, 54 and 57.

**92.** Berlin, *Contemporary Composition, supra* note 82, at 13–14.

**93.** *Id.* Recall I.A. Richards' view that words have the meaning ascribed to them by the *listener*, not the speaker or writer. *See supra* at 63.

**94.** *See, e.g.,* ALEXANDER BAIN, ENGLISH COMPOSITION AND RHETORIC (Scholars' Facsimiles & Reprints 1996) (1871); Robert J. Connors, *The Rise and Fall of the Modes of Discourse*, 32 C. COMPOSITION & COMM. 444 (1981), *reprinted in* THE WRITING TEACHER'S SOURCEBOOK 24 (Gary Tate & Edward P.J. Corbett eds., 2d ed. 1988); JOHN F. GENUNG, PRACTICAL ELEMENTS OF RHETORIC (1885); YOUNG, *supra* note 89, at 31.

**95.** BAIN, *supra*, note 94, at 153, 166, 185, and 212.

**96.** Bain described the paragraph as "the division of discourse next higher than the sentence" and the topic sentence as the first sentence that "is expected to indicate with prominence the subject of the paragraph. *Id.* at 142, 150.

**97.** A traditional five-paragraph essay is comprised of an introduction and thesis statement, three supporting examples in three separate paragraphs, and a conclusion. Far from extinct, this form of writing is still taught today in elementary and secondary education.

among certain theorists for elevating form over substance and leading students to believe writing is essentially a mechanical process.[98] By focusing on *what* to write instead of *how* to write, the four "types" of writing

> represent an unrealistic view of the writing process, a view that assumes writing is done by formula and in a social vacuum. They turn the attention of both teacher and student toward an academic exercise instead of toward a meaningful act of communication in a social context.[99]

Drawing again on Blair, Campbell, and Whately, early current-traditionalists focused on style as well, with an emphasis on spelling, punctuation, clarity, and brevity.[100] These "mechanics" of writing reduced the elegant and elaborate schemes and tropes of classical rhetoric[101] to the most commonly used figures of speech, such as simile, metaphor, and alliteration. Current-traditionalism has led generations of writers to believe that writing consists of putting pre-formed thoughts down on paper using the proper arrangement and checking for mechanics errors. "Your [law school] classes, unless you are extremely fortunate, are full of students whose perceptions of what is important in writing have been shaped by such teachers."[102]

Despite its inherent limitations, current-traditionalism influences and informs legal writing. Because legal writers tend to write for a specific purpose in a real live context, their focus must be on the end-product as well as the extent to which it accomplishes its purpose. The legal profession uses distinct types of writing, such as contracts, memoranda, and briefs, to achieve specific goals. Although beginning legal writers often feel stifled by their "rigidity," these types of writing telegraph their purpose to the reader and are not incompatible with creativity. Legal writers also strive to achieve a clear and concise writing style.[103] Clarity and conciseness convey meaning efficiently with the precision needed to

---

**98.** *See, e.g.*, CONNORS, *supra* note 94, at 32; KINNEAVY, *supra* note 1, at 28–30.

**99.** CONNORS, *supra* note 94, at 33 (quoting ALBERT KITZHABER, RHETORIC IN AMERICAN COLLEGES, 1850–1900 (1990)).

**100.** *See* YOUNG, *supra* note 89, at 31.

**101.** Both schemes and tropes were defined as any deviation in language from the ordinary and simple method of speaking. CORBETT & CONNORS, *supra* ch. 2, note 1, at 379. Specifically, a scheme was a deviation from the ordinary pattern or arrangement of words, while a trope was a deviation from the ordinary meaning of words. *Id.* Renaissance rhetoricians articulated more than 200 figures of speech. *Id.* at 378. For a fuller discussion of schemes and tropes, *see* Ch. 4, *infra*, pp. 131–33.

**102.** Donald C. Stewart, *Some History Lessons for Composition Teachers*, 3 RHETORIC REV. 134, 135 (1985).

**103.** *See, e.g.*, ANNE ENQUIST & LAUREL CURRIE OATES, JUST WRITING: GRAMMAR, PUNCTUATION, AND STYLE FOR THE LEGAL WRITER (2d ed. 2005); BRYAN A. GARNER, THE REDBOOK: A MANUAL ON LEGAL STYLE (2d ed. 2006); MARY RAY & JILL J. RAMSFIELD, LEGAL WRITING: GETTING IT RIGHT AND GETTING IT WRITTEN (4th ed. 2005); WILLIAM STRUNK, JR. & E.B. WHITE, THE ELEMENTS OF STYLE (4th ed. 1999); JOSEPH WILLIAMS, STYLE: LESSONS IN CLARITY AND GRACE (9th ed. 2006); RICHARD WYDICK, PLAIN ENGLISH FOR LAWYERS (5th ed. 2005). *See also infra*, ch. 9.

avoid misunderstanding.[104]

# 3. NEO–PLATONISM OR EXPRESSIVISM

Neo–Platonism or expressivism developed in response to current-traditionalism's assumption that a writer acquires truth outside herself and then memorializes it in writing.[105] Expressivism is based on the idea that truth is "discovered through an internal apprehension, a private vision of a world that transcends the physical."[106] This theory of teaching writing is reminiscent of Plato's belief that a philosopher discovers truth as he engages in the process of reasoning.[107] Like philosophers, writers achieve truth through their inner vision. An expressivist might say that the truth a writer discovers can never be fully communicated. The most a gifted writer can hope to do is communicate a sense of truth through metaphor, which the reader attempts to confirm through personal experience.[108] More often, however, writing serves to correct error in the reader's understanding of truth.[109] Thus a writer does not convey knowledge by direct transmission but by negating a reader's formerly held truths.

The expressivist view, which peaked in the 1960s and 1970s, presented substantial challenges for the writing teacher. In theory, if truth could be learned but not communicated, writing could be learned but not taught. Expressivist writing teachers thus tried to provide an appropriate environment for students to discover their inner visions. Students were often required to keep journals "to get the student to see the way she perceive[d] and structure[d] her experience."[110] They also used peer-group editing to discover what [was] inauthentic in their writing."[111]

Peter Elbow's *Writing Without Teachers* exemplifies the expressivist approach to teaching writing. Elbow, an English professor at the University of Massachusetts, has said that writing is an "organic, developmental process in which you start writing at the beginning—before you know your meaning at

---

104. A classic example is the ambiguous use of a comma in a will: "I leave $120,000 to be divided equally among my husband, my daughter and son-in-law." In this case, without the placement of a comma after "daughter," the husband has a good argument that the daughter and son-in-law are together entitled to $60,000. Had the drafter of the will inserted a comma after daughter, both the daughter and the son-in-law would each be entitled to $40,000.

105. *See* Berlin, *Contemporary Composition, supra* note 82, at 14–15.

106. *Id.* at 15.

107. *See* JAMES A. BERLIN, RHETORIC AND REALITY: WRITING INSTRUCTION IN AMERICAN COLLEGES, 1900–1985, 12 (1987).

108. *Id.; see also supra,* at 63 on I. A. Richards' theory of the metaphor, which Berlin claims made expressionism possible.

109. *See* Berlin, *Contemporary Composition, supra* note 82, at 15; BERLIN, RHETORIC AND REALITY, *supra* note 107, at 152–53.

110. BERLIN, RHETORIC AND REALITY, *supra* note 107, at 14.

111. *Id. See also, e.g.,* Special Issue, COMPOSITION AS ART, 15 C. COMPOSITION & COMM. 1 (1964); DONALD C. STEWART, THE AUTHENTIC VOICE: A PRE–WRITING APPROACH TO STUDENT WRITING (1972).

all—and encourage your words gradually to change and evolve."[112] Since truth resides in the writer, traditional writing teachers are unnecessary:

> The teacherless writing class is a place where there is learning but no teaching. It is possible to learn something and not be taught.[113]

Elbow has encouraged writers to engage in free-writing and create multiple drafts from which themes emerge and ideas transform. He calls this process "growing and cooking."[114]

Expressivism has had little application to teaching legal writing because authority in the legal profession is thought to exist outside the self. To be effective, legal writing must be supported by legal authority: constitutions, statutes, cases, administrative law, and the like. A judge, for example, must be convinced that the law supports a party's position before she decides what is right or true. Although for this reason expressivism applies more to creative than to professional writing, some of its practices—generating multiple drafts and soliciting peer responses—are used in all types of writing courses. In legal as much as other types of writing, a writer needs to have a sense of the extent to which the writing conveys her intended meaning.

# 4. NEW RHETORIC

At the same time Toulmin and Perelman were developing their theories on practical reasoning, a new writing pedagogy emerged. James Berlin referred to it as New Rhetoric,[115] which he later divided into Cognitive and Social-Epistemic rhetoric.[116] Like Toulmin and Perelman, the new rhetoricians argue that rhetoric creates knowledge just as much as philosophy does. Knowledge resides neither in the external nor the internal world; instead, it is created by the interaction of speaker, audience, message, and the reality the message represents. The writer both creates meaning and shapes reality.[117] Cognitive rhetoric focuses on the relationship between a writer's cognitive development and the writing process.[118] Social-epistemic rhetoric views writing as a social act that can lead to knowledge.[119]

---

**112.** PETER ELBOW, WRITING WITHOUT TEACHERS 15 (1973).

**113.** *Id.* at ix.

**114.** *See, e.g., id.* at 3, 22–23, 48–56.

**115.** *See* Berlin, *Contemporary Composition, supra* note 82, at 16. Perelman and Olbrechts–Tyteca called their work new rhetoric too. *See supra* at 69.

**116.** *See* Berlin, *Rhetoric and Ideology, supra* note 84, at 10.

**117.** *See* Berlin, *Contemporary Composition, supra* note 82, at 19.

**118.** *See* Berlin, *Rhetoric and Ideology, supra* note 84, at 12–15.

**119.** *See id.* at 19. In *Legal Writing: A Revised View,* Christopher Rideout and Jill Ramsfield describe twentieth century composition slightly differently, grouping expressivism and the cognitivists together as the process perspective and distinguishing cognitivism with a particular focus on the social nature of knowledge as the social perspective. *See* 69 WASH. L. REV. 35, 51, 56 (1994). Although expressivism and cognitivism do emphasize process, grouping those theories that make similar assumptions about the nature of truth seems to make sense for the purpose of relating writing pedagogies back to their philosophical and rhetorical origins.

## a. COGNITIVE RHETORIC

Cognitive rhetoric grew out of an interest in how people acquire knowledge, particularly language, and how that process affects the way they reason and write. In contrast to current-traditionalists, cognitive rhetoricians focus on the writing process versus the end-product. To understand the composing process is "to understand the role of reality, audience, purpose, and even language in the rhetorical act."[120] In 1971, Janet Emig published a landmark study on the composing process of twelfth-grade students.[121] Emig discovered that the writing process is not linear, as was previously assumed, but recursive. She thus rejected current-traditionalism because it ignores the writing process as it actually exists. Instead, she recommended that teachers intervene at all stages of student writing: pre-writing, writing, and rewriting.[122] Intervention at these stages in the process permits students' cognitive skills to develop appropriately and improve their writing.

Nine years later, Linda Flower and John Hayes explored the writer's creative process by studying the different pre-writing processes used by novice and expert writers in response to a given writing assignment.[123] They observed a dramatic difference between the way good and poor writers conceive of assignments or, to use their phrase, the rhetorical problem.[124] While good writers pay particular attention to all aspects of the assignment, including audience and the writer's own goals, poor writers tend to concentrate more on the product, such as the format and number of pages required.[125] In contrast to Elbow,[126] Flower and Hayes concluded that creativity "is not a totally mysterious or magical act."[127] By understanding the differences in novice and expert writing approaches, writing teachers can actually help students become more "creative."[128]

By 1982, Patricia Bizzell, an English professor at the College of the Holy Cross, had identified two types of cognitivists: those interested in the development

---

**120.** Berlin, *Rhetoric and Ideology, supra* note 84, at 12.

**121.** *See* JANET EMIG, THE COMPOSING PROCESS OF TWELFTH GRADERS (1971).

**122.** Berlin, *Rhetoric and Ideology, supra,* note 84, at 12.

**123.** Linda Flower & John R. Hayes, *The Cognition of Discovery: Defining a Rhetorical Problem,* 31 C. COMPOSITION & COMM. 21–32 (1980), *reprinted in* THE WRITING TEACHERS' SOURCEBOOK 92 (Gary Tate & Edward P.J. Corbett eds., 2d ed. 1988).

**124.** *Id.* at 94.

**125.** *Id.* at 99.

**126.** In *Writing Without Teachers,* Elbow described writing as "unusually mysterious to most people." ELBOW, *supra* note 112, at 12. In Elbow's view, the writer solves that mystery by freeing herself from what she thinks at the outset of the writing process and letting meaning evolve. *See id.* at 15.

**127.** Flower & Hayes, *supra* note 123, at 102.

**128.** *See id.* For additional readings in cognitivist theory, see, for example, Andrea A. Lunsford, *Cognitive Development and the Basic Writer,* 41 C. ENGLISH 38 (1979); Sondra Perl, *Understanding Composing,* 31 C. COMPOSITION & COMM. 363 (1980), *reprinted in* THE WRITING TEACHERS' SOURCEBOOK, *supra* note 94, at 113; Nancy Sommers, *Revision Strategies of Student Writers and Experienced Adult Writers,* 31 C. COMPOSITION & COMM. 378 (1980), *reprinted in* THE WRITING TEACHERS' SOURCEBOOK, *supra* note 94, at 119.

of the writer as an independent actor and those, such as she, interested in the effect of writing in specialized discourse communities.[129] Flower and Hayes fall into the former group because they examined the writing process without studying the influence of the community or audience on the writer.[130] Bizzell, on the other hand, studied the effect of audience on a writer's development. In her view, poor writers have an underdeveloped "knowledge of the ways experience is constituted and interpreted in the academic discourse community and of the fact that all discourse communities constitute and interpret experience."[131] For Bizzell, it makes no sense to talk about writing without "the social-rhetorical situations in which writing gets done, from the conditions that enable writers to do what they do, and from the motives writers have for doing what they do."[132]

The social-cognitivists' interest in discourse communities led Joseph Williams to write about the development of novice legal writers.[133] According to Williams, expertise in legal writing develops as the writer interacts with and becomes socialized into the legal community.[134] When a pre-socialized writer (Williams' phrase for a novice writer) first enters the legal writing community, her legal writing is likely to be poor.[135] A novice legal writer tends to state the obvious, use awkward sentence structure, or sound like she swallowed a legal dictionary. More often than not, Williams explained, this writer simply needs to become socialized into the legal writing community. Once socialized, good legal writers become post-socialized, which enables them to think abstractly and write plainly.[136] In 1994, Rideout and Ramsfield, two professor-rhetoricians, recognized the impact Williams' article would have on teaching legal writing and urged legal writing programs to embrace Williams' "social perspective."[137]

As Rideout and Ramsfield would have predicted, cognitive rhetoric permeates the teaching of legal writing today. Courses tend to incorporate multiple drafts of a given assignment, recognizing the recursive nature of writing. Good teachers

---

**129.** Patricia Bizzell, *Cognition, Convention, and Certainty: What We Need to Know About Writing*, 3 PRE/TEXT 213, 230–31 (1982). *See also* Lisa Ede & Andrea Lunsford, *Audience Address/Audience Invoked: The Role of Audience in Composition Theory and Pedagogy*, reprinted in THE WRITING TEACHERS' SOURCEBOOK, *supra* note 94, at 169.

**130.** *See, e.g.*, Bizzell, *supra* note 129, at 231.

**131.** *Id.* at 230.

**132.** James A. Reither, *Writing and Knowing: Toward Redefining the Writing Process*, reprinted *in* THE WRITING TEACHERS' SOURCEBOOK, *supra* note 84, at 286.

**133.** Joseph Williams, *On the Maturing of Legal Writers: Two Models of Growth and Development* 1 J. LEG. WRITING INST. 1 (1991).

**134.** *Id.* at 13.

**135.** In Williams' experience, novice legal writers often latch onto the most concrete aspects of the assignment and incorporate them into their writing, state what socialized writers consider to be self-evident, deteriorate in basic skills as they manage several new cognitive demands at the same time, and try to sound like lawyers. *Id.* at 15.

**136.** *Id.* at 27–29. Post-socialization is the unstated goal of most legal writing programs. Although, as Williams recognizes, students struggle in their first year to "talk the talk" of the law, most legal writing professors discourage the use of legalese, long sentences, and flowery language almost immediately.

**137.** *See* Rideout & Ramsfield, *supra* note 119, at 61–74.

ask law students to examine their own writing process and determine where their process is weak. Equally important, practical legal writing is taught with a conscious awareness of the intended audience, be it a client, opposing counsel, or judge. The feedback students receive on their writing is not intended to reflect the authenticity of the writer's vision, as Elbow would urge, but to reflect the legal community's likely response—the meaning ascribed by the audience—to the writing.

## b. SOCIAL–EPISTEMIC RHETORIC

Social-epistemic rhetoric is the most progressive and complicated of the composition theories,[138] but it has the greatest potential to change the way law students and law schools think about legal writing. In contrast to each of the foregoing theories, social-epistemic rhetoric views knowledge as the product of the interaction between speaker, subject matter, and audience. "Knowledge, then, is a matter of mutual agreement appearing as a product of the rhetorical activity, the discussion, of a given discourse community."[139] From this point of view, knowledge is derived solely from linguistic interaction. Since it is acquired neither by reason nor science, it is probable, not absolute.[140] Knowledge is relative too: it differs among discourse communities and changes over time, as cultural attitudes change.[141] Social-epistemic knowledge is the antithesis of Plato's universal truth, but it is no less valuable because it provides a way "to understand and change the world."[142]

Phillip Kissam, a law professor at the University of Kansas, has argued that in the act of writing, law students "develop new connections or new ideas about what the law is and how it should be applied in particular situations,"[143] and these ideas are knowledge in the social-epistemic sense. Unfortunately, new rhetoric has had little impact on teaching legal writing. Linda Berger, a professor at Mercer University School of Law, asserts that legal writing programs have "missed the best part of New Rhetoric: the theory that reading and writing could be used to construct meaning."[144] For this reason, she recommends that students be encouraged to rethink the relationship between reading and writing:

---

**138.** *See* Berlin, *Rhetoric and Ideology, supra* note 84, at 19–22.

**139.** BERLIN, RHETORIC AND REALITY, *supra* note 107, at 166.

**140.** Berlin, *Contemporary Composition, supra* note 82, at 19.

**141.** *See, e.g.,* Richard E. Young & Alton L. Becker, *Toward a Modern Theory of Rhetoric, reprinted in* CONTEMPORARY RHETORIC: A CONCEPTUAL BACKGROUND WITH READINGS 123, 140 (W. Ross Winterowd ed., 1975) (arguing that writers function within specific discourse communities and all writing choices, from content to style, contribute to meaning); Ann E. Berthoff, *From Problem–Solving to a Theory of Imagination*, 33 C. ENGLISH 636, 646 (1972) (stating that reality is not something "out there" but the product of a dialectic involving observer and observed).

**142.** BERLIN, RHETORIC AND REALITY, *supra* note 107, at 177.

**143.** Phillip C. Kissam, *Thinking (By Writing) About Legal Writing*, 40 VAND. L. REV. 135, 140 (1987).

**144.** Linda L. Berger, *Applying New Rhetoric to Legal Discourse: The Ebb and Flow of Reader and Writer, Text and Context*, 49 J. LEGAL EDUC. 155, 168 (1999).

By generating an ebb and flow of reader and writer within the student's head, New Rhetoric offers a way to engage students in "the dialogue that is at the heart of all composing: a writer is in dialogue with his various selves and with his audience." At times, the "inside reader's eye" predominates as the student reads texts to interpret the information with which to work. At times, the "inside writer's eye" predominates as the student explores his readings and develops thoughts, ideas, plans, and goals as well as when he monitors his writing to see if it meets his purposes. The "outside reader's eye" predominates when the focus shifts to reviewing the emerging text to see whether it meets the purposes of an outside reader, and the "outside writer's eye" is used when the writer concentrates on having an intended effect on an outside reader.[145]

The net effect of this complicated internal dialogue is to create knowledge. When a student reads a series of cases to articulate or synthesize a rule of law in a given jurisdiction, she "creates" that rule of law. When a student disagrees with the interpretation of the case holding and says, "I read that case to mean something else," she too creates meaning.

Social-epistemic rhetoric teaches us that legal writing is a creative process. Beginning legal writers understandably assume that "the law" exists out there apart from themselves, and their job is simply to find and report it. They also assume also that creating new ideas and the authority to do so lie outside their reach, and their job is to focus solely on "style." As a legal writer becomes socialized, however, she begins to understand that she can and does invent meaning. The meaning she creates is constrained only by her need to gain the audience's assent.

---

### QUESTIONS FOR CONSIDERATION

1. **According to Burke, rhetoric consists of all action, verbal and non-verbal, that has a persuasive quality. Do you agree? How do lawyers try to persuade in non-verbal ways? Can those choices be evaluated and expressed in ethical terms?**

2. **Compare Burke's pentad (act, scene, agent, agency, purpose) to Kinneavy's communications triangle (encoder, signal, decoder). How do they differ in terms of their emphasis? What does the pentad contribute to your understanding of your role as a legal advocate?**

3. **What composition theories influenced your writing teachers in elementary school, high school, and college? Did your writing teachers focus on product, process, or both?**

---

145. *Id.* at 168–69.

4. Williams said that as novice legal writers learn the language of the legal discourse community, they often seem to be poor writers, but they are really becoming socialized. Have your writing skills or confidence deteriorated as you struggle to learn this new language? How can you hasten the socialization process?

5. Do you agree with Phillip Kissam and Linda Berger that the writing process creates new ideas? If writing generates knowledge, what does that say about the traditional distinction between philosophy and rhetoric?

# F. TWENTIETH CENTURY LEGAL PHILOSOPHIES

Many twentieth-century legal scholars reject the notion of a natural law or one right outcome in a given case. Although Plato would argue that a true philosopher could discover "just" laws or outcomes, many modern legal scholars would disagree. As Chaim Perelman suggests, modern theories about the law are both philosophical and rhetorical. Primarily through scholarship, legal philosophers use informal reasoning methods to persuade their audience about the best (if not absolute) truths about law. In this sense, the legal scholar's philosophy and rhetoric are indistinguishable. Lloyd Bitzer, a prominent rhetorician at the University of Wisconsin, has stated, "Rhetoric can never be innocent, can never be a disinterested arbiter of the ideological claims of others because it is always already serving certain ideological claims."[146] In Bitzer's view, rhetoric and ideology, of which philosophy is a part, are not separate pursuits but one and the same.

As early as the 1920s, legal scholars began to question the existence of true principles of law and the predictability of judicial decisions. These questions led first to a group of theories known collectively as American Legal Realism (hereafter "realism"). Realism evolved into critical legal studies, whose proponents argued that the U.S. legal system serves to perpetuate the power of the ruling class. These revolutionary ideas generated a host of new theories on the extent to which race and gender influence the law. A familiarity with these theories as well as the law and economics movement is essential to the legal writer. Political issues are rarely discussed and cases are rarely decided without some reliance on these theories.

## 1. REALISM

By the late nineteenth century, epistemologists were interested in how people learn and think about the law.[147] The prevailing idea at that time was

---

146. Berlin, *Rhetoric and Ideology, supra* note 84, at 9.

147. *See supra* ch. 2, at 52–56.

that law could be learned and taught like a science: one could discover true and enduring principles of law by examining judicial decisions. Christopher Langdell, the Dean of Harvard Law School from 1875–95, championed this view and developed the Socratic teaching method adopted by modern law schools. In a speech to the Harvard Law School Association in 1887, Langdell stated that "law is a science":

> [A]ll the available materials of that science are contained in printed books. If law be not a science, a university will consult its own dignity in declining to teach it. If it be not a science, it is a species of handicraft, and may best be learned by serving an apprenticeship to one who practices it.[148]

Langdell's goal was twofold. First, he had been hired in part to improve the perceived value of a Harvard law degree, which had been a source of embarrassment to the university as a whole due to its lack of rigor. Second, he sought to distance the study of law from the study of rhetoric. Recall that Plato had criticized rhetoric for being merely a knack (craft), not a techne (science) because it could not discover truth with certainty.[149] In an attempt to distance the study of law from rhetoric, Langdell decided law should be taught by scholars, not practitioners. Harvard law professors were thereafter hired for their scholarly potential as opposed to their success in practicing law.[150]

Prior to Langdell, law students learned about the law from legal treatises. In the early 1870s, Langdell introduced the case method, which substituted judicial decisions for treatises. Langdell's new method was Socratic; in the classroom, he questioned students about the cases they had read for class and encouraged them to articulate and critique the court's reasoning. At first, students were opposed to Langdell's method because he was not teaching them black letter law.[151] Despite these complaints, Columbia, Northwestern, Cornell, and Stanford adopted the case method by the mid–1890s.[152] Langdell thus converted the process of training lawyers from an apprenticeship to an academic system[153] and the conception of law school as a trade school to a scholarly endeavor.

As early as 1897, Justice Oliver Wendell Holmes questioned Langdell's belief that law is a science. He rejected the notion that "the only force at work in the development of the law is logic."[154] In contrast to Langdell, Holmes argued that the law is no more than the prediction of what courts will do in a given case. In *The Path of the Law*, a speech Holmes made at the dedication of a new hall at Boston University Law School, he stated, "You will find some text writers telling

**148.** Christopher C. Langdell, *Teaching Law as a Science*, 21 AM. L. REV. 123 (1887) (Langdell's after-dinner speech to the Harvard Law School Association).

**149.** *See supra* ch. 2, at 15.

**150.** ROBERT STEVENS, LAW SCHOOL: LEGAL EDUCATION FROM THE 1850S TO THE 1980S, 38 (1983).

**151.** *See* Bruce A. Kimball, Christopher Langdell: The Case of an 'Abomination' in Teaching Practice, THOUGHT & ACTION 23, 31 (2004).

**152.** *Id.* at 34.

**153.** WILLIAM P. LAPIANA, LOGIC & EXPERIENCE: THE ORIGIN OF MODERN AMERICAN LEGAL EDUCATION 7 (1994).

**154.** Oliver Wendell Holmes, *The Path of the Law*, 10 HARV. L. REV. 457, 465 (1897).

you that [the law] is ... a system of reason, that it is a deduction from principles of ethics or admitted axioms or what not, which may or may not coincide with the decisions."[155] However, in Holmes' view, "The prophecies of what the courts will do in fact, and nothing more pretentious, are what I mean by the law."[156] In Holmes' view, Langdell's case method was too detached from reality to be helpful to law students. As far as Holmes was concerned, the purpose of studying law was to predict outcome in the future, and knowledge of the law alone was insufficient to do that.

By the early 1900s, Holmes' views on the law had taken root. In 1913, Arthur Corbin, a well-known contracts professor at Yale, argued that law changes over time and that judges rely on factual circumstances in deciding cases as much as they do on legal doctrine.[157] Similarly, Walter Cook, Underhill Moore, and Herman Oliphant, then professors at Columbia University Law School, stated that although legal doctrine could not predict case outcomes, a study of the sociological factors that affect judicial decision-making could. Oliphant, in particular, recommended that law students study the way judges decide cases, not their opinions, to learn the law:

> This is the field for scholarly work worthy of best talents because the work to be done is not the study of vague and shifting rationalizations but the study of such tough things as the accumulated wisdom of men taught by immediate experience in contemporary life,—the battered experiences of judges among brutal facts.[158]

Oliphant believed that judicial opinions were merely ad hoc justifications for the judges' decisions, and for that reason, they did not help students discover real rules of law.

Karl Llewellyn, a law professor at Columbia University, was one of realism's greatest scholars. In 1930, he published *The Bramble Bush*,[159] a series of lectures he gave to incoming students. Llewellyn echoed Holmes in telling students that judges say one thing but do another:

> It will be [the judges'] *action* and the available means of influencing their action or of arranging your affairs with reference to their action which make up the "law" you have to study. And *rules*, in all of this, are important to you so far as they help you see or predict what judges will do or so far as they help you get judges to do something. That is their importance. That is all their importance, except as pretty playthings.[160]

Llewellyn argued that the common law system contributes to the indeterminacy of case outcomes. Because precedent can be read either narrowly or broadly,

---

155. *Id.* at 460.

156. *Id.* at 461.

157. Arthur Corbin, *The Law and the Judges*, 3 YALE REV. 234, 238–39 (1914).

158. Herman Oliphant, *A Return to Stare Decisis*, 14 A.B.A. J. 71, 159 (1928).

159. KARL N. LLEWELLYN, THE BRAMBLE BUSH: ON OUR LAW AND ITS STUDY (1960).

160. *Id.* at 5.

it permits a of multitude of outcomes. Llewellyn fully developed these ideas in *Remarks on the Theory of Appellate Decision and the Rules or Canons About How Statutes Are to Be Construed*,[161] in which he set forth twenty-eight canons of statutory interpretation and their twenty-eight equal and opposite canons, all of which could be found in reported opinions or treatises.[162]

Jerome Frank, another famous realist, believed that personality was the critical factor in judicial decision-making. He and other "psychological realists" rejected the idea that sociological factors explained case outcomes. In *Law and the Modern Mind*, Frank portrayed the legal system as chaotic, driven primarily by the biases of juries and judicial hunch.[163] Frank believed that rules of law and the facts of a particular case were indeterminate: witnesses often have imperfect recollections, false testimony can be credible, and judges and juries act on sympathy and bias. Indeterminate law is thus applied to uncertain fact.[164] The myth that law has certainty, Frank wrote, stems in part from a deep-rooted childish desire for a world of stability, where law plays the father-figure.[165] Laymen, lawyers, and judges all participate in the creation of this myth, even though their participation is largely unconscious. Judges assume that their standards are neutral and they act as impartial logic machines, but in fact, they deceive themselves.[166]

# 2. CRITICAL LEGAL STUDIES

While realism established that truth in law is relative in each case, many critical legal studies (CLS) scholars argued that truth in law is non-existent.

---

**161.** Karl N. Llewellyn, *Remarks on the Theory of Appellate Decision and the Rules or Canons About How Statutes Are to Be Construed*, 3 VAND. L. REV. 395 (1950).

**162.** For example, one canon for interpreting statutes is that "[a] statute cannot go beyond its text," but courts have also stated that "[t]o effect its purpose a statute may be implemented beyond its text." *Id.* at 401.

**163.** JEROME FRANK, LAW AND THE MODERN MIND (1949).

**164.** "[I]n most cases in the trial courts the parties do dispute about the facts, and the testimony concerning the facts is oral and conflicting. In any such case, what does it mean to say that the facts of a case are substantially similar to those of an earlier case? It means, at most, merely that the trial court regards the facts of the two cases as about the same. Since, however, no one knows what the trial court will find as the facts, no one can guess what precedent ought to be or will be followed." *Id.* at xiv.

**165.** *See, e.g., id.* at 19–21. Frank used "childish" here in the Freudian sense. Frank linked the desire for stability to the trauma that is experienced by a child when she realizes that her parents (particularly the father) cannot take care of her. The law and the judge then become a kind of a substitute father figure, an entity that will protect and make everything right.

**166.** *See id.* at 3–12. *See also* Joseph C. Hutcheson, Jr., *The Judgment Intuitive: The Function of the 'Hunch' in Judicial Decision*, 14 CORNELL L.Q. 274, 278 (1928–29), in which Hutcheson stated that when deciding a difficult case, a judge "wait[s] for the feeling, the hunch—that intuitive flash of understanding which makes the jump-spark connection between question and decision."

Influenced by realism and the law and society movement,[167] a small group of law professors held a conference on critical legal studies at the University of Wisconsin in 1977.[168] The goal of the conference was to oppose traditional legal scholarship and methods of teaching law. Three main criticisms of the U.S. legal system emerged.[169] The first was that the idea of neutral rules of law is a myth because law is fundamentally at odds with our notions of individual freedom.[170] Since we live in a pluralistic society, one rule of law cannot possibly be fair to a multiplicity of people with differing political and moral views. The second criticism was that the law is internally inconsistent, providing multiple solutions to a single problem and striving to serve both individuals and society as a whole.[171] The third criticism was that the law serves to keep the political majority in power and oppress minority groups.[172]

## a. THE RULE OF LAW AS MYTH

In 1975, Roberto Unger used the word "liberalism" to refer to conventional thinking about truth and the law, which he thought stifled progress.[173] Critical legal studies adopted this term to refer to the mistaken belief that rules of law are neutral and can be applied fairly.[174] CLS scholars argued that the notion of a neutral set of laws is inconsistent with the notion of individual freedom. Because rules of law are the result of a political process, they protect only the freedoms of the ruling class. Moreover, when judges interpret the law, using terms like "due process" and "good faith," they choose among competing and subjective ideas of justice, relying primarily on their own sense of what is just and fair.[175]

Unger's colleague, Duncan Kennedy, took Unger's views one step further. Kennedy stated that

[t]eachers teach nonsense when they persuade students that legal reasoning

---

167. The law and society movement began in the late 1800s. It refers to the interest of social scientists—sociologists, anthropologists, political scientists, and psychologists—in understanding law as a social phenomenon. Earlier theories about the law assumed that law exists independent from the cultures that use it. Law and society scholars assume that law is man-made and changes as cultural norms and values change. *See, e.g.,* Lawrence M. Friedman, *The Law and Society Movement,* 38 Stan. L. Rev. 763 (1986).

168. The group included Richard Abel, Tom Heller, Duncan Kennedy, Rand Rosenblatt, David Trubeck, and Mark Tushnet, all of whom had been at Yale Law School "either as teachers or students" from 1967–72. Louis B. Schwartz, *With Gun and Camera Through Darkest CLS–Land,* 36 Stan. L. Rev. 413, 415 (1984).

169. Andrew Altman, Critical Legal Studies: A Liberal Critique 13 (1990).

170. *Id.* at 13.

171. *Id.* at 14–15.

172. *Id.* at 15–16.

173. *See* Roberto M. Unger, Knowledge & Politics (1975). Unger believed that society's understanding of itself and the world was so limited by conventional thinking that it had become "the guard that watches over the prison house." *Id.* at 3.

174. For an elaborate defense and discussion of the liberal view of law, see the works of H.L.A. Hart and Ronald Dworkin. *E.g.,* H.L.A. Hart, The Concept of Law (1961); Ronald Dworkin, Law's Empire (1986).

175. *See* Altman, *supra* note 169, at 27–28.

is distinct, *as a method for reaching correct results,* from ethical and political discourse in general ... There is never a "correct legal solution" that is other than the correct ethical or political solution to that legal problem.[176]

In the late 1970s, Kennedy published a detailed criticism of Blackstone's *Commentaries,* which summarized English common law in the 1760s and greatly influenced British and American legal thought.[177] Kennedy argued that Blackstone's work legitimized the political status quo by characterizing a system of oppressive rules as neutral and necessary for the good of society.[178] For example, Blackstone distinguished between two kinds of rights: absolute and relative. According to Blackstone, absolute rights were akin to natural, universal rights that are afforded more protection under the law than relative rights, which "aris[e] from particular relationships."[179] Kennedy argued the distinction was false but permitted Blackstone to describe commercial laws designed to maintain the prevailing socio-economic order as laws relating to relative rights. Kennedy said, "Slavery," for example, "violated natural law and could not exist in England, though Blackstone seemed to regard a lifetime contract to labor in exchange for support as perfectly legal."[180]

## b. THE LAW AS FUNDAMENTAL CONTRADICTION

Both Unger and Kennedy were instrumental in formulating the idea that legal doctrine is riddled with contradiction. Kennedy, for example, argued that the chief contradiction in law is the tension between rules and standards.[181] Whereas rules of conduct are determinate, leaving little room for judicial discretion, standards of conduct, such as "good faith" and "reasonableness" are indeterminate, allowing for a wide range of discretionary choices.[182] Rules and standards are contradictory because they represent different belief systems about the self, a person's duty to others, the role of law in society, and the nature of individual freedoms.[183] A rule-based approach to law primarily benefits the individual, because a person is given advance notice of the kinds of conduct that are prohibited and thus punishable. In contrast, a standards-based approach tends to benefit society as a whole because its flexibility allows decision-makers to tailor their approach to specific circumstances and promote society's overall goals.[184]

---

**176.** Duncan Kennedy, *Legal Education as Training for Hierarchy, in* THE POLITICS OF LAW 47 (D. Kairys ed., 1982).

**177.** SIR WILLIAM BLACKSTONE, BLACKSTONE'S COMMENTARIES ON THE LAWS OF ENGLAND (Cavendish 2001) (1768).

**178.** Duncan Kennedy, *The Structure of Blackstone's Commentaries,* 28 BUFF. L. REV. 205, 234–56 (1979).

**179.** BLACKSTONE, *supra* note 177, bk. 1, p. 123.

**180.** Kennedy, *Structure of Blackstone's Commentaries, supra* note 178, at 283.

**181.** Duncan Kennedy, *Form and Substance in Private Law Adjudication,* 89 HARV. L. REV. 1685 (1976).

**182.** *Id.* at 1687–88.

**183.** *See* ALTMAN, *supra* note 169, at 109.

**184.** *Id.* at 108.

Unger, too, argued that legal doctrine competes with itself in its pursuit of various goals. Unger claimed that liberalism viewed legal doctrine as a set of guiding principles with exceptions. Whereas the guiding principles promote economic interests, the exceptions protect the often conflicting sphere of family and friends.[185] Unger too cited contract law to demonstrate his theory: The guiding principle of contract law is to ensure the freedom of individuals to form contracts and establish their terms. An exception to this principle is recognized only where enforcing a contract would violate social order or seem unfair.[186] Like standards and rules, principles and exceptions represent the competing goals of furthering the good of society and individual interests.

### c. THE LAW AS AN INSTRUMENT OF DOMINATION AND OPPRESSION

The third major criticism of liberalism was that it assumes our legal system prevents the improper exercise of political power. From the CLS point of view, the idea that governments exist independent of the people who create them is absurd.[187] Because law and politics are synonymous, legal institutions operate to keep the political majority in power: "Law is an instrument of social, economic and political domination, both in the sense of furthering the concrete interests of the dominators *and* in that of legitimizing the existing order."[188] In 1982, David Kairys, a civil rights attorney and professor of law at Temple University argued:

> The law is a major vehicle for the maintenance of existing social and power relations ... The law's perceived legitimacy confers a broader legitimacy on a social system ... characterized by domination. ... This perceived legitimacy of the law is primarily based ... on the distorted notion of government by law, not people.[189]

As Unger had suggested in 1975, this mistaken belief enslaves us to the institutions over which we should be masters.[190]

## 3. CRITICAL RACE THEORY

Critical race theory argues that racial identity is the "deciding factor in determining social standing and access to society's resources" in the United States.[191] Although CLS scholars acknowledged that the law perpetuates the

---

**185.** *See* Roberto Unger, The Critical Legal Studies Movement 58–90 (1986).

**186.** *Id.* at 61.

**187.** *See* Altman, *supra* note 169, at 16.

**188.** *See* Schwartz, *supra* note 168, at 417 (*quoting* Invitation to First Conference on Critical Legal Studies, Jan. 17, 1977).

**189.** The Politics of Law, *supra* note 176, at 5–6.

**190.** *See* Unger, Knowledge & Politics, *supra* note 173, at 3.

**191.** Derrick Bell, Race, Racism and American Law 1 (4th ed. 2000). Like CLS, Critical Race Theory rejects the idea of neutral law but in the racial context. According to this view, the law is an instrument that entrenches white supremacy.

power of the political majority, they did not identify themselves as members of that majority. Most CLS scholars were white men who attended Ivy League schools, had tenured positions at top-ranking law schools, and had published in the most prestigious American law journals. Critical race theorists picked up where CLS scholars left off, exploring racial equality under law.

Just as CLS criticizes the legal system for its corruptness, critical race theory (CRT) criticizes the legal system for its racism. CRT scholars argue that although discrimination is illegal, lawmakers and judges unconsciously discriminate on the basis of color. According to Charles Lawrence, III, unconscious racism is taught and perpetuated by our culture through parents, peers, and authority figures. With regard to racist beliefs, Lawrence argues:

> Because these beliefs are so much a part of the culture, they are not experienced as explicit lessons. Instead, they seem part of the individual's rational ordering of her perceptions of the world. The individual is unaware, for example, that the ubiquitous presence of a cultural stereotype has influenced her perception that blacks are lazy or unintelligent.... Even if a child is not told that blacks are inferior, he learns that lesson by observing the behavior of others.[192]

According to Lawrence, unconscious racial motivation influences judges, who must choose between competing arguments and potential outcomes in deciding cases.

Central to CRT is the idea that a "color-blind" approach to making law perpetuates racism. In the 1970s, many thought that "color-blindness" was the way to eliminate discrimination and promote democratic ideals. Since the goal of the Civil Rights Movement was to make society's resources available to all citizens, legislators and courts thought it made sense to distribute those resources on the basis of merit, not color. By eliminating race-based classifications, however, it became impossible to create "race-based remedies for discrimination while leaving untouched discriminatory action conducted through means that do not mention race."[193] What's more, CRT argues, the idea of an objective form of merit is problematic. Since the majority defines and interprets "merit" from its own perspective, it can perpetuate its own privilege. Notions of merit that are ostensibly neutral act instead as "repositories of racial power."[194]

The fallacy of "objective merit" became the focus of several scholars of color in the mid–1980s. In 1984, Richard Delgado, a professor of law at the University of Pittsburgh, observed that not one of the top twenty law review articles on civil

**192.** Charles R. Lawrence III, *The Id, the Ego, and Equal Protection Reckoning with Unconscious Racism*, IN CRITICAL RACE THEORY: THE KEY WRITINGS THAT FORMED THE MOVEMENT 235, 238 (Kimberlé Crenshaw et al. eds., 1995).

**193.** BELL, *supra* note 191, at 132.

**194.** CRITICAL RACE THEORY: THE KEY WRITINGS, *supra* note 192, at xxvi.

rights had been written by a scholar of color.[195] Although there were at least 133 scholars of color teaching at law schools, many of whom were publishing in that field, not one of the top twenty articles even cited their work.[196] Surprisingly, the authors of all top twenty articles were white men who had cited exclusively to the work of other white men. According to Delgado, these articles were often factually inaccurate, lacked empathy, and focused on procedural issues.[197] In this instance, Delgado would argue, the facially-neutral idea of merit served to discriminate against scholars of color. Randall Kennedy, a black law professor at Harvard, disagreed with Delgado,[198] but Duncan Kennedy, a noted white CLS scholar, agreed with Delgado and advocated for affirmative action in legal academia.[199]

# 4. FEMINIST LEGAL THEORY

With its focus on gender and discrimination, feminist legal theory (FLT) explores the extent to which the legal system subordinates women. Like its predecessor movements, FLT scholars differ on how best to achieve their goal, which in this case is equality for women under the law. In the early 1970s, liberal feminists advocated for gender neutral laws on the basis that men and women should be treated alike, whereas cultural feminists, who emerged in the 1980s, argued that the rule of law should account for significant differences between men and women.

In the 1970s, legal feminists tried to achieve equality for women by eliminating sex-based classifications in law and giving women equal access to legal rights and responsibilities, such as education, employment, and public benefits.[200] As an outgrowth of this effort, the U.S. Senate and House of Representatives passed the Equal Rights Amendment in 1972, but the states failed to ratify it. The Women's Rights Project of the ACLU, led by Justice Ruth Bader Ginsburg, was particularly influential at this time, arguing before the United States Supreme Court that gender classifications were unlawful, even when they benefited women.[201] The result of the Women's Rights Project was a "system of 'formal' equality, in the sense of requiring that the form of the law

---

**195.** Richard Delgado, THE IMPERIAL SCHOLAR: REFLECTIONS ON A REVIEW OF CIVIL RIGHTS LITERATURE, 132 U. PA. L. REV. 561 (1984). Delgado defined leading articles as those cited most often, published in major law journals, and concerned with theoretical as opposed to practical concerns.

**196.** *Id.* at 561.

**197.** *Id.* at 567–68.

**198.** *See* Randall L. Kennedy, *Racial Critiques of Legal Academia,* 102 HARV. L. REV. 1745, 1770–78 (1989).

**199.** Duncan Kennedy, *A Cultural Pluralist Case for Affirmative Action in Legal Academia,* 1990 DUKE L.J. 705, 706.

**200.** *See, e.g., Califano v. Goldfarb,* 430 U.S. 199 (1977); *Frontiero v. Richardson,* 411 U.S. 677 (1973); and *Reed v. Reed,* 404 U.S. 71 (1971).

**201.** *See, e.g.,* Dr. Ruth B. Cowan, *Women's Rights Through Litigation: An Examination of the American Civil Liberties Union Women's Rights Project,* 1971–1976, 8 COLUM. HUM. RTS. L. REV. 373 (1976).

be gender neutral—that, on its face, the law make no distinction between the sexes."[202] States could no longer discriminate on the basis of sex regarding the administration of estates, Social Security benefits, or jury duty.[203] As a result, women began to gain access to traditionally male professions and Ivy League schools. By the end of the 1970s, some believed that gender equality had been achieved and the work of the women's liberation movement was done.

In the 1980s, however, feminist scholars acknowledged that although gender-based classifications had been eliminated, discrimination continued in the areas of female sexuality and reproduction.[204] The dilemma for FLT was "whether to continue to urge equality, or instead to concede difference."[205] The ensuing debate focused on special maternity leave provisions for workers that bothered equality feminists. Wendy Williams, a leading liberal feminist, disagreed with laws giving women special treatment: "If we can't have it both ways, we need to think carefully about which way we want to have it."[206] In contrast, cultural feminists argued that because only women get pregnant, they need to be treated differently.[207] The difference debate was supported in part by the work of Carol Gilligan, a psychologist whose work on moral development demonstrated that men and women reason differently.[208] Whereas men tend to view moral problems as a "hierarchy or ladder of rights," women tend to view them "through a web of connection" or relationships.[209] Gilligan's work supported the argument that the legal system is essentially male in its point of view, and true equality cannot be achieved until the system reflects both the male and the female perspective.[210]

Not all feminists in the 1980s believed that the difference debate was the proper focus of FLT. Catherine MacKinnon, for example, argued that the

**202.** MARTHA CHAMALLAS, INTRODUCTION TO FEMINIST LEGAL THEORY 35 (1999).

**203.** *Id.* at 34–35.

**204.** *Cf. supra* p. 90.

**205.** Clare Dalton, *Where We Stand: Observations on the Situation of Feminist Legal Thought,* 3 BERKELEY WOMEN'S L.J. 1, 5 (1988). *See also* Lucinda M. Finley, *Transcending Equality Theory: A Way Out of the Maternity and the Workplace Debate,* 86 COLUM. L. REV. 1118 (1986); Ann C. Scales, *The Emergence of Feminist Jurisprudence: An Essay,* 95 YALE L.J. 1373 (1986).

**206.** Wendy W. Williams, *The Equality Crisis: Some Reflections on Culture, Courts, and Feminism,* 7 WOMEN'S RTS. L. REP. 175, 196 (1981–82).

**207.** *See* Jenny Morgan, *Feminist Theory as Legal Theory,* 16 MELB. U. L. REV. 743, 745 (1988), *reprinted in* 1 FEMINIST LEGAL THEORY (Frances E. Olsen ed., 1995).

**208.** *See, e.g.,* CAROL GILLIGAN, IN A DIFFERENT VOICE: PSYCHOLOGICAL THEORY AND WOMEN'S DEVELOPMENT (1982). In her famous "Amy and Jake study," Gilligan presented male and female subjects, ages 11 and 15, with a moral dilemma. The subjects were asked whether a husband should steal a drug he cannot afford to save his wife. Gilligan discovered that male subjects tended to treat the problem as "moral arithmetic." Jake concluded that life is more important than money, so stealing the drug would be acceptable. In contrast, the female subjects tended to view the problem multi-dimensionally, wanting to satisfy the need to save the husband's wife without stealing. Amy, for example, asked lots of questions and struggled to find a way to work out the problem.

**209.** Morgan, *supra* note 207, at 747.

**210.** *See, e.g.,* Carrie Menkel–Meadow, *Toward Another View of Legal Negotiation: The Structure of Problem Solving,* 31 U.C.L.A. L. REV. 754 (1984); Robin West, *Jurisprudence and Gender,* 55 U. CHI. L. REV.1 (1988).

problem for women was not whether they were being treated differently (either for a good or bad reason) but whether their interests were subordinated to men's. MacKinnon sought to demonstrate that the legal system was "fundamentally opposed to women's interests and designed principally to perpetuate male dominance."[211] What cultural feminists viewed as difference between the sexes was the construct of a male-dominated society. In MacKinnon's view, nowhere was the male perspective more dominant than in the law's response to issues of sexuality, such as rape, pornography, and sexual harassment (a concept she coined) in the workplace. MacKinnon argued that sexual harassment violated both Title VII of the Civil Rights Act of 1964 and the Equal Protection clause of the Fourteenth Amendment.[212] According to MacKinnon, sexual harassment perpetuates women's inferior status in the workplace.[213] The Equal Employment Opportunity Commission ultimately adopted MacKinnon's definition of sexual harassment.[214] However, when she and others targeted pornography, seeking to restrict it through local ordinances, her support waned. MacKinnon's opponents argued that women should make their own choices about participating in such behavior without governmental interference.[215]

Beginning in the late 1980s, diversity feminists argued that the predominantly white voices of 1970s and 1980s feminists do not speak for all women, especially those of color. In their view, differences in race, ethnicity, sexual orientation, and socio-economic status among women are as important as gender.[216] Kimberle Crenshaw, for example, argued that cultural assumptions about female passivity and dependence are tied primarily to white women.[217] Martha Minow argued that efforts to ignore or accommodate differences between men and women reinforce those differences.[218] From Minow's point of view, we should rethink the Golden Rule: "The goal should not be to treat others as you would have them treat you ... we should listen to the other person to discover how he or she wants to be treated and determine the justness of that request in the context of the other's situation."[219] Similarly, Mari Matsuda has written about "multiple consciousness," the experience of the world from several perspectives at once, including gender and race.[220] Matsuda urges legal scholars and practitioners

---

**211.** CHAMALLAS, *supra* note 202, at 53. *See also* CATHERINE A. MACKINNON, FEMINISM UNMODIFIED: DISCOURSES ON LIFE AND LAW (1987).

**212.** CATHERINE A. MACKINNON, SEXUAL HARASSMENT OF WORKING WOMEN 5–6 (1979).

**213.** *Id.* at 47–56.

**214.** CHAMALLAS, *supra* note 202, at 55.

**215.** *Id.* at 60–62.

**216.** *Id.* at 85.

**217.** Kimberlé Crenshaw, *Demarginalizing the Intersection of Race and Sex: A Black Feminist Critique of Antidiscrimination Doctrine, Feminist Theory and Antiracist Politics*, 1989 U. CHI. LEGAL F. 139, 154–56 (1989).

**218.** MARTHA MINOW, MAKING ALL THE DIFFERENCE: INCLUSION, EXCLUSION, AND AMERICAN LAW 20 (1990).

**219.** CHAMALLAS, *supra* note 202, at 96 (interpreting MINOW, *supra* note 218, at 373–90).

**220.** Mari J. Matsuda, *When the First Quail Calls: Multiple Consciousness as Jurisprudential Method*, 14 WOMEN'S RTS. L. REP. 297, 299 (1992).

to see the world from the eyes of the privileged as well as the oppressed. This multiple consciousness "allow[s] us to operate both within the abstractions of standard jurisprudential discourse *and* within the details of our own special knowledge."[221]

Postmodern feminists emerged in the early 1990s. Although they represent a variety of viewpoints, postmodern feminists generally agree that to identify women as "women" for the purpose of achieving equality is counter-productive. In contrast to sex, which is a biological act, "gender" differences between men and women are socially constructed and perpetuated through language, including the law. In *Gender Trouble,* Judith Butler argued that gender is "performative— that is, constituting the identity it is purported to be."[222] Similarly, Mary Jo Frug rejected the idea that gender is an essential part of human nature and explored the extent to which "legal rules and discourse constitute a system that 'constructs,' or engenders the female body."[223] Many postmodern feminists also reject MacKinnon's premise of a male-dominated society with its attendant injuries to women. Janet Halley, for example, argues that these perceived injuries, such as sexual harassment in the workplace, inflict little, if any, real harm.[224] What's more, they represent a moralistic view about human sexuality that is distinctly heterosexual.[225] In Halley's view, dominance theory feminists do not speak for all women, some of whom might actually enjoy being dominated.[226] These postmodern feminists conclude that to characterize all women as victims is a self-fulfilling prophecy.

# 5. LAW AND ECONOMICS

Law and economics is more a methodology for problem solving than a political movement, but it is included here because of its immeasurable impact on contemporary legal rhetoric. The fundamental principle of law and economics is that common law rules should be efficient. "Efficiency" refers to the distribution of legal entitlements so as to maximize the benefit to society as a whole with as little waste as possible. Many law and economics scholars explicitly reject the idea that law should be used to redistribute income and entitlements so that specific sub-groups of society receive their "fair share."

Economic analysis can be used to analyze legal problems in two ways:

---

**221.** *Id.* at 299. *See also* Lama Abu–Odeh, *Post–Colonial Feminism and the Veil: Considering the Differences,* 26 NEW ENG. L. REV. 1527 (1992) (exploring the various reasons women in post-colonial Arab society wear traditional clothing in order to raise the consciousness of feminists and help them relate to the Arab woman's dilemma).

**222.** JUDITH BUTLER, GENDER TROUBLE 33 (1990).

**223.** MARY JO FRUG, POSTMODERN LEGAL FEMINISIM 130 (1992).

**224.** *See* Janet Halley, *The Politics of Injury: A Review of Robin West's Caring for Justice,* 1 UNBOUND: HARV. J. LEGAL LEFT 65, 83–84 (2005) http://www.legalleft.org/?cat=1 and Janet Halley, *Sexuality Harrassment, in* DIRECTIONS IN SEXUAL HARRASSMENT LAW 197–98 (Catherine A. MacKinnon & Reva B. Siegel, eds., 2003).

**225.** *See* Halley, DIRECTIONS IN SEXUAL HARRASSMENT LAW, *supra* note 224, at 101–02.

**226.** *See* Halley, *The Politics of Injury, supra* note 224, at 91.

descriptive or positive theorists use a cost-benefit form of analysis to explain and predict individuals' responses to legal rules and the impact of those decisions on society as a whole,[227] whereas prescriptive or normative theorists use economics to assist lawmakers in fashioning legal rules.[228] Law and economics theory has been used by positive and normative theorists to study virtually every area of law, including torts, contracts, property, criminal, family, and equal protection.[229] Judge Richard Posner brought economic analysis into the mainstream of legal academics and helped found what is called the Chicago School of law and economics. Posner is particularly known for his work on judicial decision-making, concluding that just as individuals make rational choices to maximize utility, judges do the same in resolving legal disputes.[230]

The modern law and economics movement emerged from Ronald Coase's article, *The Problem of Social Cost*.[231] Coase was a professor of Economics at the University of Virginia and interested in the problem of regulating businesses that adversely affect others, such as manufacturing companies that pollute neighboring lands. These adverse effects are commonly referred to as externaltities. Until that time, economists assumed that the best way to deal with externalities was to make businesses liable for the damage they caused or to tax them in an amount equal to the damage.[232] In contrast, Coase theorized that regardless of who is given the legal right—either the business to operate or the neighbors to prevent its operation—the ultimate outcome will be the same. Assuming no transaction costs,[233] Coase argued that the parties would bargain privately to correct the problem.[234] For example, if a business is not legally entitled to pollute, it may still operate if it is willing to pay its neighbors an amount equal to the cost to clean up the pollution. As long as the business is willing to pay the clean-up costs and that amount exceeds the neighbors' costs,

---

227. *See, e.g.*, Robert C. Ellickson, *Property in Land*, 102 YALE L.J. 1315 (1993); Henry Hansmann, *Condominium and Cooperative Housing: Transactional Efficiency, Tax Subsidies, and Tenure Choice*, 20 J. LEGAL STUD. 25 (1991).

228. Gillian K. Hadfield, *Judicial Competence and the Interpretation of Incomplete Contracts*, 23 J. LEGAL STUD. 159 (1994); Richard L. Hasen, *The Efficient Duty to Rescue*, 15 INT'L REV. L. & ECON. 141 (1995).

229. *See, e.g.*, Guido Calabresi & Jon T. Hirschoff, *Toward a Test for Strict Liability in Torts*, 81 YALE L.J. 1055 (1972); Charles J. Goetz & Robert E. Scott, *Enforcing Promises: An Examination of the Basis of Contract*, 89 YALE L.J. 1261 (1980); Harold Demsetz, *Toward a Theory of Property Rights*, 57 AM. ECON. REV. 347 (1967); Steven Shavell, *Criminal Law and the Optimal Use of Nonmonetary Sanctions as a Deterrent*, 85 COLUM. L. REV. 1232 (1985); RICHARD A. POSNER, ECONOMIC ANALYSIS OF LAW (7th ed. 2007).

230. *See, e.g.*, Richard A. Posner, *What Do Judges and Justices Maximize? (The Same Thing Everybody Else Does)*, 3 SUP. CT. ECON. REV. 1, 3 (1993).

231. Ronald Coase, *The Problem of Social Cost*, 3 LAW & ECON. 1 (1960).

232. *Id.* at 1. For the origin of this theory, see A.C. PIGOU, THE ECONOMICS OF WELFARE (4th ed. 1958). Pigou was an economist at Cambridge University from 1908 to 1943; he theorized that governments could intervene to rectify externalities, which he defined as one person or business imposing a cost on someone else.

233. Transaction costs are those costs incurred in purchasing the goods and services themselves (*e.g.*, commission due a realtor on the purchase of a home).

234. Coase, *supra* note 231, at 2–8.

the business will continue to pollute. According to Coase, economists should not assume which is the greater harm, and governments should not intervene when the market can correct itself.[235] Although Coase was criticized because transaction costs are almost always present in a bargained-for exchange, the theory "focused attention on what type of intervention is justified in the face of (nearly) ubiquitous transaction costs."[236]

In the early 1970s, then Professor Calabresi and Douglas Melamed argued that for the Coase theorem to be useful, it was necessary to articulate the relative rights, what they call entitlements, among private parties as precisely as possible.[237] Focusing on the law of property and torts, Calabresi and Melamed considered three types of entitlements: those protected by property rules, those protected by liability rules, and those that are inalienable.[238] Property rules grant rights to parties who may then decide the value of that right, such as a homeowner who decides at what price to sell his home. Liability rules, on the other hand, give the party who does *not* own the entitlement the right to violate the owner's rights and then compensate him. Liability rules encompass much of tort law. Inalienable entitlements are those that cannot be bargained for under any circumstances, such as civil rights. According to Calabresi and Melamed, entitlements should be assigned to the party in the best position to prevent externalities at the lowest possible cost.[239] As for the appropriate nature of the entitlement, they concluded that where transaction costs are likely to be high, a liability rule is most desirable.[240] The chief example is that of eminent domain, where a group of landowners' inability to reach agreement on a sale price would preclude the government from buying it for a presumably more valuable purpose. In that case, the law of eminent domain steps in, applies a liability rule as opposed to a property rule, and permits the government to purchase the property and compensate the owners for its fair market value.[241]

Despite the enormous success of these and other related theories, using economic analysis to shape law and policy has been criticized on several grounds. Some scholars argue that traditional economic analysis makes unrealistic assumptions about human nature. Christine Jolls, Cass Sunstein, and Richard Thaler argue, for example, that because people make irrational choices, law and economics theory needs to incorporate "a more realistic conception of human

---

**235.** *Id.* at 9–10.

**236.** 1 LAW AND ECONOMICS xii (Jules Coleman & Jeffrey Lange eds., 1992).

**237.** Guido Calabresi & A. Douglas Melamed, *Property Rules, Liability Rules, and Inalienability: One View of the Cathedral*, 85 HARV. LAW REV. 1089 (1972).

**238.** *Id.* at 1092–93.

**239.** *See* CALABRESI & MELAMED, *supra* note 237, at 1096–97.

**240.** *See id.* at 1106–09.

**241.** *See id.* at 1106–1107.

behavior."[242] Others, like Duncan Kennedy, have argued that "efficiency" is inadequate to guide lawmakers choosing among a number of potential solutions to a given problem, each of which allocates resources and wealth differently.[243] Ronald Dworkin, a professor of jurisprudence at University College London and New York University, has argued that law and economic theory's explicit goal of maximizing wealth is inappropriate, and judges should not use it to justify their decisions.[244] In Dworkin's view, it is a mistake to assume that a society with more wealth is better off than a society with less wealth.[245]

---

### QUESTIONS FOR CONSIDERATION

1. Do you agree with Oliver Wendell Holmes and Karl Llewellyn that rules of law are less important than being able to predict the subjective view of judges? What is the effect of this view on the idea that law is natural and fixed?

2. Critical Legal Studies argued that law is an instrument of the majority used to dominate the minority. Does that mean that laws of democracies are inherently unfair? How else should laws be created other than by majority vote?

3. Critical race theory assumes that race is still a negative factor in American life. In your opinion, is it more or less fair to consider race explicitly in making law and deciding cases?

4. In the struggle to gain equality for women, do you think it is more important to be mindful of women as equal to men or as significantly different?

5. How do attitudes about discrimination against economic, race, and gender minorities affect the kinds of arguments you will make as an advocate? What rhetorical and ethical considerations do you think are important in this context?

---

**242.** Christine Jolls, Cass R. Sunstein, & Richard Thaler, *A Behavioral Approach to Law and Economics*, 50 STAN. L. REV. 1471, 1545 (1998). *See also* Martha C. Nussbaum, *Flawed Foundations: The Philosophical Critique of (a Particular Type of) Economics*, 64 U. CHI. L. REV. 1197 (1997).

**243.** Duncan Kennedy, *Cost–Benefit Analysis of Entitlement Problems*, 33 STAN. L. REV. 387 (1981).

**244.** Ronald M. Dworkin, *Is Wealth A Value?*, 9 J. LEGAL STUD. 191 (1980).

**245.** *Id.* at 195.

# CHAPTER 4

## THE TRADITIONAL CANONS
## OF RHETORIC

■ ■ ■

*"Rhetoric is the faculty of discovering in the particular case what are the available means of persuasion. This is the function of no other art."*—Aristotle

Chapters Two and Three discuss the history of rhetoric, highlighting different viewpoints on rhetoric's ability to produce knowledge, its changing role in education, and its long-standing focus on legal argument. This chapter describes the substance of rhetoric itself, the "rules," so to speak, that Aristotle first articulated in a comprehensive way more than 2,400 years ago. As you read this chapter, remember that rhetoric is not a set of arbitrary rules to be followed blindly. Rather, it is a methodology for persuasive speaking and writing that was first observed in successful orators and then preserved in writing by Aristotle and others for those who wanted to develop similar skills of persuasion.

In contrast to Plato, Aristotle believed that rhetoric encompasses both the creation and delivery of argument; it is not just the process of delivering arguments acquired elsewhere (*i.e.*, through dialectic or some other process of acquiring knowledge). For that reason, Aristotle considered rhetoric the counterpart to dialectic, a separate but coherent and valuable pursuit in the course of human affairs. Although rhetoric produces only probable "truths," Aristotle argued it achieves something akin to certainty in law and politics:

> [W]e should be able to argue on either side of a question; not with a view to putting both sides into practice—we must not advocate evil—but in order that no aspect of the case may escape us, and that if our opponent makes unfair use of the arguments, we may be able in turn to refute them.[1]

Social-epistemic rhetoricians argue that rhetoric involves more than the invention and delivery of ideas, it actually creates them.[2] Chaim Perelman and others, too, have argued that philosophers use argument just as much as lawyers do to persuade their audiences about truth. Thus all forms of reasoning—even

---

1.   ARISTOTLE, RHETORIC, *supra* ch. 2, note 34, at bk. 1, ch. 1, p. 6.
2.   *See supra* ch. 3, at 81.

philosophical—belong to the realm of rhetoric.[3]

# A. TYPES OF RHETORIC AND FORMS OF PROOF

## 1. TYPES OF RHETORIC

- **Deliberative (political)**
- **Forensic (judicial)**
- **Epideictic (ceremonial)**

Aristotle was the first to divide persuasive speech into three types: deliberative or political, forensic or judicial, and epideictic or ceremonial.[4] He based these divisions on the nature of the audience to which each form of speech appeals:

> The kinds of Rhetoric are three in number, corresponding to the three kinds of hearers to which speeches are addressed; for, a speech being the joint result of three things—the speaker, his subject, and the person addressed— the end or object has reference to this last, namely the hearer.[5]

According to Aristotle, political oratory is addressed to people who make decisions about the future, such as legislators. He defined the subject of political speech as that which affects the public purse, war and peace, national defense, imports and exports, and legislation of a given body politic.[6] Judicial oratory is addressed to those who make decisions about the past, such as judges. Aristotle described judicial speech as concerned primarily with wrongdoing, understanding the motives of wrong-doers, and ascribing blame.[7] Finally, ceremonial oratory is directed at those whose job is merely to decide the force and merit of the speech itself. Aristotle said it is designed to praise or blame public figures and inspire audiences. Edward P.J. Corbett and Robert J. Connors cite President Lincoln's 1863 Gettysburg Address[8] as a relatively modern example of ceremonial speech.[9] Martin Luther King, Jr.'s 1963 I Have A Dream Speech,[10] which refers to President Lincoln, is another more recent example.

---

**3.** *See supra* ch. 3, at 71.

**4.** ARISTOTLE, RHETORIC, *supra* ch. 2, note 34, bk. 1, ch. 3, p. 17.

**5.** *Id.* at 16.

**6.** *Id.* at 21.

**7.** *Id.* at 55.

**8.** *See* Abraham Lincoln, The Gettysburg Address (November 19, 1863), *available at* http://showcase.netins.net/web/creative/lincoln/speeches/gettysburg.htm.

**9.** CORBETT & CONNORS, *supra* ch. 2, note 1, at 23.

**10.** *See* Martin Luther King, Jr., *I Have A Dream* (Aug. 28, 1963), *in* RIPPLES OF HOPE: GREAT AMERICAN CIVIL RIGHTS SPEECHES (Josh Gottheimer ed., 2003).

## 2. FORMS OF PROOF

| Artistic Appeals | Non-Artistic Appeals |
|---|---|
| • *Logos*— appeal to logic or reason | • Witnesses |
| • *Pathos*— appeal to audience's emotions | • Admissions under torture |
| • *Ethos*— appeal to speaker's credibility and character | • Written Contracts |
| | • Oaths |

FIGURE 8

Aristotle described two forms of proof or evidence a speaker uses to persuade her audience: artistic and inartistic. *See Figure 8, above.* Artistic forms of proof are those the speaker actually *creates* or discovers. Aristotle further divided artistic proofs into three types or modes: appeals to *logos*, appeals to *pathos*, and appeals to *ethos*.[11] Appeals to *logos* rely on logic or analytical reasoning. Appeals to *pathos* appeal to the audience's emotions. Aristotle said, "Persuasion is effected through the audience, when they are brought by the speech into a state of emotion; for we give very different decisions under the sway of pain or joy, and liking or hatred."[12] Appeals to *ethos* are those aspects of the speaker's character that lead the audience to believe she is credible.

Inartistic forms of proof are not invented; a speaker simply uses them to help persuade her audience.[13] Aristotle identified five types of inartistic proof: laws, witnesses, coerced confessions (although he firmly believed that any confession made under torture was not to be trusted), written contracts, and oaths.[14]

## B. THE CANONS OF RHETORIC

Ancient Greeks and Romans viewed rhetoric as both a substantive art and a process that could be imitated. In *Rhetoric*, Aristotle described the stages of the process as invention, arrangement, style, memory, and delivery.[15] Regardless of the subject matter of the speech, be it political, judicial, or ceremonial, he said the process remained the same. The great Roman orators and teachers of rhetoric adopted Aristotle's view. Cicero, Quintilian, and the author of *Rhetorica*

---

11. ARISTOTLE, RHETORIC, *supra* ch. 2, note 34, at bk. 1, ch. 1, pp. 8–9.

12. *Id.* at 9.

13. *Id.* at 8.

14. *Id.* at bk. 1, ch. 15, p. 80.

15. *See id.* at 143–81, 220–41, 182–219.

*Ad Herennium* described rhetoric using the same terms Aristotle used.[16] The stages of the process are commonly referred to as the canons, and they comprise the building blocks of rhetoric. *See Figure 9.*

| Canon | Definition | Greek Term | Latin Term |
| --- | --- | --- | --- |
| **Invention** | the creation or discovery of arguments | *heuresis* | *inventio* |
| **Arrangement** | the effective and orderly arrangement of arguments | *taxis* | *disposition* |
| **Style** | the style of the speaker's language or writing | *lexis* | *elocution* |
| **Memory** | the process of memorizing a speech | *mneme* | *memoria* |
| **Delivery** | the effective delivery of a speech | *hypokrisis* | *pronuntiatio* |

FIGURE 9

Invention is the most complex and time-consuming of the canons. Cicero described it as the "discovery of valid or seemingly valid arguments to render one's cause plausible."[17] In classical terms, the orator first consults various "topics"[18] and creates those arguments most likely to persuade her audience. Next, she must arrange or organize her speech. Aristotle thought the essence of a well-arranged speech was the statement of facts and the argument: "A speech

---

**16.** *See, e.g.,* Author unknown, RHETORICA AD HERENNIUM, *supra* ch. 2, note 53, at bk. 1, ch. 2, p. 7; CICERO, DE INVENTIONE, *supra* ch. 2, note 49, at bk. 1, ch. 7, ¶ 9, p. 19; QUINTILIAN, INSTITUTIO ORATORIO, *supra* ch. 2, note 61, at bk. 3, ch. 3, p. 23.

**17.** CICERO, DE INVENTIONE, *supra* ch. 2, note 49, at 19. This is Aristotle's definition of rhetoric. *See supra* at 99.

**18.** *See infra,* at 105.

has two parts. Necessarily, you state your case, and you prove it."[19] He recognized though that orators often add an introduction and a conclusion.[20] To Aristotle's arrangement of a speech, the Roman rhetoricians added the statement of the issue, an outline of the argument, and counter-arguments. *See Figure 10.* The elements of a traditional legal memorandum or brief in the twenty-first century are strikingly similar.[21]

| Arrangement of a Speech | Taxis (Greek) | Dispositle (Latin) |
|---|---|---|
| Introduction | Proem | exordium |
| Statements of Facts | narration | narratio |
| Definition of Issues | | explicatio |
| Outline of the Arguments | | divisio or partitio |
| Argument | argument | confirmatio |
| Counter-argument | | refutatio or confutatio |
| Conclusion | telos | peroration |

**FIGURE 10**

Once the orator decides how to arrange her speech, she must choose an appropriate speaking style. *Lexis* or *elocutio* referred to the canon of style. As Aristotle put it, "[I]t is not enough to know *what* to say—one must also know *how* to say it. The right way of doing this contributes much to the right impression

---

19.  Aristotle, Rhetoric, *supra* ch. 2, note 34, bk. 3, ch. 13, p. 220.

20.  Corbett & Connors, *supra* ch. 2, note 1, at 20.

21.  *See infra* ch. 8, at 216–218.

of a speech."[22] As a result of the scientific revolution of the seventeenth century, rhetorical theorists focused on style.[23] The great rhetoricians of the eighteenth and early nineteenth centuries, such as Blair, Campbell, and Whately, focused on arrangement as well as style.[24] Aristotle's views on style were rather straightforward; he said a speaker's words and overall effect should be clear and appropriate to the circumstances.[25] He said:

> Thus we see the necessity of disguising the means we employ, so that we may seem to be speaking, not with artifice, but naturally. Naturalness is persuasive, artifice just the reverse.[26]

The Romans divided style into three types: simple or low, middle or forcible, and grand or high.[27] The *Rhetorica Ad Herennium* defined them as follows:

> The Grand type consists of a smooth and ornate arrangement of impressive words. The Middle type consists of words of a lower, yet not of the lowest and most colloquial, class of words. The Simple type is brought down even to the most current idiom of standard speech.[28]

The simple or low style was thought to be most effective for teaching or proof, the middle style was appropriate for delighting or moving an audience, and the grand style was reserved for persuasion.[29] Cicero was particularly well known and often criticized for his grandiloquent or Asiatic style.[30]

Although Aristotle did not write about the canons of memory or delivery in great detail, delivery was a critical part of an orator's education in ancient Greece and Rome.[31] Aside from acknowledging the need to memorize and practice giving speeches to be effective, rhetoricians devoted little time to either of these subjects until the eighteenth century, when the elocutionists first explored the impact of body language on audience.[32] With the invention of the printing press in 1436, most communications were written. As as result, the need to teach memory and delivery as part of rhetoric diminished greatly. Today, these canons survive in the form of speech and communications classes. Because this book focuses on legal writing, neither of these canons is addressed in detail here.

---

**22.** ARISTOTLE, RHETORIC, *supra* ch. 2, note 34, bk. 3, ch. 1, p.182.

**23.** *See supra* ch. 2, at 46–47.

**24.** *See supra* ch. 2, at 52–58.

**25.** ARISTOTLE, RHETORIC, *supra* ch. 2, note 34, bk. 3, ch. 2, p. 185.

**26.** *Id.* at 186.

**27.** *See, e.g.,* Author unknown, RHETORICA AD HERENNIUM, *supra* ch. 2, note 53, at bk. 4, ch. 8, p. 253; CICERO, ORATOR, *supra* ch. 2, note 49, at ch. 5, ¶ 20, p. 319; QUINTILIAN, INSTITUTIO ORATORIO, *supra* ch. 2, note 61, at bk. 8, ch. 3, pp. 345–47.

**28.** RHETORICA AD HERENNIUM, *supra* ch. 2, note 53, at bk. 4, ch. 8, p. 253.

**29.** CORBETT & CONNORS, *supra* ch. 2, note 1, at 21; RHETORICA AD HERENNIUM, supra ch. 2, note 53, at bk. 4, ch. 8, p. 252 n.c.

**30.** *See supra* ch. 2, at 22.

**31.** CORBETT & CONNORS, *supra* ch. 2, note 1, at 22. Isocrates, was one of the first teachers of rhetoric to have his students learn its principles and practice on their feet. *See supra* ch. 2, at 14.

**32.** *See supra* ch. 2, at 58–59.

# C. INVENTION OF ARTISTIC ARGUMENTS

For classical rhetoricians, invention was a two-step process. First, the orator identified the issue to be resolved,[33] and then he consulted a range of ideas or topics to create the best arguments. Aristotle conceived of the topics (*topoi*) as places where ideas for arguments are stored.[34] The topics establish "the 'grounds' of argument. Hence, by using various topics, a rhetor is able to invent lines of argument and take a 'stand' on an issue."[35] What Aristotle called common topics, he considered useful for all kinds of argument. The special topics were reserved for specific types of argument. *See Figure 11.* Much of Aristotle's work on the *topoi* appears in his *Topics*,[36] and *Rhetoric* assumes the reader's familiarity with it.

## Common Topics

- *Definitions—*
  genus, species

- *Comparisons—*
  size, similarity, and difference

- *Relationships—*
  cause and effect, contraries,
  contradictions

- *Circumstances—*
  possible or impossible, future
  and past facts

- *Testimony—*
  authority, statistics, documents,
  laws, precedent

## Special Topics

- Political—
  the good, the unworthy,
  the advantageous and
  disadvantageous

- Judicial—
  wrongdoing and justice

- Ceremonial—
  the noble and the base

**FIGURE 11**

# 1. THE COMMON TOPICS

Aristotle listed the following common topics in *Rhetoric*: possible or impossible, future fact, past fact, and size or degree.[37] Reading the *Topics* and *Rhetoric* together, rhetoricians have since reorganized Aristotle's common topics into the following categories: definition, comparison, relationship, circumstance,

---

**33.** *See* CICERO, DE INVENTIONE, *supra* ch. 2, note 49, at bk. 1, ch. 8, ¶ 10, p. 21.

**34.** THOMAS J. KINNEY, THE COMMON TOPICS (2003–04), http://www.u.arizona.edu/?tkinney/pdf/handouts/commontopics.pdf.

**35.** *Id.*

**36.** This work, together with *Prior and Posterior Analytics, On Interpretation, Sophistical Refutations*, and *Categories*, comprise *The Organon*, a collection of Aristotle's essays on logic. These essays were published together c. 350 BCE. *See supra* ch. 2, note 31.

**37.** *See* ARISTOTLE, RHETORIC, *supra* ch. 2, note 34, at bk. 2, ch. 19, p. 143.

and testimony.[38] By consulting these potential areas for argument, the orator would be sure to leave out nothing relevant.[39]

## a. DEFINITION

Aristotle said the best way to know the nature of the subject matter or the scope of the issue is to define it. He said a "*definition* is a phrase which signifies the what-it-is-to-be" something.[40] Quoting Socrates from Plato's *Apology*, Aristotle illustrates: " 'What is the divine'? It must be either a god or the work of a god. Well, then, any one who believes in the existence of a work of a god must needs believe in the existence of gods."[41] According to Aristotle, arguments based on definition rely on the essential meaning of something and proceed "to reason from it on the point at issue."[42] You may recall that Richard Weaver ranked arguments based on definition as the most ethical because they try to capture the essence of something.[43]

Legislatures, judges, and parties to a dispute use definitions to identify behavior that is or is not prohibited and to distinguish between seemingly similar objects or circumstances. In 1998, President Clinton attempted to define "is" in such a way as to prove he had not committed perjury in prior testimony. Clinton had been called before a grand jury to answer questions relating to his testimony given the year before in a sexual harassment case filed by Paula Jones.[44] During the grand jury proceedings, federal prosecutors asked Clinton whether he had lied when he testified that he told his aides he was not having an intimate relationship with White House intern Monica Lewinsky. In the earlier *Jones* case, Clinton had testified, "[T]here's nothing going on with us." When asked before the grand jury whether that statement was true, President Clinton said that its truth depended on the definition of "is" (the use of which was implicit in "there's"):

> It depends on what the meaning of the word "is" is. If the—if he—if "is" means is and never has been, that is not—that is one thing. If it means there is none, that was a completely true statement.... Now, if someone had asked me on that day, are you having any kind of sexual relations with Ms. Lewinsky, that is, asked me a question in the present tense, I would have said no. And it would have been completely true.[45]

---

**38.** *See* KINNEY, *supra* note 34 (citing CORBETT & CONNORS, *supra* note 1, at 85–86).

**39.** For various discussions of the topics by Roman rhetoricians, see, for example, CICERO, DE ORATORE, *supra* ch. 2, note 49, at bk. 2, ch 34, pp. 315–323 and QUINTILIAN, INSTITUTIO ORATORIO, *supra* ch. 2, note 61, bk. 5, ch. 10, pp. 375–429.

**40.** ARISTOTLE, TOPICS, *supra* note 36, at bk.1, ch. 5, p. 4.

**41.** ARISTOTLE, RHETORIC, *supra* ch. 2, note 34, at bk. 2, ch. 23, p. 163.

**42.** *Id.*

**43.** *See* WEAVER, LANGUAGE IS SERMONIC, *supra* ch. 3, note 14, at 212–213.

**44.** SEE CLINTON V. JONES, 520 U.S. 681 (1997).

**45.** Independent Counsel's Report to Congress on the Investigation of President Clinton, Part XIV.D.2 n. 1091 (Sept. 9, 1998), *available at* http:// thomas.loc.gov/icreport/.

Clinton thus defined "is" in such a way as to exclude behavior he later admitted to but was no longer engaging in at the time he testified in the *Jones* case. Although inarticulate, this definition is a memorable example of the use of definition in legal argument.

## b. COMPARISON

Aristotle said comparisons are used to show the degree to which a particular action should be considered good or evil, honorable or disgraceful, and just or unjust.[46] The "tendency to compare things is as natural for people as the tendency to define things."[47] By comparing two objects or ideas for similarity or difference, we attempt to order and understand our world. Perceived similarity forms the basis for both inductive and analogical reasoning. If two things are sufficiently similar, we feel comfortable making an inference about the relationship between the two.[48] Aristotle's term for arguments based on similarity was "example," and he identified two types: examples based on historical fact and examples based on invented similarities in the form of a hypothetical, parable, or fable.[49] Aristotle said that examples based on historical fact "function like witnesses—and there is always a tendency to believe a witness."[50]

Arguments based on similarity are ubiquitous in legal argument because of the nature of common law systems.[51] The principle of *stare decisis* requires that like cases be treated alike. If a party can argue convincingly that the facts and circumstances of her case are similar to those of a prior case, a judge or jury is bound to treat both cases the same way. Uniformity of outcome in similar cases ensures predictability and fairness. In legal argument, a case is said to be on "all fours" with a prior case if the facts and circumstances as well as the legal issues of both cases are seemingly identical or strikingly similar. *"To be on all four or to stand on all four"* is an eighteenth century phrase meaning "to be on a level with another, to present an exact analogy or comparison with something else (presumably the image is of two animals standing together, both on all four legs, hence in closely similar situations)."[52]

## c. RELATIONSHIP

Arguments based on the relationship between two or more things are expressed in classical rhetorical terms as cause and effect, antecedent and consequence,

---

**46.** *See* ARISTOTLE, RHETORIC, *supra* ch. 2, note 34, at bk. 1, ch. 3, p. 19.

**47.** CORBETT & CONNORS, *supra* ch. 2, note 1, at 92.

**48.** *See id.* at 92–93; *see also infra* ch. 5, at 170.

**49.** *See* ARISTOTLE, RHETORIC, *supra* ch. 2, note 34, at bk. 2, ch. 20, p. 147.

**50.** *Id.* at 149.

**51.** For a detailed discussion of arguments based on similarity and difference in legal argument, see *infra* ch. 5, at 170–178.

**52.** Michael Quinion, *World Wide Words* (April 25, 2008), http://www.worldwidewords.org/qa/qa-ona1.htm.

contradictions, and contraries.[53] Aristotle recognized the power of "arguing from the presence or absence of the cause to the existence or non-existence of the effect. If you prove the cause, you at once prove the effect."[54] Closely related to cause and effect is antecedent and consequence. Arguments based on antecedent and consequence often appear in the form of "if, then" arguments, such as "if it rains, we will need our umbrellas." Although there is no strict causal relationship between rain and the use of umbrellas, the existence of one tends to increase the presence of the other.[55] Contradictory and contrary propositions are based on opposites. An argument based on contradictions assumes that two things cannot both exist and not exist at the same time. For example, if a light is turned off, it cannot be turned on at the same time. To prove the light is off is also to prove it is not on. An argument based on contraries assumes that two things in the same general category are incompatible. Connors and Corbett explain the difference between contradictions and contraries using the following example: The concepts of "liberty" and "license" (the latter of which connotes some limitation on the actor's freedom) are contradictory because a right cannot be both unlimited and limited at the same time. "Liberty" and "slavery" are contrary notions because they both relate to individual freedom, but they are incompatible with each other.[56]

Arguments based on relationships are also common in legal argument. Cause and effect, for example, is a critical legal concept. The question of who is responsible for the plaintiff's harm may rest entirely on the concept of causation: Did the defendant's illegal dumping of pesticides in the river *cause* the plaintiff's cancer? Did the manufacturing defect in the air conditioner that fell from the window *cause* the car to crash? Arguments based on antecedent and consequence are also common. If a defendant had sufficient motive, means, and opportunity to commit murder, he may be found guilty. If he was not at home at the time of the murder, as he said he was, then he could have been at the scene of the crime, and so on. An argument based on contradiction, for example, would be the following attempt to convince a jury that the defendant lied in court: "Either he lied, or he didn't lie, and we have heard countless witnesses say he lies." Finally, "separate" and "equal" are contrary legal concepts. Although "separate but equal" was used in *Plessy v. Ferguson*, 163 U.S. 537 (1896), to justify racial segregation in public accommodations, the United States Supreme Court rejected it in *Brown v. Board of Education of Topeka*, 347 U.S. 483 (1954), finding these concepts incompatible with each other.

## d. CIRCUMSTANCE

Arguments based on circumstance include the possible and impossible, past

53.   CORBETT & CONNORS, *supra* ch. 2, note 1, at 100–07.

54.   ARISTOTLE, RHETORIC, *supra* ch. 2, note 34, at bk. 2, ch. 23, p. 170.

55.   *See* CORBETT & CONNORS, *supra* ch. 2, note 1, at 104.

56.   *Id.* at 105.

fact, and future fact.[57] Aristotle explained arguments based on possibility as follows: "[I]f two things are alike, and one is possible, then so is the other. And if the harder of two things is possible, then so is the easier."[58] As for the impossible, Aristotle said, "the speaker obviously will have his stock of arguments in the opposites of the [possible]."[59] Aristotle gave the following examples of arguments based on "past facts":

> [Y]ou may argue that a man has done a thing, if he wished to do it, and if there was no external hindrance; or if he could have done it, and was in a state of anger; or if he was in a position to do it, and was spurred on by desire."[60]

Aristotle said that arguments based on future facts are used most often by politicians trying to influence legislators. He said, "[Y]ou may argue ... the intended result is likely to come, if the means to it have been effected: 'If the foundation is laid, there will be a house.' "[61]

Like arguments based on relationships, arguments based on circumstance play a vital role in legal argument. Just as a defendant may be guilty because the consequence (murder) is related to the antecedent (motive, means, and opportunity), the antecedent makes it possible that the defendant committed the crime. Although neither an argument based on antecedent/consequence nor on possibility proves the defendant's guilt with certainty, each can be persuasive to a jury. Juries may convict entirely on the basis of circumstantial evidence as long as they are persuaded beyond a reasonable doubt. On the other hand, an argument based on the impossibility that the defendant committed the murder because he was in the hospital at the time would likely prove his innocence. Arguments based on Aristotle's "past facts" are the bread and butter of litigation, where liability or guilt depends on whether the defendant acted as alleged. In a case of rape, for example, "granted the occurrence of the act, you argue that it was preceded ... by the necessary force or deceit or other means to its accomplishment."[62]

## e. TESTIMONY

Aristotle distinguished between arguments that are created (artistic) and arguments that exist outside the speaker's imagination (inartistic). According to Aristotle, inartistic arguments are comprised of laws, witnesses, contracts, torture, and oaths. Quintilian said that "though these things themselves involve no art, it generally takes high powers of eloquence to support or refute them."[63] Aristotle recognized that an advocate must use the law to support his position

---

**57.** *See id.* at 108–12.

**58.** Aristotle, Rhetoric, *supra* ch. 2, note 34, at bk. 2, ch. 19, p. 143.

**59.** *Id.* at 145.

**60.** *Id.*

**61.** *Id.* at 146.

**62.** *Id.* at 145–46.

**63.** Quintilian, Institutio Oratorio, *supra* ch. 2, note 61, bk. 5, ch. 1, p. 325.

even when the law works against him:

> It is clear that if the written law is adverse to our case, he must appeal
> to the universal law, and to the principles of equity as representing a higher
> order of justice.... On the other hand, if the written law favors his case, the
> speaker ... may say that, if a law is not to be enforced, it might as well not
> have been enacted."[64]

As for witnesses, Aristotle identified two types: ancient witnesses, "poets and
other men of note whose judgments are on record,"[65] and fact witnesses. Fact
witnesses, Aristotle said, are useful for determining if a thing exists or has
occurred.[66] Aristotle's word for all kinds of agreements was "contracts," and he
said that for them to be upheld, they must be both credible and valid.[67] "Torture"
referred to coerced confessions, which Aristotle said are just as likely to be false as
true.[68] Finally, Aristotle described arguments based on oaths (sworn testimony).
For example, in a case where prior testimony is used to impeach your witness,
Aristotle advised, "[[Y]ou must argue] that there is no perjury; for wrong-doing
must be voluntary, and perjury is such, but things done under compulsion, and
through being tricked, are involuntary; [you must therefore argue that either
the former oath or the present one is the result of force or trickery, so that you
cannot be held responsible for perjury.]"[69]

## 2. THE SPECIAL TOPICS

Although the common topics provide lines of argument useful in all contexts,
special topics are used for particular purposes. "In these special regions," Aristotle
said, "the orator hunts for arguments as a hunter pursues game. Knowing where
a particular kind of game (or argument) is to be found, he will hunt for it there,
and not in some other place or places."[70] Since the aim of political speech is to
advise, Aristotle described its special topics as the good and the expedient: "Now
the aim of one who gives counsel is utility [what is expedient]; for men deliberate,
not about the ends to be attained, but about the means of attaining these; and
the means are expedient things to do."[71] The special topics of ceremonial speech
he described as the noble and the base, since its aim is to praise or blame.[72]
Finally, because judicial speech aims to address wrongdoing and assign fault, its
special topics are justice and injustice.[73] In conjunction with the special topics of
justice and injustice, Aristotle examined the motives for human action and the

---

**64.** ARISTOTLE, RHETORIC, *supra* ch. 2, note 34, at bk. 1, ch. 15, p. 80–81.

**65.** *Id* at 82.

**66.** *Id.* at 83.

**67.** *Id.* at 84.

**68.** *Id* at 86.

**69.** *Id* at 88.

**70.** *Id.* at bk. 2, ch. 22, p. 155.

**71.** *Id* at bk. I, ch. 6, p. 29.

**72.** *Id* at bk. I, ch. 9, p. 46.

**73.** *Id.* at bk. 1, ch. 3, p. 18.

states of mind in which people act.[74] In this regard, *Rhetoric* is considered one of the earliest texts on the psychology of human behavior.

---

### QUESTIONS FOR CONSIDERATION

1. How accurately does Aristotle's notion of the topics portray the actual process of inventing legal argument? Does that matter?

2. How does one become adept at employing the various lines of argument Aristotle articulated?

3. What do you think Richard Weaver would say about President Clinton's use of the definition of "is" in his testimony before the grand jury? Would you have made that argument as counsel for Clinton?

4. Much of Aristotle's discussion in Rhetoric on the special topics of justice and injustice is an attempt to understand the psychology of human behavior. To what extent must an advocate also be an expert in human behavior to be persuasive?

5. Reread Aristotle's advice on how to deal with prior inconsistent testimony (see p. 110). Do you get the sense Aristotle believed that for each and every argument, there is a counter-argument? A valid and ethical one?

---

## 3. APPEALS TO LOGOS

Appeals to *logos* (reason) are the first of Aristotle's three forms of artistic proof. Aristotle said that all appeals to reason are either inductive or deductive. Induction and deduction are used in dialectic as well, but the results are theoretically different. Both deduction and induction in rhetoric produce probable truth, whereas in dialectic, deduction produces scientific or certain truth. As Aristotle said, the subject of rhetoric is not capable of certainty because who would bother to debate matters "which admit of no alternative?"[75] Aristotle assigned different names to induction and deduction based on the context in which they are used. In the *Posterior Analytics,* he referred to "induction" in dialectic as "example" in rhetoric.[76] Today, we think of arguments by example as arguments by analogy. What Aristotle called deductive syllogisms in dialectic he called the enthymeme in rhetoric.[77] "Whenever men in speaking effect persuasion through proofs," Aristotle said, "they do so either with examples or enthymemes;

---

74. *See id.* at chs. 10–12, pp. 55–70.

75. *Id.* at bk. 1, ch. 2, p. 11.

76. *See* ARISTOTLE, POSTERIOR ANALYTICS, *supra* ch. 2, note 31, bk. 1, ch. 1; bk. 1, ch. 18; and bk. 2, ch. 19; *see also* ARISTOTLE, RHETORIC, *supra* ch. 2, note 34, bk. 1, ch. 2, p. 10.

77. *See* ARISTOTLE, THE TOPICS, *supra* ch. 2, note 31, bk. 1, chs. 1, 12. *See also* ARISTOTLE, RHETORIC, *supra* ch. 2, note 34, bk. 1, ch. 2, p. 10.

they use nothing else."[78]

## a. INDUCTION

*"Inductive reasoning is critical in the common law tradition. It lies at the heart of the judicial process and is the most distinctive characteristic of that process."—Judge Ruggero J. Aldisert*

Induction generally refers to probable as opposed to conclusive proof. It serves as the model for the scientific method, whereby a series of observations lead to a hypothesis or rule. For example, every man who has ever been born has died. Therefore, we can hypothesize that all men are mortal. However, our hypothesis cannot be proved with certainty. Induction in legal analysis often involves a similar process of hypothesizing or synthesizing rules from a series of particular case outcomes.[79] In this context, inductive reasoning can be represented visually by an equilateral triangle, with one tip of the triangle pointing up. *See Figure 12.* The particular outcome in each case is examined and compared to prior outcomes to synthesize a general rule.

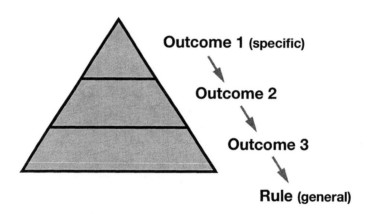

## FIGURE 12

The seventeenth-century epistemologists argued that Aristotelian logic could demonstrate the relationship between objects or ideas already known, but it could not generate *new* knowledge.[80] Bacon said the only way to acquire knowledge was by induction, and he encouraged scientists to rely on their observations rather than the logic of ancient philosophers.[81] Despite the ability of

---

78. ARISTOTLE, RHETORIC, *supra* note 34, p. 10.

79. *Id.* In modern logicians' terms, these two forms of induction are distinct processes. The scientific method, also known as enumerative induction, creates a hypothesis about future outcomes, whereas rule synthesis hypothesizes a rule to explain past outcomes. *See, e.g.,* WAYNE A. DAVIS, AN INTRODUCTION TO LOGIC 94, 138 (2007). The two processes are similar, however, because they use particular outcomes to form a general premise.

80. *See supra* ch. 2, at 45–50.

81. *See id.*

induction to generate knowledge, it does not do so conclusively. As Hume argued, despite the number of times a particular outcome is observed, one cannot be sure that future outcomes will always be the same.[82] Unlike the scientific method of induction, rhetoric relies on statistically insignificant numbers of outcomes when synthesizing general rules and giving examples for purposes of illustration. At best, rhetoric proves truth on a scale of more or less probable. In order to be persuasive, induced rules of law must be reasonable and examples apt. If they are based on inadequate, unreliable, irrelevant, or atypical data, they will not succeed.[83]

### i) RULE SYNTHESIS IN LEGAL ARGUMENT

Inductive reasoning occurs at two key points in the argumentation process, the first of which Aristotle did not address and which remains largely invisible to the legal reader. As legal writers gather research to create arguments in a given case, they piece together statutes, cases, regulations, and other relevant materials to derive a general rule or rules of law. Lawyers often refer to the process of piecing together case outcomes to form a general rule as rule synthesis or case synthesis.[84] Each statute, each case, each regulation, and so on is like the piece of a puzzle or a tile from a mosaic that the writer puts together to form a complete picture. Once complete, the writer has a synthesized rule that applies to her case.[85] *See Figure 12.*

### ii) ANALOGICAL REASONING IN LEGAL ARGUMENT

The second point at which induction occurs is when legal writers compare the facts and circumstances of their case to the facts and circumstances of precedent cases. The legal doctrine of *stare decisis* requires that like cases be treated alike. Therefore, legal writers must demonstrate how applicable common law rules should be applied in their case based on how they have been applied in past cases. By comparing how prior cases and their own case are similar, they argue that their case should be decided the same way. Although Aristotle described this form of reasoning as argument by example or rhetorical induction,[86] we commonly refer to it today as analogical reasoning. As Corbett and Connors state:

> Analogy revolves around the principle that two things which resemble one another in a number of respects resemble one another in a further,

---

82. HUME, AN ENQUIRY CONCERNING HUMAN UNDERSTANDING, *supra* ch. 2, note 196, at § 4, pt. 1, ¶ 25, p. 29.

83. *See* CORBETT & CONNORS, *supra* ch. 2, note 1, at 60–62.

84. *See, e.g.,* LINDA H. EDWARDS, LEGAL WRITING AND ANALYSIS 36–43 (2d ed. 2007); Jane Kent Gionfriddo, *Thinking Like a Lawyer: The Heuristics of Case Synthesis*, 40 TEX. TECH L. REV. 1, 3 (2007); RICHARD K. NEUMANN, JR., LEGAL REASONING AND LEGAL WRITING 167–68 (5th ed. 2005).

85. For a more detailed discussion of rule synthesis and legal argument, see *infra* ch. 5, at 144–49.

86. *See* ARISTOTLE, RHETORIC, *supra* ch. 2, note 34, bk. 1, ch. 2, p. 10.

unconfirmable respect.[87]

The ultimate persuasiveness of the argument depends on how significant the audience perceives the factual similarities between the two cases and whether any differences strike the reader as even more significant. An analogy can fail as much because an advocate ignores significant differences between two cases as because of a dearth of similarities.[88]

## b. DEDUCTION

*"When presented with the properly framed major and minor premises of a syllogism, the human mind seems to produce the conclusion without any additional prompting."*—James Gardner

In Aristotelian logic, deduction is different from induction because it proves truth with certainty. In contrast to rule synthesis and analogy, deduction often consists of applying a general rule to a set of facts to reach a particular conclusion.[89] Where, as here, it moves from general to specific concepts, deduction can be represented visually by an equilateral triangle, with one side facing up and one tip of the triangle pointing down. *See Figure 13.* The acronym IRAC is often taught in law school as a shorthand for deduction—issue, rule, application, conclusion.

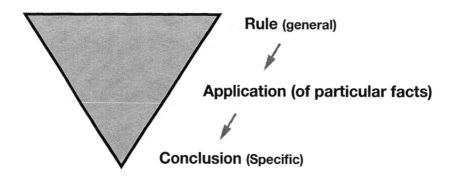

**Rule** (general)

**Application (of particular facts)**

**Conclusion** (Specific)

### FIGURE 13

Arguments that consist of two premises, a conclusion, and no more than three terms are called categorical syllogisms. In legal analysis, the first or major premise is usually the general rule of law, and the second or minor premise is comprised of the facts to which the rule applies. *See Figure 13.* What makes syllogistic argument so appealing is its seemingly ironclad quality. "[T]he peculiar force of a syllogistic argument resides in this: if we assent to the truth

---

**87.** *See* CORBETT & CONNORS, *supra* ch. 2, note 1, at 94. *See also supra* at 111.

**88.** *See* CORBETT & CONNORS, *supra* ch. 2, note 1, at 95. For a more detailed discussion of analogical reasoning and legal argument, see *infra* ch. 5, at 170–78.

**89.** Although deductive reasoning in other contexts may move from the specific to the general or the specific to the specific, it is helpful in the context of legal analysis to think of it as moving from a general rule of law to the proposed outcome in a specific case.

of the premises and if we agree that the reasoning is valid, we must grant the conclusion."[90] Although the premises in legal argument are rarely indisputably true, legal writers try to argue as syllogistically as possible to achieve maximum persuasiveness. As James Gardner explains, the legal syllogism is based on the mathematical principle of transitivity: If A = B, and B = C, then A = C. Accordingly, if Socrates (A) = man (B), and man (B) = mortal (C), then Socrates (A) = mortal (C).[91]

### i) THE TEST OF A SOUND SYLLOGISM

The soundness of a syllogism refers both to the truth of the premises and the validity of the reasoning (*i.e.,* whether it makes sense). The following rules can be used to test the soundness of a syllogism:

*1) The premises must be indisputably true;*

Premises in legal analysis are rarely, if ever, indisputably true. As explained more fully below and in Chapter Five, the premises of a legal syllogism must be probably or reasonably true for the syllogism to be persuasive.

*2) Only three terms of comparison may be used;*

*3) The rules of distribution must not be violated:*

　　*a) The middle term must be distributed at least once.*

　　*b) No term is distributed in the conclusion that was not distributed in at least one of the premises;*

*4) No conclusion can be drawn from two premises where the subject terms of the premises are undistributed;*

*5) Valid conclusions are rarely drawn from two negative premises; and*

*6) If one premise is negative, the conclusion usually needs to be negative too.*

### ii) THE DISTRIBUTION OF TERMS

"Distributed" means the extent to which a term encompasses all or some of the named objects or individuals. "All men" is a distributed term, because it refers to all of the named individuals. *See Figure 14A.* "Some men" is an undistributed term—something less than the total number of men. *See Figure 14B.*

---

90.  CORBETT & CONNORS, *supra* ch. 2, note 1, at 43–44. *See also* JAMES A. GARDNER, LEGAL ARGUMENT: THE STRUCTURE AND LANGUAGE OF EFFECTIVE ADVOCACY 6 (1993).

91.  GARDNER, *supra* note 90, at 6–7.

**Distributive Term**

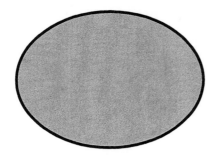

"all men"

FIGURE 14A

**Undistributive Term**

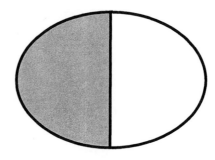

"some men"

FIGURE 14B

Whether a term is distributed depends, in part, on whether it acts as the subject or predicate of the premise.

## a) *Subject terms (the actor in the sentence)*

Usually, it is easy to determine if subjects terms are distributed. For example, in Figure 15, on page 117, the subject term of the major premise is "all men." Since "all men" refers to all the named individuals, it is distributed.[92] The subject term of the minor premise in Figure 15 is a proper noun, "Socrates." Proper nouns are considered distributed. The subject term of the conclusion, "Socrates," in Figure 15 is thus also distributed.

## b) *Predicate terms (terms that modify the subject)*

To determine if predicate terms are distributed is less easy. The predicate term of an affirmative proposition is usually undistributed. The predicate term of a negative proposition is usually distributed.[93] In Figure 15, the predicate term in the major premise is "mortal." Since the major premise is an affirmative proposition (i.e., it states the positive of something), "mortal" is undistributed. This makes sense because the major premise does not attempt to define the entire class of mortals; it merely identifies men as a member of that class.[94] The predicate terms in the minor premise ("man") and the conclusion ("mortal") are also undistributed

> **To determine if predicate terms are distributed**
>
> • *For affirmative propositions, assume predicate terms are undistributed.*
>
> • *For negative propositions, assume predicate terms are distributed.*

92.    As in Figure 15, the subject terms of affirmative propositions will often be distributed.

93.    CORBETT & CONNORS, *supra* note 1, at 44.

94.    Another way to think about why "mortal" is undistributed is because the major premise tells you something about "all men" but only "some mortals." Therefore, the subject is distributed while the predicate is not. In contrast, negative propositions always say something about all subjects and predicates. "No men are immortal" tells you something about all men and all immortal beings (they are not men). Thus, both the subject and predicate terms of the premise are distributed. *See id.*

because the propositions are affirmative.[95]

---

### SHORT EXERCISE ON DISTRIBUTED TERMS

Identify whether the underlined terms in the following premises are distributed or undistributed:

1. Reasonableness is an objective measure.

2. The Food and Drug Administration followed its own rulemaking procedures.

3. The jury did not have a reasonable doubt.

4. Some parts were defective.

5. Congress delegated some of its authority to a sub-committee on ethics.

---

### iii) APPLYING THE SOUNDNESS TEST TO A SAMPLE SYLLOGISM

A sample syllogism is set forth below in Figure 15:

*Major Premise: All **men** are **mortal**.*

*Minor Premise: **Socrates** is a **man**.*

*Conclusion: **Socrates** is **mortal**.*

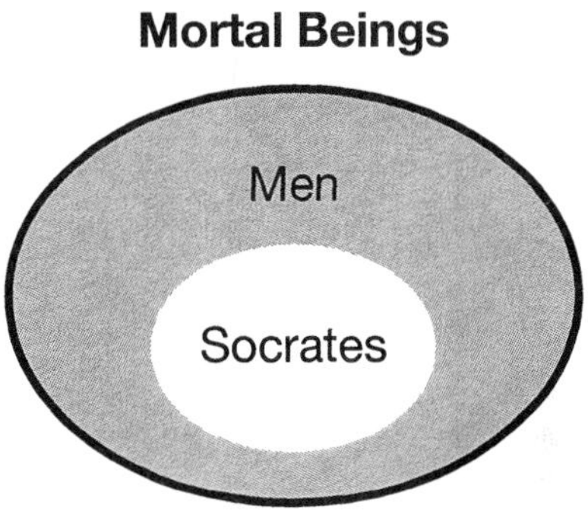

**FIGURE 15**

Applying the soundness test to this syllogism yields the following analysis:

**1. *Premises must be indisputably true.***

In this syllogism, we readily assent to the truth of the premises.

**2. *Three terms of comparison are used.***

As illustrated above, only three terms of comparison are used: "man/men," "mortal," and "Socrates."

---

**95.** "Man" appears as the predicate term of the minor premise and is undistributed because the minor premise does not attempt to define the entire class of men; it merely identifies Socrates as a member of that class. The predicate term of the conclusion, "mortal," is undistributed because it does not attempt to define the entire class of mortals, it merely identifies Socrates as a member of that class.

### 3. The rules of distribution are not violated.

#### a) The middle term must be distributed at least once.

Here, the middle term is "men/man" because it does not appear in the conclusion. "All men" is the subject of the major premise and is distributed.[96]

#### b) No term is distributed in the conclusion that was not distributed in at least one of the premises;

The subject term "Socrates" is the only term in the conclusion that is distributed. This term is also distributed in the minor premise. Therefore, no term is distributed in the conclusion that is not also distributed in one of the premises.

#### 4) No conclusion can be drawn from two premises where the subject terms of the premises are undistributed;

The subject terms of the premises are distributed, so this rule does not apply.

#### 5) Valid conclusions are rarely drawn from two negative premises; and

Neither premise is negative, so this rule does not apply.

#### 6) If one premise is negative, the conclusion usually needs to be negative too.

Neither premise is negative, so this rule does not apply.

*Conclusion:* The syllogism is sound.

### iv) THE LEGAL SYLLOGISM

Because our legal system is comprised of general rules applied to particular facts and circumstances, the legal syllogism (Aristotle called it an enthymeme) is the essential component of legal analysis. Keep in mind that legal syllogisms differ from categorical syllogisms in two major respects. First, the premises in legal syllogisms are rarely, if ever, indisputably true. Two advocates, representing opposing parties, are likely to articulate different, yet reasonable rules of law from the same statute, case, or line of cases. In that sense, neither advocate's rule (*i.e.,* major premise) can be *true.* Moreover, the parties may advocate for the application of two *different* rules of law, both of which arguably apply to the same situation. In that sense, although both rules may be stated accurately, it cannot be said that one is truer than the other. The parties are even more likely to disagree about the facts, making it difficult to know with any certainty which characterization of the facts (*i.e.,* minor premise) is accurate. Because the premises cannot be proved with certainty, the legal syllogism produces only probable truth.

Second, the physical form of legal syllogisms tends to differ from that of the categorical syllogism. Legal argument does not look like a mathematical proof. As Aristotle recognized, rhetorical syllogisms may leave out the major premise

---

**96.** *See supra,* p. 116.

because the audience will readily supply it themselves.[97] For example, the categorical syllogism in Figure 15 could be expressed as a rhetorical syllogism: Because Socrates is a man, he is mortal. Here, the major premise—that all men are mortal—is implicit in the argument. The Roman rhetoricians, too, recognized that orators rarely speak in purely syllogistic form. They described rhetorical syllogisms as epicheirema. Although both Cicero and *Rhetorica ad Herennium* outlined the form for epicheirema, it is not clear whether they were actually used by Roman orators.[98] The epicheireme was said to be comprised of five parts, the proposition, the reason, the proof of the reason, the embellishment, and the conclusion.[99] The proposition states what the orator intends to prove (the conclusion of a syllogism), and the reason sets forth the basis for the claim:[100]

**Proposition:** **Socrates is mortal.**

**Reason:** **All men are mortal.**

As *Rhetorica ad Herennium* explained, the proof of the reason presents additional arguments that corroborate the stated reason, and the embellishment adorns and enriches the argument:[101]

**Proof of the reason: Every man who has been born has died.**

**Embellishment: For example, Socrates' parents died as well as his grandparents, aunts, and uncles.**

Finally, the conclusion draws together all parts of the argument:[102]

**Therefore, because all men die, such as Socrates' family has died, all men must be mortal, including Socrates.**

Recall that Toulmin articulated a model of informal reasoning based on legal argument that includes claims, data, and warrants.[103] *See Figure 16.* A claim is a statement to be proved (the conclusion of a syllogism). Claims are based on data, such as the fact that Socrates is a man (the minor premise of a syllogism). Just as rules of law determine the outcome of a given case, warrants explain why the claim follows from the data: Socrates is mortal because all men are mortal (the major premise of a syllogism). If the warrant is not absolute as it is in this case, a qualifier can be used to indicate that the statement is probably true. The argument is even more convincing if a rebuttal or counter-agreement is anticipated, such as Socrates is mortal unless he is a god. Finally, if the warrant is not convincing on its face, a backing might also be used, such as every man who has ever lived has also died.

---

97. *See* ARISTOTLE, RHETORIC, *supra* ch. 2, note 34, bk. 2, ch. 22, p. 155–56.

98. RHETORICA AD HERENNIUM, *supra* ch. 2, note 53, bk. 2, ch. 18, ¶ 28, p. 107, n.b.

99. *See, e.g., id.* at 107; CICERO, DE INVENTIONE, *supra* ch. 2, note 49, bk. 1, ch. 37, ¶ 67, p. 111.

100. *See, e.g.,* RHETORICA AD HERENNIUM, *supra* ch. 2, note 53, bk. 2, ch. 18, ¶ 28, pp. 107–09.

101. *Id.* at 109.

102. *Id.*

103. *See supra* ch. 3, at 66.

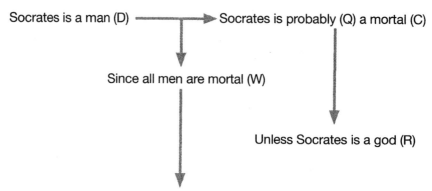

**FIGURE 16**

---

*QUESTIONS FOR CONSIDERATION*

1. Aristotle said that the only forms of reason are induction and deduction. Can you think of any process of reasoning that is neither?

2. Do you agree with Bacon that syllogisms do not produce knowledge? Is induction any more or less reliable than deduction?

3. What kinds of reasoning do you use when you drive a car? Study? Answer questions in class? Decide what to wear? Grocery shop?

4. Which model of deduction makes more sense to you— Aristotle's syllogism, the epicheireme, or Toulmin's informal logic? Which one more closely resembles legal argument? The way you think?

5. When an advocate relies on a similar case to argue for similar treatment in her case, how does she know which similarities matter and which ones do not?

---

# 4. APPEALS TO PATHOS

Aristotle's second form of artistic proof was appeals to *pathos*—the audience's emotion. Aristotle devoted more space in *Rhetoric* to emotions than he did to logical reasoning. He recognized that an audience is motivated to act only when it becomes emotionally involved and will make a decision in your favor only if it feels you have the better case. When we ask people why they decided to take a particular job, voted in a certain way, chose to marry, and so on, they invariably explain the nature of their feelings as well as their thought process. Thus the two are inextricably linked.

Legal writers have as much a need to make their audiences favorably disposed to their arguments as courtroom attorneys do. As Aristotle put it, a speaker must get his audience "into the right state of mind."[104] He thought appeals to emotion were the most critical in legal (as opposed to other forms of) argument. Referring to the need to appeal favorably to the judge's emotions in a criminal trial, Aristotle said, "To the friendly judge, the [defendant] will seem either quite innocent or guilty of no great wrong; to the inimical judge, the [defendant] . . . will seem just the opposite."[105] He thought attorneys needed to familiarize themselves with the range and complexity of human emotion so they can arouse emotion in others.

According to Aristotle, there are three components to understanding emotional appeals: (1) the nature of the emotion itself, (2) the types of people and situations that make that emotion likely to occur, and (3) the causes of that emotion.[106] In Book 2 of *Rhetoric,* he examined the three components of anger, calmness, love, hatred, fear, confidence, shame, benevolence, pity, indignation, envy, and emulation.[107] He defined anger as "an impulse attended by pain, to a revenge that shall be evident, and caused by an obvious, unjustified, slight with respect to the individual or his friends."[108] He observed that people become angry with those who insult or injure them in some way, and they are more likely to get angry with their friends than their enemies.[109] Aristotle concluded by advising the courtroom attorney to "represent the adversary as obnoxious in those things which make men angry, and as the sort of person who arouses anger."[110]

Classical and modern scholars continued to explore Aristotle's interest in the effect of emotion on decision-making. In Book 6 of *Institutio Oratorio*, Quintilian said:

> [T]he man who can carry the judge with him, and put him in whatever frame of mind he wishes, whose words move men to tears or anger, has always been a rare creature. Yet this is what dominates the courts, this is the eloquence that reigns supreme.[111]

The seventeenth century epistemologists explored the idea that argument needs emotion to be effective. John Locke, for example, said that when a person is at ease, he is content without action. A person must be in a state of uneasiness, therefore, before he will act. To stir a person to uneasiness and action requires arousal of emotion.[112] George Campbell, writing in the eighteenth century, believed that emotion is needed to stimulate action. To Aristotle's list of useful

---

**104.** ARISTOTLE, RHETORIC, *supra* ch. 2, note 34, at bk. 2, ch. 1, p. 91.

**105.** *Id.*

**106.** *Id.* at 92.

**107.** *Id.* at 93–131.

**108.** *Id.* at bk. 2, ch. 2, p. 93.

**109.** *Id.* at 96–98.

**110.** *Id.* at 99.

**111.** QUINTILIAN, INSTITUTIO ORATORIO, *supra* ch. 2, note 61, bk. 6, ch. 2, p. 47.

**112.** *See supra* ch. 2, at 48–49.

emotional appeals, he added both humor and wit.[113]

# 5. APPEALS TO ETHOS

Aristotle's third form of artistic appeals was appeals to *ethos*—a speaker must have a good character and be credible. Aristotle said:

> [H]e must give the right impression of himself, and get his judge into the right state of mind. This is true above all in deliberative speaking, but it is true in forensic [*i.e.*, judicial] speaking also; for in conducing to persuasion it is highly important that the speaker should evince certain character, and that the judges should conceive him to be disposed towards them in a certain way, and further, if possible, that the judges themselves should have a certain attitude towards him.[114]

Aristotle understood that for people to be persuasive, the audience must like and respect them; they must appear to know what they are talking about and possess a certain amount of integrity. If they are not worthy of belief, their arguments will be rejected outright.

In Book 1 of *Rhetoric*, Aristotle explored "the means by which a speaker may produce in his audience the impression that he is of such and such a character."[115] He said a speaker must exude virtue because the audience will then consider him trustworthy. He defined virtue as "a faculty tending to provide and preserve 'goods,' or a faculty tending to confer many great benefits."[116] The goods conferred by the virtuous man include justice, courage, temperance, magnificence, magnanimity, liberality, gentleness, prudence, and wisdom.[117] Cicero said that a speaker must use language calculated to work his way into the good graces of his hearers.[118] Quintilian developed an even broader view of *ethos* than Aristotle or Cicero. Appeals to *ethos* encompassed more than the speaker's appeal at the time a speech was delivered. Quintilian said a "a good man skilled in speaking" is a person free from vice, a lover of wisdom, a sincere believer in his cause, and a servant of the people.[119]

Legal writers, too, must make their audience "well-disposed, attentive, and receptive."[120] First and foremost, the claims they make must ring true. Their characterizations of the facts and the law must be reasonable to be credible. Assumptions, speculation, and exaggeration serve only to discredit the writer and lose the reader's respect. Legal writers must also have integrity; they have

---

113. *See supra* ch. 2, at 53. For a more detailed discussion of appeals to *pathos* in legal writing, see *infra* ch. 6, at 179.

114. ARISTOTLE, RHETORIC, *supra* ch. 2, note 34, bk. 2, ch. 1, p. 91.

115. *Id.* at bk. 1, ch. 9, p. 46.

116. *Id.* at 47.

117. *Id.*

118. CICERO, DE INVENTIONE, *supra* ch. 2, note 49, bk. 1, ch. 15, ¶ 21, p. 43.

119. QUINTILIAN, INSTITUTIO ORATORIO, *supra* ch. 2, note 61, bk. 12, ch. 1, p. 197.

120. CICERO, DE INVENTIONE, *supra* ch. 2, note 49, bk. 1, ch. 15, ¶ 20, p. 41.

an ethical obligation to disclose binding law that supports the opposition's case, and they must prove the law is what they say it is by citing supporting authority. Failure to do either of these weakens their case and credibility. Finally, legal writing must *look* credible, meaning it must be polished and professional. If the writing looks sloppy, the reader will assume the arguments are sloppy as well.[121]

---

*EXERCISE IN ARTISTIC APPEALS*

1. **Pick one of the topics set forth below, or select one of your own, and write a paragraph or two that argues for or against it.**

   a. **Lawyers are not to be trusted because they advocate for their clients regardless of the rectitude of their client's position.**

   b. **The rule of law represents the majority view and thus excludes the opinions and values of the minority.**

   c. **Judges decide cases on the basis of the result they hope to achieve, and judicial opinions serve to justify their choices.**

2. **Exchange your argument with that of a colleague and answer the following questions:**

   a. **How did the writer characterize the issue in this case?**

   b. **Does the writer make appeals to logos? Can you identify the form of reasoning as deductive or inductive?**

   c. **Does the writer make appeals to pathos? What themes, words, or other devices does she use to engage the reader's emotions? Does a theme emerge?**

   d. **Does the writer make appeals to ethos? In what ways does the writer seek to appear credible? Is she successful?**

   e. **What type of appeals dominates the argument? Did that strike you as appropriate?**

---

# D. ARRANGEMENT OF ARGUMENTS

Once a speaker's arguments are "invented," they must be arranged. Aristotle said the essential parts of a speech are the statement of the facts and the argument itself, but he acknowledged that speakers often add an introduction and conclusion.[122] The Romans, who focused primarily on the arrangement of courtroom speeches, added the following elements: the statement of the issues to

---

121. For a more detailed discussion of appeals to *ethos* in legal writing, see *infra* ch. 7, at 204.

122. ARISTOTLE, RHETORIC, *supra* ch. 2, note 34, bk. 3, ch. 13, p. 220.

be addressed, an outline of the arguments, and counter-arguments.[123] *See Figure 10, p. 103*. As you will see, these ancient divisions of speech survive today in modern legal writing and practice.[124] As the orator arranges her speech, she must choose among the various arguments she has invented and decide which ones to put first, to emphasize, or to leave out. Cicero said the orator must "manage and marshal his discoveries, not merely in orderly fashion, but with a discriminating eye for the exact weight as it were of each argument."[125] These choices provide as much opportunity for creativity as the invention of the arguments themselves.

# 1. INTRODUCTION

Aristotle said the introduction to a speech "pave[s] the way for what follows"[126] and secures the audience's good will and attention.[127] Like a prelude to music, the introduction prepares the audience for the speech to follow. Comparing a trial attorney's opening statement to the prologue to a poem or drama, Aristotle said:

> [T]he [introduction] gives a hint at the plot, so that we may promptly know what the story is about, and our minds must not be left hanging—since the indefinite is bewildering. So when the teller puts the gist of the action into your hand, as it were, he enables you with this hold to follow the story.[128]

Quintilian, too, said the purpose of the introduction is "to prepare the hearer to be more favourably inclined towards us for the rest of the proceedings."[129] Like Plato, Aristotle understood that audiences often have to be plied to be persuaded. "Men pay attention to things of importance, to their own interests, to anything wonderful, to anything pleasant; and hence, you must give the impression that your speech has to do with the like."[130] Although not strictly relevant to the introduction, these "tricks" were necessary for an "audience that is weak enough to accept utterances beside the point; and if audiences were not what they are, there would be no need of any [introduction] beyond a summary statement of the matter in question."[131]

Like oral arguments, written legal analysis begins with an introduction, regardless of whether it is objective or persuasive. The opening of a memorandum or brief is often called the question presented or the issue presented for review. The purpose of this section is to highlight the controlling law, significant facts,

---

**123.** *See, e.g.,* CICERO, DE INVENTIONE, *supra* ch. 2, note 49, bk. 1, ch. 14, ¶ 19, p. 41; QUINTILIAN, INSTITUTIO ORATORIO, *supra* ch. 2, note 61, bk. 3, ch. 9, p. 149.

**124.** *See infra* ch. 8, pp. 216, 237.

**125.** CICERO, DE ORATORE, *supra* ch. 2, note 49, bk. 1, ch. 31, ¶ 142, p. 99.

**126.** ARISTOTLE, RHETORIC, *supra* ch. 2, note 34, bk. 3, ch. 14, p. 221.

**127.** *Id.* at 223–24.

**128.** *Id.* at 222.

**129.** QUINTILIAN, INSTITUTIO ORATORIO *supra* ch. 2, note 61, bk. 4, ch. 1, pp. 182–83. *See also* CICERO, DE INVENTIONE, *supra* ch. 2, note 49, bk. 1, ch. 15, ¶ 20, p. 41.

**130.** ARISTOTLE, RHETORIC, *supra* ch. 2, note 34, bk. 3, ch. 14, p. 224.

**131.** *Id.*

and legal issue. By articulating these at the outset, the writer prepares the reader for the analysis or argument to follow and puts her in the right frame of mind to understand it.[132]

## 2. STATEMENT OF FACTS

Aristotle said statements of fact are critical in courtroom oratory because trials often involve "the past facts" of the case.[133] As you know, trial attorneys typically set forth the facts they intend to prove in conjunction with their opening statements. Aristotle instructed plaintiffs to "narrate whatever tends to your own credit, or to the discredit of the other side."[134] A defendant, he said, "needs less narration. Here you have to contend that the act did not occur, or that it did no harm, or that it was not unjust, or that it had not the importance alleged."[135] Aristotle said the facts statement should "depict character" (*i.e.*, appeal to *ethos*) and "employ the traits of emotion" (*i.e.*, appeal to *pathos*).[136]

Cicero, Quintilian, and *Rhetorica ad Herennium* further specified that statements of fact be brief, clear, and plausible.[137] To be brief is to say no more than necessary to engage the audience and inform it of the relevant facts. Quintilian said the statement of facts should begin at the point where the facts "first concern the judge," avoid stating irrelevant facts, and leave out everything that "can be removed without in any way damaging either the process of judgement or our own interest."[138] On the subject of clarity, he said to use "normal but expressive words—not vulgar of course, but not out of the way and [obtuse] either" and to give "a distinct view of facts, persons, times, places, and causes."[139] Cicero advised that the facts be stated chronologically, in a straightforward manner, and in clear language.[140] Cicero said that the statement of facts is plausible "if it seems to embody characteristics which are accustomed to appear in real life" and "the story fits in with the nature of the actors in it, the habits of ordinary people

---

**132.** For a more detailed discussion of the Question Presented in legal writing, see *infra* ch. 8, at 216, 238.

**133.** ARISTOTLE, RHETORIC, *supra* ch. 2, note 34, bk. 1, ch. 3, p. 17 & bk. 3, ch. 13, p. 220.

**134.** *Id.* at bk. 3, ch. 16, p. 229.

**135.** *Id.* at 230.

**136.** *Id.* at 230–31.

**137.** CICERO, DE INVENTIONE, *supra* ch. 2, note 49, bk. 1, ch. 20, ¶ 28, p. 57; QUINTILIAN, INSTITUTIO ORATORIO, *supra* ch. 2, note 61, bk. 4, ch. 2, p. 235; RHETORICA AD HERENNIUM, *supra* ch. 2, note 53, bk. 1, ch. 9, ¶ 14, p. 25. Aristotle was not convinced that the statement of facts had to be brief. He said, "[T]he right thing is neither rapidity nor brevity, but the proper mean. And the mean consists in saying just so much as will make matters plain." ARISTOTLE, *supra* ch. 2, note 34, bk. 3, ch. 16, p. 229.

**138.** QUINTILIAN, INSTITUTIO ORATORIO, *supra* ch. 2, note 61, bk. 4, ch. 2, p. 241.

**139.** *Id.* at 239.

**140.** CICERO, DE INVENTIONE, *supra* ch. 2, note 49, bk. 1, ch. 20, ¶ 29, p. 59. *See also* RHETORICA AD HERENNIUM, *supra* ch. 2, note 53, bk. 1, ch. 9, p. 27.

and the beliefs of the audience."[141]

As Aristotle might have predicted, statements of fact are a mainstay of contemporary legal writing. Whether imparting legal advice to their clients or drafting briefs, legal writers include statements of fact to put the legal issue in context and delineate the facts on which the analysis is based. In advising clients, the facts statement protects the writer as well, for if the client leaves out critical information, the writer can demonstrate that she was unaware of it. Today we give the same advice the ancient Greeks and Romans gave for drafting effective statements of fact: Include significant legal facts and those background facts necessary for the context to be understood, state the facts succinctly so as not to confuse the reader or lose her interest, and tell an interesting and believable story.[142]

## 3. DEFINITION OF ISSUES AND OUTLINE OF ARGUMENTS

Aristotle said that the argument section of a speech did not need to be divided. The Romans, however, inserted a definition of the issues and an outline of the arguments as a point of transition between the statement of the facts and the argument itself. *See Figure 10, p. 103.* These were designed 1) to specify the disputed issues to be resolved, and 2) to enumerate for the audience the arguments to follow.[143] The author of *Rhetorica Ad Herennium* explained the definition of issues as follows:

> When the Statement of Facts has been brought to an end, we ought first to make clear what we and our opponents agree upon, ... and what remains contested as follows: "Orestes killed his mother; on that I agree with my opponents. But did he have the right to commit the deed, and was he justified in committing it? That is in dispute."[144]

Cicero said that by enumerating the disputed issues, the speaker points out for the listener that "on which he ought to have his attention fixed."[145] Quintilian said that the definition of issues also indicates to the audience "that the Narrative is over and the Proof is beginning."[146]

The outline of arguments identifies the arguments the speaker intends to give and briefly explains them. Cicero said that in the outline

the matters which we intend to discuss are briefly set forth in a methodical

---

**141.** CICERO, DE INVENTIONE, *supra* ch. 2, note 49, bk. 1, ch. 21, ¶ 30, p. 61. *See also* QUINTILIAN, INSTITUTIO ORATORIO, *supra* ch. 2, note 61, at bk. 4, ch. 2, pp. 245–47; RHETORICA AD HERENNIUM, *supra* ch. 2, note 53, bk. 1, ch. 9, ¶ 16, p. 29.

**142.** For a more detailed discussion on drafting Statements of Fact, see *supra* ch. 8, at 217, 238.

**143.** *See* CICERO, DE INVENTIONE, *supra* ch. 2, note 49 bk. 1, ch. 22, ¶ 31, p. 63; RHETORICA AD HERENNIUM, *supra* ch. 2, note 53, bk. 1, ch. 10, p. 31.

**144.** RHETORICA AD HERENNIUM, *supra* ch. 2, note 53, bk. I, ch. 10, p. 31.

**145.** CICERO, DE INVENTIONE, *supra* ch. 2, note 49, bk. 1, ch. 22, ¶ 31, p. 63.

**146.** QUINTILIAN, INSTITUTIO ORATORIO, *supra* ch. 2, note 61, bk. 4, ch. 4, p. 297.

way. This leads the [listener] to hold definite points in his mind, and to understand that when these have been discussed the [speech] will be over.[147]

*Rhetorica Ad Herennium* instructed orators not to list more than three arguments because a long list "instills in the hearer the suspicion of premeditation and artifice."[148] Quintilian disagreed; he thought it made no sense to limit the number of arguments to three since "a Cause may well need more."[149] He advised that the outline be brief, however, because the goal was just to highlight the arguments, not make them.

In legal writing, a brief definition of the issues and an outline of the writer's arguments often appear in a summary of the writer's analysis or argument, usually called the Brief Answer in a memorandum and the Summary of Argument in a brief. This section is usually separate and appears between the Statement of Facts and the Discussion or Argument that follows. The writer briefly summarizes the issues relevant to the legal question and her analysis with respect to each. Typically, the writer speaks in her own voice, without citation to authority.

At the beginning of the Discussion section of a memorandum or the Argument section of a brief, the writer may also include a short introduction that sets forth the issues to be discussed and the major rules of law applicable to the analysis. In legal writing textbooks, this section, often referred to as a roadmap or umbrella section for the reader,[150] foreshadows the arguments and the order in which the reader should expect them. As to the order of individual arguments, Quintilian said, "It is a particularly disgraceful mistake to treat your points in a different order from that which was given in your [definition of the issues]."[151] In keeping with Quintilian's advice, we often advise writers to analyze the issues in the order they listed them so as not to confuse the reader.[152]

# 4. ARGUMENT

The argument section is the focal point of oral and written argument. Deciding what arguments to make and how to arrange them is perhaps the most difficult part of the process. Aristotle said simply that arguments should function like proofs, either inductive or deductive, and the choice of arguments depends on the nature of the issues involved.[153] Aristotle advised against stringing too many

---

147. CICERO, DE INVENTIONE, supra ch. 2, note 49, bk. 1, ch. 22, ¶ 31, p. 63.

148. RHETORICA AD HERENNIUM, *supra* ch. 2, note 53, bk. 1, ch. 10, p. 31.

149. QUINTILIAN, INSTITUTIO ORATORIO, *supra* ch. 2, note 61, bk. 4, ch. 5, p. 299.

150. *See, e.g.*, VEDA R. CHARROW ET AL., CLEAR AND EFFECTIVE LEGAL WRITING 142 (4th ed. 2007); LINDA H. EDWARDS, LEGAL WRITING AND ANALYSIS 111 (2d ed. 2007); RICHARD K. NEUMANN, JR., LEGAL REASONING AND LEGAL WRITING 122 (5th ed. 2005).

151. QUINTILIAN, INSTITUTIO ORATORIO, *supra* ch. 2, note 61, bk. 4, ch. 5, p. 311.

152. For a more detailed discussion of the Brief Answer, Summary of Argument, and introductory paragraphs in a Discussion or Argument, see *infra* ch. 8, at 217, 239–41.

153. ARISTOTLE, RHETORIC, *supra* ch. 2, note 34, bk. 3, ch. 17, pp. 232–33.

proofs together at once or "your arguments will damage each other's effect."[154] He thus recommended that speakers weave appeals to *pathos* and *ethos* throughout appeals to *logos* for maximum effect.[155]

Neither the Greeks nor the Romans explored in detail what we consider to be large-scale organization. Focusing on the nature of argument and the small scale organization of inductive and deductive proofs, they virtually ignored the question of how to choose one argument over another or in what order to present them. Quintilian acknowledged that "just as much care should be taken in deciding what to put forward as in working out how what you have put forward should be proved."[156] He concluded, however, that because the choice of argument depends so heavily on the specifics of each case and personal preference, "this is something that cannot be covered by textbooks."[157] He advised to avoid making every conceivable argument because that approach will bore the audience and damage one's credibility.[158] As for the ordering of arguments, Quintilian said, "The question is also asked, whether the most powerful Arguments should be put at the beginning, so as to take possession of the judge's mind, or at the end, so as to leave a final impression on him."[159] Quintilian said the answer depends on the nature of the case, but a speech should "never descend from the strongest argument to the weakest."[160]

The conventional wisdom in legal writing today is rooted in these ancient concepts. Writers should make conscious choices about which arguments to advance and in what order. With regard to which arguments to make, time and space constraints help the writer choose, but the strongest and most relevant arguments should be advanced. The question, of course, is which arguments are strongest? Most relevant? These questions seem unanswerable at first, due in part to an expectation that there are "right" answers to these questions. As you gain experience and confidence, you will begin to understand that you have the ability, the authority, and the obligation to answer these questions in a variety of ways. With regard to the order of the arguments, a 2002 survey revealed that 74 percent of the federal judiciary considers it either essential or very important for an advocate to make her strongest arguments first.[161] Although this is only one survey, and it speaks only to one kind of audience, it suggests that Quintilian's advice to end an argument with the strongest proof is just one man's opinion. Finally, in accordance with Aristotle's advice, most experienced legal writers

---

154. *Id.* at 234.

155. *Id.*

156. QUINTILIAN, INSTITUTIO ORATORIO, *supra* ch. 2, note 61, bk. 5, ch. 10, p. 421.

157. *Id.* at 423.

158. *Id.* at bk. 5, ch. 12, p. 459.

159. *Id.* at 463.

160. *Id.*

161. Kristen K. Robbins (now Robbins–Tiscione), *The Inside Scoop: What Federal Judges Really Think About the Way Lawyers Write*, 8 J. LEG. WRIT. INST. 257, 273 (2002). For more information on choosing and arranging legal arguments, see *infra* ch. 8, at 218, 241.

recommend that arguments based on principles of equity and public policy (*i.e.*, appeals to *pathos*) be woven throughout appeals to *logos* as opposed to stand alone.

## 5. COUNTER–ARGUMENT

Unlike Aristotle, the Roman rhetoricians conceived of counter-argument as separate from the argument itself. Quintilian said that each side uses counter-arguments "to rebut what is said by the other."[162] Counter-arguments can be of two types: The first denies the opponent's allegations (an argument based on an issue of fact), and the second takes issue with the legal ramifications of the action itself (an argument based on an issue of law).[163] Quintilian said that it is always harder to rebut than to make an argument because "wounding is easier than curing the wound."[164] For that reason, "even moderate speakers have done well enough in prosecutions, but there has never been a good defence advocate who has not been first class as a speaker."[165] Legal writers, too, must rebut their opponent's arguments, sometimes in advance of knowing what they are. The challenge of selecting the best counter-arguments to make and when to make them is similar to that of the writer making her own affirmative arguments.[166]

## 6. CONCLUSION

Aristotle said the conclusion of a speech should (1) make the audience "well-disposed to yourself, and ill-disposed to your opponent," (2) emphasize those points favorable to your case and de-emphasize unfavorable points, (3) put the audience in the right frame of mind, and (4) refresh their memories.[167] To make the audience well-disposed, Aristotle said to "commend yourself, censure [your opponent], and drive the difference home."[168] He said to refresh the audience's memory as to your arguments so they "learn them well."[169] Cicero said judicial orators should summarize their arguments in a conclusion when "owing to the lapse of time or the length of your speech you distrust the memory of your audience, and when your case will be strengthened by recapitulating and briefly setting forth the main points of your argument."[170]

Formal conclusions are often used in traditional memoranda for the reasons

---

162. QUINTILIAN, INSTITUTIO ORATORIO, *supra* ch. 2, note 61, bk. 5, ch. 13, p. 467.

163. *Id.* at 469–73. *See also* CICERO, DE INVENTIONE, *supra* ch. 2, note 49, bk. 1, ch. 42, ¶ ¶ 78–79, pp. 123–25.

164. QUINTILIAN, INSTITUTIO ORATORIO, *supra* ch. 2, note 61, bk. 5, ch. 13, p. 469.

165. *Id.*

166. For a more complete discussion of the nature of counter-arguments and their placement in legal writing, see *infra* ch. 8, at 220, 244.

167. ARISTOTLE, RHETORIC, *supra* ch. 2, note 34, bk. 3, ch. 19, p. 240.

168. *Id.*

169. *Id.* at 241.

170. CICERO, DE PARTITIONE ORATORIA, ch. 17, ¶ 59, pp. 355–56 (H. Rackham trans., 1968) (c. 46 BCE). *See also* RHETORICA AD HERENNIUM, *supra* ch. 2, note 53, bk. 2, ch. 30, ¶ 47, p. 145.

Aristotle gave, but they are rare in written legal argument. Most conclusions in briefs are not substantive; they simply state the precise relief sought.[171]

---

### QUESTIONS FOR CONSIDERATION

1. **Does it trouble you that much of the advice in constructing speeches aims to help the speaker ingratiate himself with the audience? Why should it?**

2. **Why is there so much repetition built into the arrangement of a speech? Should legal writing be repetitive for the same reasons?**

3. **Why do you suppose the classical rhetoricians paid little attention to the overall organization of the arguments themselves?**

4. **What principles of organization have you learned as a student or professional that will affect the choices you make about ordering arguments in legal writing? Do you think it always best to put your strongest arguments first or last? How do you decide?**

5. **Do you agree with Quintilian that it is always harder to defend than accuse? Is there a way to compensate for this problem? How?**

---

# E. STYLE OF ARGUMENTS

The last canon of classical rhetoric relevant to legal writing is style. Aristotle said "[I]t is not enough to know *what* to say—one must also know *how* to say it."[172] He also said the orator's language should be clear and appropriate to the purpose of the speech.[173] According to Aristotle, clarity is achieved by using ordinary words, without being too plain or vulgar, and avoiding the overuse of poetic devices.[174] The orator must disguise his means so as to appear natural. "Naturalness is persuasive, artifice just the reverse."[175] He also advised orators to construct sentences that are easy to follow, be as specific as possible, avoid ambiguous language, and follow rules of grammar and punctuation.[176]

---

171. For a complete discussion of the conclusion in legal memoranda and briefs, see *infra*, ch. 8, at 218, 241.

172. ARISTOTLE, RHETORIC, *supra* ch. 2, note 34, bk. 3, ch. 1, p. 182.

173. *Id.* at bk. 3, ch. 2, p. 185.

174. *See id.* at 185–86.

175. *Id.* at 186.

176. *See id.* at bk. 3, ch. 5, pp. 194–95.

Cicero added that an orator should alter his style based on the goal of his speech. An orator's goal could be to prove, please, or persuade, and he therefore identified three different speaking styles:

> [T]here are three styles, the plain style for proof, the middle style for pleasure, the vigorous style for persuasion; and in this last is summed up the entire virtue of an orator.[177]

Quintilian, on the other hand, did not think the orator was limited to three styles. "Just as a third type was inserted between the slender and the strong,"[178] he said, "so also there are intervals between the three, and in these intervals is found a style which is a blend of those on either side."[179]

A speaker's style was considered low, middle, or high depending on the complexity of his sentence structure and the use of figures of speech. "Poetic devices," the basic figures of speech, were typically divided into two categories: schemes and tropes. A scheme is a "deviation from the ordinary pattern or arrangement of words."[180] An example of a scheme is alliteration, which is the repetition of a leading consonant sound in two or more adjacent words (*e.g.,* "Peter Piper picked a peck of pickled peppers.").[181] A trope is a "deviation from the ordinary and principal signification of a word."[182] The most common examples of tropes are metaphors and similes, which compare two things of unlike nature but seem to have something in common (*e.g.,* "He was a bear this morning when he got up," and "He acted like a bear this morning.").[183] A low style was characterized by short sentences, plain language, and little use of figures of speech, whereas a high style was characterized by complex sentence structures, ornate language, and the use of various figures. The Attic orators, like Isocrates, used a low style, whereas the Asiatic orators, like Cicero, used a high style.[184]

As the focus of rhetoric shifted from invention to style in the nineteenth century, scholars became interested in identifying and cataloging figures of speech. A chart of the figures with which you are probably familiar is set forth in Figure 17, below.

---

**177.** CICERO, ORATOR, *supra* ch. 2, note 49, ch. 21, ¶ 69, p. 357. *See also* RHETORICA AD HERENNIUM, *supra* ch. 2, note 53, bk. 4, ch. 8, ¶ 11, p. 253.

**178.** Quintilian refers here to the middle style identified by Cicero and RHETORICA AD HERENNIUM.

**179.** Quintilian, *supra* ch. 2, note 61, bk. 12, ch. 10, p. 317.

**180.** CORBETT & CONNORS, *supra* ch. 2, note 1, at 379.

**181.** *See id.* at 388–89.

**182.** *Id.* at 379.

**183.** *Id.* at 396.

**184.** *See supra* ch. 2, at 22.

## Common Figures of Speech

1. Schemes

    a. Parallelism—similarity of structure in a pair or series of words or phrases.
    *Example: The plaintiff claiming slander must prove that the defendant made a false statement and that the defendant knew it was false when he made it.*

    b. Parenthesis—insertion of a word or phrase that interrupts the normal flow of the sentence.
    *Example: The Food and Drug Administration (hereafter "FDA"), brings this motion for summary judgment.*

    c. Apposition—placing two related words or phrases side-by-side, where the second explains or modifies the first.
    *Example: The plaintiff, the Food and Drug Administration, filed this appeal.*

    d. Alliteration— the repetition of a leading consonant sound in two or more adjacent words.
    *Example: The defendant had means, motive and opportunity to commit the murder.*

    e. Assonance—the repetition of similar vowel sounds in the stressed syllables of adjacent words.
    *Example: He continues to be innocent in his own mind.*

2. Tropes

    a. Metaphor—the implied comparison between two things of unlike nature that have something in common.
    *Example: The defendant was a monster, brandishing a weapon and screaming at the top of his lungs.*

    b. Simile—the explicit comparison between two things of unlike nature that have something in common.
    *Example: For the defendant companies, the Tax Relief Act was like an angel from heaven.*

    c. Personification—attributing human qualities or abilities to inanimate objects.
    *Example: It's as if the company chewed up its employees and spit them out.*

    d. Hyperbole—the use of exaggeration to emphasize or heighten effect.
    *Example: If looks could kill, this police officer would be dead.*

    e. Rhetorical Question—asking a question for the purpose of making a point indirectly.
    *Example: Did the defendant act this way because he wanted to or because he had to?*

**FIGURE 17**

Although Cicero advocated the use of a high style for persuasion, good legal writing in the twenty-first century is characterized by an elegant, middle style.[185] As a result of the plain English movement of the mid-twentieth century,[186] good writers eschew legalese and long-windedness in favor of concise writing in plain and simple terms. A Ciceronian style would be out of place in the practice of law today, but legal writers employ schemes and tropes (*e.g.,* parallelism, metaphor, and hyperbole) to great effect. Used sparingly, they can have tremendous impact in persuasive writing. As Aristotle advised, the legal writer must also follow basic rules of grammar and punctuation. Legal readers are demanding: they expect legal writing to be proofed, polished, and professional. Sloppy documents signal sloppy thinking. Finally, the legal writer must be familiar with certain writing conventions within the legal writing community. Knowing these conventions hastens the beginning legal writer's socialization into the legal community.[187]

---

### QUESTIONS FOR CONSIDERATION

1. **How would you describe the writing style of the appellate opinions you read—low, middle, or high? How about the style of a car rental agreement? A plane ticket? Your lease?**

2. **How would you describe your own writing style? Should it be the same as that of judges?**

3. **Does it surprise you that figures of speech are common in legal writing? In what other ways does legal writing allow for creativity?**

4. **When you came to law school, did you anticipate that legal writing would be just like other kinds of writing you had done in the past? Did you think it would be like learning a foreign language? What do you think now?**

5. **People are easily offended by comments intended to improve their writing. Can you identify the kinds of arguments they feel most defensive about? Are they appeals to logos, pathos, or ethos? Do they involve organization? Mechanics? Unfamiliarity with the discourse community?**

---

**185.** *See supra* ch. 2, at 22.

**186.** *See infra* ch. 9, at 260.

**187.** For a more detailed discussion of stylistic concerns in legal writing, see *infra* ch. 9, at 276–280.

# PRACTICAL APPLICATIONS OF RHETORICAL THEORY TO LEGAL WRITING

■ ■ ■

# CHAPTER 5

## INVENTION: *LOGOS* IN LEGAL WRITING

■ ■ ■

*"Argument is proof-giving, by which one thing is inferred from another, and which confirms what is doubtful by means of what is not doubtful."*
*—Quintilian*

Appeals to *logos* (reason) are either inductive or deductive. In creating arguments, legal writers engage in both types of reasoning. As Quintilian's quotation suggests, legal arguments are not iron-clad proof, but they can have the same psychological impact as logical proofs if made in syllogistic form. The first step in creating effective legal analysis or persuasive legal argument is to induce the applicable rule or rules of law. To do that, the writer must identify the legal issue or issues to be resolved and conduct thorough research. This process is a form of induction: the writer pieces together statutes, cases, regulations, and any other relevant information to form a generalrule of law that explains the outcomein the prior cases. Legal writers oftenrefer to this process as rule or case synthesis. *See Figure 18.*

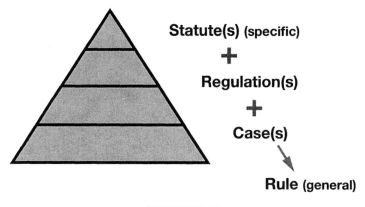

**Statute(s)** (specific)

**+**

**Regulation(s)**

**+**

**Case(s)**

**Rule** (general)

**FIGURE 18**

The second step is to apply the induced or synthesized rule(s) of law to the facts of the case in order to anticipate or argue for a specific outcome. *See Figure*

137

*19.* Aristotle called these deductive proofs rhetorical syllogisms or enthymemes.[1] The major difference between categorical and rhetorical syllogisms is their degree of proof. A categorical syllogism proves truth with certainty, whereas a rhetorical syllogism proves truth only on a scale of more or less probable.

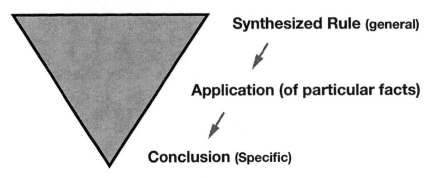

**Synthesized Rule** (general)

**Application (of particular facts)**

**Conclusion** (Specific)

FIGURE 19

The third step in legal analysis or argument involves *stare decisis*, the legal doctrine that like cases be treated alike. The client's case must be compared to prior case law in the appropriate jurisdiction to predict or argue why the outcome in the client's case should be the same or different. These comparisons are commonly referred to today as analogies: Based on a number of identifiable similarities or differences between the two cases, the writer predicts or advocates for similar or different treatment. *See Figure 20.* Aristotle called these comparisons "examples" in rhetoric because they do not represent a statistically significant number of cases from which any sort of scientific conclusion can be drawn.[2] Analogies are related to rule synthesis because they both draw conclusions based on a number of observed instances (rule synthesis looks to prior case outcomes, whereas analogies look to similarities or differences in prior cases). However, analogy differs from rule synthesis in a significant respect. While rule synthesis uses case outcomes to explain the outcome of past cases, analogy uses case outcomes to predict the outcome in the case at hand. Unlike case synthesis, analogy moves from the specific facts and holdings of past cases to the specific outcome predicted in the present case.[3]

---

1.    *See supra* ch. 4, at 111.

2.    *See id.*

3.    *See* ARISTOTLE, RHETORIC, *supra* ch. 2, note 34, at bk. 1, ch. 2, p. 10.

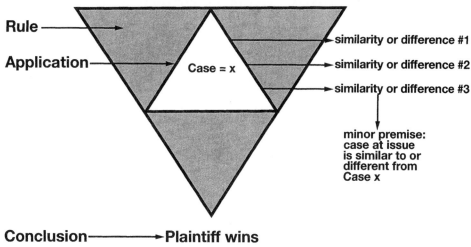

**FIGURE 20**

# A. RULE SYNTHESIS

## 1. IDENTIFY THE ISSUE(S)

In legal writing, the "issue" refers to the legal question that arises from some form of conflict.[4] The conflict may give rise to one or more questions, and, as Cicero said, they may be questions of fact, questions of law, or mixed questions of fact and law.[5] Rarely do clients present situations that solely involve questions of fact (*e.g.,* was the light red or green when the defendant drove through the intersection?). More often, the situation involves fact and legal questions (*e.g.,* If the light was red, but the defendant was driving his wife to the hospital because she was in labor, is he still responsible for the plaintiff's injuries?). Sometimes, the client knows or has a good idea what the legal questions are. More often, though, the client presents a story—a set of facts and circumstances—along with a perceived injury and a desire to be compensated in some way.

Whether or not you think you know what the legal questions are, it is helpful to analyze the client's story by asking the following questions. They may help identify issues you did not anticipate at the outset.

---

4.    *See, e.g.,* QUINTILIAN, INSTITUTIO ORATORIO, supra ch. 2, note 61, bk. 3, ch. 6, ¶ 5, p. 51.

5.    *See supra* ch. 2, at 21.

### a. WHO IS INVOLVED IN THIS CONFLICT? WHAT HAPPENED? WHEN DID IT OCCUR? WHERE DID THE CRITICAL EVENTS TAKE PLACE? WHY DID THIS BECOME A PROBLEM?

The answers to these questions will reveal the facts you know as well as those you must seek out. The best way to answer them is to ask the client directly (*e.g.*, interview anyone with relevant knowledge, read all existing files and documentation, and speak with colleagues who have any familiarity with the client or situation).

### b. WHAT LEGAL QUESTIONS NEED TO BE RESOLVED?

Even if you do not yet know whether the conflict involves constitutional, statutory, regulatory, or common law, find a way to express the basic legal questions in descriptive terms. In common vernacular, think of these as keywords. For example, if the client's dispute involves a broken contract to sell the assets of her business, search for disputes relating to assets, breach, and contracts. If the situation involves injury due to an allegedly false statement, you do not need to know in advance the legal terms defamation, libel, or slander. Simply look for rules of law relating to false statements. Your search will produce rules of law relating to these specific causes of action. Even if you were to suspect the cause of action is slander, do not limit your search to that term alone. If you are wrong (*i.e.*, the statement was written), you may miss better, more relevant law on related causes of action such as libel.

### c. WHAT JURISDICTION'S LAW APPLIES TO THIS CONFLICT?

The controlling or binding jurisdiction is often obvious. In some cases, however, you may not know whether federal or state law applies or which of two states' law applies. As between federal and state law, federal law may pre-empt applicable state law, so you will need to check for both and see if the state law is pre-empted. As between two states' laws, search for rules on choice or conflicts of law in the jurisdiction(s) where the dispute might be resolved. Then use those rules to research the substantive law that might apply.

## 2. CONDUCT THOROUGH RESEARCH

Just as the classical orator consulted the common and special topics, lawyers consult legal resources. The goal of legal research is to find binding, relevant law. To be relevant, it must relate to the legal issues involved and help resolve the conflict. Because current constitutions, statutes, and regulations take precedence over pre-existing case law, *these sources of law should always be consulted first*. It is possible to "back into" these sources of law by reading about them in relevant cases, but that approach is not reliable.

## a. CONSULT PRIMARY AND SECONDARY SOURCES OF LAW IN YOUR JURISDICTION

Depending on personal preference, you may decide to begin your search with primary law sources and then consult secondary sources to further explain their import and broaden your search. Alternatively, you may consult secondary sources first to familiarize yourself with a particular area of law and then search primary sources of law in your jurisdiction. Either path works. Most sources today are available in print and online. *See Figure 21* for the various primary and secondary sources available.

### Sources of Primary and Secondary Law

Primary

- Constitutions

- Statutes

- Administrative Regulation/
  Agency Decisions

- Case Law

Secondary

- Legal Encyclopedias
  (*e.g.*, Am. Jur.2d)

- Treatises/Hornbooks

- Legal Periodicals
  (*e.g.*, law journals)

- American Law Reports

- Legislative History

- Loose-leafs/Newsletters
  (*e.g.*, BNA's *Product Safety & Liability Reporter*)

**FIGURE 21**

## b. APPROACH THE PROBLEM FROM MULTIPLE ANGLES

The key to good research is to approach it from many angles. When consulting primary and secondary law sources, choose two or more alternative paths and pursue each, keeping meticulous notes on where you have been and where you plan to go. When you see something that looks interesting, take note of it—never assume you will be able to find it again! If you approach your research from different angles, including online and print sources, you should begin to see the same results. Once you feel you have come full circle, you will be confident you have conducted a thorough and comprehensive search. Again, based on personal preference, you may start with print or electronic sources; all roads should lead to Rome.[6] *See Figure 22.*

---

**6.** The roads of the Roman Empire radiated out from the capital, like the spokes on a wheel, so all roads did literally lead to Rome.

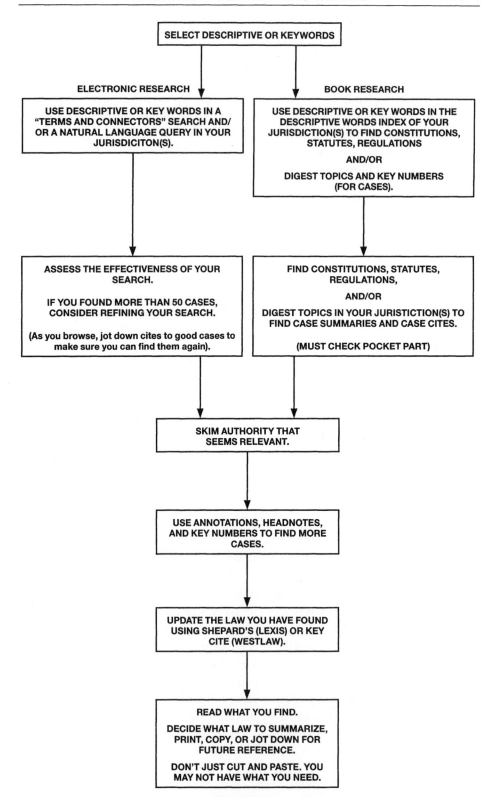

FIGURE 22

## c. BE SURE TO GET A CURRENT AND REPRESENTATIVE SAMPLE OF BINDING CASE LAW

As you look for relevant case law, you are looking for the *best* cases, but which cases are best? Ideally, you are looking for the most recent cases decided by the highest court in your jurisdiction that actually discuss the applicable rules of law and are factually similar to your case. Since cases that good rarely exist, follow these guidelines, more or less in this order:

- **Look for the most recent cases from the highest and intermediate appellate courts of your jurisdiction. Usually, the newer the case, the better (unless the older case is from a higher, binding court or very similar factually). Cases more than ten years old are virtually *ancient*.**

- **Read the cases you find to see if they discuss and/or apply the rules of law as opposed to simply restate them. Read the cases cited within these cases.**

- **Look for factually similar cases from your jurisdiction (or a federal court applying your state's law) *regardless of the age of the case*, as long as the rules of law in your jurisdiction have not changed significantly.**

- **If you cannot find any factually similar cases in your jurisdiction, broaden your search to other jurisdictions where the law is substantially the same. Federal courts applying state law and neighboring jurisdictions are usually preferred.**

Figure 23 below illustrates the best cases to find in terms of the deciding court. Assume your problem is based on Illinois state law. Assuming the case is relevant (*i.e.*, is recent, discusses the law, or is factually similar), the "bull's-eye" would be case law from the Illinois Supreme Court. The next best cases would be from the Illinois Appellate Court, and so on. Most often, you will need to piece together the rule of law from a series of recent, older, highest appellate court, intermediate appellate court, and factually similar cases.

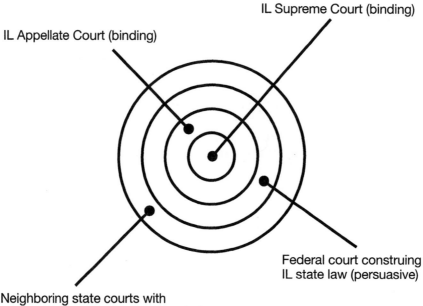

IL Supreme Court (binding)

IL Appellate Court (binding)

Federal court construing
IL state law (persuasive)

Neighboring state courts with
substantially similar law (persuasive)

**FIGURE 23**

## 3. INDUCE (PIECE TOGETHER) A COMPREHENSIVE RULE OF LAW

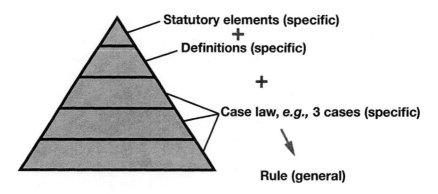

**Statutory elements (specific)**
**+**
**Definitions (specific)**

**+**

**Case law, *e.g.,* 3 cases (specific)**

**Rule (general)**

**FIGURE 24**

Once you complete and review your research, you must piece together rules
of law. The rules you synthesize will guide your analysis or argument. You
may need to piece together statutes; statutes plus regulations; statutes plus
regulations plus cases; and so on. Each rule is like the tile of a mosaic or the
piece of a jigsaw puzzle. Once you examine all the pieces and put them where
you think they belong, you will have a complete picture of the applicable legal
rules. Although not truly scientific, this inductive process resembles Bacon's

methodology of using particular observations to reach more general conclusions.[7] The following example is a simple form of induction:

*Example 1: You go outside on Day 1, and the sun is shining. You go outside on Day 2; it is raining and you get wet. On Day 3, it is raining again, and again you get wet when you go outside. On Day 4, it is sunny, and you do not get wet when you go outside. On Day 5, it is raining, but you use an umbrella when you go outside, and, lo and behold, you do not get wet.*

**Day 1    +  Day 2    +  Day 3    +  Day 4    +  Day 5=**

sun →dry    rain →wet    rain →wet    sun →dry    rain + umbrella →dry

**Piecing these observations together, you form the following conclusion:**

**Synthesized rule: You will get wet if you go outside in the rain without an umbrella.**

Although inducing legal rules is usually more complicated, the basic process is the same as in *Example 1*. Courts rarely state comprehensive rules of law applicable to your situation, and you are likely to need to form your own rules. At first, you may feel uncomfortable synthesizing a rule that is not explicitly stated elsewhere or that requires you to resolve inconsistencies in the law. However, not only should you do that, you will be *expected* to do that. The law "is what you say it is," meaning you have both the right and the obligation to put that jumble of law into words. Your authority is limited only by a need to be accurate and reasonable in the statement of your rule. Aristotle might say that the "truth" of the rule need not be certain, but it must at least be reasonable. Your opponent may take issue with your rule on the grounds that it fails to provide the best explanation for the outcomes in the prior cases or it fails to include information relevant to the outcome of the cases that cannot be explained by your rule.[8]

The second example (based on a Texas statute) is more complicated and requires the synthesis of several legal rules. The cases cited are fictitious:

*Example 2: You represent a Starbucks franchise in Dallas, Texas, that uses only organically grown coffee beans. A local consumer advocacy group, "Consumers for Safe Products (CSP)," recently published its monthly newsletter, indicating that your client's coffee beans are grown using pesticides. Your client's sales have dropped, and the owner is furious.*

**In the course of your research, you discover the following relevant materials:**

---

7.    *See supra* ch. 2, at 45. The main difference between the two processes is that the scientific method is used to predict future cases, whereas the synthesized rule is used to explain past cases.

8.    *See* DAVIS, *supra* ch. 4, note 79, at 139–40.

(1) Section 96.2 of a Texas statute prohibits making false statements about food products that cause harm to the plaintiff. In order to prevail in a claim for food disparagement, the statute requires plaintiffs to prove the following elements:

(a) the person disseminates in any manner information relating to a perishable food product to the public;

(b) the person knows the information is false; and

(c) the information states or implies that the perishable food product is not safe for consumption by the public.[9]

(2) the definition of "perishable food product" in the definitions section of the same statute, section 96.1:

"perishable food product" means (a) a food product (b) of agriculture or aquaculture that is (c) sold or distributed in a form that will perish or decay beyond marketability within a limited period of time.

(3) *The Pet Barn, Inc. v. Holmes* (Tex. 2004). The plaintiff, the owner of a pet food store, sued a disgruntled employee who suggested the store's most popular product was unsafe. The product was baked from all natural ingredients including flour, chicken stock, and salt. Even though the ingredients were harvested from the ground or derived from livestock, the court held the product at issue was not a food product of agriculture or aquaculture. The court stated, "The product sold is a *combination* of products of agriculture, not a *sole* product of agriculture, as the statute contemplates."

(4) *Green's Grocer v. Janus* (Tex. App. 2007). The plaintiff, a farm stand owner, sued a local newscaster who stated during one of his broadcasts that his wife choked on an apple he bought at the farm stand. The court held that the statement made on television reached "a large enough audience" to constitute "dissemination to the public." However, even if the defendant's statement was false, he did not state or imply that the product itself was unsafe. The court said, "The statute intends to protect producers from false accusations that the produce is tainted in some way. People choke on all sorts of foods. We have no authority to interpret the statute so broadly."

(5) *Thomas Meats v. Safeway* (Tex. 2008). The plaintiff meat distributor sued Safeway for posting a sign in its window. The sign stated that the ground beef Safeway purchased from the plaintiff the week before was unsafe and advised customers to throw it away. Safeway had heard rumors that the beef was tainted but did not investigate them before

---

9.    This example is based on a Texas statute prohibiting the false disparagement of perishable food products. *See* TEX. CIV. PRAC. & REM. CODE ANN. §§ 96.001–.004 (2007).

**posting the sign in its window. The court stated that although Safeway employees did not have actual knowledge that the statements were false, their "reckless indifference to the truth was tantamount to knowledge of falsity" and held for the plaintiff.**

To synthesize the legal rules for *Example 2*, it is easiest to begin by laying out the elements the plaintiff must prove under the statute.[10] *See (1), (2), and (3) in Figure 25 below.* Then read the entire statute, including the definitions, and the case law. Use them to flesh out what the elements mean and how they have been interpreted by the courts. Keep track of the sources of your information. Piecing the rules together, you might come up with something that looks like Figure 25:

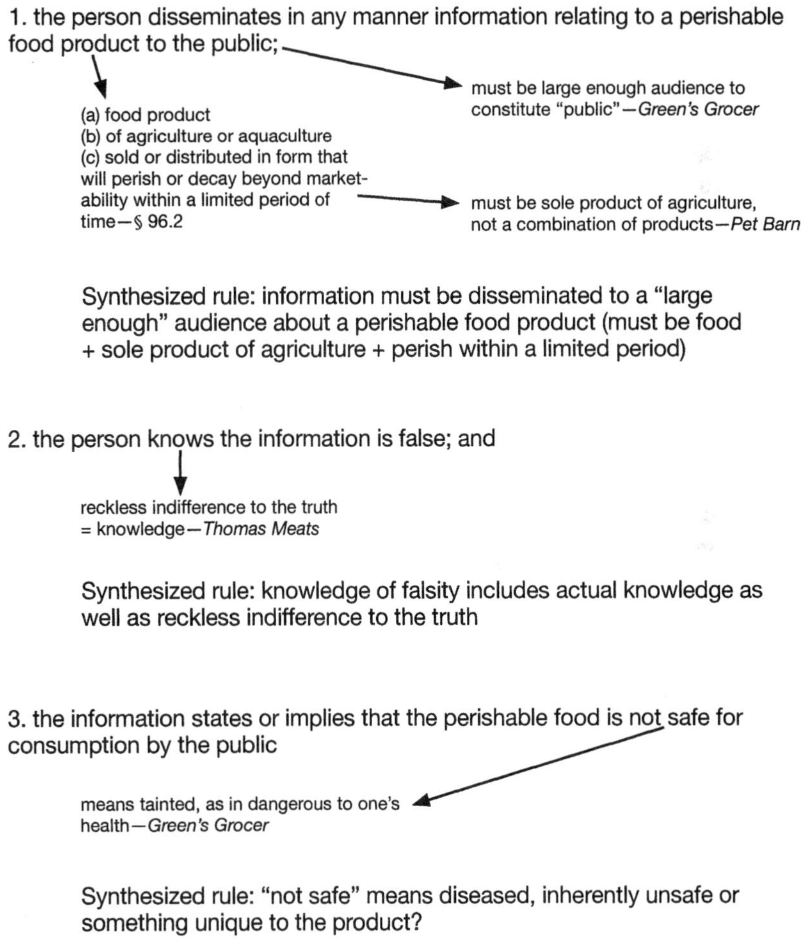

1. the person disseminates in any manner information relating to a perishable food product to the public;

(a) food product
(b) of agriculture or aquaculture
(c) sold or distributed in form that will perish or decay beyond market-ability within a limited period of time—§ 96.2

must be large enough audience to constitute "public"—*Green's Grocer*

must be sole product of agriculture, not a combination of products—*Pet Barn*

Synthesized rule: information must be disseminated to a "large enough" audience about a perishable food product (must be food + sole product of agriculture + perish within a limited period)

2. the person knows the information is false; and

reckless indifference to the truth = knowledge—*Thomas Meats*

Synthesized rule: knowledge of falsity includes actual knowledge as well as reckless indifference to the truth

3. the information states or implies that the perishable food is not safe for consumption by the public

means tainted, as in dangerous to one's health—*Green's Grocer*

Synthesized rule: "not safe" means diseased, inherently unsafe or something unique to the product?

**FIGURE 25**

---

**10.** The elements of a statute or a common law cause of action are those components of the claim that must be proved in order to win the case. In *Example 2*, they are listed in sub-sections (a), (b), and (c) of section 96.2 of the statute.

Having synthesized the rules of law, you can begin to determine if CSP is liable to Starbucks for its drop in sales. Did CSP disseminate information about a perishable food product to the public? Did it know its statement was false? Did the information state or imply that the product was unsafe for consumption by the public? How could Starbucks prove CSP's newsletter caused its drop in sales? Is there anything else you need to know to answer these questions? Do you think Starbucks would succeed in a claim against CSP?

---

### CASE SYNTHESIS EXERCISE

A. For this exercise, assume there is a common law cause of action for making false statements about perishable food products in Illinois. Synthesize the following cases into a comprehensive rule either in graphic or paragraph form:

1. *Big Burgers, Inc. v. Seinfeld*, 35 N.E.2d 45 (Ill. 1999).

   Plaintiff sued a comedian for food disparagement for making jokes during a stand-up routine insinuating the meat the plaintiff used to make its hamburgers was not fresh. The court found for the defendant. The court said that the plaintiff must prove (1) the person disseminated the information about a perishable food product to the public; (2) that the defendant knew the information was false; and (3) the information stated or implied the food product was not safe for consumption by the public. Although the defendant stated that the beef was unsafe to a large number of people, the information regarding the staleness of the meat had been announced the day before in a press release issued by the federal government, and the defendant had heard the announcement.

2. *Small v. Little*, 100 N.E.2d 87 (Ill. 2002).

   Plaintiff sued defendant for statements made to plaintiff's neighbors regarding the plaintiff's produce. The court held that although the defendant caused the plaintiff's damages, they were minimal, and a statement made to five people does not qualify as dissemination to the public.

3. *Pet Snacks v. Seymour*, 124 N.E.2d 2 (Ill. App. Ct. 2004).

   Plaintiff sued a famous actress for telling a few friends that her dog ate Doggy Jerk, a beef jerky snack for dogs, and got sick. Assuming without deciding that Doggy Jerk was a perishable food product, the court nevertheless held for the defendant. The court explained, "Although the actress told a few friends about her dog's experience without knowing if Doggy Jerk caused her dog to become ill, the plaintiff cannot win its case. In order to be liable, the defendant must claim the product is unsafe for human, not animal, consumption."

4. *Gatorade v. Citizens for Health*, 320 N.E.2d 1 (Ill. App. Ct. 2006).

Plaintiff sued an environmental group for claiming plaintiff's beverages contained harmful chemicals. The court held that even though Gatorade has calories and may be a food product as such, it does not perish within a limited period of time. For that reason, the court found for the defendant.

B. Apply your synthesized rule to predict the outcome in the following case:

*Smoothies, Inc. v. Bernson*—The editor of a large city newspaper stated recently at a meeting of his top twenty reporters that he heard the "guy who sells smoothies at the entrance to our building washes his fruit in contaminated water. I saw the cooler myself—that water looked nasty. Don't tell anyone," he said, "but I wouldn't buy those if I were you." One of the reporters told the smoothie vendor what the editor said. The vendor then sued the editor. At trial, the vendor proved he had lost about $500 in sales the day the reporter told him about the editor's statements. How should the court rule?

# 4. FALLACIES OF INDUCTIVE REASONING

The kinds of mistakes people make when they reason tend to follow a predictable pattern. These mistakes are known as fallacies in logic. The word "fallacy" usually refers to an error in reasoning as opposed to a false premise, but premises can be fallacious as a matter of fact. One of the most common fallacies of induction or rule synthesis is the "faulty generalization," when one "jumps to a conclusion" from inadequate evidence.[11] In legal writing, the faulty generalization often occurs when the writer synthesizes an incomplete or inaccurate rule due to inadequate research. If, in *Example 2* above, you found the statutory section that sets forth the elements of the potential claim but missed the definition of perishable food product, a synthesized rule that omitted the definition would be fallacious and misleading.

---

11. CORBETT & CONNORS, *supra* ch. 2, note 1, at 68.

# B. RULE APPLICATION

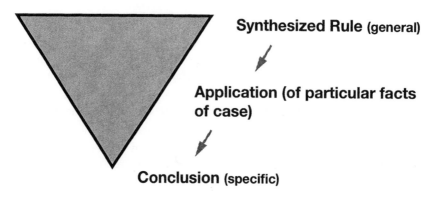

**Synthesized Rule** (general)

**Application (of particular facts of case)**

**Conclusion** (specific)

FIGURE 26

Because the law is primarily a system of rules applied to facts, rhetorical or legal syllogisms are the *sine qua non*[12] of legal analysis. General (often synthesized) rules of law are applied to specific facts to predict or argue for a particular outcome (a process that can, in turn, engender new law). *See Figure 26.* As if with mathematical precision, legal writers try to prove that one premise applied to another yields a certain result. Aristotle knew the power of the syllogism to persuade: If the audience grants the truth of the stated premises and the reasoning is valid, it will accept the conclusion as sound.[13] Presented with reasonable premises grounded in the law, the reader jumps easily and quickly to the desired conclusion, even though it is at best likely to be true.[14] As Chapter Four explains, legal syllogisms are generally sound as long as the premises are probable or reasonable, no more than three terms of comparison are used, and the principle of distributed terms is not violated.[15]

## 1. EXAMPLE 1: THE APPLICATION OF A SIMPLE RULE

Reconsider the synthesized rule from *Example 1*, page 145:

**You will get wet if you go outside in the rain without an umbrella.**

Assume I need to go outside today. It is raining, but I do not have an umbrella. When I apply the rule to these facts, I predict I will get wet.

## a. FORMULATE THE SYLLOGISM

My reasoning can be put in syllogistic form:

---

**12.** *Sine qua non* was a phrase Aristotle used to mean that which is essential or an integral part of something. *See, e.g.,* 3 ARISTOTLE, *On Memory and Reminiscence, in* THE WORKS OF ARISTOTLE 452a (W.D. Ross ed., 1952) (remembering is the "sine qua non of recollecting.").

**13.** *See supra*, ch. 4, at 114–15.

**14.** GARDNER, *supra* ch. 4, note 90 at 6.

**15.** *See supra*, ch. 4, at 115.

Major premise:    **Going outside in the rain without an umbrella (B) causes one to get wet (C).**

Minor premise:    **I (A) am going outside today without an umbrella (B).**

Conclusion:    **I (A) will get wet (C).**

Formulating syllogisms can be confusing at first. The major premise is the synthesized rule, and the minor premise comes from the specific facts of your case. To be sound, the legal syllogism must contain only three terms of comparison: A, B, and C. The legal syllogism is based on the mathematical principle of transitivity: *if A = B and B = C, then A = C.* Notice though, that when you convert the equation into a formal syllogism, the equation becomes *if B = C, and A = B, then A = C.* To determine which term is which, use the letter A to represent the subject term of your conclusion (also called the *minor term* because it appears in the minor premise), the letter B to represent the middle term (the one that does not appear in the conclusion), and the letter C to represent the predicate term of your conclusion (also called the *major term* because it appears in the major premise). It is often easiest to begin with your conclusion and work backwards from there.

## b. TEST THE SYLLOGISM

Major premise:    **Going outside in the rain without an umbrella (B) causes one to get wet (C).**

Minor premise:    **I (A) am going outside today without an umbrella (B).**

Conclusion:    **I (A) will get wet (C).**

As explained earlier in Chapter Four, the syllogism must comply with the following rules in order to be sound:[16]

(1) The premises must be indisputably true or, in the case of legal reasoning, at least probably or reasonably true;

(2) There must be only three terms or phrases being compared so that a valid conclusion can be drawn about the relationship of the terms to each other;

(3) The rules of distribution[17] must not be violated:

    (a) the middle term must be distributed at least once;

    (b) no term is distributed in the conclusion that is not also distributed in one of the premises;

(4) No conclusion can be drawn from two premises where the subject terms

---

16. *See supra*, ch. 4, at 115.

17. "Distributed" means the extent to which the term applies to the named objects or individuals. "All men" is a distributed term, whereas "some men" is not. *See supra*, ch. 4, at 116, and Figures 14A and 14B.

of the premises are undistributed;

(5) Valid conclusions are rarely drawn from two negative premises; and

(6) If one premise is negative, the conclusion usually needs to be negative too.

Applying these rules to *Example 1* yields the following analysis:

**(1) Question the premises.**

Although it is possible that my major premise fails to provide the best explanation for my getting wet (*i.e.*, I got wet on Days 2 and 3 for reasons unrelated to rain),[18] it seems unlikely based on the facts. In addition, my minor premise might fail to include relevant information about me (*i.e.*, I have decided to go outside wearing a raincoat with a hood). However, assuming I have no umbrella and no such coat, both premises seem reasonably true.

**(2) Determine the number of terms.**

There are only three terms of comparison: If going out in the rain without an umbrella (B) makes you wet, (C), and I (A) go out in the rain without an umbrella (B), I (A) will get wet (C).

**(3) Consult rules of distribution.**

**Rule (a):** The middle term (B) appears in both premises but not in the conclusion. It must be distributed at least once. Here, the middle term, "going out in the rain without an umbrella," is distributed in the major premise because all trips outside are meant to be included. The middle term is undistributed in the minor premise because it is the predicate term of an affirmative proposition.

**Rule (b):** Since the middle term is distributed at least once, the syllogism is sound as long as no term in the conclusion is distributed that was not distributed in one of the premises. The subject term in the conclusion, "I," is distributed in the conclusion and in the minor premise because "I" is a proper

> ## Soundness Test for Syllogisms:
>
> 1. *Premises must be probably or reasonably true;*
>
> 2. *Only three terms of comparison may be used;*
>
> 3. *Distribution rules are not violated:*
>
>    a. *The middle term must be distributed at least once.*
>
>    b. *No term is distributed in the conclusion that was not distributed in at least one of the premises.*
>
> *"Distributed" means the extent to which a term encompasses all or some of the named objects or individuals.*
>
> *Tips:*
> * *Subject terms of affirmative propositions are often distributed. Proper nouns are distributed.*
>
> * *Predicate terms of affirmative propositions are undistributed, whereas predicate terms of negative propositions are distributed.*

---

18. *See supra* p. 145.

noun. The predicate term in the conclusion, "will get wet" is undistributed in the conclusion because it is the predicate term of an affirmative proposition. Because the predicate term is undistributed in the conclusion, it need not be distributed in one of the premises.

**(4) No conclusion can be drawn from two premises where the subject terms of the premises are undistributed.**

The subject terms of the premises are distributed, so this rule does not apply.

**(5) Valid conclusions are rarely drawn from two negative premises.**

Neither premise is negative, so this rule does not apply.

**(6) If one premise is negative, the conclusion usually needs to be negative too.**

Neither premise is negative, so this rule does not apply.

**Conclusion:** the syllogism is sound.

## 2. EXAMPLE 2: MORE COMPLICATED APPLICATIONS

*Example 2*, taken from the Starbucks case on page 145, provides a more realistic example of syllogistic reasoning in legal writing. Reconsider the facts:

> ***There is a Starbucks franchise in Dallas, Texas, that uses only organically grown coffee beans. A local consumer advocacy group, "Consumers for Safe Products (CSP)," recently published its monthly newsletter, indicating that your client's coffee beans are grown using pesticides. Starbucks' sales have dropped, and the owner is furious.***

To predict whether Starbucks will succeed in its claim against CSP, each element of the statute must be analyzed separately. Element by element, the synthesized rules can be applied to the facts in syllogistic form. *See Figure 27.*

**(1) Synthesized rule: information must be disseminated to a "large enough" audience about a perishable food product (must be food + sole product of agriculture + perish within limited period)**

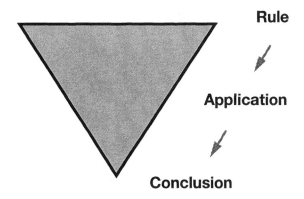

Rule

Application

Conclusion

**(2) Synthesized rule: knowledge of falsity includes actual knowledge and reckless indifference to the truth**

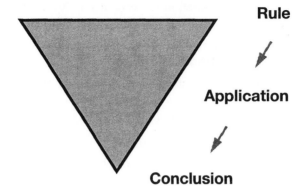

**(3) Synthesized rule: to state or imply that food is not safe means diseased, inherently unsafe, or a danger unique to that product**

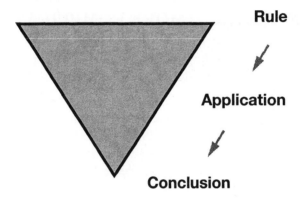

FIGURE 27

Assume an attorney for Starbucks has already drafted a memorandum on this question. Review the following analysis of the first element:

**The first element Starbucks must prove is that CSP disseminated information regarding a perishable food product to the public. *See* Tex. Civ. Prac. & Rem. Code Ann. § 96.2(a) (Vernon 2007). Since CSP published information about Starbucks coffee in a local newsletter, the dissemination is likely to be considered to the "public."[19] *See Green's Grocer v. Janus* (Tex. App. 2007) (holding that a statement made on a television newscast was disseminated to the public). Information on the number of subscribers to the newsletter would be helpful to validate this conclusion.**

**The only remaining issue under the first element is whether**

---

**19.** This sentence is a typical enthymeme as Aristotle defined it. It is an argument based on probable premises that combines the minor premise and the conclusion. *See supra*, ch. 4, at 118–19. The major premise—that distribution to the newsletter subscribers is equivalent to dissemination to the public—is implicit here.

Starbucks coffee drinks are perishable food products. In order to be a perishable food product, the coffee drinks must be (a) a food product, (b) of agriculture or aquaculture, (c) that is sold or distributed in a form that will perish or decay beyond marketability within a limited period of time."[20] Tex. Civ. Prac. & Rem. Code Ann. § 96.1. The statute does not further define food products. Although coffee is a beverage, Starbucks could argue that its coffee drinks are food products because they contain calories from the addition of cream, syrups, and sugar.[21]

To be food products of agriculture under (b) though, the drinks must be sole products of agriculture, not a combination of products. *See The Pet Barn, Inc. v. Holmes* (2004) (holding that a baked combination of agricultural products was not "a product of agriculture"). Although the ingredients added to the coffee drinks may convert the drinks into food, the drinks might be disqualified as products of agriculture under *Pet Barn.* Although products of agriculture, these ingredients are not likely to be considered "a product of agriculture" in combined form.[22]

Even if a court were to consider the coffee drinks a product of agriculture, they probably do not perish or decay beyond marketability within a limited period of time. Although the statute does not define this phrase, to decay within a limited period of time probably means to rot within a few days, as lettuce or other fresh produce might. Since the drinks cannot be said to "rot," they do not "decay or perish" within a limited period of time.[23] As to the first element, CSP probably disseminated information to the public, but that information probably did not concern a perishable food product because coffee drinks are not a product "of agriculture," and they cannot be said "to rot" within a few days.[24]

Do you agree with the writer that Starbucks cannot prove the first element? With which parts of the analysis do you agree or disagree? Does the writer employ sound, deductive reasoning? Are the premises reasonable? Is the logic valid?

The analysis of the first element contains four legal syllogisms—one for each sub-issue the writer identified. Each of these can be formulated and tested for soundness.

---

**20.** The writer here sets forth the three requirements that must be met to qualify as a perishable food product. Each is then addressed separately below.

**21.** This sentence concludes the writer's analysis of the first requirement—food product.

**22.** This sentence concludes the writer's analysis of the second requirement—of agriculture.

**23.** This sentence concludes the writer's analysis of the third requirement—perishes or decays beyond marketability within a limited period of time.

**24.** This sentence is the writer's overall conclusion as to the three requirements for being a perishable food product.

**Sub-Issues of First Element**

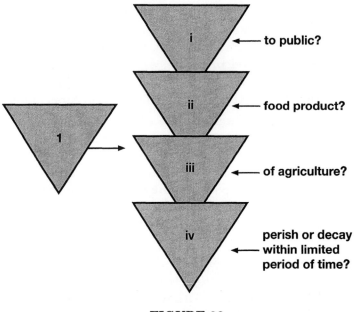

FIGURE 28

## a. SUB–ISSUE (i): DID CSP DISSEMINATE TO THE PUBLIC?

| | |
|---|---|
| Major premise: [implied] | Publication of information in a newsletter (B) is dissemination to the public (C). |
| Minor premise: | CSP (A) published information in a newsletter (B). |
| Conclusion: | CSP (A) disseminated information to the public (C). |

### (1) Question the premises.

CSP might argue that publishing information in a local newsletter is not nearly as "public" as broadcasting information on television because the size of the audience is significantly smaller. The major premise seems reasonable, however, because the newsletter was likely distributed to enough people that patronize Starbucks to affect its sales. Since CSP did publish information about Starbucks in its newsletter, the minor premise is accurate.

### (2) Determine the number of terms.

The syllogism contains only three terms or phrases of comparison: If publication of information in a newsletter (B) equals dissemination to the public (C), and CSP (A) published information in a newsletter (B), then CSP (A) disseminated information to the public (C).

**(3) Consult rules of distribution.**

*Rule (a):* The middle term (B) appears in both of the premises but not in the conclusion. It must be distributed at least once. Here, the middle term, "publication of information in a newsletter," is distributed in the major premise because the term is intended to include all such publications.

*Rule (b):* Since the middle term is distributed at least once, the syllogism is valid as long as no term in the conclusion is distributed that was not distributed in one of the premises. The subject term in the conclusion, "CSP," is distributed in the conclusion and in the minor premise because CSP is a proper noun. "Dissemination to the public" is undistributed in the conclusion as the predicate term of an affirmative proposition. Since "dissemination to the public" is undistributed, it does not need to be distributed in one of the premises.

**(4) No conclusion can be drawn from two premises where the subject terms of the premises are undistributed.**

The subject terms of the premises are distributed, so this rule does not apply.

**(5) Valid conclusions are rarely drawn from two negative premises.**

Neither premise is negative, so this rule does not apply.

**(6) If one premise is negative, the conclusion usually needs to be negative too.**

Neither premise is negative, so this rule does not apply.

**Conclusion:** the syllogism is sound. Figure 29 illustrates the validity of this reasoning.

---

Soundness Test for Syllogisms:

1. *Premises must be probably or reasonably true;*

2. *Only three terms of comparison may be used;*

3. *Distribution rules are not violated:*

   a. *The middle term must be distributed at least once.*

   b. *No term is distributed in the conclusion that was not distributed in at least one of the premises.*

*"Distributed" means the extent to which a term encompasses all or some of the named objects or individuals.*

*Tips:*
- *Subject terms of affirmative propositions are often distributed. Proper nouns are distributed.*

- *Predicate terms of affirmative propositions are undistributed, whereas predicate terms of negative propositions are distributed.*

**Forms of Dissemination to Public**

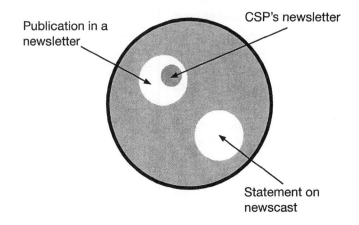

Publication in a newsletter

CSP's newsletter

Statement on newscast

**FIGURE 29**

## b. SUB–ISSUE (ii): ARE STARBUCKS COFFEE DRINKS FOOD PRODUCTS?

Major premise:    **Products with calories (B) are food products (C).**

Minor premise:    **Starbucks coffee drinks (A) have calories (B).**

Conclusion:    **Starbucks coffee drinks (A) are food products (C).**

### (1) Question the premises.

CSP might take issue with one or both of the premises here. First, CSP might argue the major premise is flawed because calories alone are not synonymous with food. Arguably, the calories must be nutritious for the product to be considered food. As to the minor premise, CSP might argue that coffee has no calories and is not food even under Starbucks' definition. Although cream and sugar (which do have calories) may be added to the coffee, CSP might argue that these secondary ingredients cannot count for purposes of making the drinks "food." If the additional ingredients do count, they disqualify the coffee drinks from being sole products of agriculture. *See supra p. 155 and sub-issue (iii) below.* How can Starbucks get around this problem? Could it argue that the drinks are food products in a way that does not prevent them from being products "of agriculture?"

### (2) Determine the number of terms.

The syllogism contains three and only three terms of comparison: If calories (B) equate to food (C), and Starbucks coffee drinks (A) have calories (B), then Starbucks coffee drinks (A) are food (C).

**(3) Consult rules of distribution.**

**Rule (a):** The middle term (B) appears in both of the premises but not in the conclusion. It must be distributed at least once. Here, the middle term, "products with calories," is distributed in the major premise because it is intended to apply to all drinks containing additional ingredients (black coffee would not qualify).

**Rule (b):** Since the middle term is distributed at least once, the syllogism is valid as long as no term in the conclusion is distributed that is not distributed in one of the premises. The subject term in the conclusion, "Starbucks coffee drinks," is distributed in the conclusion and in the minor premise because the terms are intended to apply to all of Starbucks drinks (even though that premise may be arguable). The predicate term in the conclusion, "food product" is undistributed in the conclusion because it is the predicate term of an affirmative proposition. Because it is undistributed, "food product" does not need to be distributed in one of the premises.

> **Rules:**
>
> a. *The middle term must be distributed at least once.*
>
> b. *No term is distributed in the conclusion that was not distributed in at least one of the premises.*
>
> *Tips:*
> * *Subject terms of affirmative propositions are usually distributed. Proper nouns are distributed.*
>
> * *Predicate terms of affirmative propositions are undistributed, whereas predicate terms of negative propositions are distributed.*

**(4) No conclusion can be drawn from two premises where the subject terms of the premises are undistributed.**

The subject terms of the premises are distributed, so this rule does not apply.

**(5) Valid conclusions are rarely drawn From two negative premises.**

Neither premise is negative, so this rule does not apply.

**(6) If one premise is negative, the conclusion usually needs to be negative too.**

Neither premise is negative, so this rule does not apply.

**Conclusion:** the reasoning is valid, but the premises may be questionable. Figure 30 illustrates the writer's reasoning.

**Food Products**

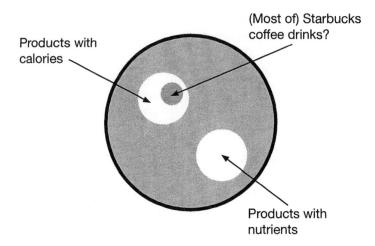

FIGURE 30

## c. SUB–ISSUE (iii): ARE STARBUCKS COFFEE DRINKS PRODUCTS OF AGRICULTURE?

Major premise: **A product that is a combination of products of agriculture (B) is not a product of agriculture under Texas law (C).**

Minor premise: **Starbucks coffee drinks (A) are a combination of products of agriculture (B).**

Conclusion: **Starbucks coffee drinks (A) are not products of agriculture under Texas law (C).**

**(1) Question the premises.**

Here CSP is likely to agree with the premises. Coffee drinks mixed with cream, syrups, and sugar cannot be harvested directly from the ground like beans or carrots. *Pet Barn* supports this premise. If the additional ingredients count for purposes of qualifying the drinks as food, *see infra, sub-issue (ii) above,* then they prevent the drinks from being a product of agriculture under Texas law.

**(2) Determine the number of terms.**

There are only three terms of comparison: Combined products of agriculture (B) are not products of agriculture under Texas law (C), and Starbucks coffee drinks (A) are combined products of agriculture (B), then Starbucks coffee drinks (A) are not products of agriculture under Texas law (C).

**(3) Consult rules of distribution.**

**Rule (a):** The middle term (B) appears in both of the premises but not in the conclusion. It must be distributed at least once. Here, the middle term, "combined products of agriculture" is distributed in the major premise because it is intended to apply to all combined products of agriculture.

**Rule (b):** The subject term in the conclusion, "Starbucks coffee drinks," is distributed in the conclusion and in the minor premise because the term applies to all of Starbucks' drinks. Finally, the predicate term in the conclusion, "product of agriculture under Texas law" is distributed as the predicate term of a negative proposition. It is distributed in the minor premise for the same reason.

**(4) No conclusion can be drawn from two premises where the subject terms of the premises are undistributed.**

The subject terms of the premises are distributed, so this rule does not apply.

**(5) Valid conclusions are rarely drawn from two negative premises.**

Only one premise is negative, so this rule does not apply.

**(6) If one premise is negative, the conclusion must also be negative.**

The major premise is negative and so is the conclusion.

**Conclusion:** the syllogism is sound. *See Figure 31 below.*

---

Rules:

a. *The middle term must be distributed at least once.*

b. *No term is distributed in the conclusion that was not distributed in at least one of the premises.*

Tips:
- *Subject terms of affirmative propositions are usually distributed. Proper nouns are distributed.*
- *Predicate terms of affirmative propositions are undistributed, whereas predicate terms of negative propositions are distributed.*

---

### Products of Agriculture

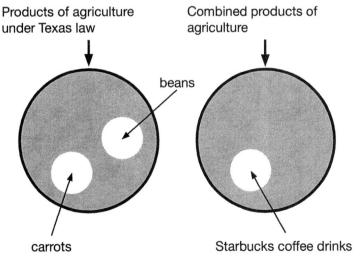

FIGURE 31

## d. SUB–ISSUE (iv): DO STARBUCKS COFFEE DRINKS PERISH OR DECAY BEYOND MARKETABILITY WITHIN A LIMITED PERIOD OF TIME?

| | |
|---|---|
| Major premise: | Food that rots within a few days (B) perishes or decays beyond marketability within a limited period of time. (C) |
| Minor premise: | Starbucks coffee drinks (A) do not rot within a few days. (B) |
| Conclusion: | Starbucks coffee drinks (A) do not decay beyond marketability within a limited period of time (C). |

**(1) Question the premises.**

CSP might agree with the major and minor premises here because both are to CSP's advantage. However, the writer's definition of what it means to perish or decay seems narrow. As demonstrated below, the reasoning is weak partly because of the writer's narrow definition of "perish or decay."

**(2) Determine the number of terms.**

There are three terms of comparison: If food that rots within a few days (B) perishes or decays beyond marketability within a limited period of time (C), but Starbucks coffee drinks (A) do not rot within a few days (B), then Starbucks coffee drinks (A) do not perish or decay beyond marketability within a limited period of time (C).

**(3) Consult rules of distribution.**

**Rule (a):** The middle term (B) appears in both of the premises but not in the conclusion. It must be distributed at least once. Here, the middle term, "rots within a few days" is distributed in the major premise because it is intended to apply to all food that rots.

**Rule (b):** The subject term in the conclusion, "Starbucks coffee drinks," is distributed in the conclusion and in the minor premise because the terms apply to all of the drinks in question. The predicate term in the conclusion, "decays beyond marketability within a limited period of time" is distributed as the predicate term of a negative proposition. However, the same term is undistributed in the major premise as the predicate term of an affirmative proposition.

> **Rules:**
>
> a. The middle term must be distributed at least once.
>
> b. No term is distributed in the conclusion that was not distributed in at least one of the premises.
>
> **Tips:**
> - Subject terms of affirmative propositions are usually distributed. Proper nouns are distributed.
>
> - Predicate terms of affirmative propositions are undistributed, whereas predicate terms of negative propositions are distributed.

**(4) No conclusion can be drawn from two premises where the subject terms of the premises are undistributed.**

The subject terms of the premises are distributed, so this rule does not apply.

**(5) Valid conclusions are rarely drawn from two negative premises.**

Only one premise is negative, so this rule does not apply.

**(6) If one premise is negative, the conclusion must also be negative.**

The major premise is negative and so is the conclusion.

**Conclusion:** the syllogism is not sound because it violates Rule 3(b).

The reasoning above is a common fallacy of deductive reasoning known as "denying the antecedent." It occurs when one argues on the basis of an "if, then" proposition, such as, "if it rains, you will get wet," or as in this case, "if food rots, it perishes or decays." The fallacy is to assume that if the antecedent clause is denied (*i.e.*, the food does not rot), then the consequence must also be denied (*i.e.*, the food does not perish or decay). For example, just because it does not rain, a person could still get wet for a variety of reasons. Similarly, just because coffee drinks do not rot, it does not mean they do not "perish or decay" in some other way. *See Figure 32 below.*

## Different Ways to Perish

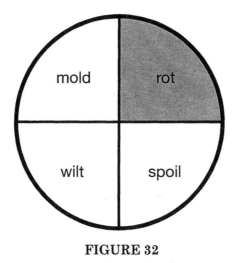

FIGURE 32

---

### *ADDITIONAL EXERCISES IN SYLLOGISTIC REASONING*

1. Review Chapter 3 on Toulmin's model of informal reasoning, *supra* pp. 66–68, based on the use of data, warrants, qualifiers, rebuttals, and backings to support claims. Diagram the writer's analysis of the first element in the Starbucks case using Toulmin's model. Which resonates more with you—diagramming legal syllogisms and testing for soundness or Toulmin's model? Why?

2. Read the analysis below of the second element in the Starbucks case, from *Example 2*, p. 145. Diagram the legal syllogism the writer uses to reach her conclusion and test the legal syllogism to see if it is sound. Be sure to apply each of the six rules for testing syllogisms. *See* p. 115.

   Starbucks is likely to prove the second element: that CSP knew its information was false. That Starbucks' coffee beans are organic and that CSP's statements are false is assumed for purposes of this discussion. Under *Thomas Meats* (Tex. 2008), a reckless indifference to the truth is equivalent to actual knowledge of falsity. CSP likely conducted little or no investigation with respect to the truth of the statements in its newsletter. Otherwise, it would have discovered that Starbucks' beans are not grown using pesticides. Therefore, Starbucks is likely to prove CPS was recklessly indifferent to the truth and thus "knew its statements were false."

3. Draft an analysis of whether Starbucks can prove the third element of its claim against CSP. Then (1) diagram your syllogism(s) and test for soundness, and (2) illustrate your analysis using Toulmin's model.

## 3. FALLACIES IN DEDUCTIVE REASONING[25]

Legal writers do not routinely test the soundness of their syllogisms as demonstrated above. With experience, some—but by no means all—legal writers develop a sort of "sixth sense" for constructing logical arguments. They can hear or read an argument and say, "Wait—that makes no sense." However, even their intuition is not always foolproof. The goal here is to help you identify sooner, rather than later, what sorts of arguments do not work and *why*. In turn, you will avoid making these mistakes yourself. Below are common fallacies seen in the deductive reasoning of legal writers.

### a. BOTH PREMISES MISSING

This fallacy is self-explanatory.[26] It looks like a legal syllogism, but it is not. The analysis fails to state or imply a major premise from the cited authority and, as a consequence, states no minor premise either. The result is simply a description of the authority perceived to support the conclusion. Without having formed the necessary premises, there is no syllogism and no real analysis. The reader is forced to infer the premises and the thought process that led to the writer's conclusion.

---

**25.** In an article written in 2002, I struggled to develop a working vocabulary for several of these fallacies. I chose names and phrases I thought would be memorable. *See* Kristen K. Robbins, *Paradigm Lost: Recapturing Classica Rhetoric to Validate Legal Reasoning*, 27 VT. LAW REV. 483, 498–531 (2003). They struck me as somewhat cutesy then and even more so now. I have renamed them here in a purely descriptive and less "clever" way.

**26.** Formerly called the "book report" because it simply "reports on" the case without providing any analysis. *Id.* at 498–505.

*Example:*

> For CSP to be liable, Starbucks must prove CSP knew its statement about the coffee beans was false. *See* § 96.2(b). In *Thomas Meats* (Tex. 2008), the defendant grocery store posted a sign indicating the meat it bought from the plaintiff was unsafe without first checking to see if that were true. Therefore, although CSP may not have had actual knowledge, Starbucks is likely to prove the second element. [conclusion]

As you can see, the writer has done little here to prove that CSP knew its statement was false. Although the writer refers to the facts of *Thomas Meats*, she does not formulate a major premise (synthesized rule) or explain how the court ruled in *Thomas Meats* and why. Although the reader could infer a rule and supply the missing analysis, the writer leaves too many holes for the reader to fill in for the analysis to be effective.

*Revised example:*

> For CSP to be liable, Starbucks must prove CSP knew its statement about the coffee beans was false. *See* § 96.2(b). Knowledge can be actual or imputed due to a reckless indifference to truth. *Thomas Meats* (Tex. 2008). [major premise] In *Thomas Meats,* the court held the defendant had been reckless in failing to investigate the truth of its statements and thus had knowledge of falsity. *Id.* Starbucks and its suppliers were not contacted by CSP about the nature of the coffee beans. [minor premise] Assuming CSP was reckless with regard to the source of the beans, Starbucks can prove CSP had the requisite knowledge. [conclusion]

## b. CONCLUSION MISSING

This fallacy has the opposite problem—although the premises are stated, the writer's conclusion is missing.[27] With the conclusion missing, the reader may miss the writer's point and, more likely, forget it. Although the reader might supply the missing conclusion herself, it may not be what the writer intended. What might seem redundant or obvious here is necessary to clarify meaning.

*Example:*

> For CSP to be liable, Starbucks must prove that CSP knew its statement about the coffee beans was false. *See* § 96.2(b). Knowledge can be actual or imputed due to a reckless indifference to truth. *Thomas Meats* (Tex. 2008). [major premise] In that case, the court held the defendant had been reckless in failing to investigate the truth of its statements and thus had knowledge of falsity. *Id.* Starbucks and its suppliers were not contacted by CSP about the nature of the coffee beans. [minor premise] Whether this amounts to reckless indifference and thus knowledge of falsity is a question for the jury to decide.

---

27. Formerly called the "fear of commitment" because it fails to reach a conclusion. *Id.* at 505.

Because the writer fails to explore the possible similarities between the efforts of the grocery store to verify its statements and those potentially taken by CSP, she does not draw an ultimate conclusion. Perhaps she is uncomfortable because so little information is available. Nevertheless, the writer must predict an outcome based on the information she has, qualifying her conclusion as she deems necessary. Only then can a productive conversation begin on how best to deal with the uncertainty. Sometimes, the reader will be able to sense what the writer's conclusion would be. However, to leave it out is to risk being misunderstood. In this situation, the writer must act as the jury herself and predict the ultimate outcome.

*Revised example:*

> For CSP to be liable, Starbucks must prove that CSP knew its statement about the coffee beans was false. Tex. Civ. Prac. & Rem. Code Ann. § 96.2(b). Knowledge can be actual or imputed due to a reckless indifference to truth. *Thomas Meats* (Tex. 2008). [major premise] In that case, the court held the defendant had been reckless in failing to investigate the truth of its statements and thus had knowledge of falsity. *Id.* Starbucks and its suppliers were not contacted by CSP about the nature of the coffee beans. [minor premise] Assuming the newsletter is false, Starbucks will have to prove CSP failed to investigate. If CSP did nothing, like the grocery store in *Thomas Meats*, Starbucks should be able to prove knowledge. [conclusion]

You should have noticed that these first two examples have at least one thing in common: The writer is engaged only superficially in the analysis and seems hesitant to venture out too far from the law itself. As you can see in the revised examples, the writer simply needed to elaborate on her reasoning. Whether or not you agree with the ultimate conclusion, the writer's reasoning provides a starting point for conversation and decision-making.

## c. DENYING THE ANTECEDENT[28]

The analysis of sub-issue (iv) of the Starbucks case, *supra* page 162, commits the fallacy of denying the antecedent. This fallacy occurs when the writer assumes that if the antecedent of an "if, then" proposition is denied, the consequence must also be denied.

*Example:*

> For CSP to be liable, Starbucks must prove CSP knew its statement about the coffee beans was false. *See* § 96.2(b). A reckless indifference to truth constitutes knowledge. *Thomas Meats v. Safeway* (Tex. 2008). CSP claims it checked with three of Starbucks coffee bean suppliers, each of whom said that the beans had been

---

**28.** Formerly called "the deceptive hypothetical" because it appears to make sense but is not logical. *Id.* at 512.

**grown using pesticides. Therefore, CSP was not recklessly indifferent to the truth of its statement, and Starbucks will be unable to prove the second element.**

The above example commits the fallacy of denying the antecedent. It assumes the only way for Starbucks to prove knowledge is to show that CSP was recklessly indifferent to the truth of its statements. However, the law indicates this is incorrect: If Starbucks can prove CSP otherwise had *actual* knowledge of falsity, Starbucks could still satisfy the second element. *See Figure 33.*

## Types of Knowledge of Falsity

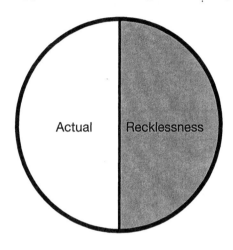

FIGURE 33

# d. THE DOUBLE NEGATIVE PROOF

The double negative proof occurs when a prior case in which a legal requirement was not met is used to claim that the legal requirement is met in the writer's case. It is as if to say, "I need to prove x. In the prior case, the court found not-x, but my case is not like that case. My case is not not-x" (thus the double negative). A legal writer makes this mistake most often when there are no factually similar cases that are decided in her favor, and her only recourse is to distinguish applicable case law on the basis of factual differences. Although this is an effective way to deal with negative case law, it does not *prove* the writer's point. She needs to find other or additional ways to support her analysis or argument.

*Example:*

**For CSP to be liable, Starbucks must prove its coffee drinks are food products of agriculture. *See* § 96.1(b). In *Pet Barn, Inc. v. Holmes* (Tex. 2004), the court held that a baked pet snack made from several different products of agriculture combined together had ceased to be a product of agriculture under the statute. Unlike the baked snack in *Pet Barn*, Starbucks coffee drinks are not made**

from ingredients baked together; instead, each ingredient retains its original nature. Since Starbucks coffee drinks are made from a mixture of agricultural products that remain chemically unaltered, they are likely to be food products of agriculture.

As Figure 34 illustrates, the reasoning here is fallacious because being unlike the baked pet snack is insufficient to qualify as a product of agriculture. The real question is whether Starbucks coffee drinks are like corn, milk, beans, or carrots, not whether they are similar to baked pet snacks. Although the coffee drinks are less likely to be products of agriculture if they are baked, the fact that they are not baked does not make them any more like products of agriculture. In fact, the drinks can at the same time be unlike the baked pet snacks and unlike products of agriculture. Starbucks coffee drinks could be most like frozen entrées, which are arguably another combination of chemically unaltered agricultural products.

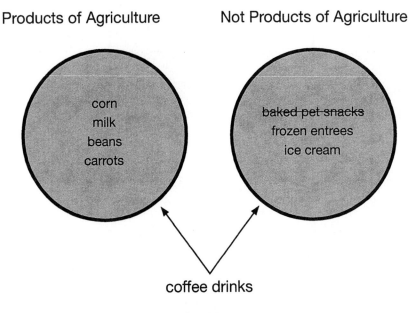

FIGURE 34

The faulty syllogism can be formulated as follows:

**Major premise:**  **Baked products of agriculture (B) are not products of agriculture under Texas law (C).**

**Minor premise:**  **Starbucks coffee drinks (A) are not baked products of agriculture. (B).**

**Conclusion:**  **Starbucks coffee drinks (A) are products of agriculture (C).**

Although the syllogism passes the first four rules for soundness, it fails Rule 5:

**(5) Valid conclusions can rarely be drawn from two negative premises.**

In this case, no valid conclusion can be drawn about the relationship of Starbucks coffee drinks to products of agriculture because whether Starbucks coffee drinks are products of agriculture has nothing to do with whether they are baked.

## e. BEGGING THE QUESTION

Most people have heard of this fallacy but may not know what it really means. To beg the question is to assume the conclusion you are trying to prove, leaving the ultimate question unanswered.

*Example:*

> **For CSP to be liable, Starbucks must prove CSP had knowledge that its statement about the coffee beans was false.** *See* § 96.2(b). **Since CSP was unaware that its statements were false, this element cannot be proved.**

This analysis begs the question of what knowledge means under the statute and whether CSP had such knowledge. The legal syllogism can be formulated as follows:

| | |
|---|---|
| **Major premise:** | **A defendant has no knowledge of falsity (C) if it is unaware of the truth of its statements (B).** |
| **Minor premise:** | **CSP (A) was unaware of the truth of its statements (B).** |
| **Conclusion:** | **CSP (A) had no knowledge of falsity (C).** |

Notice that the minor premise essentially repeats what the conclusion says using slightly different words. This is akin to saying that CSP had no knowledge because it had no knowledge. Also known as circular reasoning, this fallacy leaves the question unanswered. Circular reasoning often appears in the questions presented in briefs, affecting both the strength of the writer's argument and her credibility.[29]

---

> ### *EXERCISE IN IDENTIFYING FALLACIES IN DEDUCTIVE REASONING*
>
> Review the following syllogisms and "if, then" propositions to determine whether they are valid. Why or why not?
>
> 1. Major premise: A fever indicates one is ill.
>    Minor premise: Jane has a fever.
>    Conclusion:     Jane is ill.
> 2. If you run a red light, you will get a ticket.
>    My professor would never run a red light.
>    My professor will not get a ticket.

---

**29.** *See infra* ch. 8, at 238.

---

3. Major premise: A food product has nutrients.

   Minor premise: Tea is not like water, which has no nutrients.

   Conclusion:    Tea is a food product.

4. If the defendant had motive, means, and opportunity, he is likely to have committed the crime.

   The defendant had the motive, means, and opportunity.

   The defendant likely committed the crime.

5. Because my client had nothing to do with the accident, he did not hit the plaintiff's car.

6. If it rains, she will get wet.

   She got wet.

   It must have rained.

---

# C. ANALOGICAL REASONING

*Stare decisis* requires that you compare or analogize your case to prior cases (where they exist) to see if they are similar or different. If there are significant similarities between the cases, your case should be treated the same way. Alternatively, if there are significant differences, the cases should be treated differently. Analogical reasoning is used in legal writing to persuade the reader how the rule of law should be applied by comparing specific similarities or differences between the cited case and the case at hand. The writer's conclusion as to overall similarity or difference forms the the minor premise. *See Figure 35.* Analogical reasoning generally takes place after the statement of the general rule (the major premise) and as part of the statement of the minor premise. The analogy thus occurs within the syllogistic framework and is often referred to as "analogy within deduction."[30]

---

**30.** *See, e.g.,* JILL J. RAMSFIELD, THE LAW AS ARCHITECTURE: BUILDING LEGAL DOCUMENTS 299 (2000). For additional reading on this subject, see RUGGERO J. ALDISERT, LOGIC FOR LAWYERS: A GUIDE TO CLEAR LEGAL THINKING (3d ed. 1997); STEVEN J. BURTON, AN INTRODUCTION TO LAW AND LEGAL REASONING 25–40 (3d ed. 2007); GARDNER, *supra* ch. 4, note 90, at 10–13.

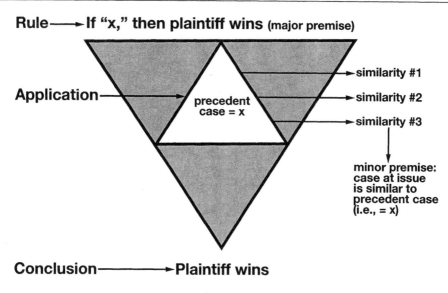

FIGURE 35

In Aristotelian terms, the use of *Case X* in Figure 35 to predict or advocate that the plaintiff should win is an *example*. As Aristotle explained, in any given argument, it is not possible to compare one's case to a statistically significant number of like cases. Therefore, the legal writer chooses one or more cases to serve as representative examples of the relevant law. The analogy derives its force from comparing two different but arguably similar situations. Due to significant factual similarities or dissimilarities between the two situations, the writer argues that the case at hand should be treated in the same or opposite manner.[31] Steven Burton, a professor of law at the University of Iowa, describes the first step in analogical reasoning as "identify[ing] a base point situation from which to reason."[32] The writer then selects the facts she believes are most pertinent to the cited case and compares them to her case. The idea behind the analogy is that "two things which resemble each other in a number of respects resemble one another in a further, unconfirmable respect."[33] Like legal syllogisms, analogies cannot prove anything with certainty. "[T]here is a leap from the known to the unknown. It is because of this inductive leap that analogy achieves probability rather than certainty."[34] Athough analogies do not provide conclusive proof of similarity or difference, they are very persuasive.

---

**31.** ALDISERT, *supra* note 30, at 51; BURTON, *supra* note 30, at 26; CORBETT & CONNORS, *supra* ch. 2, note 1, at 119.

**32.** BURTON, *supra* note 30, at 28. Of course, an advocate may analogize to several cases that are arguably similar to her case and dispense with a full textual comparison to an individual case. For purposes of understanding the analogy, however, it is best to begin by learning what makes a case-to-case comparison effective and then build outward from there. A combination of these approaches gives the legal writer the versatility she needs on a case-by-case basis to respond to the relevant law and write creatively and efficiently.

**33.** CORBETT & CONNORS, *supra* ch. 2, note 1, at 94.

**34.** *See id.*

Recall that in *Example 2*, the Starbucks case, supra, p. 145, Starbucks must prove CSP stated or implied that its coffee was unsafe for consumption by the public. *See* § 96.2(c). The only case interpreting the third element held that the defendant must state or imply that the food product is tainted in some way. *See Green's Grocer v. Janus* (Tex. App. 2007) (holding a statement by the defendant that his wife choked on an apple did not imply the apple was unsafe for consumption). Because the court in *Green's Grocer* held for the defendant, Starbucks will need to distinguish it and argue for different treatment. CSP will analogize to it and argue for similar treatment. Here are sample analogies to *Green's Grocer* that the parties might make in the course of their arguments:

| Starbucks | CSP |
|---|---|
| CSP implied that Starbucks coffee drinks are unsafe for public consumption. This court has interpreted "unsafe for consumption" to mean the defendant implies that the product is dangerous to the public's health. *[major premise] See Green's Grocer v. Janus* (Tex. App. 2007). In Green's, the defendant stated in a television newscast that his wife had choked on an apple he purchased from the plaintiff. The court ruled for the defendant, stating that the statute does not apply when the statement does not indicate the product itself is tainted in some way. *See id.* Here, CSP did just that: It stated that Starbucks coffee beans are grown using pesticides, implying that the beans are tainted or poisoned in some way. *[comparison → minor premise]* That the public understood the implication of CSP's newsletter is evidenced by the precipitous drop in Starbucks' sales. In accordance with Green's, CSP implied that Starbucks coffee drinks are unsafe for public consumption. *[conclusion]* | CSP neither stated nor implied that Starbucks coffee is unsafe for public consumption. In *Green's Grocer*, this court held that in order to be liable under the statute, the defendant must indicate the product is tainted in some way. *[major premise] See Green's Grocer v. Janus* (Tex. App. 2007). In that case, the defendant stated on television that his wife had choked on an apple he bought from the plaintiff. The plaintiff grocer sued for false disparagement, and the court ruled for the defendant. *Id.* The court stated, "People choke on all sorts of foods, but that does not imply they are unsafe. We have no authority to interpret the statute so broadly." *Id.* Similarly, CSP's newsletter did not imply that the defendant's product was unsafe—just that the beans used to make its drinks are not organically grown as advertised. It is well known that many foods are grown using pesticides; that fact alone does not make them unsafe. *[comparison → minor premise]* As in *Green's Grocer*, the statute was not intended to apply in this context. *[conclusion]* |

Which analogy do you find more convincing? Why? What does Starbucks think is the essential difference between the newscaster's statement, which

*Green's Grocer* held did not fall within the statute, and CSP's statement? What is CSP's theory that the statements are similar enough to warrant similar treatment? How would *you* rule?

# 1. THE PROBLEM OF IMPORTANCE

The success of an analogy depends on how strong the reader perceives the factual similarities between the two cases and whether any differences strike the reader as even more significant.[35] Deciding precisely what makes one case similar to or different from another can be difficult. When it comes to identifiable similarities and differences, how do you know which ones matter and which ones do not?

*Example:*

> Assume the facts and circumstances of a precedent case (Case 1) and your case (Case 2) are similar in some ways and different in others. Assume they can be visually represented as follows:

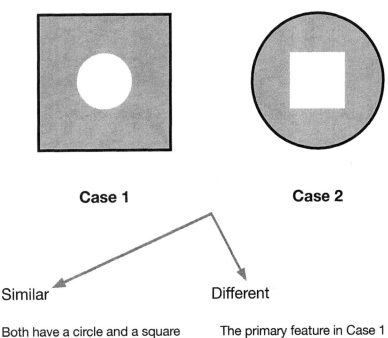

**Case 1**          **Case 2**

Similar                       Different

Both have a circle and a square

Both cases have the same two defining features and no more

Their overall size is roughly the same

The primary feature in Case 1 is a square, and the primary feature in Case 2 is a circle

The sizes of the circles and squares are different

**FIGURE 36**

---

**35.** *Id.* at 95 ("Most of the time when we say, 'Your analogy doesn't hold,' we are exposing an analogy that has avoided consideration of important differences."). *See also* DAVIS, *supra* ch. 4, note 79, at 77–79.

For purposes of *stare decisis*, do you think these cases are similar or different?[36]

As Figure 36 illustrates, there is no way to conclusively decide which factors are more important—the similarities or the differences. In the U.S. legal system, these decisions are generally left to the discretion of the lawyers and judges involved in the case. Burton calls the resolution of these competing factors a "judgment of importance."[37] As Burton states, analogical reasoning tends to "leave the crucial judgment of importance ... unconstrained by the law and open to abuse."[38] In Burton's view, though, the law does not permit reasons relating to a judge's personal bias to determine the final outcome, thus keeping potential abuse in check.[39] Judge Hutcheson has indicated that the problem of importance is much harder for the judge to solve than it is for the lawyer, who "having a predetermined destination in view,—to win his law suit for his client—looks for and regards only those hunches which keep him in the path that he has chosen."[40] As a legal writer, you too will be challenged to decide what makes your case more or less similar to binding case law. On what will you rely?

## 2. RECURRING PROBLEMS IN ANALOGICAL REASONING

A weak analogy is weak not because the reasoning is invalid but because in the reader's view, the writer has misinterpreted the facts. Edward P.J. Corbett and Robert J. Connors state that weak analogies often "concentrate on irrelevant, inconsequential similarities" and "overlook pertinent, significant dissimilarities."[41] As a result, the minor premise is so improbable that the syllogism fails to persuade, even if the reasoning is valid. In my view, analogies are weak both when writers fail to include *enough information* and when they rely on insignificant details. Below are common fallacies seen in the analogical reasoning of legal writers.

### a. TOO MUCH MISSING INFORMATION[42]

When too many of the details of the cases being compared are left out, the reader is unable to make the leap to similarity or difference. In an effective analogy, the writer must explain or infer the court's reasoning in the cited case and then explain how it compares to her case. In the example below, the writer relies on *Thomas Meats* in concluding that Starbucks can prove the second

---

**36.** Remember that the cases need not be identical; if they were, there would be no need for an analogy. They only need to be "alike" to be treated the same way.

**37.** *See* Burton, *supra* note 30, at 27, 52.

**38.** *Id* at 27–28. *See also* Cass R. Sunstein, Commentary, *On Analogical Reasoning*, 106 Harv. L. Rev. 741, 773 (1993).

**39.** Burton, *supra* note 30, at 90.

**40.** Hutcheson, Jr., *supra* ch. 3, note 166, at 278.

**41.** Corbett & Connors, *supra* ch. 2, note 1, at 69.

**42.** Formerly called the "missing link" because it leaves too much for the reader to infer. Robbins, *supra* note 25, at 535.

element of its claim:

> Starbucks can likely prove that CSP knew its statement about the coffee beans was false. Knowledge can be actual or imputed due to a reckless indifference to truth. *[major premise] Thomas Meats v. Safeway* (Tex. 2008). In *Thomas,* the court held the defendant had been reckless in failing to investigate the truth of its statements and was thus charged with knowledge. *Id.* Similarly, CSP was reckless with regard to the truth of the statements in its newsletter. *[comparison → minor premise]* Therefore, Starbucks can establish knowledge. *[conclusion]*

The problem with this analysis is not the validity of the reasoning, it is with the analogy. Without any specific information about the facts or the holding of *Thomas Meats*, the reader cannot draw any comfortable conclusion about the similarity of that case to Starbucks' case. The link between these two cases is missing. What did the defendant in *Thomas Meats* fail to investigate? Specifically, how is CSP's behavior similar to that of the defendant in *Thomas Meats?*

*Revised Example:*

> Starbucks can likely prove that CSP knew its statement about the coffee beans was false. Knowledge can be actual or imputed due to a reckless indifference to truth. *[major premise] Thomas Meats v. Safeway* (Tex. 2008). In *Thomas Meats,* the defendant posted a sign in its window stating that the plaintiff's meat was contaminated. *[facts of case explained]* The court held that since the defendant failed to investigate the truth of its statements before the signs were posted, its reckless indifference was equivalent to knowledge. *Id. [holding and court's reasoning]* Similarly, CSP was reckless with regard to the truth of the statements in its newsletter. *[comparison → minor premise]* To Starbucks' knowledge, CSP "failed to investigate" the nature of the coffee beans by contacting either Starbucks or its suppliers before publishing its newsletter. Therefore, Starbucks can likely establish knowledge as a result of reckless indifference to truth. *[conclusion]*

## b. RELIANCE ON CASE WITH ADVERSE OUTCOME[43]

When there is not much favorable case law, you may be forced to rely on cases with adverse outcomes. Although it is natural to want to cite to cases that are factually similar or that have favorable statements of the law, the adverse outcome of the case can destroy the analogy. Here, the writer analyzes whether Starbucks can prove the third element of its claim:

> CSP probably stated or implied that Starbucks coffee beans are unsafe for public consumption. *See* § 96.2(c). "Unsafe for

---

**43.** Formerly called the "house of cards" because the missing information could cause the analysis to collapse. *Id.* at 542.

consumption" means the defendant has stated or implied that the product is dangerous to the public's health. *[major premise] Green's Grocer v. Janus* (Tex. App. 2007). In *Green's,* the appellate court held that if the defendant states or implies that the product is tainted in some way, that is sufficient. *See id.* Similarly, CSP suggested that Starbucks coffee beans are tainted by claiming they are grown using pesticides. *[comparison → minor premise]* That the public assumed the beans are tainted is evidenced by the precipitous drop in Starbucks' sales. Thus, CSP implied that Starbucks coffee drinks are unsafe for public consumption. [conclusion]

The problem here is that the writer fails to focus on the holding of the cited case. The reader does not know that the *Green's* court held for the *defendant* in that case, which tends to undercut Starbucks' reliance on it. In addition, the reader is unable to evaluate the nature of the defendant's conduct in *Green's* and its similarity to or difference from that of CSP without knowing what the court decided. The writer's credibility here is damaged when she cites a case in support of proposition x (*e.g.,* the defendant stated or implied that the product was unsafe) when the court in the cited case held that proposition x did not exist (*e.g.,* the defendant did not state or imply the product was unsafe).

## c. THE PROBLEM WITH TOTALITIES

Certain rules of law are fluid. They allow the parties, judge, and jury to gauge activity against a standard of conduct as opposed to a rigid rule or definition. "The reasonable person" and "what a person knew or should have known" are examples of standards of conduct in tort law. When evaluating behavior measured against such standards, courts look at the totality of the circumstances. Factors the court deems relevant to its decision may be explicitly stated or inferred.[44] Analogies to cases involving the application of standards can be weak if they ignore relevant or unfavorable factors.

*Example:*

An eighteen-year-old man is charged with unlawful possession of a firearm. He has moved to suppress the gun at trial because the officer obtained it without a warrant or his voluntary consent to a search. Only one officer was present during the encounter, and the search was conducted at 5:00 p.m. The officer did not have a warrant, nor did he tell the suspect he could refuse consent.

Voluntariness of consent is based on whether a reasonable person in the defendant's position would have felt free to refuse consent. Consent may not be the product of duress or coercion.[45] Assume the deciding court in this example examines the following factors to determine voluntariness of consent:

---

44. The choice as to which factors to rely on is another example of a "judgment of importance." *See* BURTON, *supra* note 30, at 52.

45. *See, e.g., Schneckloth v. Bustamonte,* 412 U.S. 218, 227 (1973).

- the individual characteristics of the defendant;
- the number of police officers present and the nature of their behavior;
- the time of day and location of the encounter with the police; and
- whether or not the officer(s) told the suspect he could refuse to consent to a search.

Assume there are three relevant cases in this jurisdiction:

*Case 1: Held:* the defendant voluntarily consented to a warrantless search in a public park, when only one officer was involved in a daytime encounter, and the officer told the suspect he could refuse consent.

*Case 2: Held:* the defendant did not voluntarily consent to a nighttime, warrantless search on the sidewalk in front of his house, when the two officers present used their weapons to intimidate him and did not tell the suspect he could refuse consent.

*Case 3: Held:* the defendant voluntarily consented to a warrantless search in the alley behind his apartment building, when one officer was involved, the suspect was twenty years old, and the officer told the suspect he could refuse consent.

In arguing that the defendant voluntarily consented to the search, the government argues as follows:

> **The motion to suppress should be denied. Factors relevant to voluntary consent are (1) the individual characteristics of the defendant, including what the defendant knew about his rights; (2) the number of police officers present and the nature of their behavior; and 3) the time of day and location of the encounter with the police. *Case 1; Case 2.* In *Case 1,* the court held the defendant voluntarily consented to a search conducted by a single officer during the day in a public park. *Case 1.* Similarly, the defendant in this case was searched by a single officer, during the day, and on the sidewalk in front of his own home. The location was such that he was likely to feel even more comfortable refusing consent than in a large, public space like in *Case 1.* Where, as here, there is no evidence of any police coercion, the search must be deemed voluntary.**

How persuasive is the government's argument? Which factors has it emphasized and which has it ignored? What factors taken together might suggest the outcome should be different? What cases support that argument? Responding to the problem with the government's totality analysis, the defendant might argue as follows:

> **In arguing that the defendant voluntarily consented to the search, the government ignores a number of factors critical to the outcome of consent cases in this jurisdiction. Although time of day and the number of officers present do affect the voluntariness of**

the consent, additional factors such as the age of the suspect and the suspect's familiarity with the legal system are also relevant. *See, e.g., Case 2; Case 3.* In *Cases 2 and 3*, where the court found involuntary consent, the suspect had no knowledge that he had the right to refuse consent. Similarly, the officer in this case failed to inform the defendant that he could refuse consent. The defendant in this case had just turned eighteen and was likely to be less familiar with his legal rights than the twenty-year-old defendant in *Case 3*. Finally, the search occurred late in the afternoon, just as it was getting dark, which would have contributed to the defendant's sense that he could not refuse. *See Case 2.*

As the defendant's argument above makes clear, the government failed to address the situation in its totality, cherry-picking *Case 1* to its advantage and ignoring relevant factors and cases. The goal in a totality of circumstances analysis is to account for both those factors that work for and against you and demonstrate how—in the context of the totality—the court should still rule in your favor. How could the government have effectively distinguished *Cases 2 and 3?*

---

### *ANALOGICAL REASONING EXERCISE*

1. Assume you represent Starbucks (see materials *supra* p. 145) and have found an additional, helpful case:

*Salad Days v. Marriott, Inc.* **(Tex. 2007)**. This case was brought by the wholesale supplier of prepared lettuce and vegetable blends for the defendant's salad bars. The defendant informed its employees that the plaintiff's product was potentially unsafe. The court held that unlike in *Pet Barn, Inc. v. Holmes* (Tex. 2004), the product at issue—a mixture of shredded lettuce, carrots, and cabbage—was comprised of products of agriculture: "To say that the plaintiff converted them into something else simply by mixing them together is nonsensical."

Taking this new case and *Pet Barn* into account, write a paragraph that uses analogical reasoning to determine whether Starbucks coffee drinks are food products of agriculture.

2. Assume you represent CSP. Your client informs you that prior to publishing its newsletter, it contacted Starbucks to verify the contents of its article, but Starbucks refused to give any comment. Write a paragraph that uses analogical reasoning to distinguish *Thomas Meats v. Safeway* (Tex. 2008).

# CHAPTER 6

---

# INVENTION: *PATHOS* IN LEGAL WRITING

■  ■  ■

*"Reason is and ought only to be the slave of the passions, and can never pretend to any other office than to serve and obey them."*—David Hume

A child breaks a vase and immediately blurts out, "I didn't mean it!" Her mother comes running to see what happened, and her daughter repeats, "I didn't mean it, Mom, I'm sorry." The child understands that if she broke the vase by accident, her mother's response is likely to be different from the one she would have if her daughter broke the vase intentionally. People tend to mitigate their mistakes by casting them in the most favorable light; it's only natural. But for some reason, when lawyers do that for clients, it feels slightly deceptive or manipulative. As discussed in Chapter 2, the idea that emotional appeals are manipulative dates back to Plato. He described rhetoric as an evil and selfish form of love that manipulates the audience to serve itself.[1] In contrast, Francis Bacon, John Locke, and David Hume said that appeals to emotion are the only way to motivate an audience. There seems to be nothing inherently wrong with a lawyer presenting her case in a way that favorably affects the opponent, judge, or jury. Why, then, was Plato so opposed to it? Is it wrong for attorneys to inject emotion into argument? Is it a matter of degree? Where does one draw the line?

Appeals to emotion are Aristotle's second form of artistic proof. He said a speaker must get his audience "into the right state of mind."[2] Aristotle said appeals to emotion are more important to legal argument than to other forms of persuasion. Just as courtroom attorneys need to put their audience in the right state of mind, legal writers need to make their readers favorably disposed to their arguments. This chapter addresses just a few of the ways a legal writer can appeal to her audience's emotion and motivate it to take action in her client's favor. They include developing an overarching theory of the case, stating the facts and rules of law from the client's point of view, using policy arguments to put the client's dispute in a larger perspective, and minimizing the impact of the opponent's arguments through effective counter-argument.

---

1.   *See Phaedrus, in* PLATO, *supra* ch. 2, note 5, at ¶¶ 237d–238c and 260a–261b.

2.   ARISTOTLE, RHETORIC, *supra* ch. 2, note 34, at bk. 2, ch. 1, p. 91.

# A. THEORY OF THE CASE

An effective means of persuasion is to develop what lawyers often call the "theory of the case." The theory of the case is the lawyer's umbrella theory or ultimate reason why the client should prevail. Having a theory of the case means being able to complete the following sentence: "My client should win because ..." All arguments, both oral and written, that support the client's position should be consistent with this theory. The theory of the case combines appeals to logic, emotion, and credibility in the form of factual, legal, and policy arguments, but the emphasis is on emotional appeals. In the Starbucks matter,[3] for example, Starbucks' theory of the case might be that the Texas statute protects all producers of agricultural products, including products that contain combinations of agricultural products. This interpretation of the statute, Starbucks might add, best protects the state's economy. Consumers for Safe Products (CSP), on the other hand, might argue that the statute is intended to protect plaintiff farmers and fishermen, who most need protection from false statements that cannot be corrected before their products spoil and can no longer be sold.

The briefs in *Clinton v. Jones*, 520 U.S. 681 (1997),[4] provide good examples of effective but competing case theories. Paula Jones, a former Arkansas state employee, sued sitting President Clinton. She alleged that he had made "abhorrent" sexual advances toward her while he was Governor of the State of Arkansas and that her rejection of those advances led to retaliatory punishment by her supervisors. The United States District Court for the Eastern District of Arkansas granted Clinton's request for temporary immunity from suit during his presidency. 869 F. Supp. 690 (E.D. Ark. 1994). Although the court held that the trial could not go forward while Clinton was still in office, it held that discovery of relevant factual information in accordance with ordinary pre-trial procedures could proceed. Both parties appealed, and the United States Court of Appeals for the Eighth Circuit reversed the district court's ruling on immunity and affirmed its ruling that discovery could proceed. 72 F.3d 1354 (8th Cir. 1996). On appeal to the United States Supreme Court, Clinton and Jones adopted unique theories of the case that helped crystallize their arguments. In the end, the Supreme Court ruled that Clinton was not immune from suit during his presidency for unofficial actions and that forcing him to defend himself while still in office did not violate separation-of-powers principles. 520 U.S. at 695, 703.

## 1. COMPETING THEORIES OF THE CASE IN *CLINTON V. JONES*

The theories of the parties were in direct opposition. Clinton's goal was to postpone the litigation, and he argued he was too busy to take time away from the presidency to defend himself. He also argued that it would be an unconstititutional violation of separation-of-powers principles for the judiciary to

---

3.  *See supra* ch. 5, at 145.

4.  *See supra* ch. 4, at 106.

tell the Chief Executive what to do. Jones, on the other hand, said the president should not be allowed to use his official position to get special treatment. She also argued that, as a practical matter, he was capable of being the president and defending himself in a lawsuit at the same time. Their theories are summarized below in one sentence:

| Clinton | Jones |
| --- | --- |
| The Presidency is a special office; Clinton should not be bothered with the demands of defending against a civil suit while he holds that office. | The president is a man like any other man; requiring him to answer for his actions in a civil suit will not interfere with his presidential duties in any way. |

Masterfully, the lawyers maintained these theories throughout their briefs to the United States Supreme Court. Excerpts from the Statements of the Issue, the Statements of the Facts, and the Headings of their arguments are set forth below. As you read them, look for the parties' recurring reliance on these theories.

## a. STATEMENTS OF THE ISSUE

| Clinton | Jones |
| --- | --- |
| Whether the litigation of a private civil damages action against an incumbent President must in all but the most exceptional cases be deferred until the President leaves office.[5] | This uncomplicated civil action for damages against petitioner, who is President of the United States, for acts committed before he became President, bears no possible relation to his official responsibilities. No showing was made in the district court that the lawsuit, or any aspect of it, would impair the functioning of the presidency.[6] |

What do you notice first about these issue statements? Perhaps that one is considerably shorter than the other. Ironically, Jones' statement of the issue, which contains almost twice the number of words that Clinton's does, states that the issue before the court is not complicated. Does the length of the issue statement matter in terms of its emotional appeal?

Clinton's statement of the issue has an objective quality to it with its use of "whether" and relatively neutral language (with the exception perhaps of "exceptional"). Clinton's issue statement makes no mention of the substance of the plaintiff's allegations, only that this is a private action for damages. By omitting the substance of the allegations, the issue statement focuses the reader

---

5.　Brief of Petitioner at i, *Clinton v. Jones*, No. 95–1853, 520 U.S. 681 (1997).

6.　Brief of Respondent at i, *Clinton v. Jones*, No. 95–1853, 520 U.S. 681 (1997).

on the "real issue" of immunity to suit. The statement suggests the answer is an obvious "yes," except in the most "exceptional" cases. That Jones' ordinary civil suit is unexceptional is implicit. Jones' issue statement, on the other hand, is more frank and conversational. It seems to make the following argument: This is an "uncomplicated civil action" despite Clinton's efforts to make it sound full of complex constitutional law issues, forcing Clinton to answer to a sexual harassment allegation "bears no possible relation" to his being president, and Clinton has been unable to demonstrate that "any aspect" of the litigation will interfere with "the functioning of the presidency." Which of these statements of the issue is more successful? Why?

## b. EXCERPTS FROM STATEMENTS OF THE FACTS

### Clinton's Statement of Facts

*Petitioner William Jefferson Clinton is President of the United States. On May 6, 1994, respondent Paula Corbin Jones filed this civil damages action against the President in the United States District Court for the Eastern District of Arkansas. The complaint was based principally on conduct alleged to have occurred three years earlier, before the President took office. The complaint included two claims arising under federal civil rights statutes and two arising under state tort law, and sought $175,000 in actual and punitive damages for each of the four counts.* [1] ...

*1. The first two counts allege that in 1991, when the President was Governor of Arkansas and respondent a state employee, he subjected respondent to sexual harassment and thereby deprived her of her civil rights in violation of* 42 U.S.C. §§ 1983, 1985 (1994)....

*The President moved to stay the litigation or to dismiss it without prejudice to its reinstatement when he left office. He asserted that such a course was warranted by the singular nature of the President's Article II duties and by principles of separation of powers. The district court stayed the trial until the President left office, but held that discovery could proceed immediately "as to all persons including the President himself."*

*The district court reasoned that "the case most applicable to this one is Nixon v. Fitzgerald, [457 U.S. 731 (1982)]", which held that a President is absolutely immune from any civil liability for his official acts as President. The district court ... concluded that a significant part of the rationale in Fitzgerald did apply here: [T]he majority opinion by Justice Powell [in Fitzgerald] is sweeping and quite firm in the view that to disturb the President with defending civil litigation that does not demand immediate attention ... would be to interfere with the conduct of the duties of the office.* [7]

Clinton's statement of the facts diverts the reader's attention from the substance of the plaintiff's claims just as his issue statement did. The statement begins by emphasizing the gravity of the case before the court: "Petitioner William Jefferson Clinton is President of the United States." It proceeds to summarize the procedural history of the case, which gives the statement an objective tone.

---

7.   Brief of Petitioner, *supra* note 5, at 1–3.

The substance of Jones' allegations is relegated to a footnote, presumably to diminish its impact. By referring to the "singular" nature of his position and the principles of separation of powers, Clinton takes the opportunity to summarize the arguments he made before the district court and echo his theory of the case. Finally, the fact statement summarizes the reasoning of the district court that Clinton will urge the Supreme Court to adopt.

**Jones' Statement of Facts**

*In Arkansas on May 8, 1991, respondent Paula Corbin Jones was a $6.35–an–hour state employee, and petitioner William Jefferson Clinton was the Governor. The complaint alleges that both were at the Excelsior Hotel in Little Rock that day for the Governor's Quality Management Conference. While working at the conference registration desk, Mrs. Jones (Miss Corbin at that time) and a coworker were approached by Danny Ferguson, a state trooper assigned to Governor Clinton's security detail. Trooper Ferguson told Mrs. Jones that "[t]he Governor would like to meet with you" in a suite in the hotel, and gave her a piece of paper with the suite number written on it.... The Governor then made a series of verbal and physical sexual advances toward Mrs. Jones ... On May 6, 1994, ... Mrs. Jones filed suit ... in the United States District Court for the Eastern District of Arkansas....*

*Mr. Clinton did not answer the complaint, but instead requested and obtained an order allowing him to defer a response pending a motion to dismiss on grounds of "presidential immunity." On August 10, 1994, he filed what he called a "Motion to Dismiss on Grounds of Presidential Immunity." ... Mr. Clinton argued that "immunity for the duration of the President's tenure is constitutionally mandated in the instant case." ... Mr. Clinton's motion was predicated simply upon his occupancy of the Office of President of the United States. He made no factual showing that any aspect of the pretrial or trial proceedings would hinder him from carrying out the duties of that Office.*[8]

Jones' statement stands in stark contrast to Clinton's. First, it begins by attempting to garner sympathy for Jones as being less powerful than Clinton and subordinate to him: "In Arkansas on May 8, 1991, respondent Paula Corbin Jones was a $6.35–an–hour state employee, and petitioner William Jefferson Clinton was the Governor." It proceeds to describe in graphic detail the events of the alleged harassment—most of which are deleted here—to cast Clinton in the worst possible light. The second paragraph explains that Clinton "did not answer the complaint, but instead requested and obtained an order" granting him "presidential immunity." The reference to Clinton "not answering" the complaint suggests Clinton has been almost evasive, and the quotations around "presidential immunity" cast doubt on the legitimacy of immunity in this case. Jones' claim that Clinton "made no factual showing" that the suit would interfere with his ability to carry out the duties of his office suggests that Clinton's immunity argument is theoretical at best.

---

8.   Brief of Respondent, *supra* note 6, at 1–4.

You may want to read the full statements of fact online to see other techniques the parties used to make their facts of the case emotionally appealing to the court.

## c. MAJOR AND MINOR HEADINGS

Headings are used to organize an argument by its issues and sub-issues. Major headings are often used to introduce discrete but related issues. They are often numbered using roman numerals and are set in capital letters. Minor headings are used under major headings to further subdivide an issue. They are often lettered "A," "B," "C," and so on and conform to *Bluebook* Rule 8 or *ALWD Citation Manual* Rule 3.1.[9] Issues can be further divided within the minor headings using numbers and, then, small roman numerals. As visual cues, headings underscore the writer's main points as the argument progresses. As you see them printed below, headings are usually set out together at the beginning of a party's brief for the court's convenience.

**Clinton's Headings**

*I. PRIVATE CIVIL DAMAGES LITIGATION AGAINST AN INCUMBENT PRESIDENT MUST, IN ALL BUT THE MOST EXCEPTIONAL CASES, BE DEFERRED UNTIL THE PRESIDENT LEAVES OFFICE*

*A. A Personal Damages Action Against An Incumbent President Would Interfere With The Discharge Of A President's Article II Responsibilities And Jeopardize The Separation Of Powers*

*1. The President, Unlike Any Other Official, Bears Sole Responsibility For An Entire Branch Of Government*

*2. To Subject An Incumbent President To Civil Litigation In His Personal Capacity Would Be Inconsistent With The Historic Understanding Of Relations Between The Executive And Judicial Branches*

*3. Civil Damages Litigation Against A Sitting President Would Seriously Impair The President's Ability To Discharge His Constitutional Responsibilities*

*4. Criminal Cases Where A President Has Been A Third–Party Witness Provide No Precedent For Requiring A Sitting President To Participate As A Defendant In Civil Damages Litigation*

*B. "Case Management" By The Trial Court Does Not Mitigate, But Instead Exacerbates, The Separation Of Power Problems Created By Suits Against An Incumbent President*

*1. "Case Management" By Federal District Courts Impermissibly Entangles The Branches Of Government By Permitting Courts To Examine, And Re-order, Executive Branch Priorities*

---

**9.** THE BLUEBOOK: A UNIFORM SYSTEM OF CITATION R. 8, at 76–78 (Columbia Law Review Ass'n et al. eds., 18th ed. 2005) [hereinafter BLUEBOOK]; ALWD CITATION MANUAL 19–20 (3d ed. 2006).

    2. *"Case Management" By State Trial Courts Is Inconsistent With Principles Of Federalism Inherent In The Constitutional Scheme*

    C. *The Relief Sought Here Is Not Extraordinary, And Would Not Place the President "Above The Law."*

        1. *Deferring Litigation Is Not Extraordinary*

        2. *Presidents Remain Accountable For Private Misconduct*

*II. THE LITIGATION OF THIS PARTICULAR PRIVATE DAMAGES SUIT AGAINST THE PRESIDENT SHOULD, IN ANY EVENT, BE DEFERRED*

    A. *Several Factors Weigh Heavily In Favor Of Deferring This Litigation In Its Entirety*

    B. *At A Minimum, The District Court's Decision To Stay Trial Should Have Been Sustained*

        1. *The Court Of Appeals Lacked Jurisdiction Over Respondent's Cross Appeal*

        2. *The Court Of Appeals Erred In Reversing The District Court's Decision To Stay Trial In This Case*

Clinton's issue statement effectively telegraphed his theory of the case at a glance. The headings, on the other hand, are quite detailed. They raise complex constitutional and other legal issues, each of which has been highlighted by a heading. Does the number of major and minor headings here effectively convey the sense that it is no simple matter for the court to force a president to defend himself in a private suit? Notice how the major headings signal the flow of Clinton's argument. The first major heading argues that the court has virtually no choice but to grant immunity in this case. The second major heading sets forth Clinton's alternative argument: Even if the court has the power to force the president to defend himself, this is not an appropriate case for exercising that discretion. Clinton's theory of the case is thus echoed in these headings: Litigation can only proceed against a sitting president in "exceptional" cases and to permit the case to proceed here would "interfere with the discharge of a president's Article II responsibilities and jeopardize the separation of powers."

### Jones' Headings

*I. THE TEMPORARY PRESIDENTIAL IMMUNITY ASSERTED BY PETITIONER IS LEGALLY INSUPPORTABLE AND IS UNNECESSARY TO PROTECT THE INTERESTS OF THE PRESIDENCY*

    A. *The immunity case law does not support petitioner's immunity claim*

    B. *Petitioner's immunity claim would be contrary to the intention of the Framers, is not supported by any decisions of this Court, and would place petitioner above the law*

    C. *Petitioner's immunity claim cannot be justified under Article II or the separation of powers*

*1. This simple civil case will not prevent the Executive Branch from accomplishing its constitutionally assigned functions*

*2. Proper judicial case management is sufficient to protect the interests of the Executive Branch in this case and would not violate the separation of powers*

## II. THE COURT OF APPEALS CORRECTLY FOUND THAT, ON THIS BARREN FACTUAL RECORD, THERE IS NO BASIS FOR A STAY OF THE TRIAL OR THE LITIGATION GENERALLY[10]

---

Although Jones' issue statement was almost twice as long as Clinton's, her argument headings are far less detailed than Clinton's. The difference between the parties' headings emphasizes Jones' view that the issues before the court are "uncomplicated." The first major heading addresses Clinton's; it argues there is no legal support for the type of immunity Clinton seeks. Moreover, Jones argues in her second major heading, the Court of Appeals correctly found no factual basis for granting a stay in this particular case. Jones' headings, too, contain her theory of the case: There is no evidence that this "simple case" will interfere with the president's ability to carry out his duties.

---

### *THEORY OF THE CASE EXERCISE*

**Formulate a theory of the case for both parties in the following cases:**

*1. A sixteen-year-old high school student, who has been arrested for shoplifting diabetic testing kit supplies for his indigent grandmother.*

*2. A food supplier to a major grocery store chain has breached its contract to deliver fresh vegetables weekly because it cannot afford the cost of gasoline to deliver them.*

*3. The CEO of a Fortune 500 company has been indicted for "shading" the truth in her company's annual reports so as to avoid consumer panic and a debilitating decline in the company's stock, which will only make matters worse.*

---

# B. CRAFTING ARGUMENTS FROM YOUR CLIENT'S POINT OF VIEW

As illustrated above, there are many ways for parties to communicate their theories of the case in writing. There is more to emotional appeals, though, than the theory of the case. At every opportunity, the advocate should characterize the case from her client's point of view. Like the child who breaks the vase, the advocate attempts to affect the outcome of the case by appealing to emotion. The

---

**10.** *Compare* Brief of Petitioner, *supra* note 5, at ii–iii, *with* Brief of Respondent, *supra* note 6, at ii-iii.

goal is to make the audience sympathetic to the client's case and motivate it to rectify the wrong the client has suffered.

Set forth below is a fictional Texas case, *State v. Opara*. As you read the parties' issue statements, statements of fact, and synthesized rules of law, notice how each is crafted from their point of view.

### State v. Opara

**Facts: Amadi Opara is a legal Nigerian immigrant. He was arrested on October 10, 2008, for possession of and intent to distribute marijuana under state law. The arresting officer, Daniel Blake, has been on the police force for ten years. He noticed Mr. Opara standing outside a gas station at about 7 p.m. on a Friday evening in a dark corner of the station's parking lot. According to Officer Blake, Opara appeared nervous, had his hands in his pants pockets, and looked up and down the street and into the station several times. The officer pulled into the parking lot with his police cruiser. When Mr. Opara saw the car, his eyes widened, and he started to walk away. Officer Blake suspected he was engaged in criminal activity and stopped him to investigate. A subsequent frisk of Mr. Opara revealed a bag of marijuana in his pocket. Counsel for Mr. Opara has moved to suppress the evidence as obtained in violation of the Fourth Amendment to the United States Constitution.**

The Fourth Amendment to the United States Constitution prohibits unreasonable searches and seizures. Since Officer Blake did not have an arrest warrant, the stop and frisk of Opara were unconstitutional unless Blake had reasonable, articulable suspicion that Mr. Opara was or was about to be engaged in criminal activity. *See Terry v. Ohio*, 392 U.S. 1 (1968). As with consent,[11] courts determine reasonable, articulable suspicion by examining the totality of the circumstances. The following factors are relevant to finding reasonable, articulable suspicion: (1) the officer's experience and training, (2) the suspect's presence in a high-crime area, and (3) the defendant's behavior, including nervousness and flight. The state's theory of the case is that Officer Blake, who has many years of experience, reasonably suspected that a man standing in the dark on a Friday evening and appearing both nervous and evasive was preparing to rob the gas station. The defendant's theory of the case is that Mr. Opara was standing outside the gas station minding his own business when an overzealous police officer assumed that a black man standing outside a gas station must be planning to rob it.

## 1. ISSUE STATEMENTS

The parties phrase the issue to the court as follows:

---

11. *See supra* ch. 5, at 176.

| Counsel for the State | Counsel for Opara |
|---|---|
| Did Officer Blake have reasonable, articulable suspicion to stop and frisk the defendant, who stood in the dark outside a gas station, appeared to be casing it, had his hands in his pockets, and began to flee when he saw the officer pull his car into the station's parking lot? | Did the officer violate Mr. Amadi Opara's Fourth Amendment rights when, without a warrant, he stopped and frisked him for standing outside a gas station waiting for a friend to pick him up? |

Notice the difference between the two issue statements: Both parties ask a question to be answered in the affirmative, but the same legal question is phrased from opposing points of view. The state's issue statement focuses on the reasonableness of the officer's actions, whereas the defendant's issue statement focuses on the violation of his constitutional rights. In the same vein, the state emphasizes the facts indicating the officer reasonably suspected Opara was engaged in imminent criminal activity, while the defendant emphasizes the facts that indicate he was minding his own business when Officer Blake stopped him. Notice also the attempts to personalize both the officer and the defendant by referring to them by name. What else do you notice about the two different issue statements?

## 2. STATEMENTS OF FACT

In both objective and persuasive writing, the statement of facts highlights the legally significant facts of the case, including those that establish context for the reader and those critical to resolving the legal issues. In persuasive writing, the statement of facts needs to tell a compelling story—a story that will stir the audience's emotion. Although it is natural to emphasize favorable facts and deemphasize unfavorable ones, the legal writer has an ethical obligation to state the facts accurately, without intentionally misleading the reader.[12] Typically, facts are set forth in chronological order unless there is a good reason to do otherwise. As you read the following statements of fact, try to identify the techniques the writers use to create a sympathetic story for their clients.

---

**Counsel for the State**

In the early evening hours of Friday, October 10, 2008, veteran Officer Randall Blake observed a young, black male loitering outside the Exxon gas station on Glebe Road in an area known for habitual drug trafficking and store robberies. The man stood in a dark corner of the parking lot, away from the spotlights that illuminated the entrance to the station. Officer

---

12. *See infra* ch. 7, at 205.

Blake noticed that the man appeared nervous: He kept his hands in his pockets, kept looking up and down the street, and glanced into the station several times. Familiar with typical "casing" behavior, the officer drove into the parking lot to investigate further. As Officer Blake's cruiser entered the lot, he saw a look of surprise cross the defendant's face. The defendant turned abruptly and walked away briskly. Believing the defendant to be acting evasively, Blake stopped the cruiser and exited. Although he had no warrant to arrest the suspect, he conducted a routine *Terry* stop and frisk. The frisk produced a bag of marijuana, which Officer Blake retrieved from one of the defendant's pants pockets and seized. The defendant was then charged with possession of and intent to distribute marijuana.

<u>Counsel for Opara</u>

The defendant, Amadi Opara, emigrated legally from Nigeria in 2004 and is working towards U.S. citizenship. On the night of October 10, 2008, Mr. Opara stood outside the Exxon gas station one block from his apartment waiting for a friend to pick him up and drive him to work. Although Mr. Opara cannot afford the luxury of a car, he earns enough money working as an office janitor to pay for his own apartment. As Mr. Opara waited for his ride, Officer Blake observed him standing at the far end of the parking lot so as to be out of the way of traffic moving in and out of the station. It was a bit chilly that night, so Mr. Opara had his hands in his pockets, and he moved about a bit to keep warm. Mr. Opara did not see the officer's cruiser before it entered the parking lot. When he did notice it, he was surprised and moved to the opposite side of the lot so as to get out of the cruiser's way. The next thing Mr. Opara knew, the officer exited his vehicle and accosted him, peppering him with questions. As soon as the officer got close enough to Mr. Opara, he spun him around and frisked him. The officer pulled a soft baggie out of the defendant's back pants pocket that contained a small amount of marijuana. At no time did the officer explain to the defendant why he had been stopped or frisked.

Notice how completely different these statements are of the same event. What is your sense of the situation from the state's and the defendant's point of view? Are the statements successful in conveying the parties' theories of the case? Do they feel misleading in any way? At this point, do you feel favorably disposed toward either party? Why?

As the statements of fact from the *Clinton* and *Opara* cases demonstrate, legal writers use them to characterize the case from their clients' point of view. As you learn to craft persuasive statements of fact, consider the following techniques used by the writers in *Opara*:

a. <u>Characterize facts to your advantage</u> and neutralize those facts that hurt your client's case.

In the state's brief, the defendant is described as **"a young, black male loitering outside the Exxon gas station,"** whereas the defendant's brief describes him as standing **"outside waiting for a friend to pick him up."** With regard to the defendant's hands in his pockets, the state describes Opara as appearing nervous: **"He kept his hands in his pockets, kept looking up and down the street ..."** In contrast, the defendant states, **"It was a bit chilly.... Opara had his hands in his pockets, and he moved about a bit to keep warm."**

b. <u>Make effective word choices</u> that suggest the image you want to project.

The state describes Opara as **"loitering"** in the parking lot, whereas the defendant says he just **"stood"** there. According to the state, Opara **"appeared nervous,"** but the defendant says he **"moved about a bit to keep warm."** Although the state describes Opara as having **"walked away briskly"** from the police car, the defendant describes himself as having **"moved to the opposite side"** of the lot. Finally, the state says Officer Blake **"called out"** to Opara, who claims the officer **"accosted him, peppering him with questions."**

c. <u>Begin and end with favorable facts.</u>

The state's statement of facts begins by emphasizing Officer Blake's experience and the defendant's allegedly suspicious behavior: **"In the early evening hours of Friday, October 10, 2008, veteran Officer Randall Blake observed a young, black male loitering outside the Exxon gas station on Glebe Road in an area known for habitual drug trafficking and store robberies."** The statement ends by highlighting that Officer Blake's suspicion was correct: **"The frisk produced a bag of marijuana, which Officer Blake retrieved from one of the defendant's pants pockets and seized. The defendant was then charged with possession of and intent to distribute marijuana."**

The defendant, on the other hand, begins his statement by casting himself in a positive light: **"The defendant, Amadi Opara, emigrated legally from Nigeria in 2004 and is working towards U.S. citizenship."** He concludes the statement by suggesting the unreasonableness of Officer Blake's behavior: **"At no time, did the officer explain to the defendant why he had been stopped or frisked."**

d. <u>Sandwich unfavorable facts between favorable facts.</u>

The state's statement does a good job of downplaying the fact that Officer Blake had no arrest or search warrant by sandwiching that fact between Opara's suspicious behavior and the fact that the officer found marijuana during the course of the frisk. Similarly, the defendant's statement does a good job of minimizing what could be characterized as flight by sandwiching that fact between Opara's status as a legal alien, who might be less familiar with the workings of law enforcement than a U.S. citizen, and the aggressiveness of the officer's behavior.

# 3. SYNTHESIZED RULES OF LAW

In addition to selecting the best cases for citing to controlling rules of law and for making favorable analogies, legal writers use cases to articulate synthesized rules of law from their clients' point of view. Although the rules of law should not be manipulated beyond recognition,[13] they can be stated in such a way as to favor your client's position. Read the opening paragraphs from both parties' arguments on the motion to suppress in *State v. Opara*:

### Counsel for the State

The Supreme Court has consistently upheld the validity of a stop and frisk when the arresting officer articulated a reasonable suspicion that criminal activity was afoot and that the defendant was armed and dangerous. *See, e.g., United States v. Cortez*, 449 U.S. 411 (1981); *Terry v. Ohio*, 392 U.S. 1, 30 (1968). A number of factors present in this case contributed to the officer's reasonable, articulable suspicion, including the officer's experience and training, the defendant's behavior, and his location in a high crime area. *Cortez*, 449 U.S. at 417–18. Based on his ten years of experience, the defendant's suspicious behavior, and the officer's knowledge of the area as a frequent site for drug trafficking and robberies, Blake had reasonable, articulable suspicion that the defendant was involved in criminal activity and potentially armed and dangerous. Officer Blake thus acted in accordance with both his duty as an officer of the law and the defendant's constitutional rights when he conducted a brief, investigatory stop and frisk.

### Counsel for Opara

Adami Opara's Fourth Amendment right to be free from unreasonable searches and seizures was violated in this case. Warrantless stops and searches are *per se* unreasonable under the United States Constitution. U.S. Const., amend. IV. Only a few well-delineated exceptions permit warrantless invasions of privacy, none of which applies in this case. The State argues the arresting officer conducted a valid investigatory stop and frisk of Mr. Opara, while he waited for his ride to work. However, *Terry v. Ohio*, 392 U.S. 1 (1968), prohibits a police officer from stopping a citizen to investigate, unless he has reasonable, articulable suspicion to believe that an individual is engaged in imminent criminal activity.

---

**13.** Legal writers have an ethical obligation to state the law accurately. *See infra* ch. 7, at 205.

*Id.* at 22. To conduct a subsequent frisk, he must also have reasonable articulable suspicion that the individual is armed and dangerous. Reasonable, articulable suspicion is determined by looking at the totality of the circumstances, including the defendant's location and behavior. *United States v. Cortez*, 449 U.S. 411, 417–18 (1981). Where, as here, the suspect, who happens to be a black man, appears to be normal and engages in common, everyday behavior, no reasonable officer could conclude that a *Terry* stop and frisk were permissible.

In these paragraphs, both parties set forth the law regarding warrantless searches and seizures and the criteria for a *Terry* stop and frisk. The difference between the paragraphs is how they articulate the law and what they emphasize. The State's paragraph refers first to the exception to the rule that officers must have warrants to search and seize. By emphasizing the exception to the rule, the state validates Officer Blake's behavior up front and highlights his experience in sensing a potential crime scene. Opara's paragraph, on the other hand, begins by emphasizing an individual's constitutional right to be free from unreasonable search and seizure. Opara characterizes a *Terry* stop and frisk as a narrow exception to the requirements of the Fourth Amendment, which the State has allegedly violated.

In what other ways do the parties set the stage for an argument that will make the audience sympathetic to them?

## 4. POLICY AND OTHER NON–LEGAL ARGUMENTS

Litigators like to say that when the facts are against you, argue the law, and when the law is against you, argue the facts. This means that when the relevant cases have been decided against the client's position, the advocate should focus on the rules of law and distinguish the cases based on factual differences. On the other hand, when the law itself is unfavorable, the advocate should focus on the facts of her case and argue that the law is inapplicable to her case, that the law no longer makes sense, or that the case was decided badly in the first place. In both instances, the real challenge is to distinguish the client's case on its facts. Sometimes neither the facts nor the law supports the client's position.

When the law fails to support an advocate's position, legal writers often turn to policy or other non-legal arguments to persuade their audience. None of these arguments alone is likely to win the case, but they can buttress an otherwise weak argument. Policy arguments come from a variety of sources, ranging from the purpose and legislative history of a particular statute to a court's need to rule consistently in similar cases and write opinions that guide future conduct. Although policy arguments may appeal to reason, credibility, and emotion, they are included in this chapter because they make the party's position *feel fairer*. There are many examples of non-legal arguments that not only helped the party win its case, they changed the course of the common law. Here are just a few:

a. The **use of economic theory to resolve private contract disputes** in *Lake River Corp. v. Carborundum Co.*, 769 F.2d 1284 (7th Cir. 1985).

In *Lake River Corp. v. Carborundum Co.*, the United States Court of Appeals for the Seventh Circuit relied on economic policy arguments to resolve a contract dispute. Lake River had agreed to store, bag, and distribute Carborundum's product (a powder used to manufacture steel) to its Midwest customers. Under the contract, Carborundum guaranteed Lake River a minimum amount of product to be bagged and shipped over a three-year period. At the end of the three years, Carborundum had shipped only 12,000 of the guaranteed 22,500 tons. The plaintiff sued to enforce the damages clause of the contract and recover the difference between the contract price for the full amount of the guaranteed product, had it been shipped, minus what Carborundum had already paid. Carborundum argued that the damages clause was an unenforceable penalty under Illinois law. It also argued that had it performed the contract, Lake River would have lost money because it underestimated its own costs to perform. Judge Posner agreed with Carborundum. Although Lake River was entitled to compensatory damages,[14] he said the damages clause discouraged breach in a situation where it was better for society as a whole than performance under the contract's original terms.[15] Although Posner acknowledged it might seem unfair to protect Carborundum from contract terms it agreed to and on which Lake River relied, it was even worse to give Lake River a huge windfall under the circumstances.[16]

b. The **use of medical-legal history and medical evidence** in *Roe v. Wade*, 410 U.S. 113 (1973).

In *Roe v. Wade*, the plaintiffs challenged the constitutionality of Texas laws that criminalized abortion. At that time, a majority of states, including Texas, prohibited abortion in all cases except where the mother's life was at risk. After three years of litigation, the Supreme Court ruled in 1973 that the Texas statute violated a woman's Fourteenth Amendment right to privacy, which includes the right to terminate a pregnancy.[17] The Court held, however, that her right was not absolute; by the end of the first trimester of pregnancy, the State's interest in protecting the health of the mother is compelling and permits it to regulate abortions performed thereafter. Similarly, once the fetus becomes viable, the State's interest in protecting the health of the unborn child permits it to regulate and even prohibit abortions.

In his opinion, Justice Blackmun referred to the Court's awareness of "the sensitive and emotional nature of the abortion controversy ... and of the deep and seemingly absolute convictions that the subject inspires," as well as the

---

**14.** 769 F.2d at 1292.

**15.** *Id.* at 1289.

**16.** *Id.* at 1288–91.

**17.** 410 U.S. at 153.

Court's desire to resolve the issue "free of emotion."[18] In an apparent attempt to diffuse the emotional intensity of the debate, Blackmun acknowledged the Court's reliance on medical-legal history and medical evidence, most of which had been presented by the plaintiffs.[19] As Blackmun explained, abortions had generally not been illegal either at English common law or in the United States until the mid-nineteenth century.[20] For Blackmun, at least, this fact put the relatively short-lived abortion statutes in some perspective. Relying again on the medical-legal history presented by appellants, Blackmun concluded these statutes were intended to protect the health of the mother more than the life of the fetus.[21] Since abortions in the early 1970s were safer than childbirth, the medical justification for prohibiting them no longer made sense.[22]

    c.  The **use of empirical data** to demonstrate the adverse psychological effects of segregated schools on African-American children in *Brown v. Board of Education*, 347 U.S. 483 (1954).

*Brown v. Board of Education* was a consolidation of several cases from Kansas, South Carolina, Virginia, and Delaware. The plaintiffs were African-American children who alleged that being forced to attend segregated public elementary schools violated their Fourteenth Amendment right to equal protection. In each of the cases, the lower federal courts denied plaintiffs relief based on the "separate but equal doctrine" established in *Plessy v. Ferguson*, 163 U.S. 537 (1896). At trial, the plaintiffs presented empirical data, and the *Brown* court found, that racial segregation in schools (1) affected the plaintiffs' ability to develop citizenship skills and adjust to integrated society, (2) denied them status, power, and privilege, and (3) interfered with their motivation for learning and instilled in the plaintiffs a feeling of inferiority.[23] Nevertheless, the lower court in *Brown* felt compelled to deny relief under *Plessy*. Relying on the lower court's finding of psychological damage to the *Brown* plaintiffs, the United States Supreme Court reversed and overruled *Plessy:* "Whatever may have been the extent of psychological knowledge at the time of *Plessy v. Ferguson*, this finding is amply supported by modern authority."[24]

    As *Lake River Corp. v. Carborundum Co.*, *Roe v. Wade*, and *Brown v. Board of Education* demonstrate, policy arguments are used to convince the court that literal application of the law can lead to unfairness. In *Lake River*, the plaintiff miscalculated its own cost to comply with the original contract. Had Carborundum performed the contract fully, Lake River would have lost money. It simply would have been unfair to enforce the damages clause and reward Lake River for its own miscalculations. In *Roe*, Justice Blackmun was convinced

---

18.  *Id.* at 116.

19.  *See* Brief of Appellants *passim*, *Roe v. Wade*, No. 70–18, 410 U.S. 113 (1973).

20.  410 U.S. at 139.

21.  *Id.* at 148.

22.  *Id.* at 149.

23.  Brief of Appellants at 9; *Brown v. Board of Educ.*, No. 1, 347 U.S. 483 (1954).

24.  347 U.S. at 494.

that the original justification for prohibiting abortions no longer existed, and he fashioned a solution that gave rights to both sides of the debate. In *Brown*, the Court was convinced that the psychological damage of segregation took precedence over *Plessy's* "separate but equal" doctrine. Forcing minority children to attend segregated schools was akin to a moral wrong.

---

### EXERCISE IN CRAFTING ARGUMENTS FROM YOUR CLIENT'S POINT OF VIEW

Your client was stopped and frisked while getting into his car, which was parked in the covered garage of a shopping mall. The arresting officer claimed he had reason to suspect the defendant had been shoplifting and was armed and dangerous. The frisk produced a small handgun in the defendant's back pocket. The defendant argues there was no reasonable suspicion to stop or frisk, and the gun should be suppressed at trial. Rewrite the following issue statement, statement of facts, heading, and rule of law from the *defendant's* point of view:

1. Is an illegal handgun seized in the course of a *Terry* stop based on reasonable, articulable suspicion admissible at trial?

2. As the officer approached the defendant, the defendant hurriedly got into his car looking nervously behind him.

3. THE TERRY STOP WAS PERMISSIBLE BECAUSE THE OFFICER HAD REASON TO BELIEVE THE DEFENDANT HAD BEEN SHOPLIFTING IN THE MALL.

4. As long as the police officer has reason to believe the suspect has engaged in criminal activity, she may conduct a brief, investigatory stop without a warrant. *Terry v. Ohio*, 392 U.S. 1, 30 (1968).

---

# C. ADDRESSING COUNTER–ARGUMENTS

## 1. TYPES OF COUNTER–ARGUMENTS

As lawyers craft their client's arguments, they need to anticipate what their opponent will argue in response. The way they characterize their opponent's arguments can help make the audience sympathetic to their client's position. Opposing arguments, also called counter-arguments, are usually one of two basic types, described below. *See Figure 37.*

> **Argument:**
>
> *If x, plaintiff wins. Plaintiff has proved x. Plaintiff wins.*
>
> *Counter-argument Type 1:*
> *If x, plaintiff wins. Plaintiff has not proved x. Therefore plaintiff loses.*
>
> *Counter-argument Type 2:*
> *Even if x, y negates x. Defendant has proved y. Therefore, plaintiff loses.*

**FIGURE 37**

## a. DENIAL OF THE ALLEGATION

The first type of counter-argument is a denial of the party's allegations: If the plaintiff must prove $x$ to prevail, the defendant argues that the plaintiff has not proved $x$ or that the opposite of $x$ has occurred. In the *Starbucks* case,[25] for example, Starbucks would argue that CSP knowingly disseminated false information to the public that stated or implied its coffee drinks are unsafe. CSP would deny most of these allegations outright. This first type of counter-argument often represents a question of fact for the judge or jury to decide. The question might also be a legal one: Whether a cited case is sufficiently similar to dictate the outcome in the case at hand. For example, Starbucks might argue that under *Thomas Meats v. Safeway* (Tex. 2008),[26] CSP had knowledge of falsity because it failed to investigate the truth of the information contained in its newsletter. CSP might counter-argue that *Thomas Meats* is distinguishable because the defendant in that case did not attempt to verify the truth of its statements, whereas CSP made some effort to do so.[27]

## b. A SUPERSEDING ARGUMENT THAT NEGATES LIABILITY EVEN IF THE ASSERTION IS PROVED

The second type of counter-argument admits the party's allegations but then presents a superseding rule of law or circumstance that negates liability in that particular case: Even if the plaintiff proves $x$, the defendant is not liable because of $y$. This second type of counter-argument often takes the form of an affirmative defense that excuses or limits the defendant's liability in a

---

**25.** *See supra* ch. 5, at 145.

**26.** *See supra* ch. 5, at 146.

**27.** *See id.*

civil or criminal context. Typical affirmative defenses in a civil context include contributory negligence, assumption of the risk, consent, and even statutes of limitation, which prevent liability if the plaintiff fails to assert its rights after a designated period of time has elapsed. Insanity, necessity, and self-defense are a few examples of affirmative defenses in a criminal context.

## 2. MINIMIZING THE IMPACT OF COUNTER–ARGUMENTS

In persuasive writing, advocates try to anticipate their opponent's arguments and minimize their impact on an emotional level. The goal is to persuade the audience that your opponent's arguments have been factored into your argument and do not present a legal or ethical problem. Although it is prudent to address your opponent's counter-arguments to some degree, only those counter-arguments that present a real problem for your client's position should be incorporated into your own argument. Under no circumstances do you want to make your opponent's argument for her—you might end up making a better argument than your opponent would. The following examples of addressing counter-arguments are taken from the *Starbucks v. CSP*, *Clinton v. Jones*, and *State v. Opara* cases that appear throughout the book.

### *Example 1: Starbucks v. CSP*

To succeed, Starbucks must argue that CSP disseminated false information about its coffee drinks.[28] It must also argue that coffee drinks are perishable food products because they are derived from products of agriculture and sold in a form that decays beyond marketability within a limited period of time.

Set forth below are two ways Starbucks might anticipate CSP's counter-argument (a type 1 counter-argument) that coffee drinks are not food products of agriculture under the Texas statute. As you read them, decide which one is more effective.

**a. CSP will argue that Starbucks coffee drinks are not food products under the disparagement statute. *See The Pet Barn, Inc. v. Holmes* (Tex. 2004). In that case, the owner of a pet food store sued a disgruntled employee, who suggested the plaintiff's pet snacks were unsafe. The snacks were made from agricultural ingredients such as flour, chicken stock, and salt. The court held that the baked snacks were not a food product of agriculture because they were a "*combination* of products of agriculture, not a *sole* product of agriculture," as the statute contemplates. *Id.* Unlike the pet snacks in *The Pet Barn*, the agricultural ingredients in Starbucks coffee drinks are not baked together in a way that changes their essential character. The fact that Starbucks mixed these ingredients together does not negate the fact that they are all agricultural products. Thus, *The Pet Barn* does not preclude a finding**

---

28.  *See supra* ch. 5, at 146.

that Starbucks coffee drinks are "food products of agriculture" under the statute.

*b.* The fact that Starbucks coffee drinks are a *mixture* of agricultural products does not prevent the drinks from being a "food product" under the disparagement statute. *See Salad Days v. Marriott, Inc.* (2007) (holding that a mixture of agricultural ingredients is still a product of agriculture for purposes of the statute).[29] To the extent CSP relies on *The Pet Barn, Inc. v. Holmes* (2004), it is distinguishable. In that case, the court held that a baked pet snack made from agricultural ingredients was not a food product under the statute. *Id.* The court relied on the fact that the baking process used to manufacture the snack converted the ingredients into something new, like a chemical compound. *See id.* In this case, the products used to make Starbucks coffee drinks are simply mixed together; the process of combining them does not convert them into something new. *See Salad Days.*

Although you may not be persuaded that *Pet Barn* is distinguishable, *Version b* does a better job of anticipating and diminishing CSP's reliance on it. Instead of making CSP's argument first and then disputing it (as *Version a* does) *Version b* begins with Starbucks' *response* to the anticipated counter-argument by citing *Salad Days* first. By demonstrating its anticipation of CSP's reliance on *Pet Barn* and distinguishing it, Starbucks minimizes the impact of that case were CSP to rely on it. *Version b* has the added advantage of literally shrinking the size of CSP's counter-argument and expanding Starbucks' response to it. What other principles about addressing counter-arguments can you discern from just this one example?

### *Example 2: Clinton v. Jones*

Recall that President Clinton sought temporary immunity in a private sexual harassment case, seeking to postpone the litigation until he was out of office.[30] He argued that being forced to defend himself while in office would interfere with his duties and violate the separation-of-powers principles. Jones argued there was no legal basis for such immunity and no evidence to suggest that Clinton could not defend himself and serve as president at the same time. Set forth below are excerpts from the parties' briefs on this issue:

#### a. *Clinton's response to Jones' counter-argument:*

*4. Criminal Cases Where A President Has Been A Third–Party Witness Provide No Precedent For Requiring A Sitting President To Participate As A Defendant In Civil Damages Litigation.*

*The respondent and the panel majority below minimized the disruptive effect of civil litigation on the Presidency by comparing the full-scale defense of a personal damages action to the few occasions when a President has testified as*

---

29. *See supra* ch. 5, at 178.

30. *See supra* at 180.

*a non-party witness in a criminal or legislative proceeding. See Pet. App. 22–23 (Beam, J., concurring). This comparison is not plausible. The isolated event of giving testimony in a proceeding to which one is not a party bears no resemblance to the burdens borne by a defendant in a civil action for damages. In fact, the lesson of cases involving Presidential testimony is more nearly the opposite of what respondent and the panel majority say: those cases show that requiring an incumbent President to submit as a defendant in a private damages action would go beyond anything a court has done before, with less justification.[31]*

### b. *Jones' response to Clinton's counter-argument:*

*As the court of appeals observed, Mr. Clinton has presented a "sweeping claim that this suit ... will violate the constitutional separation of powers doctrine ... without detailing any specific responsibilities so [sic] explaining how or the degree to which they are affected by the suit." Pet. App. 12. He made no attempt in the district court to show how this case could possibly keep him from carrying out his official duties. He did not do so for a very simple reason—he cannot.*

*It is not even necessary to look to Mr. Clinton's duties to establish the point. Given its simple factual predicate and the utterly barren record, this case could not be deemed to impose hardship upon the Executive Branch. It has nothing to do with Mr. Clinton's official duties. It is at bottom a very simple dispute about what happened in a very short encounter between two people in a room.[32]*

One of the most striking features of these opposing arguments is their lack of supporting case law. Because there was no case law directly on point, the parties simply made factual arguments. At the outset, Clinton acknowledged Jones' reliance on cases that permitted a president to testify but emphasized that those were cases where the president was not a party to the litigation. He also used the absence of case law to argue that forcing a president to testify as a party to suit while still sitting as president was literally unprecedented. In the end, Clinton seemed to argue that defending himself in the *Jones* case while president would be unfair because it had never happened before. Jones, on the other hand, made a forceful argument that Clinton could not specify how his participation in the litigation would make it hard for him to carry out his official duties. Since no examples of the case's interference with Clinton's duties had been proffered, Jones concluded that it would be fair for the president to defend himself while still in office.

### *Example 3: State v. Opara*

*Opara* involved the *Terry* stop of a defendant arrested for marijuana possession.[33] Officer Randall Blake conducted a *Terry* stop and frisk of the defendant, claiming he had reasonable, articulable suspicion that Opara was engaged in imminent criminal activity as well as armed and dangerous. Blake relied, among other things, on the fact that Opara had acted evasively when he

---

31. Brief of Petitioner, *Clinton v. Jones, supra* note 5, at 26.

32. Brief of Respondent, *Clinton v. Jones, supra* note 6, at 27.

33. *See supra* at 187.

observed Blake approaching. In seeking to suppress the evidence at trial, *Opara* argued that he had simply been walking away from the police cruiser so as to get out of its way.

An example of how the parties might anticipate and try to diminish the impact of their opponent's argument is set forth below. The state's argument is first.

### a. *Opara's Suspicious Behavior Reasonably Led Officer Blake to Believe the Stop and Frisk Were Justified.*

Officer Blake had reason to believe the defendant was engaged in imminent criminal activity because Opara acted both nervously and evasively. *See Illinois v. Wardlow*, 528 U.S. 119 (2000) (holding that flight is suggestive of wrongdoing); *United States v. Mayo*, 361 F.3d 802 (4th Cir. 2004) (holding that nervous behavior can justify a Terry stop). Officer Blake observed the defendant standing in the dark near the gas station in a high-crime area, where he might be attempting to remain unobserved. He had his hands in his pockets, looked into the station and up and down the street several times, and his eyes widened as he observed Officer Blake enter the lot. As in *Mayo*, where the defendant acted nervously by putting his hands in his pockets and avoiding eye contact with the officer, see 362 F.3d at 807–08, the defendant appeared nervous with his hands in his pockets and movement away from the officer. His movement away from the officer further was suggestive of flight, another factor that contributes to reasonable, articulable suspicion. *See Wardlow*, 528 U.S. at 124–25 (holding that running from the scene constituted suspicious behavior); *United States v. Sims*, 296 F.3d 284 (4th Cir. 2002) (holding that the defendant's jerking his head away to avoid eye contact with the officer was evasive).

In contrast, the defendant might argue as follows:

### b. *Officer Blake Has No Reason to Believe Mr. Opara Was Engaged in Criminal Activity.*

The State's attempt to convert Mr. Opara's behavior into nervous and evasive action is just that—an attempt. Although nervousness and flight can be suggestive of wrongdoing, *see Illinois v. Wardlow*, 528 U.S. 119 (2000); *United States v. Mayo*, 361 F.3d 802 (4th Cir. 2004), Mr. Opara did not appear to be either nervous or evasive. In *Mayo*, the Fourth Circuit held that the stop was justified in part because the defendant avoided eye contact with the officer, was breathing heavily, and kept putting his hands into his pockets. Id. at 807–08. In contrast, Mr. Opara stood out of the way in a corner of the parking lot looking for his friend's car. When he noticed the cruiser enter the lot, he simply moved to the other side. The fact that his eyes widened when he saw a police car approaching does not make him suspicious. Moreover, his movement from one side of the lot to the other in no way resembles "flight" as that term is understood. *See Wardlow*, 528 U.S. at 124–25 (holding that running from the scene constituted suspicious behavior); *United States v. Sims*, 296 F.3d 284 (4th Cir. 2002) (holding that the defendant's jerking his head away to avoid eye contact with the officer was evasive).”

Notice how the parties anticipate their opponent's arguments and use the best cases to their advantage. The State takes advantage of the case law on nervousness and flight, arguing that these behaviors contributed to Officer Blake's suspicion and that they are similar to the defendants' behavior in *Mayo* and *Sims*. The defendant acknowledges up front that nervousness and flight can lead to reasonable, articulable suspicion but argues that Opara's behavior did not rise to the level of nervousness in *Mayo* or flight in *Wardlow* or *Sims*.

As these examples from the *Starbucks, Clinton,* and *Opara* cases demonstrate, counter-arguments can be managed or anticipated to minimize their impact. Although an opponent's argument may have a strong logical appeal, a counter-argument can be used to change the audience's emotional response. As between two competing arguments, that which feels the most fair is the one likely to succeed.

---

### AN EXERCISE IN CRAFTING ARGUMENTS FROM YOUR CLIENT'S POINT OF VIEW

**James Hall is the four-year-old son of Dana Hall, who has been convicted of attempted murder and will be incarcerated at least until James is seventeen. Dana Hall's husband (James' father) is deceased; he died soon after James was born. Ms. Hall argued at trial that she acted in self-defense because the victim, her live-in boyfriend, pushed her down the stairs earlier on the same day after repeated emotional and physical abuse (although James never witnessed any of these incidents). While the victim was sleeping, Dana hit him with a shovel, but she does not have a clear memory of the attack. Under state law, James' paternal grandparents have sought to terminate Dana's parental rights and adopt James. Both paternal grandparents are sixty-eight-years-old but in good health and retired. Dana's twenty-year-old brother, Steven Clark, is a personal trainer who works out of his apartment. Steven has temporary custody of his nephew, James, until his mother's release from prison.**

**To terminate Dana's parental rights, James' grandparents must prove that Dana is unfit and that adoption by his grandparents is in James' best interest. Specifically, they argue that Dana's rights should be terminated because she has "failed to maintain a reasonable degree of interest, concern, or responsibility as to [James'] welfare" while in prison. *In re Syck*, 562 N.E.2d 174, 182 (Ill. 1990). They claim that Dana has written only two letters to James and that James has visited Dana only once in the thirteen months since her conviction. Dana argues that she has written only two letters because James cannot read yet, and the prison has denied her requests to send him**

taped messages. As for James' visits, Dana argues that since she was transferred to a prison 300 miles from home, it is nearly impossible to arrange visits for James, but she and her brother, Steven, are doing the best they can. They hope to have enough money saved for James to visit in a month.

For each party, either Dana Hall/Steven Clark or the Hall grandparents, craft (1) a theory of the case, (2) a statement of the issue, (3) a statement of facts, (4) an argument that Dana has or has not maintained a "reasonable degree of interest, concern, or responsibility as to [James'] welfare," and a response to the opposing party's anticipated counter-arguments on this issue. Do no additional research.

# CHAPTER 7

## INVENTION: *ETHOS* IN LEGAL WRITING

■　■　■

*"For the man who seems bad when he speaks must inevitably speak badly."*—**Quintilian**

Aristotle defined *ethos* as "a cause of persuasion when the speech is so uttered as to make [the orator] worthy of belief."[1] Aristotle thought that the audience's trust "should be created by the speech itself, and not left to depend" on the orator's reputation.[2] Successful appeals to *ethos* thus require the orator to be familiar with what his audience is likely to find convincing. Writing some 450 years later, Quintilian, influenced both by Aristotle and Cicero, developed a broader view of *ethos*: The orator's *character*, not just his speech, must appeal to the audience. Only a good man who is free from vice, a lover of wisdom, a sincere believer in his cause, and a servant of the people, can be an orator.[3] *Ethos* "in all its forms" requires that an orator be a "good and even-tempered person. Since the orator needs to demonstrate these qualities, if he can, in his client too, he must at any rate possess, or be thought to possess, them himself."[4]

Twenty-first century lawyers must appeal to *ethos* too. Unlike orators though, they usually have to rely on written argument to persuade their audience. In the context of appellate litigation, for example, oral argument is rare. To complicate matters, the adversarial nature of our legal system creates readers who are inclined to doubt. Invariably, they want proof that facts and law are represented accurately. Opponents in particular will question the truth of the writer's premises and the validity of the logic.

To "be worthy of belief," legal writers must be credible and honest. To be credible, a legal writer should not speculate as to facts, and she must cite an adequate amount of authority accurately, comprehensively, and without exaggeration. The writing itself must be professional. In order to file a document

---

1.　Aristotle, Rhetoric, *supra* ch. 2, note 34, bk. 1, ch. 2, at 8.

2.　*Id.* at 8–9.

3.　Quintilian, Institutio Oratorio, *supra* ch. 2, note 61, bk. 12, ch. 1, ¶¶ 3–10, at 199–203.

4.　*Id.* at bk. 6, ch. 2, ¶ 18, p. 55.

with a court or agency, the writer must comply with applicable rules regarding the format of the document. Finally, the writer must conform to rules of grammar, punctuation, and usage, and cite appropriately to legal authority. To be honest is to act in good faith. As members of a bar association, lawyers have an ethical obligation to act in good faith and with candor in all aspects of their clients' representation. Lawyers may not represent two clients who have an interest in the outcome of the same dispute, they must ground allegations in fact and law, and they must disclose to the court any binding authority that is contrary to their client's position.

# A. GAINING CREDIBILITY

## 1. CITE ADEQUATE SUPPORTING LAW

Since legal readers invariably challenge the truth of your premises, you need to provide proof that you have adequately represented the facts and law. In particular, you will need to prove that the law is as you say it is (*i.e.,* that your major premises are at least probably true). As discussed in Chapter Five,[5] legal writers have both the right and the obligation to articulate synthesized rules of law. Their authority is limited only by their need to be accurate and reasonable in their representations. For the rule to be *credible* to the reader, it must be supported by citation to relevant authority and produce arguably fair results. A quick way to lose credibility with the reader is to fail to cite to law that supports your argument or to misrepresent the law in some way.

*Example:*

Assume that in the Starbucks case,[6] you make the following argument that your client's coffee drinks are food products under Texas law:

> **Starbucks coffee drinks are perishable food products.** *See* § 96.1. **The statute defines a perishable food product as "(a) a food product (b) of agriculture or aquaculture that is (c) sold or distributed in a form that will perish or decay beyond marketability within a limited period of [time]."** *Id.* **Although coffee drinks are beverages, which are not normally considered "food" in the ordinary terms, they are food products for purposes of the statute because any ingestible product that contains calories and nutrients is [food]. Although not a sole product of agriculture, they are derived from products of agriculture that are grown and harvested (*i.e.,* the coffee beans) or obtained from farm animals (*i.e.,* milk and cream). Once prepared, the drinks perish or decay beyond marketability within a limited period of [time]. At the very least, they get cold in a few minutes and form mold within a few days. Thus, Starbucks' products qualify for protection under the statute as food products of agriculture.**

---

5.    *See supra* Ch. 5 at 145.

6.    *Id.*

Although the writer has developed good arguments that her client's products are "perishable food products," they are unsupported. In fact, they raise more questions than they answer. Although the statute itself is cited, there is no law cited in support of the synthesized rule on the meaning of "perishable food product." In the absence of authority, the arguments read more like an editorial than a legal argument. Common sense arguments are legitimate when there is no authority to flesh out the meaning of the legal rules, but that is not the case here. For example, *The Pet Barn, Inc. v. Holmes* (Tex. 2004) held that products of agriculture cannot be combinations of products of agriculture and still qualify for protection under the statute. The writer's failure to acknowledge the holding of this case misrepresents the law and weakens her credibility. If she is forced to distinguish *Pet Barn* for the first time in response to her opponent's counter-argument (*i.e.,* that Starbucks coffee drinks combine agricultural products), she will lose more credibility with her audience than she would have if she attempted to distinguish it from the beginning.

Where there is indeed no helpful authority, and you must rely on common sense or policy arguments, explain that to your reader. Only then will your reader give any credence to your seemingly unsupported arguments.

## 2. AVOID HYPERBOLE OF FACTS AND LAW

Exaggeration destroys credibility. Remember Clinton's argument on what the meaning of "is" is?[7] To stretch the truth with regard to the facts or the law is to risk being unworthy of belief. In the *Starbucks* case, it would be an exaggeration to say that coffee drinks are literally "products of agriculture" because they do not grow in the ground and you cannot harvest a coffee drink. The argument is that they are derived or created from products of agriculture, such as coffee beans and milk, and should be treated like products of agriculture regardless of the fact that they have been mixed together. As we have seen, though, that argument requires Starbucks to distinguish *Pet Barn* convincingly. The only way to make a credible argument is to acknowledge *Pet Barn*, distinguish it on the basis of factual differences, and argue that the policy behind the statute supports its application in Starbucks' case. Failure to acknowledge *The Pet Barn* could even be construed as a breach of an attorney's ethical obligation to disclose contrary authority.[8]

## 3. DO NOT SPECULATE ABOUT FACTS, SUCH AS MOTIVE OR OTHER MENTAL STATES

To speculate about missing facts is to walk a tightrope. If your argument relies on facts that do not exist in the record, your audience will assume they are false, and you will fall.

---

7.   *See supra* Ch. 4, at 106.

8.   *See infra* at 210.

*Example:*

In the Opara case,[9] you argue that Officer Blake did not have reasonable, articulable suspicion to stop and frisk Mr. Opara:

> The State's attempt to convert Mr. Opara's behavior into nervous and evasive action must fail. Although nervousness can suggest wrongdoing, *see United States v. Mayo*, 361 F.3d 802 (4th Cr. 2005), Mr. Opara did not appear either nervous or evasive. In *Mayo*, the Fourth Circuit held that a stop was justified in part because the defendant avoided eye contact with the officer, was breathing heavily, and kept putting his hands in his pockets. *Id.* at 807–08. In contrast, Mr. Opara stood in a corner of the parking lot, wondering where his friend, who was taking him to work, could be. When he noticed the cruiser enter the lot, Mr. Opara simply moved to the other side. Just because this was a high crime area and Mr. Opara was a black man, Officer Blake assumed he was about to commit a crime. That Mr. Opara opened his eyes widely when he saw Officer Blake approach does not automatically make him suspicious. Anyone would be startled and afraid under those circumstances, particularly an immigrant experiencing this country's current backlash against illegal immigrants.

Although this argument has a great deal of emotional appeal, it is not grounded in the facts and thus not credible. First, there is no evidence that Mr. Opara wondered where his friend could be. Although this fact would help make Mr. Opara's behavior seem more benign, it is not in the record. This form of speculation is inappropriate and borders on a violation of the ethical obligation to have evidentiary support for each factual allegation made to the court.[10] Second, if Officer Blake suspected Mr. Opara of wrongdoing in part because he is black, that could violate Mr. Opara's equal protection rights under the Fourteenth Amendment to the United States Constitution. Without any factual support, this allegation is even more outrageous. Finally, it is stretching the truth to say that Mr. Opara was afraid of Officer Blake because all immigrants are afraid of police officers.

# B. PROFESSIONALISM

The lawyer's first opportunity to make a good impression is the physical appearance of the document that she sends to opposing counsel or that she files with a court or agency. The professionalism of the document itself is like the icing on a cake: It is the first thing the reader sees. If the icing is sloppy or unappealing, the reader will suspect there is something wrong with the cake too. Many of the issues relating to professionalism in writing are addressed later in Chapter Nine on style, including common legal writing conventions; grammar, punctuation, and usage; and proper citation to legal authority. Proficiency

---

9.   *See supra* Ch. 6 at 187.

10.   *See infra* at 209.

in these areas helps the writer communicate professionally and effectively, signaling her socialization into the legal community. For the moment, though, read the following sample paragraph from the *Starbucks* case on coffee drinks qualifying as perishable food products:

### I. Starbuck's coffeedrinks are perishable food product

**Starbucks' coffee drinks are perishable food products as defined by the Texas statue. § 96.1 The statue defines a perishable food product as "a food product of agriculture or aquaculture that is sold or distributed in a form that will perish or decay beyond marketability within a limited period of time. *Id.* Although coffee drinks is a beverage, which are not normally considered 'food' in ordinary terms, they are food products in this context.because they contain calories and nutrients. Although not a sole product of agriculture, they are derived from products of or obtained from farm animals such as milk and cream. Once prepared, they perishes or decay within a limited period of time. Thus, Starbucks' products thus qualifyies for protection under the statute.**

Did you find this paragraph frustrating and hard to read? It is riddled with inconsistencies and typographical, grammatical, and punctuation errors. The lack of professionalism calls into question the integrity of the writer's analysis, even though the analysis is basically sound (even if unsupported). Maintaining a high degree of professionalism is thus essential to maintaining credibility with your reader.

Courts have not hesitated to comment on and, in some cases, dismiss complaints and impose sanctions for unprofessional submissions. For example, in *In re Generes,* the Court of Appeals for the Seventh Circuit imposed sanctions for pursuing a frivolous appeal in part because " 'the briefs ... submitted to this court [were] poorly organized, replete with typographical and grammatical errors, and sorely lacking in relevant legal authority.' "[11] With regard to a criminal indictment riddled with grammatical errors, the Supreme Court of Mississippi said it "would receive an 'F' from every English teacher in the land."[12] The document was so "grammatically unintelligible," the court was moved to quote Shakespeare: "It cannot be gainsaid that all the perfumes of Arabia would not eviscerate the grammatical stench emanating from this indictment. *Cf.* W. Shakespeare, Macbeth, Act V, sc. 1, lines 56–57."[13] As one might expect, grammatical, punctuation, and spelling errors have led courts to find the lawyers who submitted them incompetent. In *In re Hawkins,* the Minnesota Supreme Court held that a lawyer's "repeated filing of documents rendered unintelligible by numerous spelling, grammatical, and typographical errors were sufficiently

---

11. 69 F.3d 821, 826 (7th Cir. 1995) (quoting the district court judge).

12. *Henderson v. State,* 445 So.2d 1364, 1365 (Miss. 1984).

13. *Id.* at 1367 n.1.

serious that they amounted to incompetent representation."[14]

# C. GOOD FAITH AND CANDOR TO THE TRIBUNAL

Just as legal writers must be credible to appeal to *ethos,* they must act in good faith and with candor to the tribunal. These obligations are set forth in the American Bar Association's Model Rules of Professional Conduct enacted in 1983 and most recently amended in 2002.[15] To date, all states except California, Maine, and New York have adopted the Model Rules. California and Maine have adopted their own rules, and New York follows the predecessor code, the ABA's Model Code of Professional Responsibility.[16] As a whole, rules of professional conduct seek to (1) identify typical ethical dilemmas faced in the ordinary course of practicing law, and (2) prescribe appropriate conduct to ensure honesty and fairness in the legal profession. Several of these rules address the lawyer's need to avoid conflicts of interest that call her arguments into question, to have a factual basis for every allegation, to have legal support for each argument she makes, and to disclose to the court any authority directly contrary to her client's argument.

## 1. AVOID CONFLICTS OF INTEREST

Rule 1.7 of the ABA's Model Rules prohibits lawyers from representing clients if doing so gives rise to a conflict of interest. A conflict of interest is a situation where the lawyer represents two (or more) opposing parties to the same dispute. Rule 1.7 states that a concurrent conflict of interest exists and a client should not be represented if

1) the representation of one client will be directly adverse to another client; or

2) there is a significant risk that the representation of one or more clients will be materially limited by the lawyer's responsibilities to another client, a former client or a third person or by a personal interest of the lawyer.[17]

Under certain circumstances, a lawyer may still represent clients where there is a "conflict of interest," but the clients involved in the conflict must give

---

**14.** *In re* Hawkins, 502 N.W.2d 770, 770–71 (Minn. 1993). For a more detailed discussion of the cases cited in notes 11–14 and other opinions that discuss unprofessional legal writing, *see, e.g.,* Judith D. Fischer, *Bareheaded and Barefaced Counsel: Courts React to Unprofessionalism in Lawyers' Papers,* 31 SUFFOLK U. L. REV. 1, 20–37 (1997).

**15.** MODEL RULES OF PROF'L CONDUCT (2008), *available at* http://www.abanet.org/cpr/mrpc/home.html.

**16.** *See* Center for Professional Responsibility of the American Bar Association, Dates of Adoption of the Model Rules of Professional Conduct by State, http://www.abanet.org/cpr/mrpc/alpha_states.html (last visited October 15, 2008).

**17.** MODEL RULES OF PROF'L CONDUCT, *supra* note 15, R. 1.7(a).

their consent to the representation.[18] This rule prevents lawyers from making arguments that advance their position at the potential cost to another one of their clients. If the lawyer stands to gain regardless of the outcome of the dispute, his arguments are suspect. Rule 1.10 even prohibits lawyers associated in the same firm from representing a client if any member of the firm would be prevented from doing so for conflict reasons.[19]

## 2. ALLEGATIONS SHOULD BE REASONABLY GROUNDED IN FACT AND LAW

Procedural rules governing the filing of documents in court as well as state ethics rules require that lawyers act in good faith with regard to the truth of all their allegations. For example, Rule 11 of the Federal Rules of Civil Procedure states that by signing or submitting any document to a federal district court, a lawyer certifies that "to the best of the person's knowledge, information, and belief, formed after an inquiry reasonable under the circumstances"

(1)  the document has not been filed for an improper purpose;

(2)  all legal arguments are grounded in the law or a non-frivolous argument that the law be changed; and

(3)  all factual allegations have or are likely to have evidentiary support.[20]

A violation of Rule 11 can result in court-imposed sanctions, including injunctive relief and monetary penalties.[21]

In determining whether Rule 11 has been violated, courts apply "a standard of objective reasonableness, focusing on whether 'a reasonable attorney in like circumstances could believe his actions to be legally justified.' "[22] In *F.D.I.C. v. Maxxam, Inc*, for example, the Fifth Circuit affirmed a Texas district's court's award of tens of millions of dollars in costs to Maxxam because the FDIC pursued litigation in an attempt to delay the resolution of a dispute between the parties.[23] *See also, e.g., Clark v. United Parcel Service, Inc.*, 460 F.3d 1004 (8th Cir. 2006) (affirming an award of $21,000 in penalties and attorney's fees for, among other things, "unsupported attempts to controvert facts ... and failures to provide citations to the record.").

Good faith also includes being certain that the law relied on is current: It has not been repealed, overruled, reversed, or otherwise called into serious doubt. As

---

**18.** With the parties' informed consent, confirmed in writing, the lawyer may proceed despite the conflict if (1) she reasonably believes that she will be able to provide competent and diligent representation to each affected client; (2) the representation is not prohibited by law; and (3) the representation does not involve the assertion of a claim by one client against another client represented by the lawyer in the same litigation or other proceeding before a tribunal. *Id.* at 1.7(b).

**19.** *Id.* at R. 1.10(a).

**20.** *See, e.g.,* FED. R. CIV. P. 11 (b)(1)-(4); MODEL RULES OF PROF'L CONDUCT, *supra* note 15, at R. 3.1; MD. CT. R. 1–341.

**21.** *See* FED. R. CIV. P. 11(c)(2), (4).

**22.** *Wallace v. Mercantile County Bank*, 514 F. Supp. 2d 776, 795 (D. Md. 2007) (quoting *In re Sargent*, 136 F.3d 349, 352 (4th Cir.1998)).

**23.** 523 F.3d 566, 589 (5th Cir. 2008).

the United States District Court for the Northern District of Illinois has stated:

> It is really inexcusable for any lawyer to fail, as a matter of routine, to Shepardize all cited cases (a process that has been made much simpler today than it was in the past, given the facility for doing so under Westlaw or LEXIS).[24]

In *Glassalum Eng'g Corp. v. 392208 Ontario, Ltd.*, a Florida state judge chastised the lawyers on both sides of the case for failure to cite binding, relevant case law.[25] Even worse, one of the parties cited *Gonzalez v. Ryder Systems, Inc.*, 327 So.2d 826 (Fla. Dist. Ct. App. 1976), which had been abolished by statute. "By shepardizing the *Gonzalez* case, one would have been alerted that its soundness or reasoning had been questioned in a later case; and by reading that later case, ... one would have discovered that *Gonzalez* is no longer the law."[26] The *Glassalum* court indicated its belief that counsel had failed to notice the Shepard's "questioned" signal (a "q") and concluded that, "as this case so dramatically shows, cases must be shepardized and that when shepardizing, counsel must mind the 'p's' and 'q's.' "[27]

## 3. DISCLOSE FALSE TESTIMONY AND NEGATIVE AUTHORITY

The Model Rules impose a duty on lawyers to speak honestly and openly. A lawyer may not make a false statement to a court or fail to correct a statement she discovers later to be false.[28] If the lawyer knows her client has presented false testimony or plans to do so, she must take remedial measures to correct the problem, including disclosing the falsehood.[29] Most important here, though, is the rule that requires lawyers in written documents

> to disclose to the tribunal legal authority in the controlling jurisdiction known to the lawyer to be directly adverse to the position of the client and not disclosed by opposing counsel.[30]

In *Smith v. United Transp. Union Local No. 81*,[31] a California district court imposed Rule 11 sanctions on defense counsel for relying on a case that had been vacated, a fact which their brief indicated they had to know:

> This is more than a merely sloppy failure to "Shepardize" a case. When confronted with the correct citations and holdings in plaintiff's reply brief

---

**24.** *Gosnell v. Rentokil, Inc.*, 175 F.R.D. 508, 510 n.1 (N.D. Ill. 1997).

**25.** 487 So.2d 87, 88 (Fla. Dist. Ct. App. 1986).

**26.** *Id.*

**27.** *Id.*; *see also Dawson v. California Dep't of Corr.*, No. C 05–2253, 2006 WL 2067078, at *2 (N.D. Cal. July 25, 2006) ("Defense counsel is reminded that she must Shepardize or otherwise check the precedential value of cases cited in briefs filed in this court to be sure they are still good law.").

**28.** *See* MODEL RULES OF PROF'L CONDUCT, *supra* note 15, R. 3.3(a)(1).

**29.** *Id.* at R. 3.3(a)(3).

**30.** *Id.* at R. 3.3(a)(2).

**31.** 594 F. Supp. 96 (S.D. Cal. 1984).

and by the Court during oral argument, counsel for the Union remained unrepentant and declared the plaintiff's motion for sanctions was "the height of arrogance." ... [T]he conduct of the Union's attorneys stands out as an appropriate case for the imposition of Rule 11 sanctions.[32]

As discussed in Chapter 9, the disclosure of contrary authority is easily accomplished through using the signal *contra*.[33] And, as the Northern District of Illinois has said, there is no longer any excuse for not finding contrary authority. Nevertheless, a lawyer may advocate zealously for her client, and she may in good faith distinguish the problematic law to the best of her ability.

---

### QUESTIONS FOR CONSIDERATION

1. In *Rhetoric*, Aristotle said that *ethos* is the orator's most powerful tool for persuasion. Why did he think that? Do you agree? What is the legal writer's most powerful tool?

2. How do you reconcile Quintilian's ideal of the orator as a "good man skilled in speaking" with the fact that lawyers often have to represent clients they do not like and make arguments they do not believe in?

3. On what basis do *you* decide, consciously and unconsciously, if a piece of writing is worthy of belief? Do any of these criteria translate to legal writing? How so?

4. Based on the *Starbucks* case (*see supra* p. 145), identify any credibility or ethical problems with the statements made below. Assume for purposes of this exercise that these statements are contained in documents filed by counsel for Starbucks or CSP in court.

   a. Starbucks: *"There is no support in the law for the claim that products of agriculture cannot be combined and qualify for protection under the false disparagement statute."*

   b. CSP: *"In order to be liable under the disparagement statute, the defendant must have had actual knowledge that the information disseminated was false."*

   c. Starbucks: *"In an effort to destroy Starbucks' reputation, CSP disseminated information stating that it sold dangerous coffee drinks."*

   d. CSP: *"For purposes of finding that the false disparagement statute is inapplicable here, there is no difference between coffee drinks and baked pet snacks."*

   e. Starbucks: *"There is no hard and fast rule in this jurisdiction on how many people must receive false information for it to qualify as "disseminated.""*

---

**32.**  *Id.* at 101.

**33.**  *See infra* p. 294.

# CHAPTER 8

## ARRANGEMENT: LARGE AND SMALL SCALE ORGANIZATION IN LEGAL WRITING

■  ■  ■

*"Neither can embellishments of language be found without arrangement and expression of thoughts, nor can thoughts be made to shine without the light of language."*—Cicero

Arrangement is the canon that guides the order of the orator's speech. In legal writing, it guides the writer's large and small scale organization. The Greeks were the first to articulate an arrangement for speeches: introduction, statement of the facts, argument, and conclusion. To this arrangement, the Romans, notably Cicero, added a statement of the issue, an outline of the arguments to follow, and counter-arguments.[1] In the 1950s, Kenneth Burke summarized the classical arrangement of a speech as

> a progression of steps that begins with an [introduction] designed to secure the good will of one's audience, next states one's own position, then points up the nature of the dispute, then builds up one's own case at length, then refutes the claims of the adversary, and in a final [conclusion] expands and reinforces all points in one's favor, while seeking to discredit whatever had favored the adversary.[2]

This basic pattern appears today in many forms of legal writing, both objective and persuasive. Redundancies were built into the classical arrangement to help the audience focus on and remember the important points of the orator's speech.[3] They appear in contemporary forms of legal writing as well. These redundancies can be frustrating to new legal writers, who feel they keep repeating themselves. It helps, though, to realize that the redundancies were built in for a reason. Legal writers should also be comforted by the fact that as the demands of law practice require lawyers to work even faster and more efficiently, some of them are being eliminated.

---

1.   *See supra* ch. 4, at 103.

2.   KENNETH BURKE, A RHETORIC OF MOTIVES, *supra* ch. 3, note 67, at 69.

3.   *See, e.g.*, ARISTOTLE, RHETORIC, *supra* ch. 2, note 34, at bk. 3, ch. 19, pp. 240–41.

# A. THE ANALYTICAL PARADIGM

## 1. LARGE–SCALE ORGANIZATION

Like a categorical syllogism, legal writing is usually organized deductively, moving from general to specific concepts. Good legal writers organize their analysis *around the issues or controlling rule(s) of law that determine the outcome of a particular case* (not the sources of the rules such as case law) and proceed to address each issue or rule of law in a logical and predictable order. Figure 38 illustrates a case with three issues that need to be resolved to answer the client's question. To learn how to identify the issues, see Chapter Five, pp. 139–40.

**Identity Issues/Rules of Law**

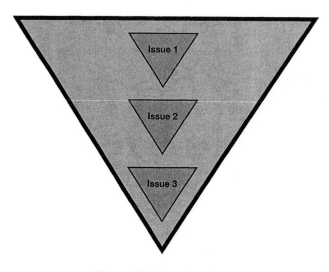

**Overall Conclusion**

**FIGURE 38**

## 2. SMALL–SCALE ORGANIZATION

Each issue has a set of legal rules that needs to be applied to the facts of the client's case. As Figure 38 indicates above, the analysis of each issue should be organized deductively. Depending on the nature of the applicable law, the analysis may involve applying rules to facts as well as comparing the client's case to prior case law. *See Figure 39 below.* Together with anticipated counter-arguments, the deductive model of *rule-application-conclusion* constitutes the paradigm for all legal analysis.

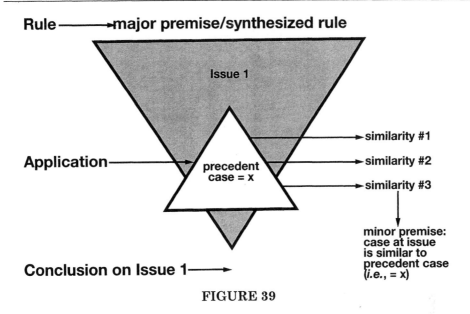

FIGURE 39

# B. OBJECTIVE LEGAL WRITING

The goal of objective legal writing is to inform clients and attorneys about controlling rules of law (or other research results) and the writer's predicted answer to a particular question. Objective analysis is usually for "inside readers" only, meaning it is shared with attorneys and others who can communicate confidentially, without disclosing the information to opposing or third parties. Objective legal writing is written in frank and simple terms, without being argumentative. This type of analysis is used in a countless variety of situations, ranging from assessing the likelihood of success in a litigation matter to whether a client should incorporate his business for tax reasons. It can take the form of a memorandum, opinion letter, or even e-mail. Although objective writing should be an unbiased assessment of your client's questions, it can be a challenge to report your honest opinion when you are trying to help your client achieve certain goals at the same time. Although realism and post-modern philosophies of law suggest that it is not possible to be truly objective in one's point of view,[4] the goal of practitioners is to weigh competing arguments and predict as best they can which argument is likely to prevail in a court of law.

## 1. THE TRADITIONAL LEGAL MEMORANDUM

Of the three forms of objective writing discussed in this chapter, the traditional legal memorandum looks the most like a classical orator's speech. The traditional memorandum has been taught to law students at least since the 1970s, when legal writing courses were first introduced. Before the advent of fax machines, the Internet, or Adobe Acrobat, lawyers often communicated with

---

4.   *See supra* at 83–97.

clients through the mail using this memorandum format. Given the cost today to produce traditional memoranda and most clients' general unwillingness to pay for them,[5] traditional memoranda have been virtually replaced by informal memoranda and e-mail transmissions.[6] A recent survey of Georgetown law graduates suggests that roughly 75 percent of lawyers practicing in a variety of fields write no more than three traditional memoranda per year.[7]

Although traditional memoranda are not as common as they used to be, you may draft them in practice. They may be sent to clients or used to prepare other documents, such as briefs or contracts. In the absence of any guidance as to what form your objective analysis should take, you can feel comfortable using this traditional format. As many respondents to the Georgetown survey indicated, there is no better way to learn how to engage in rule synthesis, deductive reasoning, and analogical reasoning than to draft a traditional memorandum.

## a. ELEMENTS OF A TRADITIONAL MEMORANDUM

The elements of a typical legal memorandum are described below. A sample memorandum in the *Starbucks* case[8] appears at pp. 221–25.

### HEADING

The Heading indicates to whom the memo is written, by whom, for what purpose, and when. *See p. 221.*

### QUESTION PRESENTED

The statement of the legal question(s) to be answered is commonly referred to as the "Question Presented." A well-crafted statement of the Question Presented includes a reference to the controlling jurisdiction or law, the precise legal question, and a short summary of the most significant facts from a legal point of view. The idea is to present the crux of the issue.

There is no one format for drafting Questions Presented as long as they contain the information described above. Typical forms include questions that ask, "Under [state or federal] law, can the client recover for [cause of action], given [these particular facts]?" Lawyers also begin Questions Presented with "whether" or write a sentence or two that describes the scope of their inquiry. Usually, a Question Presented that begins with "whether" ends with a period, not a question mark, because it is a declarative sentence, not a question. *See p. 221.*

---

5.   At a billing rate of $500 per hour, a ten-page memorandum that took five business days to research and write could cost $20,000.

6.   *See* Kristen Konrad Robbins–Tiscione, *From Snail Mail to E–Mail: The Traditional Legal Memorandum in the Twenty–First Century,* 58 J. LEGAL EDUC. 32 (2008).

7.   *Id.* at 36.

8.   *See supra* ch. 5, at 145. All citations to authority in the sample memorandum are fictitious.

## BRIEF ANSWER

The Brief Answer is just what it sounds like: a brief summary of the writer's answer to the question presented. Brief answers should include the basic, overarching rules of law (*e.g.*, the elements of a false disparagement claim), the writer's ultimate conclusion on the application of those rules to the facts (*i.e.*, your answer), and the writer's *reasoning*. The reader is interested in what the law "is," how it applies, and why. Brief Answers summarize the writer's analysis. Lawyers typically do not include formal citations or quotations in their Brief Answers. Even the doubting legal audience will wait for proof (*i.e.*, citations) in the Discussion section. A typical Brief Answer begins with a short phrase like "Probably not," "Unlikely," or "Yes," and then proceeds in a paragraph or two to summarize the writer's analysis in her own words. *See p. 221.*

## STATEMENT OF FACTS

The Statement of Facts should contain just enough background information to provide a context for the client's question and all legally significant facts. At either the beginning or the end of the statement, lawyers typically include the procedural history of the case, if any, and what the client hopes to achieve. The legally significant facts are not always obvious. Some legal writers prefer to write the facts section *after* the Discussion section for that reason. Any facts used in the Discussion section should appear in the Statement of Facts so as not to confuse or surprise the reader. A good technique is to read the Statement of Facts once the Discussion is written to make sure they conform to each other. *See p. 221.*

## DISCUSSION

The Discussion contains the bulk of the writer's analysis: the synthesized rules of law; their application, including potential arguments and counter-arguments; and a predicted outcome for each issue or sub-issue. Citations to all legal authority relied on and signals, where necessary, are included in this section.

Legal readers have certain expectations with respect to objective legal analysis. Most legal readers are impatient; they want to know from the beginning what the writer's ultimate conclusion will be (this is communicated through the Brief Answer as well as at the outset of the Discussion). The typical legal reader also expects an overview of the applicable law at the outset of the Discussion, so she can easily follow the analysis. This overview is the Romans' version of the "outline of arguments" to follow.[9] Thus, it is typical to begin the Discussion section with an introductory paragraph or two that states the writer's ultimate conclusion and summarizes the general rules of law (*e.g.,* elements of a cause of action for false statements under Texas law) that apply to the question presented. This introductory paragraph is also commonly referred to as a "roadmap" for the reader because it foreshadows the analysis. An introductory or roadmap

---

9.  *See supra* at 213 of this chapter and ch. 4, at 103.

paragraph also encourages the writer to proceed deductively, moving from one issue to the next, applying general rules of law to reach specific conclusions. *See p. 222.*

## CONCLUSION

The conclusion summarizes the writer's analysis in more detail than the Brief Answer. It tends to assume the reader's familiarity with the analysis in the Discussion and is thus more specific in summarizing the writer's analysis. The length of the conclusion will vary depending on the complexity of the question(s) presented, but one to two pages are common. As with Brief Answers, Conclusions do not contain signals or citations to authority. *See p. 225.*

## b. ORGANIZATION OF THE DISCUSSION SECTION

The legal writer needs to consider both large-and small-scale organization in the Discussion section, preferably in that order.

### i) LARGE SCALE ORGANIZATION

As stated at the beginning of this chapter, legal analysis is usually organized first by issue and second by the rules of law that determine the outcome of that issue. The easiest way to think about large scale organization is to organize the Discussion according to the synthesized rules of law. For example, if a common law claim has three elements, the Discussion could be organized into three sections, one for each element. *See Figure 38, at 214.* If, for example, the first element had two sub-elements, both would be discussed in order in the first section. Resist the temptation to organize your discussion of the issues around the cases you plan to discuss. Organizing by case law and not by issue may prevent you from synthesizing the cases to form a comprehensive rule at the outset and cause you to repeat or contradict yourself. Once you have figured out the large-scale organization, you are ready to draft the introductory (or roadmap) paragraph that provides the reader with an outline of the discussion to follow.[10] In the *Starbucks* case,[11] for example, the Texas statute contains three elements to be proved. Accordingly, the sample memorandum has an introductory paragraph that outlines the statutory elements for the reader, and each element is discussed in turn. *See Sample Memorandum, p. 221.*

Unless there is a good reason to do otherwise, introductory paragraphs should outline the elements in the same order they appear in the statute, regulation, or case law, and should be discussed in that order as well. An inconsistent organizational pattern is likely to confuse the reader. The rules of law relating to each element, rule, requirement, and the like must then be defined or explained, applied to the facts, and tested with counter-arguments. *See Small*

---

**10.** The roadmap paragraph is akin to the outline of arguments in the Roman speech. *See supra* ch. 4, at 103 and 213.

**11.** *See supra* ch. 5, at 145.

*Scale Organization below.* For complicated analyses, it may help to use headings to divide the discussion visually. Roman numerals are commonly used for that purpose. The convention in memo writing is to cite to legal authority in the text of the document and avoid placing citations in footnotes. *See Figure 40, below.*

## LARGE SCALE ORGANIZATION

• *Organize around rules of law (elements, rules, requirements, etc., NOT cases), moving from general to more specific rules.*

• *Analyze elements, rules, requirements, etc. in order unless a good reason exists for doing otherwise. If so, explain why.*

• *Include an introductory or roadmap paragraph that outlines the analysis for the reader.*

• *Where helpful, use headings to divide the analysis visually.*

*I. ISSUE 1*

　　*A. Sub-issue*

　　*B. Sub-issue*

*II. ISSUE 2*

• *Cite in text as opposed to footnotes.*

### FIGURE 40

## ii) SMALL SCALE ORGANIZATION

The small scale organization of a legal issue may feel awkward or confining at first. Most novice legal writers are unfamiliar with formal deductive reasoning and common law analysis. Generally speaking, the small scale organization of a legal issue should contain the following:

• **a topic sentence that identifies the issue or sub-issue that** the paragraph(s) discuss(es) (it may also include the writer's prediction of the outcome on that issue);

- a statement of the relevant synthesized rule, requirement, element, and the like (and any sub-parts) to be discussed;

- if necessary, an explanation or definition of what the rule, requirement, element, and the like means, including the facts and holding(s) of cited case law;

- the application of the rule and the like to the facts of the client's case, and, where common law applies, comparisons to case law to analogize or distinguish cases; and

- a conclusion on that issue.

The paragraph below is taken from the *Starbucks* sample memorandum, where the writer analyzes the knowledge of falsity element. Although there is no one right way to organize a legal syllogism, this paragraph contains the essentials of good analysis: a topic sentence; a statement of the synthesized rule and an explanation of what the rule means; the application of the rule to the facts of the case, including an analogy to the cited case; and a firm conclusion.

> Turning to the second element, Starbucks is likely to prove that CSP knew the information it disseminated is false. **[TOPIC SENTENCE THAT INCLUDES WRITER'S PREDICTION OF OUTCOME]** Knowledge of falsity can include actual knowledge as well as a reckless indifference to truth. *Thomas Meats v. Safeway*, 10 S.W.3d 45 (Tex. 2007). **[SYNTHESIZED RULE ON KNOWLEDGE]** In *Thomas Meats*, the defendant grocery store posted a sign in its windows saying that the plaintiff's meats were unsafe. **[FACTS OF CITED CASE]** Because the defendant had relied solely on rumors and failed to investigate the truth of those rumors, the court held Safeway's "reckless indifference to the truth was tantamount to knowledge of falsity." *Id.* at 46. **[HOLDING AND COURT'S REASONING IN THOMAS MEATS]** Similarly, CSP's statements regarding the nature of Starbucks' beans are unfounded. Not only is Starbucks unaware of any other source indicating that its beans are not organically grown, CSP "failed to investigate the truth of its statements at least insofar as it did not contact Starbucks to verify them. **[COMPARISON → MINOR PREMISE]** Therefore, Starbucks can argue that CSP's "reckless indifference to the truth" constitutes knowledge of falsity. **[CONCLUSION]**

As you practice deductive writing and analogy within deduction, use this sample as a guide, not as a template, for each paragraph you write. Some issues can be resolved in one paragraph with one simple rule of law, whereas other issues will require several pages of analysis of several rules and sub-rules.

As you become more comfortable with this process and encounter a variety of different legal issues, you may develop other effective patterns of analysis. However, to ensure that your analysis is persuasive, learn at the outset to think and write deductively.

**SAMPLE MEMORANDUM IN *STARBUCKS V. CSP***

To:        Supervising Attorney

From:     Junior Associate

Date:     June 22, 2008

Re:       Starbucks/False disparagement

### QUESTION PRESENTED

Under Texas statutory [law], can Starbucks recover against Consumers for Safe Products [(CSP)] for false [disparagement] when CSP published a statements in its newsletter that Starbucks' organic coffee beans are grown using [pesticides]?

### BRIEF ANSWER

Probably [not]. In order to succeed in a claim for false disparagement, Starbucks must prove three [elements]. With regard to the first element, Starbucks can prove that CSP disseminated information to the public through its newsletter, but [it] is unlikely to prove that the information related to a "perishable food product." Perishable food products must be products of agriculture or aquaculture, and coffee drinks are probably not a product of agriculture but a combination of products, which disqualifies them from protection under the [statute]. Nevertheless, Starbucks is likely to prove the second element, which requires that CSP knew its information was false. Since CSP does not appear to have conducted any investigation as to the truth of its statements, it demonstrated a reckless indifference to the truth that equates to actual knowledge. [ Starbucks can probably also prove the third element, that the information states or implies that the product is unsafe for consumption by the public, by showing that most people associate pesticides with health [risks].

### STATEMENT OF FACTS

Our client is a Starbuck's franchise located in Dallas, Texas. Part of this particular franchise's success is attributed to its campaign advertising the store's exclusive use of organically-grown coffee beans from fair trade sources. CSP is a Dallas-based consumer advocacy group that publishes a monthly newsletter about products sold directly to

**Comment:** Identifies controlling law.

**Comment:** This abbreviation creates a short form to be used throughout the memorandum.

**Comment:** Identifies legal issue.

**Comment:** Identifies significant legal facts which will help resolve issue.

**Comment:** States up front the writer's bottom line.

**Comment:** By stating there are three elements, this sentence creates an outline for the Brief Answer to follow.

**Comment:** Corporations are referred to as "its." Ch. 9, C.11, p. 278.

**Comment:** This part of the Brief Answer summarizes the legal rule of the first element and the writer's analysis and conclusion.

**Comment:** Summary of the legal rule of the second element and the writer's analysis and conclusion.

**Comment:** Summary of the legal rule of the third element and the writer's analysis and conclusion.

**SAMPLE MEMORANDUM**

consumers in the Dallas area. CSP's most recent newsletter contained an article stating that despite Starbuck's advertisements to the contrary, Starbucks' coffee drinks are made from beans that are gown using pesticides. Immediately after the newsletter was distributed, Starbucks' coffee sales dropped significantly, and Starbucks believes the drop in sales is attributable to the newsletter. To Starbucks' knowledge, CSP made no effort to contact Starbucks to verify the statements in its newsletter. Starbucks is interested in filing suit against CSP. This memo addresses just one of several potential [claims].

> **Comment:** The statement identifies the parties, sets forth background as well as significant legal facts, and states the client's goal.

### DISCUSSION

Starbucks is unlikely to succeed in an action against CSP, because it will not be able to prove a portion of the first element that requires it to sell or distribute a "perishable food product." Under Section 96.2 of the Texas false disparagement statute, a person is liable for false disparagement if

> (a) the person disseminates in any manner information relating to a perishable food product to the public;
>
> (b) the person knows the information is false; and
>
> (c) the information states or implies that the perishable food product is not safe for consumption by the public.

Tex. Civ. Prac. & Rem. Code Ann. § 96.2 (Vernon 2007).

Although CSP disseminated information relating to Starbucks' coffee drinks to the public, coffee drinks do not "perish" in the sense that fresh fruits and vegetables do. For that reason, the court is likely to conclude that the statute is not intended to protect Starbucks in this [case].

> **Comment:** This paragraph introduces the reader to the cause of action and its required elements. By stating each of the elements in order, it creates a natural outline for the Discussion to follow. It also makes clear the writer's ultimate conclusion that Starbucks will not succeed in this case and why. An introductory paragraph such as this is often called a "roadmap" paragraph because it indicates to the reader where the analysis is going.

As for the first element, Starbucks must prove that CSP disseminated information regarding a perishable food product to the public. § 96.2(a). [RULE OR MAJOR PREMISE] Since CSP published information about Starbucks' coffee beans in a widely circulated newsletter [MINOR PREMISE RE DISSEMINATION TO PUBLIC], CSP likely disseminated information to the [public]. [CONCLUSION] There is no case law in

> **Comment:** This sentence applies the rule of law on dissemination to the public to the facts to yield a conclusion.

**SAMPLE MEMORANDUM**

this jurisdiction suggesting that publication does not amount to dissemination.

The only real issue here is whether Starbucks' coffee is a perishable food [product]. The statute defines a perishable food product as "a food product of agriculture or aquaculture that is sold or distributed in a form that will perish or decay beyond marketability within a limited period of time." § 96.1 [RULE OR MAJOR PREMISE RE PERISHABLE FOOD PRODUCT] Although coffee is a beverage, Starbucks could argue that its prepared coffee drinks are food products of [agriculture]. Because they are ingestible and contain both calories and nutrients, they are arguably food, although the Texas courts have not defined "food" as [such]. [MINOR PREMISE AND CONCLUSION RE FOOD] As for coffee drinks being products "of agriculture," the argument is less certain. Certainly Starbucks' coffee drinks are derived from products of agriculture, because coffee beans and other natural ingredients Starbucks uses are grown and harvested, and milk and cream are dairy products. [MINOR PREMISE RE "OF AGRICULTURE"] However, the fact that these single ingredients are combined to form a new product could destroy Starbucks' ability to recover under the statute. [ANTICIPATED COUNTER-ARGUMENT RE "OF AGRICULTURE"] In *The Pet Barn, Inc. v. Holmes,* 224 S.W.2d 99, 102 (Tex. 2004), the Court held that a baked pet snack was not a product of agriculture even though it contained products of agriculture: "The result is a *combination* of products of agriculture, not a sole product of agriculture as the statute contemplates." *Id.* Starbucks may try to distinguish *Pet Barn* on the ground that its coffee drinks are different from the baked snack because the ingredients of the drinks are not chemically altered as they were in that case. This argument is likely to fail unless Starbucks can convince the court that for policy reasons, it should be treated differently from the plaintiff in *Pet Barn.* [CONCLUSION RE "OF AGRICULTURE"]

Finally, with regard to the "perish or decay" portion of the definition of perishable food product, the drinks do perish or decay beyond marketability within a limited period of time in the sense that they get cold in a few minutes and form mold within a few [days]. [MINOR PREMISE RE "PERISH OR DECAY BEYOND MARKETABILITY"] CSP is likely to argue that coffee beans do not perish or decay in a short period of time, and Starbucks can prevent its losses

**Comment:** The topic sentence signals to the reader that this paragraph will discuss the rest of the first element: Whether the information regarded a perishable food product.

**Comment:** Here, the writer addresses the first part of the definition of perishable food product set forth above: "food product of agriculture."

**Comment:** The writer acknowledges that she has no authority for this common sense argument, preventing her from losing credibility for failure to provide a cite here.

**Comment:** The topic sentence of this paragraph indicates that the writer is moving to the last part of the definition of perishable food product: "perish or decay beyond marketability within a limited period of time."

**SAMPLE MEMORANDUM**

simply by not grinding the beans and preparing drinks ahead of time. Moreover, the rate at which coffee beans do decay is slow compared to the rate at which fresh produce decays, and therefore, coffee beans do not "perish or decay in a limited period of time." [ANTICIPATED COUNTER-ARGUMENT] Despite these strong arguments, if Starbucks can argue that it has a large shipment of beans in storage that will mold soon or that their ingredients perish or decay in some way of which we are not aware, it may succeed in proving this last part of the [definition]. [CONCLUSION RE: PERISH OR DECAY]

> **Comment:** This sentence sets forth a tentative conclusion based on information the writer does not have but wants to be sure to ask the client about.

Turning to the second element, Starbucks is likely to prove that CSP knew the information it disseminated is false. Knowledge of falsity can include actual knowledge as well as a reckless indifference to truth. *Thomas Meats v. Safeway,* 10 S.W.3d 45 (Tex. 2007). [SYNTHESIZED RULE ON KNOWLEDGE] In *Thomas Meats,* the defendant grocery store posted a sign in its windows saying that the plaintiff's meats were [unsafe]. Because the defendant had relied solely on rumors and failed to investigate the truth of those rumors, the court held Safeway's "reckless indifference to the truth was tantamount to knowledge of falsity." *Id.* at [46]. Similarly, CSP's statements regarding the nature of Starbucks' beans are unfounded. Not only is Starbucks unaware of any other source indicating that its beans are not organically grown, CSP "failed to investigate" the truth of its statements at least insofar as it did not contact Starbucks to verify [them]. [MINOR PREMISE] Therefore, Starbucks can argue that CSP's "reckless indifference to the truth" [constitutes] knowledge of falsity. [CONCLUSION]

> **Comment:** The writer explains here the significant facts of the analogous case. Since the case has already been cited, there is no need to cite. You should provide cites to rules of law but not to cases.

> **Comment:** The writer here provides a statement of the court's holding. A cite here is thus necessary.

> **Comment:** The writer compares the significant similarities between *Thomas Meats* and the Starbucks case.

> **Comment:** Notice that the writer's analogy is strengthened by describing the facts of her case using the same words the *Thomas Meats* court used.

With regard to the third element, Starbucks is likely to prove that CSP stated or implied that its coffee drinks are not safe for consumption by the public. In order to state or imply that a perishable food product is unsafe, the defendant must indicate that the product is inherently dangerous in some way. *See Green's Grocer v. Janus,* 228 S.W.2d 94 (Tex. 2006). [SYNTHESIZED RULE] The only Texas case to have construed this part of the statute, *Green's Grocer,* rejected a disparagement claim where the defendant newscaster claimed his wife choked on the plaintiff's apples. *Id.* at 96. Because the newscaster had not suggested that the apples themselves were tainted or unsafe, the court dismissed the plaintiff's complaint. *Id.* Unlike the newscaster in *Green's Grocer*, CSP did imply that the coffee drinks were

**SAMPLE MEMORANDUM**

inherently unsafe. For years, the public has associated pesticides and other chemicals used to grow crops as either carcinogenic or otherwise [harmful]. CSP might argue that its information states only that the beans are not organic as advertised without making any statement as to their safety. [ANTICIPATION OF COUNTER-ARGUMENT] Given the fears associated with chemicals in our food supply, Starbucks probably has the better argument. To say that chemicals are used to grow Starbucks' coffee beans likely suggests that their consumption poses a risk to consumers' health. [CONCLUSION]

> **Comment:** Here the writer attempts to distinguish *Green's Grocer v. Janus* on the basis of significant dissimilarities.

## CONCLUSION

Although Starbucks can probably prove the second and third elements of a false disparagement claim under Texas statutory law, it is unlikely to prove the first element. The first element requires that CSP disseminated information regarding a perishable food product to the public. Although CSP likely disseminated information to the public through its monthly newsletter, it is doubtful that the information related to a perishable food product as that phrase is defined by the false disparagement statute. A perishable food product must be a food product of agriculture or aquaculture that perishes or decays beyond marketability within a limited period of time. Although Starbucks can probably establish that its coffee drinks are "food" for purposes of protection under the statute, the drinks are probably not a product of agriculture because they are a combination of products of agriculture. Assuming that CSP did not investigate the truth of the statements in its newsletter, Starbucks is likely to be able to prove the second element, which requires that CSP knew the information was false. Finally, the third element requires that CSP stated or implied that the product was unsafe for consumption by the public. Since most consumers associate pesticides with a health risk, Starbucks is likely to establish that CSP implied its coffee drinks are unsafe for [consumption].

> **Comment:** The Conclusion summarizes in more detail than the Brief Answer the writer's analysis regarding the three elements. Notice that it assumes the reader's knowledge of information contained in the Discussion.

## SAMPLE MEMORANDUM

## c. STUDENT–WRITTEN, SAMPLE MEMORANDUM WITH COMMENTS

Attached at Appendix B is a student-written, sample memorandum on an issue of tort law. The question presented is whether the plaintiff, a former employee of a hospital, has a cause of action for retaliatory discharge under Michigan law. The employee threatened to report the hospital's blood bank to the FDA for distributing potentially unsafe blood, and the hospital fired her. Comments in the margin of the sample memorandum address the writer's analysis, organization, and mechanics.

# 2. THE INFORMAL MEMORANDUM

Although not necessarily the top choice among practitioners for communicating with clients, informal memoranda are more common today than traditional ones.[12] For example, roughly 35 percent of Georgetown graduates from 2003 report writing twenty or more informal memoranda per year.[13] Sixty-two percent of the same graduating class report writing no more than three traditional memoranda per year.[14] Although the format of informal memoranda varies widely by practice, most contain some of the elements of traditional memoranda. All forms of informal memoranda appear to eliminate the conclusion. The Georgetown survey indicates that the most popular type of informal memorandum contains a Brief Answer and a Discussion.[15] Other combinations of traditional elements are popular too. Figure 41 below lists them in the order of most to least commonly used by survey respondents.[16]

### Typical Elements of an Informal Memorandum
### (in order from most to least common)

1. Brief Answer and Discussion

2. Statement of Facts and Discussion

3. Question Presented, Brief Answer, and Discussion

4. Question Presented, Brief Answer, Statement of Facts, Discussion

### FIGURE 41

---

12. *See* Robbins–Tiscione, *supra* note 6, at 39–40.

13. *Id.* at 39.

14. *See id.* at 32.

15. *Id.* at 41.

16. *See id.*

## 3. THE SUBSTANTIVE E–MAIL

In today's global economy and with high-tech options at their disposal, lawyers are far more likely to communicate with clients by substantive e-mail than by any form of memorandum.[17] A substantive e-mail contains legal analysis and/or advice in the body of the message as opposed to a short message that serves as a cover letter and attaches an electronic version of a formal or informal memorandum. Although the form of substantive e-mails varies widely, their collective goal is simplicity: "Unlike a legal memo [the e-mail] will tend to be organized around the question itself. In other words, the sections are dictated by the substance of the question and not a prescribed formula."[18] Several respondents to the Georgetown survery described their e-mails as looking like an informal memorandum: "I usually start with a brief statement of the question ... and the relevant facts. Sometimes I also include a sentence indicating what I did to find the answer. The focus is on the conclusion, with brief supporting analysis."[19] Others said their e-mails look like letters.[20] Figure 42 is a sample substantive e-mail that looks like a letter.

---

From: Sara Jan                        Sent: Th 10/12/08 4:18 p.m.

To: jelkins@starbucks.com

CC:

Subject: CSP/False Statements

Attachments:

Jim:

You asked us to look into the possibility of suing CSP for stating in its newsletter that your beans are not organic. I understand your sales have dropped significantly since the newsletter came out, and we are looking into several options for you. As for a claim under the Texas statute, my associate's preliminary results do not look encouraging. Under state statute, there are three things you need to prove in order to bring a successful action:

(1) that CSP disseminated the information to the public about a "perishable food product" (PFP);

(2) that CSP knew its information was false; and

(3) that the newsletter stated or implied that your products are unsafe for consumption.

---

17. *See id.* at 41–44.

18. *Id.* at 43.

19. *Id.* at 44.

20. "My e-mails read like a letter. 'We investigated whether the communication constituted 'fraud' under Texas law.' I then give the answer and a brief analysis." *Id.*

The first element will be most difficult to prove. "Perishable food product" basically means a sole product of agriculture, like beef, milk, green beans, etc. There is a recent Texas case holding that a baked pet snack was not a PFP because it was a combination of products of agriculture and not a sole product. We might be able to distinguish this case, but that seems unlikely. We would also have to prove that your products are really "food" and that they "perish or decay" beyond marketability "within a limited period of time." What percentage of your drinks do you sell without added ingredients (i.e., black coffee or espresso)? Also, how quickly do you need to dispose of prepared coffee before it can no longer be sold?

As for the second and third elements, we have good arguments. I understand that CSP did not attempt to verify its information with your office before publishing its newsletter. This probably qualifies as "a reckless indifference to the truth," which counts for actual knowledge. Finally, since people tend to associate pesticides with health risks, the newsletter at least implied that the drinks are unsafe for consumption.

If you can get back to me with answers to my questions, that would be great. Let's talk next week after we complete our research on other options. I will be in touch.

Sara

Sara Jan

Jan & Associates

874 Main Street, Suite 130

Frisko, Texas 75034

214-993-9012

sjan@jan.com

*This e-mail is confidential, privileged, and intended only for recipients listed above.*[21]

## FIGURE 42

The tone of the e-mail is more casual and conversational than that of a traditional or informal memorandum. It concisely identifies the issue and communicates the essence of the writer's analysis and conclusion. Notice, though, that this format does not preserve detailed legal analysis the way a traditional or even informal memorandum would. That information must be retained either in informal notes or the writer's memory and is therefore more likely to be lost. You will have to decide what form of advice makes the most sense under the circumstances.

Although e-mail is an easy and quick way to deliver advice, it should not be used haphazardly. Just like personal e-mail, once you send it, you cannot get it back. Moreover, as illustrated above, the analysis is often truncated, which can make the attorney vulnerable to criticism. As one Georgetown Law

---

**21.** E-mails can easily be forwarded to third parties. This line reminds the recipient not to forward it indiscriminately and jeopardize client confidentiality.

survey respondent wrote, "To the extent it's not a complete explanation of the analysis, ... it's important to specify what is being left out. Most importantly, the e-mail should be well-written and proofed just as any other memo would be."[22] Remember, too, that e-mails can easily be forwarded to third parties, which endangers the client's privilege to keep attorney-client communications confidential.

---

### QUESTIONS FOR CONSIDERATION

1. **How can you analyze objectively and advocate zealously for your client at the same time? Is "objectivity" even possible?**

2. **Why do you think the format of a classical Roman speech was adopted for legal memoranda? Was that a good decision?**

3. **Are there any advantages still to writing a traditional as opposed to an informal memorandum or substantive e-mail?**

4. **On what bases will you choose among the three conventions for objective analysis?**

5. **What other formats for written objective analysis might you propose?**

---

# C. PERSUASIVE WRITING

The goal of persuasive legal writing is to convince the audience to take proposed action. All modes of appeal—*logos, ethos,* and *pathos*—are important to the persuasive legal writer. Since transactional documents, such as asset purchase agreements or real estate contracts, represent an agreement already reached by the involved parties, they do not fall within the category of persuasive writing. Most often, persuasive writing occurs in the midst of a dispute, whether the context is traditional litigation, arbitration, or an agency investigation. The quintessential forms of persuasive writing in this context are motions and briefs. A motion is a party's request that the judge or arbitrator grant some form of interim or final relief based on legal argument. The object of a motion can range from dismissing a case for failure to state a claim to setting aside a jury verdict. "Brief" refers generically to any form of written legal argument submitted for consideration at any court level, trial or appellate. Briefs are often submitted in support of motions or to inform the court about the legal support for the party's claims.

## 1. MOTIONS

A typical motion is a short document that states in numbered paragraphs and plain terms the precise relief the party seeks. A proposed order for the court to use if the motion is granted is often included for the court's convenience.

---

22. *Id.* at 45.

Recall that in the fictional *Opara* case, Mr. Opara was charged with possession of marijuana under state law. His goal was to exclude from the evidence at trial the marijuana seized by the officer at the time of his arrest. Opara claimed that the seizure of the marijuana violated his Fourth Amendment rights under the United States Constitution. A motion to exclude evidence at a criminal trial is commonly called a motion to suppress. Assume that the *Opara* case arose in Frisco, Texas, outside of Dallas. A sample motion to suppress in *Opara* appears below. *See Figure 43.*

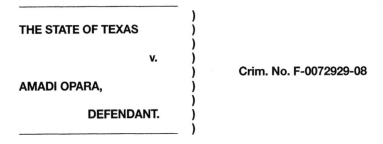

**IN THE DISTRICT COURT FOR COLLIN COUNTY, TEXAS**

| | | |
|---|---|---|
| **THE STATE OF TEXAS** | ) | |
| | ) | |
| | ) | |
| **v.** | ) | |
| | ) | **Crim. No. F-0072929-08** |
| | ) | |
| **AMADI OPARA,** | ) | |
| | ) | |
| **DEFENDANT.** | ) | |
| | ) | |

**MOTION TO SUPPRESS EVIDENCE**

      Comes now the Defendant in the above-entitled case and moves the court for an order to suppress the evidence seized from the Defendant by Officer Randall Blake on October 10, 2008. *See* Tex. Code Crim. Proc. Ann. § 38.23(a) (Vernon 2005). This Motion is made on the grounds that Officer Blake seized the evidence without a warrant and subsequent to an unlawful Terry stop and frisk that violated the Defendant's right to reasonable search and seizure under the Fourth Amendment to the United States Consitutition.

      Wherefore, the court is hereby requested to suprress the aforementioned evidence at the trial scheduled for January 12, 2009.

                                  Respectfully submitted,

                                  _____

                                  Sara Jan
                                  Jan & Associates
                                  874 Main Street
                                  Suite 130
                                  Frisko, Texas 75034

                                  Attorney for the Defendant

**FIGURE 43**

      The motion includes the caption of the case, the docket number assigned to the case when it was filed, a title that identifies the purpose of the motion, the actual request that the court suppress the evidence, and a brief explanation of the basis for the motion. The lawyer's signature at the bottom satisfies the ethical requirement that she certify the document is reasonably grounded in both fact and law.[23]

# 2. BRIEFS

Although the format of legal memoranda can be tailored to suit the client's needs and budget, the format for filing documents with the same agency or court tends to be uniform. All state and federal courts, as well as agencies, have their own local rules that govern both the form and substance of the motions and briefs filed within their jurisdiction. Typically, these "local rules" specify in detail the elements each brief should contain, as well as the page limits, font size, and the process for filing.[24] Many state and federal courts now accept electronic filing of documents and have rules regulating electronic submissions.[25]

## a. MEMORANDA OF POINTS AND AUTHORITIES

Despite their name, memoranda of points and authorities are briefs; they are typically used at the trial court level and filed in support of a motion. They provide the legal argument a party hopes will persuade the court to grant the motion in its favor. As with the Discussion section of a memorandum, the Argument in a brief is the focal point of the document. It should be organized deductively: first by issue and second by the rules of law that determine the outcome of that issue. Similar to that in a legal memorandum, the introductory or roadmap paragraph of a brief states the client's ultimate argument and outlines the arguments to follow. *See Figure 40*, at 219.

Unlike in objective memoranda, the order in which supporting arguments are made can be important. If there are three reasons why the client should prevail, for example, conventional wisdom dictates that the strongest argument be made first.[26] The writer must then decide whether to make the weakest argument last (which is the one the reader is left with) or sandwich it in the middle. There is no right answer to this question; in fact, there are as many different answers to this question as the number of people asked. Again, the legal writer must decide what makes the most sense under the circumstances. A sample memorandum in support of the defendant's motion to suppress in *Opara* appears below at 232–36.

The sample relies on three factors indicating that Officer Blake did not have

---

23. *See supra* ch. 7, at 209.

24. *See, e.g.*, Fed. R. App. P. 27 (stating that motions "must be double-spaced, but quotations more than two lines long may be indented and single-spaced" and that motions "must not exceed 20 pages"); Md. R. 2–501 (stating that in response to a motion for summary judgment, a party must "(1) identify with particularity each material fact as to which it is contended that there is a genuine dispute and (2) as to each such fact, identify and attach the relevant portion of the specific document, discovery response, transcript of testimony (by page and line), or other statement under oath that demonstrates the dispute.").

25. *See, e.g.*, Ariz. Sup. Ct. R. 124 (Electronic filing, delivery and service of documents).

26. *See, e.g.*, Kristen K. Robbins (now Robbins–Tiscione), *The Inside Scoop: What Federal Judges Really Think About the Way Lawyers Write, supra* ch. 4, note 161, at 273.

reasonable, articulable suspicion to stop the defendant. From the defendant's point of view, the factors are addressed from strongest to weakest. The State might argue the factors in a different order.

**IN THE DISTRICT COURT FOR COLLIN COUNTY, TEXAS**

| | |
|---|---|
| **THE STATE OF TEXAS,** )<br>)<br>v.                          )<br>)<br>**AMADI OPARA,**        )<br>)<br>Defendant.        )<br>) | **Crim. No.**<br>**F-72929-08** |

**MEMORANDUM IN SUPPORT**
**OF DEFENDANT'S**
**MOTION TO SUPPRESS**

The State seeks to introduce evidence against Mr. Opara at trial, which is scheduled for January 12, 2009. There is no dispute that at the time of Mr. Opara's arrest, Officer Blake did not have a search warrant. He had never met Mr. Opara, nor did he know anything about him. The State argues that the evidence was seized subsequent to a *Terry* stop and frisk, which if valid, would permit a warrantless seizure. However, as the argument below demonstrates, neither the stop nor the frisk of Mr. Opara in this case was valid under *Terry* or any cases in this jurisdiction construing [*Terry*].

> **Comment:** This introduction to the memorandum creates the context of the dispute for the reader and outlines the two major arguments to follow.

**I. STATEMENT OF FACTS**

Amadi Opara emigrated legally from Nigeria in 2004 and is working towards U.S. citizenship. Early in the evening of October 10, 2008, Mr. Opara stood outside the Exxon gas station one block from his apartment in a low-income area waiting for a friend to pick him up and drive him to work. Although Mr. Opara cannot afford the luxury of a car, he earns enough money working as an office janitor to pay for his own apartment. As Mr. Opara waited for his ride, Officer Blake observed him standing off to the side of the parking lot so as to be out of the way of traffic moving in and out of the station. It was a bit chilly that night, so Mr. Opara had his hands in his pockets, and he moved about a bit to keep warm. Mr. Opara did not initially see the officer's cruiser as it entered the lot. When he did notice it, he was surprised and moved to the opposite side of the lot so as to get out of the cruiser's way.

The next thing Mr. Opara knew, the officer exited his vehicle and accosted him, asking questions. "Hey you—what are you doing?" were Officer Blake's

**SAMPLE MEMORANDUM OF POINTS AND AUTHORITIES**

first words to Mr. Opara. Unfamiliar with police procedures in the United States, Mr. Opara became nervous and started to back away from Officer Blake. As he testified at the preliminary hearing, Mr. Opara was not even sure that the officer was addressing him in particular. Still a bit confused, Mr. Opara decided that Officer Blake was indeed speaking to someone else. Since his friend had failed to pick him up from work, Mr. Opara decided to walk home in case there was going to be any trouble. As he turned around, Officer Blake touched his shoulder, spun him around and frisked him. Officer Blake then seized a small bag of marijuana from Mr. Opara's pants [pocket].

> **Comment:** The statement of the facts here is given from the defendant's point of view. The story should have emotional appeal but not exaggerate or stretch the truth in a way that detracts from the writer's credibility.

## II. ARGUMENT

The evidence seized by Officer Blake must be suppressed because it was obtained in violation of Mr. Opara's Fourth Amendment rights. Warrantless search and seizure are *per se* unreasonable under the United States Constitution. U.S. Const. amend. IV (2004). Only a few well-delineated exceptions permit warrantless invasions of privacy, none of which applies in this [case].

> **Comment:** In this first paragraph of the argument, the writer again provides the context for the argument: that the defendant's Fourth Amendment rights were violated, and the evidence should be suppressed.

The State argues that Blake conducted a valid investigatory stop and frisk of Mr. Opara, while he waited for his ride to work. However, *Terry v. Ohio*, 392 U.S. 1, 22 (1968), requires that in order for a police officer to stop a person to investigate, he must have reasonable, articulable suspicion to believe that individual is engaged in imminent criminal [activity]. *See also Baldwin v. Texas,* 237 S.W.3d 808, 812 (Tex. App. 2007). In order to conduct a subsequent frisk, he must have reasonable, articulable suspicion that the individual is armed and [dangerous]. *Terry,* 392 U.S. at 24; *Griffin v. State*, 215 S.W.3d 403, 409 (Tex. Crim. App. 2006). In both instances, reasonable, articulable suspicion is determined by looking at the totality of the circumstances, including the defendant's location and behavior. *United States v. Cortez,* 449 U.S. 411, 417-18 (1981). Where, as here, the suspect, who happens to be a black man, appears perfectly ordinary and engages in common, everyday behavior, no reasonable officer could conclude that a *Terry* stop and frisk was permissible.

> **Comment:** The writer provides here a synthesized rule on what makes a stop permissible.

> **Comment:** The writer provides a synthesized rule on what makes a frisk permissible.

### A. The *Terry* Stop Was Not Based on Reasonable Articulable Suspicion that Mr. Opara Was Engaged in Any Unlawful Activity].

> **Comment:** The first minor heading visually indicates at a glance that the validity of the stop will be addressed first.

## SAMPLE MEMORANDUM OF POINTS AND AUTHORITIES

Officer Blake did not have reasonable articulable suspicion to believe that Mr. Opara was engaged in imminent criminal activity. In determining whether reasonable suspicion exists, this Court looks at the defendant's behavior, whether he is in a high-crime area, and the officer's experience in similar [circumstances]. *See Cortez,* 449 U.S. at 417-18; *Gurrola v. State,* 877 S.W.2d 300, 302 (Tex. Crim. App. 1994). None of the factors that contribute to reasonable articulable suspicion of imminent criminal activity is present in this case.

> **Comment:** The writer here explains how courts have interpreted what the rule means. In this case, the courts look at a series of factors to determine reasonableness of a stop.

1. First, Mr. Opara's behavior in the parking lot was wholly consistent with innocent [activity]. Where the defendant's behavior does not give rise to a reasonable suspicion of criminal activity, a *Terry* stop is not justified. [RULE OR MAJOR PREMISE RE FIRST FACTOR] *See, e.g., Gurrola,* 877 S.W.2d 300. In *Gurrola,* an officer was patrolling a high-crime neighborhood when he was informed by a passerby about a disturbance in a nearby parking lot. The officer observed four people arguing; when they saw him, they stopped arguing and began to walk away. The officer stopped and searched them. The defendant was arrested for possession of cocaine. In that case, the court ruled that the officer did not have reasonable, articulable suspicion to stop the defendant because the defendant's behavior was innocent. *Id.* at 302. As the court explained, the officer saw "no more than a heated discussion," and it was the defendant's "constitutional right to walk away" without creating suspicion. *[Id.]*

> **Comment:** The topic sentence indicates which factor this paragraph discusses and makes the writer's argument on that factor.

> **Comment:** This paragraph illustrates when an officer might reasonably rely on the defendant's behavior to form a suspicion of criminal activity.

The nature of Mr. Opara's activity was equally innocent. Like the defendant in *Gurrola,* Mr. Opara was standing in a parking lot, but Officer Blake did not even observe him arguing with anyone. He was just standing there waiting for a ride. The fact that Mr. Opara began to walk away when Officer Blake approached did not make him suspicious. [COMPARISON◻MINOR PREMISE] As this court has recognized, he had a "constitutional right to walk away" without subjecting himself to suspicion and a *Terry* stop. [CONCLUSION] *See also Hawkins v. State,* 758 S.W.2d 255 (Tex. Crim. App. 1988) (holding there was nothing suspicious about a man standing in a parking lot and walking away when the officer asked him to stop). That the state should attempt to characterize Mr. Opara's walking away as flight is unfounded. Flight alone cannot justify a stop. *Reyes v. State,* 899 S.W.2d 319, 324 (Tex. App. 1995); *Gurrola,* 877 S.W.2d at 303. Moreover, flight requires more than casual walking. In cases where Texas courts have found behavior to rise to the level of flight and contribute to reasonable

# SAMPLE MEMORANDUM OF POINTS AND AUTHORITIES

suspicion, the defendants have, in combination with other suspicious activity, directly attempted to evade contact with law enforcement officers. *See, e.g., Davis v. State*, 829 S.W.2d 218, 219 (Tex. Crim. App. 1992) (holding that when men selling narcotics "made a hasty effort to get into a nearby vehicle" to avoid speaking with the arresting officer, the *Terry* stop was justified).

2. Second, the fact that Mr. Opara lives in a low-income area does not make him a likely [criminal]. Although the presence of a suspect in a high-crime area can contribute to reasonable suspicion, a high-crime area alone does not. [MAJOR PREMISE] *Gurrola*, 877 S.W.2d at 303. In *Gurrola*, the court dismissed the idea that a parking lot in the late afternoon could give rise to suspicion in the way an empty parking lot at a department store might at 1:30 a.m. *Id.* As in *Gurrola*, the parking lot in which Mr. Opara stood did not reasonably raise any suspicion of criminal activity. Mr. Opara simply stood in the lot at dinnertime,waiting for his ride. [COMPARISON→MINOR PREMISE] The location at that time did not make Mr. Opara suspicious simply by virtue of the fact that crime occurs in that area. [CONCLUSION]

> **Comment:** The topic sentence indicates which factor this paragraph discusses and makes the writer's argument on that factor.

3. Finally, no amount of experience can convert Officer Blake's suspicion into a reasonable [one]. In some circumstances, the experience of the arresting officer can be a factor in finding a *Terry* stop reasonable, but the officer must have acted on more than a hunch. [MAJOR PREMISE] *Brother v. State*, 166 S.W.3d 255, 257 (Tex. Crim. App. 2005). In this case, there were no indications that Mr. Opara was engaged in imminent criminal activity: no suspicious behavior on Mr. Opara's part, no eyewitnesses of any such behavior, and no tips of any kind. [COMPARISON→MINOR PREMISE] Officer Blake acted on a mere hunch that Mr. Opara was suspicious simply by virtue of standing in a parking lot in low-income neighborhood. As in this case, a string of baseless inferences cannot add up to suspicion. [CONCUSION]

> **Comment:** Topic sentence indicates which factor this paragraph discusses and makes the writer's argument on that factor.

### B. Even if the *Terry* Stop Were Valid, Officer Blake Had No Right to Frisk Mr. Opara Because He Had No Reason to Believe Mr. Opara Was Armed and Dangerous.]

> **Comment:** The second minor heading visually indicates at a glance that the validity of the frisk will be addressed second.

Officer Blake did not have reasonable, articulable suspicion to believe that Mr. Opara was armed and dangerous. *Griffin v. State*, 215 S.W.3d 403, 409. The Court evaluates the lawfulness of a

## SAMPLE MEMORANDUM OF POINTS AND AUTHORITIES

frisk by looking at the totality of the circumstances, including the defendant's behavior, the nature of the crime suspected, and the officer's familiarity with the [suspect]. *See, e.g., id.* Only where the officer can articulate a basis for believing the suspect presents a threat to himself or others can he conduct a limited pat-down search for weapons. [MAJOR PREMISE] *Id.* (holding that a frisk was reasonable where the officer suspected the defendant was selling narcotics, because weapons are commonly used in such transactions); *O'Hara v. State,* 27 S.W.3d 548, 551 (Tex. Crim. App. 2000) (holding that frisk was reasonable where defendant had a knife clipped to his belt). Where, as here, there is no reason to believe the individual presents a threat, the officer is not entitled to search him.

> **Comment:** The writer here explains how the courts have interpreted what the rule means. In this case, the courts look at a series of factors to determine reasonableness of a frisk.

In this case, Mr. Opara engaged in no behavior that would lead a reasonable officer to conclude that he was a threat to anyone. Mr. Opara exhibited no signs of violence, nor did Officer Blake observe any weapons on him. In fact, Officer Blake had no experience with Mr. Opara, no information indicating he could be dangerous, and no reason to suspect he was engaged in a dangerous drug transaction. [COMPARISON→MINOR PREMISE] Thus, Officer Blake had no basis for frisking Mr. Opara, thus violating once again his Fourth Amendment rights. [CONCLUSION]

Respectfully submitted,

_____

Sara Jan
Jan & Associates
874 Main Street
Suite 130
Frisko, Texas 75034

Attorney for the Defendant

**SAMPLE MEMORANDUM OF POINTS AND AUTHORITIES**

## b. APPELLATE BRIEFS

### i) ELEMENTS OF AN APPELLATE BRIEF

Appellate briefs are more formal than memoranda of points and authorities or other types of briefs filed at the agency or trial court level. Federal Rule of Appellate Procedure 28, for example, sets forth the elements that an appellant's brief must contain. It serves as a good model for all appellate briefs, but always consult the local rules of any court in which a brief is to be filed. Rule 32 sets a limit of thirty pages for each party's principal brief, whereas Texas appellate courts set a limit of fifty pages.[27] The sample appellate brief at 245–54, appeals the order of the District Court for Collin County, Texas granting the defendant's motion to suppress in *Opara*.

### COVER PAGE

The Cover Page usually includes the caption of the case, the title of the brief, and the names of the attorneys filing the brief. *See p. 245.*

### TABLE OF CONTENTS

The Table of Contents lists the elements or parts of the brief and the page numbers they begin on. All headings (discussed *infra* at 244) are reprinted in the Table of Contents. They summarize the writer's argument and act as a detailed, visual outline for the reader. Page one of the brief typically begins with the jurisdictional statement, *see below*, or the first substantive element of the brief. All pages before page one are numbered with small roman numerals (*e.g.*, i, ii, etc.). *See p. 245.*

### TABLE OF AUTHORITIES

The Table of Authorities provides an alphabetical list of the cases, statutes, and other authorities cited to and relied on by the brief writer. Typically, the authorities are separated by type. The Table of Authorities should include the page number(s) on which each of the cited sources appears. Some local rules require the parties to indicate in the Table of Authorities which sources they primarily rely on. *See p. 246.*

### JURISDICTIONAL STATEMENT

The Jurisdictional Statement provides the basis for the court's exercise of subject matter jurisdiction (subject matter jurisdiction refers to the nature of the cases a court can hear). The parties should cite to the applicable regulation or statute and the relevant facts that establish the court's jurisdiction. In the *Opara* case, Article 44.01 of the Texas Code of Criminal Procedure allows the state to appeal the order of a lower court that grants a motion to suppress evidence in a

---

27. *Compare* FED. R. APP. P. 32(a)(7) *with* TEX. R. APP. P. 38.4.

criminal case. *See p. 247.*

## STATEMENT OF THE ISSUES PRESENTED FOR REVIEW

The Statement of the Issues Presented for Review is akin to the Question Presented of a memorandum. It specifies the controlling rules(s) of law, the precise legal question, and the significant facts. Unlike the Question Presented, though, the Statement of the Issues should not be objective.[28] To be persuasive, it should suggest that the outcome the client desires is the obvious outcome. A good way to frame the Statement of the Issues is to ask a question that suggests an affirmative answer. From Opara's point of view, for example, the issue would be whether the officer violated Opara's rights (*yes*) as opposed to whether the officer acted lawfully (*no*). Affirmative arguments are usually easier to write and less confusing to read. The legal writer first begins to develop her theory of the case with the statement of the issues.[29] *See p. 247.*

## STATEMENT OF THE CASE

The Statement of the Case describes the procedural history of the case. It usually includes the nature of the case (civil or criminal, tort or contract), the history of the proceedings, and the disposition below. *See p. 247.*

## STATEMENT OF FACTS

The Statement of Facts serves the same function as it does in the legal memorandum, but again, it should be persuasive, appealing to reason, emotion, and credibility. The writer should include enough background facts to provide context for the reader and those facts significant to resolve the legal issues. Consistent with the theory of the case, the Statement of Facts should also tell an interesting and compelling story from the client's point of view. It should stir the audience's emotion and make the audience want to act in the client's favor.[30] Although it is appropriate to emphasize favorable facts and deemphasize unfavorable ones, facts must be stated accurately, without intentionally misleading the reader.[31] Typically, facts are set forth in chronological order unless the writer has a good reason to do otherwise. Beginning and ending with favorable facts is also a good idea.[32] All facts should be supported by citation to the record below, which consists of testimony, exhibits, and the like. A typical citation format, indicating page seven of the record, would be as follows: (R. 7). *See p. 247.*

---

**28.** *See supra* at 216.

**29.** *See supra* ch. 6, at 180.

**30.** *See id.* at 179.

**31.** *See supra* ch. 7, at 205.

**32.** *See supra* ch. 6, at 190.

## SUMMARY OF ARGUMENT

Like the Brief Answer in a memorandum, the Summary of Argument previews the writer's reasoning. It should "contain a succinct, clear, and accurate statement of the arguments made in the body of the brief" and not "merely repeat the argument headings."[33] A summary that merely restates the writers' conclusions is less effective than one that incorporates the writer's reasons as well. Typically, cites are not included in the Summary of Argument. *See p. 248.*

## STANDARD OF REVIEW

The standard of review is the level of deference the reviewing court must give to the lower court's decision. The standard of review differs depending on the nature of the question before the reviewing court. Questions of fact are usually entitled to the greatest level of deference on appeal. The trial court—either the judge or the jury—is in the best position to evaluate the strength and credibility of the evidence, including documents and live testimony. Since a complete review of the evidence on appeal would be an inefficient use of judicial resources and akin to retrying the case, factual findings are not usually reversed unless clearly erroneous. Because agencies have highly specialized knowledge of the industries they regulate, agency findings are usually not reversed unless they are arbitrary and capricious. In contrast, questions of law are often reviewed without any deference at all. Because the reviewing court is not at a disadvantage in assessing pure legal questions, the standard of review is usually *de novo,* meaning the reviewing court can review the question entirely "anew." *See Figure 44, below.* There is no universal standard of review for mixed questions of fact and law, and different courts treat these questions differently.

---

**33.** FED. R. APP. P. 28(a)(8).

```
┌─────────────────────────────────────┐
│                                     │
│         TYPICAL STANDARDS           │
│            OF REVIEW                 │
│          (from most to              │
│          least deferential)         │
│                                     │
│  • Arbitrary and capricious—        │
│    Usually for agency findings      │
│    because agencies have            │
│    specialized knowledge and        │
│    direct access to the evidence.   │
│                                     │
│                                     │
│  • Clearly erroneous/Against        │
│    the manifest weight of the       │
│    evidence—                        │
│    Usually for findings of fact     │
│    because judge or jury had        │
│    direct access to the evidence.   │
│                                     │
│                                     │
│  • De novo—                         │
│    Usually for questions of         │
│    law, where direct access to      │
│    evidence is not necessary        │
│    and the reviewing court has      │
│    an interest in uniformity and    │
│    predictability of decisions in   │
│    its jurisdiction.                │
│                                     │
└─────────────────────────────────────┘
```

**FIGURE 44**

In a given case, the standard of review may be different for different issues. Moreover, the standard of review for a particular issue may be unclear. Different decisions from the same level court may articulate different standards of review for the same type of question on appeal. In that situation, the parties will have to argue for the application of the standard of review they think applies in their case. When beneficial, the standard of review can be incorporated into the theory of the case and relied on explicitly. When the standard of review puts the party at a disadvantage, that party needs to explain to the court why the applicable standard should not prevent the reviewing court from ruling in that party's favor. *See p. 249.*

## ARGUMENT

The Argument is to the brief what the Discussion is to the memorandum. As Federal Rule of Appellate Procedure 28 states, the Argument should contain "the appellant's contentions and the reasons for them, with citations to the authorities and parts of the record on which the appellant relies."[34] Just as with memoranda, the legal reader expects an overview of the Argument at the outset. For that reason, briefs usually begin with an introductory section or "roadmap" that states the client's ultimate argument and outlines the law (*e.g.*, Fourth Amendment law governing the validity of a *Terry* stop) that governs the issue presented for review. As discussed more fully below, the argument section should proceed deductively, moving issue by issue from general rules of law to specific conclusions. *See pp. 249–54.*

## CONCLUSION

Conclusions in briefs are short. Since a court will not grant relief that is not requested, the relief sought must be stated precisely. *See p. 254.*

## ii) ORGANIZATION OF THE ARGUMENT

The legal writer needs to consider both large and small scale organization in the Argument section of the brief, preferably in that order. As discussed below, strategic considerations not relevant to memo writing affect the organization of the argument.

### (a) Large Scale Organization

As with all legal analysis, the argument should generally be organized first by issue and second by the rules of law that determine the outcome of each issue. In a brief, however, a number of additional considerations are relevant to the brief's organization. First, the theory of the case should be considered. How does the theory itself suggest the brief ought to be organized? Recall that in Clinton v. Jones, the parties' theories of the case significantly affected each part of their briefs.[35] In the sample appellate brief below, the state seeks to reverse the lower court's order granting the defendant's motion to suppress. The standard of review is in the State's favor, but the State still needs to prove the lower court erred. The State had the choice of characterizing its case as comprised of one or two issues, namely whether the stop and frisk was legal or whether the stop was legal and if so, whether the frisk was legal. From a psychological point of view, it seems an easier burden for the State to clear if the case is characterized as having just one issue.[36] In contrast, the defendant might characterize the case as having two hurdles for the State to clear.

In addition to the theory of the case, the nature of the issues on appeal should be considered. The conventional wisdom is to argue dispositive issues first. If one issue would dispose of the case, that one should be argued first. If the court resolves the issue in a way that disposes of the case, it will not even need to address the rest of the issues. Assume, for example, that the appellant in a civil case claims that the plaintiff's motion for summary judgment should have been

---

34. *Id.* at 28(a)(9(A).

35. *See supra* ch. 6, at 180–86.

36. *See infra*, p. 247.

denied because the statute of limitations precluded the plaintiff from bringing the action in the first place. Even if the statute does not preclude the plaintiff's claim, the defendant might argue, summary judgment is improper for other reasons. In that case, the defendant-appellant might make the limitations argument first. If the court agrees with the appellant, it need not consider the appellant's argument on the merits of the motion. Since courts are interested in acting efficiently and limiting their review of a lower court's decision, this organizational choice serves the reviewing court's interest as well as the appellant's. Where the issues to be argued are on an equal level (*e.g.*, the various factors that make up a totality of circumstances inquiry or several required elements for a statutory cause of action), most writers recommend that the strongest arguments be made first. A decision then needs to be made about whether to sandwich weak arguments between stronger ones (as in the sample appellate brief) or end with the weakest arguments. Whatever the decision, it should be made intentionally. *See Figure 45, below.*

## LARGE SCALE ORGANIZATION

- *Always organize around rules of law elements, rules, requirements, etc., NOT cases), moving from general to more specific rules.*

- *When planning the organization of the issues, consider your theory of the case.*

- *Consider making dispositive arguments first, for the court's sake.*

- *Where the arguments are equally important, consider making the strongest arguments first.*

- *Consider sandwiching weak arguments between stronger ones and ending with a relatively strong argument.*

- *Use Major and Minor Point headings to divide your analysis visually:*

*I. MAJOR HEADING RE: ISSUE 1*

*[textual explaniation for further subdivision]*

*A. <u>Minor Heading</u>*

*[textual explaniation for further subdivision]*

*1. sub-heading*
*2. sub-heading*

*II. MAJOR HEADING RE: ISSUE 2*

- *Each time you divide your argument into major or minor point headings, provide text that explains the reason for the division so as not to confuse your reader.*

**FIGURE 45**

For each issue, it is customary to provide a major heading that encapsulates the legal issue, the gist of the argument, and a brief supporting reason.[37] The major headings should provide the gist of the argument at a glance, but they should not act as a substitute for strong topic sentences at the beginning of the argument. If the reader skips the heading, its point will be lost, necessitating the use of a topic sentence. Including the word "since" or "because" in the heading forces the writer to articulate her reasoning. Where the issue subdivides into smaller issues, each of which requires its own analysis, minor headings and even sub-headings can be used. Major headings are usually set in all capital letters. Consult ALWD Rule 3.1 or Bluebook Rule 8 for the format of minor headings. According to both of these rules, all words except articles and conjunctions are capitalized. Bluebook Rule 8 also requires that prepositions containing more than four letters be capitalized.

Where an issue is further divided into minor headings, it is a good idea to provide additional context for the reader to understand the reason for the division. A mini introduction or roadmap can be helpful here. *See Opara sample appellate brief, at 249.*

### *(b) Small Scale Organization*

The small scale organization of an argument in a brief resembles that of analysis in objective writing. The major difference in organization tends to be the way arguments are introduced. As discussed earlier,[38] rules of law are articulated from the client's point of view, and the tone of the writing should be argumentative. Typically, an argument on a particular issue contains the following:

- **a topic sentence that identifies the issue or sub-issue that the paragraph(s) argue(s) (it should also include the writer's argument regarding the outcome on that issue);**
- **a statement of the relevant synthesized rule, requirement, element, and the like (and any sub-parts) from the writer's point of view;**
- **if necessary, an explanation or definition of what the rule, requirement, element, and the like means, including the facts and holding(s) of cited case law;**
- **the application of the rule and the like to the facts of your case, and, where common law applies, comparisons to case law to analogize or distinguish cases; and**
- **a (re-)conclusion on that issue.**

Read the sample appellate brief below. Notice that the structure of each individual argument is slightly different. Differences in the law and the parties'

---

**37.** *See* major headings I and II in the sample appellate *Opara* brief, at 249 & 252.

**38.** *See supra* ch. 6, at 191.

arguments lead to differences in organization. As the sample illustrates, the topic sentence and rule can be stated separately or together. A comparison to case law may be made in text or by use of a parenthetical, and so on. Despite these differences, each argument contains the essentials of good legal analysis.

**IN THE COURT OF APPEALS FOR THE
FIFTH DISTRICT OF TEXAS AT DALLAS**

| | |
|---|---|
| **THE STATE OF TEXAS,**<br>           **Appellant,**<br><br>    **v.**<br><br>**AMADI OPARA,**<br><br>      **Appellee.** | **Crim. No.<br>N/2-2008 68** |

**BRIEF FOR APPELLANT**

Victor Kelsen, J.D.
300 W. 15th Street
Austin, Texas 78701

Attorney for the
Appellant

March 17, 2009

· · · · · · · · · · · · · · · · · · · · · · · · · · · · · · · · · · · · · · · · · · · · · · · · · · · · · · ·

**TABLE OF CONTENTS**

# SAMPLE APPELLATE BRIEF

. . . . . . . . . . . . . . . . . . . . . . . . . . . . . . . . . . . . . . . .

## TABLE OF AUTHORITIES

## SAMPLE APPELLATE BRIEF

| | |
|---|---|
| *Griffin v. State*, 215 S.W.3d 403 (Tex. Crim. App. 2006) | 4, 9, 10 |
| *Guzman v. State,* 955 S.W.2d 85 (Tex. Crim. App. 1997) | 3,7 |
| *Illinois v. Wardlow,* 528 U.S. 119 (2000) | 6 |
| *O'Hara v. State*, 27 S.W.3d 548 (Tex. Crim. App. 2000) | 9 |
| *Terry v. Ohio,* 392 U.S. 1 (1968) | 3,5,6,8,10 |
| *United States v. Cortez*, 449 U.S. 411 1981) | 4,7 |
| *Vanderhorst v. State,* 52 S.W.3d 237 (Tex. App. 2001) | 6 |
| *Woods v. State,* 956 S.W.2d 33 (Tex. Crim. App. 1997) | 8 |

. . . . . . . . . . . . . . . . . . . . . . . . . . . . . . . . . . . . . . . . . . . . . . . . .

## JURISDICTIONAL STATEMENT

The Court has jurisdiction over this appeal pursuant to Tex. Code Crim. Proc. Ann. art. 44.01(a)(5) (Vernon 2006 & Supp. 2007).

## STATEMENT OF THE ISSUE
## PRESENTED FOR REVIEW

Did the District Court err in suppressing the marijuana seized from the defendant subsequent to a routine *Terry* stop and frisk, when the arresting officer observed the defendant stand nervously in the dark in the corner of a gas station parking lot and then begin to flee when the officer approached [him]?

> **Comment:** The question is framed to be answered in the affirmative, drawing on those facts most beneficial to the State's case.

## STATEMENT OF THE CASE

The defendant was arrested for possession of marijuana on October 10, 2008. The defendant moved on December 12, 2008 to suppress the evidence, and the District Court for Collin County granted the [motion] on December 22, 2008. The State now appeals.

> **Comment:** Provides the procedural history of the case.

## STATEMENT OF THE FACTS

Early in the evening of Friday, October 10, 2008, veteran Officer Randall Blake observed a young, black male loitering outside the Exxon gas station on Glebe Road in an area known for habitual drug trafficking and store [robberies]. (R. [7].) The man stood in the dark, away from the spotlights that illuminated the entrance to the station. Officer Blake noticed that the man appeared nervous: He kept his hands in his pockets, kept looking up and down the street, and glanced into the station several times. (R. 9.)

> **Comment:** Statement begins with favorable facts regarding defendant's suspicious behavior.

> **Comment:** Cite here is to the source in the record where these facts were established (*e.g.,* Blake's testimony).

## SAMPLE APPELLATE BRIEF

Familiar with typical "casing" behavior, the officer drove into the parking lot to investigate further. As Officer ¬ Blake entered the lot, he saw a look of surprise cross the defendant's face. The defendant then turned and walked away quickly. Believing the defendant to be acting evasively, Blake stopped the cruiser and exited. (R. 9.)

Although he had no warrant to arrest the [suspect], he proceeded to conduct a routine *Terry* stop to investigate the situation. Officer Blake has performed several such stops over the years in this neighborhood. (R. 21.) When Officer Blake exited the vehicle, the defendant paused momentarily, giving the officer a chance to call out to him and ask the defendant where he was going. As soon as Officer Blake asked the question, the defendant began to back away, keeping his back hidden from the officer's view. (R. 10.) Suddenly, he turned and started walking again, this time even more quickly than before. Suspecting that the defendant might not only be involved in criminal activity but concealing a weapon behind his back, Officer Blake ran up to the defendant and performed a quick pat-down frisk. (R. 10, 13.) The frisk produced a glassine bag of marijuana in the defendant's right back pants pocket, and the defendant was arrested. (R. [20].)

> **Comment:** Acknowledges but downplays unfavorable fact.

> **Comment:** Ends with favorable fact that suspicion of criminal activity was ultimately confirmed.

### SUMMARY OF ARGUMENT

The District Court erred in suppressing the marijuana seized from Defendant Opara, because Officer Blake had reasonable, articulable suspicion to conduct a *Terry* stop and [frisk]. Under *Terry* and the Texas cases construing it, an officer may conduct a brief investigative stop without a warrant as long as he has reason to believe the Defendant is involved in imminent criminal activity. On the night of October 10, 2008, several factors combined led Officer Blake, a seasoned veteran, to have that belief. First, he ¬ observed the Defendant standing in the dark in the corner of a gas station parking lot, acting nervous, and having seemingly nothing to do and nowhere to go. As Officer Blake entered the parking lot with his cruiser, the Defendant immediately began to walk quickly away. [His] reasonable suspicion aroused that a robbery might be in progress, Officer Blake called out to the Defendant to see what he was doing, and the Defendant started to back away. When the Defendant turned suddenly and began to flee, Officer Blake conducted a brief pat-down frisk based on the belief that the Defendant might be armed and [dangerous]. Since the stop and frisk were justified, this Court should reverse the District Court's [order].

> **Comment:** Strong topic sentence reiterating the State's ultimate argument.

> **Comment:** Summarizes facts justifying stop.

> **Comment:** Summarizes facts justifying frisk.

> **Comment:** Specific conclusion as to what Court should do.

## SAMPLE APPELLATE BRIEF

## STANDARD OF REVIEW

The standard of review for determinations of reasonable suspicion to conduct a *Terry* stop and frisk is de novo. *Guzman v. State*, 955 S.W.2d 85, 87 (Tex. Crim. App. 1997). Where as here, the lower court's ruling does not depend on the resolution of factual issues relating to the credibility and demeanor of witnesses, the Court owes no deference to the lower court's ruling and is free to [reverse]. *Id.*

**Comment:** Standard of review is favorable to the state since there are no disputed facts below. The only question is whether the facts added up to reasonable suspicion. This section underscores the Court's ability to substitute its judgment for that of the District Court.

## ARGUMENT

The District Court's order granting the Defendant's Motion to Suppress should be reversed. In keeping with the Defendant Opara's Fourth Amendment rights, Officer Blake had the requisite suspicion needed to conduct a valid *Terry* stop and frisk without a warrant. *See* U.S. Const., amend. IV; *Terry v. Ohio*, 392 U.S. 1, 22 (1968). As long as a police officer has reasonable, articulable suspicion to believe that an individual is engaged ¬ in imminent criminal activity, he may conduct a brief stop to investigate and alleviate his concerns. *See also Baldwin v. Texas*, 237 S.W.3d 808, 812 (Tex. App. 2007). This minimal form of intrusion strikes the proper balance between the needs of law enforcement and a citizen's reasonable expectation of privacy. *Terry*, 392 U.S. at 22. Moreover, where the officer has reason to believe that the suspect may be armed and dangerous, he may conduct a brief pat-down frisk for weapons in order to ensure his safety and that of others nearby. *Id.* at 24; *Griffin v. State*, 215 S.W.3d 403, 409 (Tex. Crim. App. 2006). Reasonable, articulable suspicion to stop and frisk is determined by looking at the totality of the circumstances. *United States v. Cortez, 449 U.S. 411, 417-18 (1981)*. As demonstrated below, Officer Blake had ample reason to stop and frisk the [Defendant].

**Comment:** This paragraph acts as a roadmap for the reader, identifying the issues as part of a Fourth Amendment inquiry and framing them as reasonable suspicion to stop and to frisk. Notice that the writer weaves argument into the introduction to the legal issues.

## I. OFFICER BLAKE HAD REASONABLE ARTICULABLE SUSPICION TO BELIEVE THAT THE DEFENDANT WAS ENGAGED IN CRIMINAL ACTIVITY AS HE STOOD NERVOUSLY OUTSIDE THE GAS [STATION].

**Comment:** First major point heading signals content of argument to follow and argues that Officer Blake conducted a valid stop. Provides the argument at a glance.

Officer Blake had more than adequate suspicion to believe the Defendant was engaged in imminent criminal activity. Reasonable suspicion is based on the totality of circumstances in each case, including the defendant's behavior, the defendant's location in a high-crime area, and the officer's experience in similar situations. *Cortez*, 449 U.S. at 417-18. As the Texas Court of Criminal Appeals has often stat-

**SAMPLE APPELLATE BRIEF**

ed, the Court must give due weight "to the specific reasonable inferences that [an officer] is entitled to draw from the facts in light of his experience." *See, e.g., Brother v. State,* 166 S.W.3d 255, 257 (Tex. Crim. App. 2005). The reviewing court must ask whether the facts available to the officer at the time of the stop would warrant a person of reasonable caution in the ¬ belief that the action taken was appropriate. *See Davis v. State,* 947 S.W.2d 240, 243 (Tex. Crim. App. 1997). As each of the factors listed above indicates and this Court should find, Officer Blake was warranted in believing that the stop was [necessary].

> **Comment:** The introductory paragraph to Heading I. introduces the rules of law relating to valid Terry stops. Here, the writer explains that the question of reasonable suspicion is determined by looking at the totality, comprised of the listed factors. The reader now expects a discussion of the factors.

## A. The Defendant's Nervous and Evasive Behavior Led Officer Blake to Believe that He Was About to Rob or in the Process of Robbing the Gas [Station].

> **Comment:** The first minor heading summarizes the argument with respect to the first factor: the defendant's behavior.

The defendant's suspicious and evasive behavior was consistent with criminal activity and thus contributed to Officer Blake's reasonable [suspicion]. *See Terry,* 392 U.S. at 22-23. In *Terry,* Officer McFadden observed two men loitering on a street corner and pacing up and down the street. Several times, he saw the two men pause outside a store front window and peer in; they also consulted briefly with a third man. Believing the men to be "casing" the store for a robbery, McFadden conducted a brief investigative stop and [frisk]. The court established not only the validity of such a stop but also held that McFadden had reason to believe the men were engaged in criminal activity and was justified in stopping them [briefly]. *Id.* at 27-28. Although the Court acknowledged that activities such as walking up and down the street and looking in store windows by themselves can be innocent, "the story is quite different where, as here, two men hover about a street corner for an extended period of time, at the end of which it becomes apparent that they are not waiting for anyone or anything." *Id.* at 23. In that case, the court ruled, McFadden was justified in stopping them. [*Id.*]

> **Comment:** This topic sentence makes an argument with regard to the first factor relevant to reasonable suspicion: nervous and evasive behavior.

> **Comment:** Discusses facts of cited case and explains what reasonable suspicion based on behavior can mean.

> **Comment:** States holding of *Terry* Court.

> **Comment:** The reasoning of the *Terry* court is explained.

Similarly, Officer Blake observed Defendant Opara standing outside the gas station, in a dark ¬ corner of the parking lot. He appeared nervous, looked up and down the street, glanced into the station several times, and kept his hands shoved firmly into his pockets. Like Officer McFadden, Officer Blake thought that the Defendant might be preparing to commit a robbery since the Defendant did not appear to be "waiting for anyone or anything." [Taken] together, the Defendant's series of acts contributed to Officer Blake's reasonable suspicion, and the

> **Comment:** The writer explicitly compares the defendants' behavior in *Terry* to Opara's behavior.

**SAMPLE APPELLATE BRIEF**

situation warranted further investigation. *See id.* at [22].

In addition to his suspicious behavior, the Defendant's evasive behavior contributed to Officer Blake's suspicion and justified the investigative [stop]. As the consummate act of evasion, flight is suggestive of [wrongdoing]. *Illinois v. Wardlow*, 528 U.S. 119, 124 (2000); *Vanderhorst v. State*, 52 S.W.3d 237, 240 (Tex. App. 2001). In *Vanderhorst*, the defendant was stopped in his pick-up by an officer responding to a call that the driver was intoxicated. When the officer arrived in his car, the defendant turned off the lights and began to back away from the police [car]. On appeal, the Court of Appeals ruled that the officer had reasonable suspicion in part because the defendant had begun to flee: "Flight from an officer also can provide a reasonable suspicion that justifies an investigative [detention]." *Vanderhorst*, 52 S.W.3d at 240.

Similarly, as Officer Blake approached Defendant Opara, Opara backed away from Blake and then turned to flee. [The] absence of a tip in this case does not make *Vanderhorst* distinguishable because there were other factors that led Blake to suspect Opara was engaged in criminal activity, and each case must be judged on its unique facts and [circumstances]. Opara's flight thus contributed to Blake's reasonable suspicion in this [case]. ¬

### B. The Fact that the Defendant Was Observed Behaving Nervously and Evasively in a High-Crime Area also Contributed to Officer Blake's Reasonable Suspicion.

The fact that Officer Blake observed Defendant Opara acting nervously and suspiciously at night in an area known for crime is another factor justifying the *Terry* [stop]. When an officer suspects the defendant is engaged in criminal activity of the sort that typically occurs where the defendant is observed, there may be reasonable suspicion to [stop]. *See Guzman*, 955 S.W.2d at 90 (holding that because defendant was observed in area known for drug trafficking, that fact contributed to probable cause for [arrest]). As in *Guzman*, Officer Blake observed Defendant Opara in an area known for habitual drug

**Comment:** Conclusion regarding effect of Opara's suspicious behavior is stated here.

**Comment:** The topic sentence makes the argument with regard to the defendant's behavior in terms of evasiveness and establishes that evasion is relevant to reasonable suspicion.

**Comment:** The writer explains here that flight can mean evasion.

**Comment:** Discusses facts of cited case to illustrate evasive behavior.

**Comment:** States holding of court that the stop was justified in *Vanderhorst*.

**Comment:** Writer explicitly compares evasive behavior in *Vanderhorst* to that of Opara.

**Comment:** Writer anticipates potential counter-argument.

**Comment:** Conclusion regarding effect of Opara's evasive behavior is stated here.

**Comment:** Second minor heading summarizes argument with respect to second factor: the defendant's location in a high-crime area.

**Comment:** The topic sentence makes clear the argument with regard to the second factor.

**Comment:** Writer states rule that the defendant's presence in a high-crime area contributes to reasonable suspicion.

**Comment:** A parenthetical is used here to discuss the basic facts/ holding of a case that illustrates what a high-crime area is. Since the specific facts of *Guzman* are not that helpful, a summary of the key fact that the defendant was observed in a drug-trafficking area is adequate and saves space.

## SAMPLE APPELLATE BRIEF

tracking and store [robberies]. Combined with the defendant's behavior, the nature of the area in which he was observed contributed to Officer Blake's reasonable [suspicion].

**Comment:** The writer compares the facts of *Opara* to facts of *Guzman*.

### C. Officer Blake's Experience on the Police Force Should Be Taken Into Account In Determining Whether "Innocent" Activity Led Him to Reasonably Suspect that the Defendant Was Engaged in Imminent Criminal [Activity].

**Comment:** Conclusion regarding effect of Opara being in a high-crime area is stated here.

Officer Blake's experience on the force in the crime-ridden area at issue here contributed to his having reasonable suspicion to stop Defendant Opara. [See] *Cortez*, 449 U.S. at 419; *Ford v. State*, 158 S.W.3d 488, 493-94 (Tex. Crim. App. 2005) (holding that an officer's experience can factor into a reasonable suspicion determination). Even ¬ innocent-looking activity can be indicative of crime, and where a trained officer suspects a crime may be underway, he may stop to [investigate]. *See, e.g., Woods v. State*, 956 S.W.2d 33, 37 (Tex. Crim. App. 1997) (holding that a private security guard trained to operate a metal detector and x-ray machine at a county courthouse had reason to suspect a woman was engaged in criminal activity based on her [behavior]). Once Opara had begun to flee, Officer Blake's function was to resolve the ambiguity raised in his mind and determine whether Opara was engaged in criminal activity. *See Woods*, 956 S.W.2d at 37. Under these circumstances, where the totality gave rise to a suspicion of imminent crime, "it would have been poor police work indeed" for an officer with Blake's training and experience "to have failed to investigate this behavior [further]" *Terry*, 392 ¬ U.S. at 23.

**Comment:** The third minor heading summarizes the argument with respect to this factor: the officer's experience in similar situations.

**Comment:** The topic sentence makes the argument with regard to the third factor.

**Comment:** Writer states rule that the officer's experience can contribute to reasonable suspicion.

**Comment:** A parenthetical is used here to discuss the basic facts and holding of a case being used to illustrate what it means to have experience reasonably affect suspicion.

**Comment:** Writer applies rule relating to officer experience to facts of Opara case and concludes.

### II. OFFICER BLAKE HAD REASONABLE, ARTICULABLE SUSPICION TO BELIEVE THAT THE DEFENDANT WAS ARMED AND DANGEROUS WHEN HIS BEHAVIOR WAS CONSISTENT WITH ROBBERY IN A HIGH-CRIME AREA.

Officer Blake's frisk of Defendant Opara was conducted lawfully. Once an officer stops a suspect under *Terry* with reasonable suspicion that he may be engaged in criminal activity, he may also conduct a brief pat-down search for weapons if he has reason to believe the suspect is armed and dangerous. *Terry*, 392 U.S. at 27. The officer need not be certain that the suspect is armed and dangerous, "the issue is whether a reasonably prudent man in the circumstances would be warranted in the belief that his safety or that of others was in danger." *Id.* As with the validity of a *Terry* stop, reasonableness is deter-

**SAMPLE APPELLATE BRIEF**

mined by looking at the totality of circumstances, including the nature of the crime suspected and the defendant's behavior toward the [officer]. *See, e.g., Terry*, 392 U.S. at 28; *Griffin*, 215 S.W.3d at 409. Each of these factors contributed to Blake's reasonable suspicion that Opara was armed and dangerous, thus justifying the frisk.

### A. The Nature of the Suspected Crime Reasonably Led Officer Blake to Believe the Defendant Might Be Armed and Dangerous].

Officer Blake's reasonable suspicion that Defendant Opara might be about to rob the gas station justified the limited frisk he conducted for weapons. Where the suspected crime usually involves weapons, the officer is entitled to frisk for his safety and that of others around him. *Terry*, 392 U.S. at 28; *O'Hara v. State*, 27 S.W.3d 548, 555(Tex. Crim. App. 2000) ("Generally, a police officer may search a suspect where there is reason to believe a suspect is armed and dangerous, and the suspect is suspected of a violent crime or dealing in large amounts of [drugs].") In *Terry*, Officer McFadden suspected that the men casing the store front were about to commit a daylight robbery. In holding the pat-down frisk McFadden conducted lawful, the Court stated, "McFadden's hypothesis [was] that these men were contemplating a daylight robbery which, it is reasonable to assume, would be likely to involve the use of weapons." *Terry*, 392 U.S. at 28. Similarly, Officer Blake believed Opara was about to commit a robbery under similar [circumstances]. Blake was reasonable assuming that the robbery might involve weapons and thus justified in frisking [Opara] . ¬

### B. The Defendant's Behavior Reasonably Led Officer Blake to Believe He Was Armed and Dangerous].

Even if Officer Blake had not suspected Opara of being engaged in an inherently dangerous crime, Opara's behavior justified Blake's belief that he was armed and dangerous. When a suspect leads an officer to believe he may be concealing and/or reaching for a weapon, a weapons frisk is [justified]. *Terry*, 392 U.S. at 27; *Griffin*, 215 S.W.3d at 409; *Dixon v. State*, 187 S.W.3d 767 (Tex. Ct. App. 2006). In *Dixon*, an officer stopped a man staggering down the street after midnight. The suspect "raised his hands to his chest area as if to conceal something, stood sideways rather than face to face with the officer, and mumbled through clenched teeth." *Id.* at 769-70. The court held the subsequent frisk valid

**SAMPLE APPELLATE BRIEF**

because the officer had reason to believe the suspect was armed. *Id.* at 770. Similarly, Officer Blake had reason to believe Opara was armed that night: When the officer called out to the Defendant, he started to back away, leading Blake to believe he too might be concealing a weapon, and then Opara took [flight]. Since it was dark, Blake could not tell if anything was behind Opara's back, and he was justified in conducted a minimal pat-down frisk for [weapons]. ¬

## CONCLUSION

For the reasons stated above, the State respectfully requests that this Court reverse the District Court's order granting the Defendant's motion to suppress.

Respectfully submitted,

_____

Victor Kelsen, J.D.
120 W. 15th Street
Austin, Texas 78701

Attorney for the Appellant

March 17, 2009

**SAMPLE APPELLATE BRIEF**

## 3. STUDENT–WRITTEN, SAMPLE APPELLATE BRIEF WITH COMMENTS

Attached at Appendix C is a student-written, appellate brief on a issue of Fourth Amendment law similar to that in the *Opara* case. The issue presented for review involved whether the arresting officer conducted a valid *Terry* stop and frisk. Comments in the margin respond to the writer's argument, organization, and mechanics.

Additional sample appellate briefs are easy to find. Databases of briefs filed in federal and state court are available on Lexis and Westlaw. They can be searched using either terms and connectors or natural language searches.

---

### *QUESTIONS FOR CONSIDERATION AND WRITING EXERCISES*

1. Did you find the State's appellate brief persuasive? Why? What are the brief's strengths and weaknesses?

2. Would you have approached any of the arguments differently? Changed the organization? How so?

3. Review Arguments II. A–B of the sample appellate brief. In the right margin, annotate the argument as shown in I. A–C to reveal its internal organization.

4. Research Texas law on *Terry* stops and frisks. Draft the appellate brief for Opara. Consider the theory of the case, how to state the law from Opara's point of view, the best cases for the defendant, and large and small scale organizational issues.

5. Once you have drafted the appellate brief, annotate the arguments as shown in the sample brief above. Do your arguments contain the essentials of good legal argument? Are they organized deductively? Are the analogies to case law effective?

6. Do you use all forms of appeal—reason, emotion, and credibility? Which do you rely on most heavily? Did you strike the right balance? Do you think the "right balance" changes on a case-by-case basis? If so, how?

---

# D. ORAL ARGUMENT

Oral argument gives advocates an opportunity to summarize their arguments and, perhaps more important, gives the judges an opportunity to ask the parties questions. Although this book focuses on written advocacy, a section on oral argument is included here because law students often practice oral argument in conjunction with persuasive writing.

Oral argument today is a *conversation* as opposed to a performance where the advocate would memorize and recite scripted lines (as in ancient Greece and Rome). When an advocate is as familiar with the law as she is once she has briefed it, oral argument becomes an exercise in marshalling the *best* arguments in an interesting and effective way (remember the importance of the theory of the case) and controlling nerves. The opportunity to give oral argument is not automatic. Courts have specific rules about requesting that privilege. Because the opportunity to meet the judges and answer their questions can be rare, advocates are grateful for the chance to explain their arguments to the court.

### *Typical Elements of Oral Argument.*

A typical courtroom speech in ancient Rome had an introduction, a statement of the issues to be addressed, a statement of the facts, an outline of the arguments, the actual arguments and rebuttal of counter-arguments, and a conclusion.[39] The orator delivered the speech without interruption. In modern appellate argument, the process is less formal. Although advocates prepare virtually the same elements for their argument, they can expect—but not plan on—to be interrupted almost immediately by the judges. Since the judges want answers to their questions and time is limited, it can be difficult to deliver prepared remarks.

## 1. INTRODUCTION

The chief judge usually invites counsel for the appellant to begin the argument. A standard introduction would be, "May it please the court, my name is _____, and I represent the appellant." If more than one attorney for the same party plans to argue, counsel might introduce her co-counsel and explain their division of the issues. The appellant usually indicates at this time whether she wishes to reserve rebuttal time and how much. The appellant is given the option to rebut the appellee's arguments once the appellee's argument is finished.

## 2. STATEMENT OF THE ISSUE(S) FROM THE CLIENT'S PERSPECTIVE

Counsel for the appellant should open with an *attention-getting characterization* of the case and the issues based on her theory of the case. A modified or shortened statement of the issues presented for review from the brief is a good starting point.

## 3. OFFER/PROCEED TO RECITE FACTS

Counsel for the appellant should offer and be prepared to recite the facts of the case from the appellant's perspective. If the judges are familiar with the facts, they often ask the appellant to skip or shorten the statement and proceed directly to the party's argument. Counsel for the appellee may take issue with the appellant's version of the facts, but a second, full statement of the facts is not required.

---

**39.** *See supra* ch. 4, at 103.

## 4. ARGUMENT/QUESTION AND ANSWER PERIOD

(a) An advocate should begin by offering reasons why the court should rule in her favor. Practitioners' materials often suggest keeping it simple: Fashion the thrust of the brief into two or three main reasons (factors, elements, etc.) why the party should prevail. The reasons should be easy to remember and consistent with the theory of the case. A simple list of the reasons at the outset helps to guide the court and keep the advocate on track.

(b) The advocate should proceed to make her arguments. Most judges expect to hear the party's strongest arguments first as opposed to last. Judges do sometimes ask for cites to supporting case law, and it is not uncommon for advocates to bring their research materials to the lectern. Where an advocate cannot locate the requested information or authority, she should offer to provide it to the court after the argument.

(c) Often, the court interrupts quickly with questions. *That's why advocates are there.* It is easy to feel annoyed by the judges' interruptions, but questions indicate the judges are engaged in the issues. The advocate's prepared argument is often less important than effectively answering the judges' questions.

(d) Advocates are advised to prepare for their arguments with note cards or an outline. A full script may tempt the advocate to read her argument (which is ineffective), and make it difficult to find her place once she has been diverted by questions.

(e) There is a universal etiquette for oral argument. The advocate must be polite, deferential—address the judges as "your Honor," assertive but not hostile, open, and honest. If an advocate cannot recall the name or facts of a case, he should not pretend to do so. The advocate who offers to provide more detailed information to the court at a later time is more credible than the one who makes it up on the spot. When the advocate sees that her allotted time is running out, she should take that as a cue to wrap up her argument (*e.g.*, summarize her second reason if she has gotten only to the first or summarize both arguments). Once the clock runs out, she must stop talking immediately and ask the court's permission to conclude.

## 5. CONCLUSION

If time permits, the advocate should summarize her arguments and state the specific relief she requests.

---

*QUESTIONS FOR CONSIDERATION AND ORAL ARGUMENT EXERCISES*

1. **What can you accomplish through oral argument that you cannot accomplish in writing?**

2. **In what kinds of cases are judges more likely to grant requests for oral argument?**

---

3. How, if at all, should the emphasis of argument change from written to oral form? How would Aristotle answer that question?

4. Once you have drafted Opara's appellate brief, prepare an oral argument in the case. Consider the theory of the case and how you will characterize the issues to the court. What will your main goal be with respect to the stop and frisk issues?

5. To anticipate the appellant's oral argument, prepare a list of questions the judges might ask to challenge your argument.

6. Practice delivering your argument, giving yourself six to eight minutes to argue. Ask your classmates to act as counsel for appellant and the appellate court.

# CHAPTER 9

## STYLE: FROM CLARITY TO POLISH IN LEGAL WRITING

■ ■ ■

*"With communication the object, the principle of simplicity would dictate that the language used by lawyers agree with the common speech, unless there are reasons for a difference."*—David Mellinkoff

Aristotle said it is not enough to know *what* to say, one must know *how* to say it.[1] Cicero said the speaker should adjust his style according to the goals of the speech and legal argument should be delivered in a grand, high style.[2] As the study of rhetoric developed into the study of style, nineteenth-century scholars catalogued a multitude of existing figures of speech,[3] several of which are used today in legal writing. Despite Cicero's views, the hallmark of good legal writing today is *simplicity*. The legal audience of the twenty-first century does not have time for ornate language or verbosity. Clients and judges alike want lawyers to write in plain, straightforward terms that can be easily understood. Like any specialized discourse community, the legal profession has its own way of speaking and writing. At first, the law can seem as indecipherable as a foreign language. However, as one becomes familiar with the language and interacts with colleagues, she quickly becomes socialized into the legal community.[4] Once socialized, new legal writers are tempted to use legal jargon and Latin phrases (*i.e.*, legalese) to demonstrate their newfound understanding, but that temptation should be resisted.

As this chapter demonstrates, today's legal audience is no less demanding than Cicero's. First, legal readers demand clarity and conciseness. These terms are not easy to define, and it can be even harder to achieve them in one's writing. Second, the legal community has its own way of doing things. A lack of familiarity with these legal writing conventions is the dead giveaway of a novice writer. Third, although many legal readers will forgive the occasional dangling modifier or misplaced comma, a good legal writer must conform to the basic rules

---

1.  ARISTOTLE, *supra* ch. 2, note 34, bk. 3, ch. 1, p. 182.
2.  CICERO, *Orator, supra* ch. 2, note 49, at 319, ch. v, ¶ 20.
3.  *See supra*, ch. 4, at 131.
4.  *See* Williams, *supra* ch. 3, at 80.

of English grammar, punctuation, and usage. It is common to encounter the client or partner who still follows the "never split an infinitive rule." Fourth, the legal reader expects the writer to cite properly to legal authority. Legal citations are unique, and the format differs depending on whether you are writing as a scholar or a practitioner. Finally, legal readers demand a high level of polish and professionalism: If a document looks sloppy, the reader will assume the reasoning is sloppy as well.

The number of demands placed on the legal writer seems daunting at first. Like any new skill, it takes time to master. This chapter begins by briefly summarizing the Plain English Movement, which explains why legal writers today aspire to a simple, elegant style. Second, it examines each of the areas outlined above—clarity and conciseness, legal writing conventions, good mechanics of writing, citation format, and professionalism—in an effort to capture their most important aspects. A short set of exercises appears after each section with suggested answers attached as an appendix. For additional reading in any of these areas, consult one of the texts footnoted below or a style manual of your choice.[5] As you endeavor to conform to the legal community's expectations, you may begin to feel there is little room for creativity in legal writing, but the opposite is true. Good legal writing is actually *rare*, and those writers who stand out do so because they are creative. Opportunities for creativity arise at every stage of the writing process: researching and choosing the "relevant law," crafting a theory of the case, articulating synthesized rules of law, choosing the "best cases" for analogy and distinction, organizing arguments, varying sentence structure, and making effective and colorful word choices. Although most appellate briefs, for example, contain basically the same elements (*e.g.*, a statement of the issues, statement of facts, summary of argument, and argument), no two briefs are alike. What differentiates them is the writer's skill and creativity.

## A. THE PLAIN ENGLISH MOVEMENT

The simple, elegant style preferred in legal writing today originated in ancient Greece. Aristotle advised orators to speak clearly,[6] and the great Attic orators of the fourth and fifth centuries B.C.E. employed a plain and direct style of speaking.[7] Cicero discussed the Attic style, but he preferred a high, florid style in his own courtroom speeches.[8] In the early seventeenth century, Francis Bacon criticized the ornate style of the Renaissance humanists who had insisted on

---

5. ANNE ENQUIST & LAUREL CURRIE OATES, JUST WRITING: GRAMMAR, PUNCTUATION, AND STYLE FOR THE LEGAL WRITER (2d ed. 2005); BRYAN A. GARNER, THE REDBOOK: A MANUAL ON LEGAL STYLE (2d ed. 2006); MARY RAY & JILL J. RAMSFIELD, LEGAL WRITING: GETTING IT RIGHT AND GETTING IT WRITTEN (4th ed. 2005); WILLIAM STRUNK, JR. & E.B. WHITE, THE ELEMENTS OF STYLE (4th ed. 1999); JOSEPH WILLIAMS, STYLE: LESSONS IN CLARITY AND GRACE (9th ed. 2006); RICHARD WYDICK, PLAIN ENGLISH FOR LAWYERS (5th ed. 2005).

6. *See supra*, ch. 4, at 130.

7. *See supra*, ch. 2, at 12.

8. *See id.* at 22.

imitating Cicero's style, aptly called the Ciceronians.[9] Bacon advocated instead a simple and functional style, rejecting what he believed to be the Ciceronians' preoccupation with form over substance.[10] Like Bacon, the eighteenth-century epistemologists favored a simple speaking style for legal argument. Campbell, for example, revived Aristotle's focus on the needs of the audience and recommended the use of words that are reputable, national, and of present use.[11] By the late eighteenth century, rhetoric had evolved into the study of literature and style, and rhetoricians like Hugh Blair sought to define taste and beauty in written language. Even Blair, though, whose primary interest was in literature, counseled lawyers to speak primarily to the faculty of understanding and avoid a "high, vehement tone."[12]

Despite centuries' worth of advice to speak in plain and simple terms, lawyers developed a language only they understand. Throughout history, the legal profession has been accused, and in some cases rightly so, of deliberate doublespeak, designed to make lawyers indispensable and justify their fees.[13] The sophists of Aristotle's time were criticized for using clever but false arguments, although the "falsity" of their arguments had more to do with their willingness to argue both sides of a dispute than the form of their speeches.[14] The second sophists of ancient Rome rejected the Attic style of the Greeks and developed a grandiloquent style designed to amaze and entertain their audiences.[15] The early Christian church rejected classical rhetoric altogether, particularly its grandiloquence, due to its pagan roots. In the fourth century, however, St. Augustine revived it to spread Christianity; and he looked primarily to the eloquence of Cicero for inspiration.[16] Centuries later, the focus shifted from eloquence to efficiency. As the medieval feudal system developed and populations exploded, form letters developed to handle a multitude of church and secular correspondence. Designed neither to entertain nor amaze, form letters aimed at precision produced wordiness and redundancy. The boilerplate language in many transactional and estate-planning documents, such as leases, bills of sale, licenses, wills, and trusts, can be traced back to these medieval form letters. By the end of the nineteenth century, traditional legal writing was characterized as

---

**9.** *See id.* at 46.

**10.** *See id.* at 47.

**11.** Reputable meant language that conforms to a standard to be measured against the language of authors of reputation, "national" meant language that was neither provincial nor foreign, and "of present use" meant language that was neither modern nor obsolete. *See supra*, ch. 2, at 54.

**12.** *See id.* at 58.

**13.** By the mid-nineteenth century, Jeremy Bentham, an English philosopher and legal scholar, said that the language of lawyers had been "wrought up to the highest possible pitch of voluminousness, indistinctness, and unintelligibility." 6 JEREMY BENTHAM, Works 232 (Bowring ed., 1843). He described lawyers as "harpies of the law" schooled in "the art of poisoning language in order to fleece their clients." 5 *id.* at 23.

**14.** *See supra*, ch. 2, at 11.

**15.** *See id.* at 27.

**16.** *See id.* at 31.

intentionally complicated and impenetrable.

In the twentieth century, the public's disillusion with legal writing gave birth to the modern Plain English Movement. In 1953, Stuart Chase wrote a book, entitled *The Power of Words*,[17] that explored the power of language in all aspects of modern society. In a chapter called "Gobbledygook," Chase complained that the practice of "squandering words" and "packing a message with excess baggage" had grown "wild and lush in the law."[18] Ten years later, David Mellinkoff, a professor of law at UCLA, published *The Language of the Law*,[19] which illustrated in 450 pages what Chase may have meant and what Mellinkoff considered the absurdities of traditional legal writing. For example, he criticized a lawyer's tendency to use commonly understood words for a different purpose:

> Nothing serves better to mark the gulf between the language of the law and the common speech than a listing of common words that mean one thing to the eye or ear of the non-lawyer, and may mean something completely different to the lawyer.[20]

A few of the words he chose as examples are listed below:

| | |
|---|---|
| *action* | law suit |
| *instrument* | legal document |
| *executed* | signed and delivered |
| *prayer* | form of pleading to the court[21] |

To this, Mellinkoff added that lawyers (as well as other poor writers) are wordy, unclear, pompous, and dull.[22] He was even more critical of the form letters and books that first appeared during the Middle Ages. In those, he said, "[a lawyer] could find anything—the good and the bad, with the accolade of precedent claimed for each."[23] He concluded that a lawyer "surrounded by old boilerplate" never felt alone.[24]

The movement toward plain language that Chase and Mellinkoff inspired is now widespread. Legal educators have encouraged their students to write in plain terms since legal writing programs began in the 1970s. Richard Wydick's *Plain English for Lawyers*[25] is one example of a text devoted to helping lawyers achieve a simple but elegant style.[26] Outside the legal academy,

---

17. STUART CHASE, THE POWER OF WORDS (1953).

18. *Id.* at 251.

19. DAVID MELLINKOFF, THE LANGUAGE OF THE LAW (1963).

20. *Id.* at 11.

21. *Id.* at 12. In addition to using common words with uncommon meanings, Mellinkoff said that lawyers characterstically use rare Old and Middle English words, Latin words and phrases, terms of art, jargon, formal words, words and expressions chosen for their flexible meaning, and language designed to achieve extreme precision of meaning. *See id.* at 11–23.

22. *Id.* at 24.

23. *Id.* at 278.

24. *Id.*

25. RICHARD WYDICK, PLAIN ENGLISH FOR LAWYERS (5th ed. 2005).

26. For additional style manuals, *see supra*, n. 5.

several administrations have worked to improve the quality of writing in legal contexts. In 1972, President Nixon ordered the Federal Register to be written in "layman's terms."[27] In 1978, President Carter signed executive orders requiring that federal regulations be written "in a simple and straightforward fashion."[28] Although President Reagan rescinded these orders, some agencies, such as the Social Security Administration, have made clear, plain writing a priority.[29] In 1998, President Clinton revived plain language as a major government initiative and issued a presidential memorandum requiring that federal employees write all new regulations in plain English.[30] The Bush Administration did not pursue a plain language initiative.[31] On the state level, half of the states had introduced legislation or administrative regulations by 1980 to make legal documents readable. By 1991, eight states had enacted such legislation.[32]

The Plain English Movement is not confined to the United States. Frustrated with unintelligible government forms, Chrissie Maher and Martin Cutts launched the "Plain English Campaign" in England in 1979.[33] In 1982, the British government issued a policy statement that its departments cull their forms and eliminate those that no longer made sense.[34] Other countries with plain language efforts include Australia, Canada, New Zealand, South Africa, and Sweden.[35]

# B. CLARITY AND CONCISENESS

If simplicity is the end of legal writing, clarity and conciseness are the means. A 2002 survey of federal judges indicates "there is a strong, recurring, and unmistakable cry for conciseness and clarity" in legal writing.[36] One judge wrote:

> You [legal writing faculty] need to stress the need to write clearly and concisely. We are *drowning* in 50 page briefs that are poorly written when

**27.** CAROL M. BALDWIN, PLAIN LANGUAGE AND THE DOCUMENT REVOLUTION 132 (1999).

**28.** *Id. See also* Exec. Order No. 12,044, 3 C.F.R. 152 (1978); Exec. Order No. 12,174, 3 C.F.R. 462 (1980).

**29.** Joanne Locke, *A History of Plain Language in the United States Government, available at* http://www.plainlanguage.gov/whatisPL/history/locke.cfm.

**30.** BALDWIN, *supra* note 27 at 132.

**31.** *See* Locke, *supra* note 29.

**32.** KARAN A. SCHRIVER, DYNAMICS IN DOCUMENT DESIGN 28 (1997). States with plain language statutes include Connecticut, Hawaii, Maine, Minnesota, Montana, New Jersey, New York, Oregon, Pennsylvania, and West Virginia. *See, e.g.*, Joseph Kimble, *Plain English: a Charter for Clear Writing*, 9 THOMAS M. COOLEY L. REV. 1 (1992) and Burt A. Leete, *Plain Language Legislation: a Comparison of Approaches*, 18 AM. BUS. L. J. 511 (2007).

**33.** SHRIVER, *supra* note 32 at 29.

**34.** MARTIN CUTTS, THE PLAIN ENGLISH GUIDE 6 (1995).

**35.** Duncan Berry, *Speakable Australian Acts*, 8 INFO. DESIGN J. 48 (1995); SHRIVER, *supra* note 32 at 29–32.

**36.** Kristen Robbins–Tiscione, *The Inside Scoop, What Federal Judges Really Think About the Way Lawyers Write, supra* ch. 4, at 278–79.

the case should have been presented in a 20 page brief.[37]

With regard to clarity, several judges surveyed said the best legal writers "state clearly ... what the case is about and why the court should affirm or reverse," "[m]ake things clear and interesting," "clearly and concisely identify and analyze the issues presented," and "state their positions clearly."[38] Conversely, the worst briefs "read like a Joycean stream-of-consciousness and seem to have no theme or clear purpose," "are anything but" clear, "muddy up the water," "cloud the main issues with trivia," or contain "fuzzy, imprecise thinking and writing, leaving the reader to guess or assume as to the meaning."[39] As for conciseness, judges complained that briefs are "almost invariably *too long* and frequently repetitious," "excessively long and incomprehensible," "too long, too repetitious and meandering," and "too long and do not focus on the critical issues in the case."[40]

# 1. CLARITY

All legal readers demand clarity, but it is not an easy term to define. What do you think it means to write clearly? The idea that writing can and should be "clear" probably comes from the current-traditionalist school of writing, which focuses on the product as opposed to the process of writing.[41] The act of writing is seen as mechanical, the simple act of transcribing pre-existing ideas. The idea is that the writing should be transparent so as not to form a barrier between the audience and the writer's ideas. Whether or not you subscribe to this view of writing, it seems fair to say that "clarity" in legal writing refers to its impact on the *reader*, and to write clearly is to convey your intended meaning as unambiguously as possible. To write in plain English, the modern legal writer should avoid unnecessary Latin phrases, old-fashioned phrases and terms of art, redundancies that add no meaning, elegant variation, and the unintentional use of passive voice. As you work to achieve precision in your writing, keep the following examples in mind.[42]

## a. AVOID LATIN WORDS AND PHRASES

Many legal terms of art are taken from Latin words and phrases. Although legal readers usually understand these terms, the trend is to translate them into English. Where there is no good substitute for the Latin phrase because it has become a part of the language of the law (*e.g.,* dicta and stare decisis), use the Latin without italics. Below are just a few Latin words and phrases that can be

---

**37.** *Id.* at 281.

**38.** *Id.* at 282.

**39.** *Id.*

**40.** *Id.* at 280.

**41.** *See supra,* ch. 3, at 75.

**42.** Of course, clear writing must be analytically sound, based on reasonable premises and valid reasoning. If these are lacking, even the simplest and most plainly written argument will be muddled. *See supra,* ch. 5.

translated into English to improve clarity. *See Figure 46, below.*

## Common Latin Phrases in Legal Writing

*a fortiori*—even more so, or with even stronger reason

*ab initio*—from the beginning

*amicus curaie*—friend of the court

*assuming arguendo*—assuming for the sake of argument

*bona fide*—good faith

*caveat emptor*—buyer beware

*de facto*—in fact, even if not prescribed by law

*de jure*—by law

*de minimus*—minimal

*et al.*—and others

*et seq.*—and those that follow

*in camera*—in private

*in toto*—entirely

*inter alia*—among other things

*ipso facto*—something done contrary to law is void

*nil*—nothing

*per se*—by itself

*prima facie*—on its face, at the first instance

*pro se*—to represent oneself

*quid pro quo*—to exchange one thing for another

*sua sponte*—of its own accord

**FIGURE 46**

## b. AVOID OLD–FASHIONED WORDS AND PHRASES

As you read judicial opinions, you may encounter old-fashioned phrases and terms of art that are no longer used in ordinary speech. Several of these come from Old and Middle English. Where there is a perfectly good modern substitute, you should use it. *See Figure 47, below.*

---

### OLD-FASHIONED WORDS AND PHRASES IN LEGAL WRITING

*aforementioned*—mentioned above or before

*aforesaid*—stated above or already

*aver*—to claim

*demur*—to object

*enclosed please find*—enclosed

*herein*—in this place

*hereinafter*—from now on

*heretofore*—until now

*instant case*—the present or current case

*"one" John Doe*—refers to the party, usually the defendant, in the case

*party of the first (or second) part*—refers to one of the parties to a contract

*purported*—reputed or claimed

*"said" individual*—named or mentioned before

*thence*—from that source

*thenceforth*—from that time

*therein*—in that place

*whereas*—considering that

*whereby*—under the terms of which

---

**FIGURE 47**

## c. AVOID REDUNDANCIES THAT ADD NO MEANING

In an effort to be precise, lawyers have a habit of saying the same thing multiple times, particularly in transactional and estate-planning documents. Saying the same thing twice not only takes up valuable space, it can mislead the reader into believing that each word is supposed to mean something different. One strong word that conveys the intended meaning will suffice. Follow the same principle when explaining what the law means or how it applies to your facts. If you find yourself writing, "in other words" or providing additional information in parentheses, you may be repeating yourself unnecessarily. Avoid confusing your reader: Say it well once. *See Figure 48, below.*

```
SAMPLE REDUNDANT
PHRASES IN LEGAL
     WRITING

first and foremost

fit and proper

force and effect

for all intents and purposes

give, devise, and bequeth

good and sufficient

if and when

null, void, and of no effect

rest, residue, and remainder

totally and completely

tried and true

true and correct
```

**FIGURE 48**

## d. AVOID ELEGANT VARIATION

Writers in the humanities are encouraged to vary word choice to make their writing more interesting. Known as elegant variation, this practice should be avoided in legal writing because using two different words or phrases to mean the same thing can confuse the reader.

*Example 1:*

In order to perform a valid *Terry* stop, an officer must have a **reasonable belief** that the suspect is engaged in imminent criminal activity. *Terry v. Ohio,* **392 U.S. 1, 20 (1968). In this case, since any ordinary officer would have thought the defendant was engaged in committing a crime, the stop was permissible.**

In this brief excerpt, the writer uses the phrase "reasonable belief" and "any ordinary officer would have thought" to mean the same thing. However, since "reasonable belief" is not defined, the writer cannot assume the reader will know that "ordinary officer would have thought" equates to a reasonable belief. It would be better to say the officer's belief was reasonable and explain why.

*Example 2:*

**... The buyer of the property agrees to apply for a mortgage loan within five days of today's date. Once the loan is approved, the mortgagor shall notify the seller in writing....**

In this real estate contract, the writer uses two different words to describe the buyer ("buyer" and "mortgagor"), which is confusing. It sounds as if there are three parties to the contract: buyer, mortgagor, and seller. Since the buyer and mortgagor are the same, it makes more sense to refer to the buyer as "buyer" throughout.

## e. USE PASSIVE VOICE INTENTIONALLY AND SELECTIVELY

Passive voice consists of some form of the verb "to be" (*e.g.,* is, was, were, been) followed by the past participle of the form of a second verb. The past participle of regular verbs is formed by adding –d or –ed to the basic verb form (*e.g.,* proved, used, explained). Passive voice expresses an action performed upon the subject of the sentence. For example, to say "the text was explained by the teacher" is passive. The act of explaining is performed on the subject of the sentence, "the text." In the active voice, "The teacher explained the text," the "teacher" is the subject, and "text" is the direct object.

Using passive voice in legal writing is not wrong, but it can confuse the reader because it is often unclear who engaged in the action (*e.g.,* "The text was explained," but by whom?). Use passive voice only when you intend to divert the readers' attention from the actor in the sentence.

*Example 1:*

*Passive:* **Each element was proved by a preponderance of the evidence.**

*Active:* **The plaintiff proved each element by a preponderance of the evidence.**

In the first sentence, "proved" follows "was," and expresses an action performed on the subject (*i.e.,* the elements were proved). However, the person who did the proving is unspecified, creating ambiguity for the reader. In the second sentence, the subject of the sentence is identified and performs the action indicated by the verb (*i.e.,* the plaintiff proved).

*Example 2:*

*Passive:* **Mistakes were made in calculating the data submitted with the pharmaceutical company's application for approval of a new drug.**

*Active:* **In reviewing the pharmaceutical company's application for approval of a new drug, the FDA made mistakes in calculating the data.**

In the first sentence, "made" follows "were," and expresses an action performed on the subject of the sentence (*i.e.,* mistakes were made but by whom? The pharmaceutical company?). As in the first example, the actor in the sentence is unspecified. Counsel for the FDA might intentionally write this sentence in the passive voice to avoid drawing attention to her client's negligence.

*Example 3:*

*Passive:* **Falsified tax returns were filed by the defendant for three fiscal years.**

*Active:* **The defendant filed falsified tax returns for three fiscal years.**

The first sentence is still in passive voice even though the actor—the defendant—is identified. Notice here that when written in active voice, the sentence is shorter.

## f. AVOID DOUBLE NEGATIVES

You might be surprised to find yourself writing in double negatives, particularly as you analogize or distinguish case law. Phrases such as "not unreasonable," "not unfair," and so on, can confuse the reader when they appear in a complicated sentence. Take out the negatives and say, "reasonable," "fair," etc.

# 2. CONCISENESS

Conciseness is a virtue in legal writing because it saves time and reduces the possibility that you will be misunderstood. Words, sentences, and paragraphs should be short and to the point. Short does not mean choppy, nor does it mean a long paragraph comprised of many short sentences. Saying no more than necessary forces the writer to make intentional choices. Both in litigation and transactional practice, less is often more.

*On a Large Scale*

### a. DISCUSS ONLY THOSE ISSUES RELEVANT TO YOUR ANALYSIS

Discuss or argue only those issues that relate directly to your analysis. The analogue in law exam writing is to answer only the question asked. For example, if you are writing a memorandum that analyzes potential defenses to a tort claim, but only two out of five defenses are applicable to your case, you need analyze only the two. Of course, if you are unsure about the scope of your analysis, err on the side of over-inclusion.

### b. DEVOTE NO MORE SPACE TO AN ISSUE THAN IT DESERVES

Not all issues are created equally. As you plan your document, think about how much space will be devoted to your analysis (*e.g.*, the Discussion section in a memorandum or the Argument section in a brief), and within that, how much space should be devoted to each issue (those most in dispute are likely to deserve the most attention).

### c. STATE ELEMENTS OF A CAUSE OF ACTION OR CRIME JUST ONCE

If your analysis requires you to list the elements of a cause of action or crime, you need to do that only once. For example, you do not need to quote the elements from a statute or case and then restate them in your own words in an introductory or roadmap paragraph. Once is enough to convey them to your reader.

### d. DO NOT SUMMARIZE THE HISTORY OF RULES OF LAW

Although you may find the evolution of a particular rule of law interesting as a historical matter, your reader does not usually care what the law used to be or why it changed. Unless the law's history is directly relevant to your analysis, begin with the current state of the law and proceed from there.

### e. DO NOT EXPLAIN TO THE READER WHAT YOU, AS WRITER, INTEND TO DO OR WHAT YOU ARE THINKING

In the process of writing, legal writers often teach themselves the law.[43] In early drafts, they tend to think out loud as writers as they realize the import of what they have written or what they ought to do next in the writing. Eliminate from rough drafts phrases where you "thought aloud."

---

**43.** *See supra*, ch. 3, at 79 on the recursive nature of the writing process.

*Example 1:*

**The plaintiff must prove each element by a preponderance of the evidence. This means that the jury must believe the existence of the element is more likely than not.**

Although it is not offensive to assume your reader has no knowledge of the substantive law you are analyzing, you may assume your audience knows certain legal terms and phrases. In this example, the second sentence provides a definition for preponderance of the evidence, which clarified its meaning in the writer's mind. Since this phrase is well understood by the legal community, the second sentence is unnecessary.

*Example 2:*

**In order to succeed, the plaintiff must prove three elements. I will proceed to analyze each of these elements in turn. First, the plaintiff must prove ...**

The second sentence in this example can be deleted. It clarified for the writer that each element needed to be addressed and reveals her thought process. The sentence can be eliminated without confusing the reader.

## f. COMBINE TOPIC SENTENCES WITH PREDICTIONS, ARGUMENT, AND RULES OF LAW

You may save space by combining a topic sentence that identifies the subject of your paragraph with other parts of the paragraph. In a memorandum, for example, you could combine the topic sentence regarding an element of your analysis with your prediction as to the outcome on that element. In a brief, you might combine the topic sentence both with your argument and the applicable rule of law.

*Example 1:*

**Starbucks is unlikely to prove that it produces a perishable food product under the Texas statute.**

*Example 2:*

**The *Terry* stop and frisk were permissible because Officer McFadden had reason to believe that the defendant was engaged in criminal activity and that he was armed and dangerous. *See Terry v. Ohio*, 392 U.S. 1, 20 (1968).**

*On a Small Scale*

## g. OMIT UNNECESSARY WORDS AND PHRASES

Writers of all kinds tend to clog their sentences with unnecessary words and phrases, particularly in first drafts. Often referred to as surplus[44] or needless words,[45] they add little or no meaning to the sentence and take up space. Others represent a tortured construction of a simpler idea. *See Figure 49, below.*

TYPICAL SURPLUS
WORDS AND PHRASES
IN LEGAL WRITING

*in spite of the fact that
(although)*

*owing to the fact that (because)*

*due, in part, to the fact that
(because)*

*it is important that*

*it is well-established that*

*the United States Supreme
Court (or any court) has held
that*

*in order to succeed, the plaintiff
must prove that*

*it is beyond question that*

*it is likely that*

**FIGURE 49**

## h. AVOID NOMINALIZATIONS

A nominalization is usually a verb being used as a noun. Nominalizations may sound more formal than the simpler verb form, but they make your sentences longer and more complicated. Use the simple verb instead. *See Figure 50, below.*

---

**44.** RICHARD C. WYDICK, PLAIN ENGLISH FOR LAWYERS, *supra* note 5, at 7.

**45.** BRYAN A. GARNER, LEGAL WRITING IN PLAIN ENGLISH 17 (2001).

```
┌─────────────────────────────────────┐
│           TYPICAL                    │
│       NOMINALIZATIONS                │
│       IN LEGAL WRITING               │
│                                      │
│   to reach agreement (to agree)      │
│                                      │
│   to take into consideration         │
│   (to consider)                      │
│                                      │
│   to make a decision (to decide)     │
│                                      │
│   to make an inquiry (to inquire)    │
│                                      │
│   to conduct an investigation        │
│   (to investigate)                   │
│                                      │
│   to give notice (to notify)         │
│                                      │
│   to make an objection (to object)   │
│                                      │
│   to make a recommendation           │
│   (to recommend)                     │
│                                      │
│   to bring suit (to sue)             │
│                                      │
│   be in violation of (to violate)    │
└─────────────────────────────────────┘
```

**FIGURE 50**

## i. IN ANALOGICAL REASONING, SUMMARIZE ONLY THE PARTS OF THE CASE(S) RELEVANT TO YOUR ANALYSIS

When you describe a case for purposes of analogy or distinction, you do not need to summarize all of the facts, or the court's holding, and reasoning. Be selective; describe only those portions of the case(s) relevant to your analysis.

*Example:*

In an action for vicarious liability of a parent for the negligence of his daughter, the plaintiff must prove the daughter was a member of his "immediate household." *Hurley v. Brown,* 564 S.E.2d 558 (Ga. Ct. App. 2002). In *Hurley,* Mr. and Mrs. Brown sued the defendant, James C. Hurley, for personal injuries and loss of consortium of their daughter, Stephanie. Stephanie was driving the Browns' car when the defendant's son, Brian, struck her with a car owned by the defendant. Hurley moved for summary judgment on the grounds that a parent cannot be liable for his child's negligence unless the child lives in the parent's "immediate household." *Id.* at 558–59. The court reversed the lower court's order denying the motion and granted it, stating, "[W]e have *never* held "that two people may be members of the same household under the family purpose doctrine even if they do not live together." *Id.* As in *Hurley,* the defendant's daughter in this case lived apart from her father and was financially independent. Therefore, the defendant is not likely to be held liable for her negligence.

The legal syllogism of this paragraph is simple,[46] but it gets lost in the unnecessary details of the cited case.

*Revised Example:*

In an action for vicarious liability of a parent for the negligence of his daughter, the plaintiff must prove the daughter was a member of his "immediate household." *Hurley v. Brown,* 564 S.E.2d 558 (Ga. Ct. App. 2002). In *Hurley,* the plaintiffs sued the owner of a car driven by the defendant's son. Since the son was not a member of the defendant's "immediate household," the court granted the defendant's motion for summary judgment. *Id.* at 558–59. As in *Hurley,* the defendant's daughter in this case lived apart from her father and was financially independent. Therefore, the defendant is not likely to be held liable for her negligence.

## j. USE PARENTHETICALS TO ADD BREADTH WITHOUT LENGTH

Supplement your research by citing to additional cases using signals and parentheticals. The goal of legal analysis is to convey the "synthesized rule" and apply it to the facts of your case. That means you must give your reader sufficient information to understand the rule. Do not assume that "one case per element" will suffice. In most situations, the body of law is too complicated to rely on just one case. When you cite to two or more cases in analyzing a given element, you can use signals to achieve conciseness. You can use a signal such as *see also* to cite to the additional cases and include explanatory parentheticals. See ALWD Rule 46 and BlueBook Rule 1.5 regarding explanatory parentheticals. They should begin with a present participle such as "finding" or "holding."[47]

*Example:*

In an action for vicarious liability of a parent for the negligence of his daughter, the plaintiff must prove the daughter was a member

---

**46.** Major rule: If a child is a member of the parent's immediate household, the parent may be liable for the child's negligence.

Minor premise: The child in this case is not a member of the parent's immediate household.

Conclusion: The parent is probably not liable.

Note: For the syllogism to be sound, there must be no other basis on which to hold the parent liable. Otherwise, the syllogism could commit the fallacy of denying the antecedent. *See supra* ch. 5, at 166.

**47.** *See infra,* at 291.

of his "immediate household." *Hurley v. Brown*, 564 S.E.2d 558 (Ga. Ct. App. 2002). In *Hurley*, the plaintiffs sued the owner of a car driven by the plaintiff's son. Since the son was not a member of the defendant's "immediate household," the court granted the defendant's motion for summary judgment. *Id.* at 558–59. *See also Hicks v. Newman*, 641 S.E.2d. 589, 590 (Ga. Ct. App. 2007) (holding a father not liable for son's car accident since son visited but was not a member of father's immediate household). As in *Hurley*, the defendant's daughter in this case lived apart from her father and was financially independent. Therefore, the defendant is not likely to be held liable for her negligence.

---

### *Exercises in Clarity and Conciseness*
#### *(Suggested answers appear in Appendix D.)*

*Revise each sentence or excerpt to be clearer and/or more concise.*

1. The defendant made a clear and unambiguous indication that he neither agreed nor consented to the aforementioned terms of the proposed contract.

2. In its opinion, the United States Court of Appeals for the Ninth Circuit held that, thenceforth, any contract to engage in illegal activity would be null, void, and of no effect whatsoever.

3. Assuming *arguendo* that Starbucks produces a perishable food product, it must be proved that CSP knew its statements were false.

4. On the night in question, one James Riley stood outside the convenience store hoping to make a connection with his said drug-dealer friend, "Slick."

5. The defendant, Hooper, Hardwick and Homer, Inc. (hereinafter "Hooper"), has engaged, *inter alia*, in a conspiracy to fix, establish, and maintain the price of new and used truck tires in the city of New York and its metropolitan areas.

6. It is beyond question that a citizen is allowed to walk away from a police officer without that fact contributing to reasonable suspicion of imminent criminal activity.

7. In order to succeed, the plaintiff must prove that he gave notice to the seller with regard to the defect within a reasonable period of time.

8. The agency cited the respondent for being in violation of the pertinent regulations set forth herein and determined *sua sponte* to assess a fine.

9. In no way did the defendant contribute or add to the confusing nature of the situation, making it highly unlikely that he had anything whatsoever to do with the cause of the accident.

> **10. In the next section of this memo, I will address the three major defenses that were discussed at the meeting.**

# C. LEGAL WRITING CONVENTIONS

These conventions may not be wholly unique to legal writing, but conforming to these will go a long way toward making you sound like a socialized member of the legal community.

## 1. AVOID USE OF FIRST PERSON

Lawyers write in the third person and rarely refer to themselves, unless it is unavoidable. For example, instead of saying, "I do not think that coffee is a perishable food product," say "Coffee is probably not a perishable food product," or "Starbucks is unlikely to prove that coffee is a perishable food product." Instead of saying, "You asked me to determine whether," say, "The issue is whether."

## 2. DO NOT USE CONTRACTIONS

Although Bryan Garner approves their limited use,[48] most lawyers still consider contractions too informal for legal writing.

## 3. SPELL JUDGMENT WITH ONE "E."

"Judgement" with two "e's" is an older English version. Lawyers consistently omit the first "e."

## 4. DO NOT POSE QUESTIONS TO THE READER

Lawyers generally do not ask their readers questions regarding the issues they need to resolve. Strictly speaking, questions posed to the reader are not rhetorical because you intend for them to be answered. Do not ask the reader, "What does it mean to be a perishable food product?" Instead, state the issue as a declarative sentence: The issue is whether coffee or coffee beans are perishable food products under the statute.

## 5. USE ADVERBS SPARINGLY

The best legal writers avoid overusing adverbs, such as "clearly," "obviously," "undoubtedly," "certainly," etc. Ironically, these words weaken your analysis. If something truly is clear, obvious, beyond doubt, or certain, you need not say so. "The lady doth protest too much, methinks," comes readily to mind here.[49]

---

**48.** *See* BRYAN A. GARNER, THE ELEMENTS OF LEGAL STYLE 81–82 (2d ed. 2002).

**49.** WILLIAM SHAKESPEARE, HAMLET act 3, sc. 2, line 230 (New Folger ed., Wash. Square Press 2003).

## 6. USE FEW DIRECT QUOTES

Whenever possible, paraphrase and cite to legal authority. Long, direct quotes from statutes and cases are generally ineffective. Readers often skip over them or cannot identify what part of the quotation is most significant. It is more effective to highlight the significant language by quoting short passages directly in your text. As a general rule, quote the original source directly only when the author articulates the matter better than you can paraphrase it. Quotations longer than forty-nine words must be set off as block quotes.[50]

## 7. USE PAST TENSE TO DISCUSS CITED CASES

When summarizing the facts or holding of a case, use the past tense. For example, "In *Terry*, the police officer observed [not observes] the defendant engage in suspicious activity, and Opara acted [not acts] similarly suspiciously."

## 8. SPELL OUT THE WORD "SECTION" IN TEXT

When referring in text to section numbers, usually from a statute, spell out the word "section." In a citation, however, "section" is indicated with the § symbol.[51] For example, in the text of a memo, you would refer to "section 96.001," but the citation would be to "§ 96.001."

## 9. USE COMMAS TO SEPARATE ALL ITEMS IN A SERIES

Commas are used to separate three or more items listed in a series, and there is usually a conjunction before the last item. Legal writers always use a comma before each item in the list, including the last one. For example, "The plaintiff must prove duty, breach, causation, and damages." The comma before "and" makes the sentence clear. With it, there are four elements to prove, but without it, the reader might be misled and think there are just three: duty, breach, and causation and damages.

## 10. USE FIRST, NOT FIRSTLY, IN A LIST OF REASONS

When listing a number of reasons that support their assertion, legal writers tend to use "first," "second," and so on, as opposed to "firstly," and "secondly." Both are adverbs, but the shorter form is more modern. Similarly, use "more important," as opposed to "more importantly."

---

**50.** *See* ALWD CITATION MANUAL, *supra* ch. 6, note 9, at R. 47.5(a), at 344; BLUEBOOK, *supra* ch. 6, note 9, at R. B12, at 23, & R. 5.1, at 68–69.

**51.** *See* ALWD *Citation Manual, supra* ch. 6, note 9, at R. 6.11, at 42; BLUEBOOK, *supra* ch. 6, note 9, at R. 12.9(d), at 113.

## 11. REFER TO CORPORATIONS AND COURTS AS "ITS"

Corporations and similar fictitious entities are referred to as "its," as opposed to "he's," "she's," or "they's." For example, "Starbucks must prove that CSP knew its statements were false," and "In its opinion, the court stated ..."

## 12. CAPITALIZE "COURT" ONLY WHEN REFERRING TO THE UNITED STATES SUPREME COURT OR THE COURT YOU ARE ADDRESSING IN A BRIEF

When referring to "the court," capitalize "court" only when you are referring to the United States Supreme Court or the same court to which you are briefing an argument. In all other cases, use a lower case "c."[52] This rule does not apply when naming a court in full (*e.g.,* The United States District Court for the Southern District of New York).

*Example 1:* **The Court declared separate but equal laws unconstitutional.** *See Brown v. Board of Educ.,* **347 U.S. 483 (1954).**

*Example 2:* **(in a memo): The court took several factors into account, including time, place, and location.** *James v. Juniper,* **99 S.E.2d 676 (Ga. 1999).**

*Example 3:* **(in a brief to the Georgia Supreme Court): This Court took several factors into account, including time, place, and location.** *James v. Juniper,* **99 S.E.2d 676 (Ga. 1999).**

## 13. USE DASHES TO SET OFF IMPORTANT PHRASES

It may surprise you to learn that dashes are used in legal writing to set off phrases both visually and for emphasis. Used sparingly, dashes can have a dramatic effect.

*Example 1:* **Only the driver of the car—a grown-man living alone—should be held responsible for the plaintiff's injuries.**

*Example 2:* **The hearing committee—comprised solely of men—determined that the victim was partially responsible for the sexual assault.**

---

**52.** *See* ALWD *Citation Manual, supra* ch. 6, note 9, at R. 3.3, at 4–5; BLUEBOOK, *supra* ch. 6, note 9, at R. 8, at 77.

## 14. AVOID COLLOQUIALISMS AND SLANG

Although legal writers should avoid unnecessary formality, they are still expected to write with a professional tone. For this reason, avoid informal colloquialisms and common slang.

*Example 1*: **In *Jones,* the plaintiff thought her boss was up to no good.**

*Revised Example 1*: In *Jones,* the plaintiff thought her employer was violating the law.

*Example 2*: **The chance that the court will rule in the FTC's favor is slim to none.**

*Revised Example 2*: The court is unlikely to rule in the FTC's favor.

## 15. NUMERALS

The Bluebook follows the traditional rule to spell out numbers zero to ninety-nine in text.[53] The ALWD Citation Manual indicates that you can use either numbers or words but be consistent.[54] However, always spell out a number where it begins a sentence.

*Example 1*: **The safe-harbor test has four requirements.**

*Example 2*: **The damages were set at $500.**

*Example 3*: **Twenty residents were affected.**

---

*LEGAL WRITING CONVENTION*

*(Suggested answers appear in Appendix E.)*

*Revise each sentence or excerpt to conform to legal writing convention:*

1. **I think the Court is unlikely to find for the plaintiff.**
2. **Under § 15.2(a) of the statute, the defendant isn't entitled to file an additional brief.**
3. **The question becomes, "Did the witness commit perjury?"**
4. **The judgement amount represented damages for medical expenses, out-of-pocket costs and attorney's fees.**
5. **The FAA accused United Airlines of violating safety regulations; they said the mechanics weren't thoroughly checking the planes before each flight.**

---

53. *See* BLUEBOOK, *supra* ch. 6, note 9, at R. 6.2(a), at 73–74.

54. *See* ALWD *Citation Manual, supra* ch. 6, note 9, at R. 4.2(a), at 29.

6. In *Terry*, the defendant is casing the outside of a store, and the officer thinks he is about to rob it.

7. My research indicates the officer's belief was reasonable. Firstly, the defendant was seen in a dark alley late at night. Secondly, his behavior was suspicious. Thirdly, he took flight as the officer approached.

8. Clearly, the officer's belief that the suspect was engaged in imminent criminal activity was entirely reasonable.

9. In so holding, this Court stated:

> In cases such as these, where the totality of the circumstances is the key to the validity of the stop, the court must look at each factor and then make a determination as to whether or not the officer's belief is reasonable.

*Jones,* 87 N.W.2d at 75.

10. We believe that our opponent's position isn't supported by the case law.

# D. ENGLISH GRAMMAR, PUNCTUATION, AND USAGE

The following rules are the most commonly misunderstood rules of grammar, punctuation, and usage in legal writing. You may find this list particularly useful at the polishing stage of the writing process.

## 1. PLACE QUOTATION MARKS OUTSIDE COMMAS AND PERIODS

Quotation marks *always* go outside commas and periods, even when quoting short phrases.

*Example 1*: "Contributory negligence," the court said, "is no longer a complete bar to recovery."

*Example 2*: Starbucks must prove it produces "perishable food products."

## 2. PLACE QUOTATION MARKS INSIDE COLONS AND SEMI–COLONS

Quotation marks *always* go inside colons and semi-colons.

*Example 1*: She claimed to be suffering from "battered women's syndrome": a form of temporary insanity.

*Example 2*: She claimed to be suffering from "battered women's syndrome"; however, there was no evidence that she had been abused.

## 3. PLACE QUOTATION MARKS OUTSIDE QUESTION AND EXCLAMATION MARKS ONLY IF THEY ARE PART OF THE QUOTATION

*Example 1*: The defendant then asked, "Did you see if the light was red?"

*Example 2*: The victim screamed, "Help!"

## 4. USE COMMAS AFTER INTRODUCTORY PHRASES

Commas should be used after introductory phrases that contain more than three or four words. Commas make these sentences easier to read and set off the main idea of the sentence.

*Example 1*: In order to prove self-defense, Mrs. Myers will need to prove two elements.

*Example 2*: Having examined the fourth factor, the Court concluded the defendant was innocent.

## 5. USE COMMAS BETWEEN INDEPENDENT CLAUSES JOINED BY COORDINATING CONJUNCTIONS

Commas should be used between two independent clauses (complete thoughts that contain a subject and verb) that are joined by any of the following coordinating conjunctions: and, or, for, nor, but, either, neither, or yet.

*Example 1*: The plaintiff filed the complaint on time, but she failed to file in accordance with the local rules.

If you eliminated the subject "she" in the second clause, you would no longer need a comma because you would now have a single clause with a compound verb:

The plaintiff <u>filed</u> the complaint on time <u>but failed</u> to file in accordance with the local rules.

*Example 2*: The seller guarantees that the product will perform as described, but in the event of a problem, the purchaser agrees to notify the seller within five days ...

These clauses are independent; for conciseness reasons, they could be separated into two sentences.

## 6. USE SEMI-COLONS TO JOIN TWO INDEPENDENT CLAUSES THAT ARE RELATED IN SOME WAY

Semi-colons join two short, independent clauses that have some relation to each other. Each is a separate sentence, and again, for conciseness reasons, could be separated into two sentences.

**Example 1: Comparative negligence apportions liability among the parties; each party pays according to his share of the fault.**

You can also use semicolons to separate independent clauses joined by a conjunctive adverb.

**Example 2: Self-defense is comprised of two elements, both of which are measured by a reasonableness standard; however, for the first element, the question is whether that particular defendant acted reasonably.**

## 7. USE SEMI-COLONS TO SEPARATE ITEMS IN A SERIES WHERE ANY ITEM OF THE SERIES CONTAINS A COMMA

Although items in a series are usually separated by commas, semi-colons should be used where any item in the series contains a comma.

**Example: The court based its decision on the fact that Eleanor had a high school education; limited experience with high-paying, professional employment; and a frustrated desire to have children.**

## 8. AVOID SPLITTING INFINITIVES

The infinitive form of a verb is usually the word "to" plus the verb itself, such as "to state," "to decide," "to go." To split the infinitive is to place a word or phrase between them. The rule against splitting infinitives appeared in the nineteenth century. Although some still adhere strictly to this rule, most modern readers will not object to a split infinitive when it makes the sentence smoother and easier to read.

**Example 1: The tenant shall not be entitled <u>to</u> without prior permission <u>paint, remodel, or renovate</u> the apartment.**

*Revised Example 1:* The tenant shall not be entitled to paint, remodel, or renovate the apartment without the landlord's permission.

**Example 2: The goal of the meeting was to further solidify the co-defendants' ideas.**

*Revised Example 2*: The goal of the meeting was to solidify further the co-defendants' ideas.

In *Example 2*, you might decide that the original phrase that includes a split infinitive sounds better.

## 9. USE "THAT" AND "WHICH" CORRECTLY; IF IN DOUBT, USE "THAT."

"That" is used with restrictive clauses. A restrictive clause narrows or limits the meaning of its subject. In the sentence, "All cars that are due for inpsection will be towed," the word "that" restricts the meaning of cars to be towed to only those due for inspection. Commas are not used to set off restrictive clauses.

"Which" is used with non-restrictive clauses. A non-restrictive clause provides additional information about the subject without restricting its meaning. In the sentence, "All cars, which are due for inspection, will be towed," the word "which" describes the cars to be towed, but it does not limit them. Commas should be used to set off non-restrictive clauses.

**Example 1: The issue that poses the greatest problem for the plaintiff is whether she gave the defendant adequate notice of the defect.**

**Example 2: The issue, which poses a great problem for the plaintiff, is whether she gave adequate notice of the defect.**

It can be hard sometimes to tell whether "that" or "which" should be used. In those cases, opt for "that," it is usually right.

## 10. USE CORRECT PLURAL FORMS FOR SINGULAR WORDS ENDING IN "S."

To form the plural of a singular noun ending in "s," simply add "es."

*Example*: **The house belongs to the Joneses.**

## 11. USE CORRECT POSSESSIVE FORMS FOR WORDS ENDING IN "S."

Add an apostrophe alone or an apostrophe and "s" to form the possessive of singular nouns already ending in "s." Add only an apostrophe to form the possessive of plural nouns already ending in "s."

*Example 1*: **Mr. Faris' (or Mr. Faris's) claim cannot succeed.**

*Example 2*: **The Newells' best hope for recovery lies in a cause of action for wrongful pregnancy.**

## 12. AVOID USING PRONOUNS WITH AMBIGUOUS REFERENTS

Excessive use of pronouns in compound sentences can be confusing to the reader, who may be unsure to whom the pronoun refers.

**Example 1: At present, Susan has custody of the children; however, she has informed her daughter that she must do nothing to jeopardize the situation.**

In this example, it is not clear whether the second "she" refers to Susan or the daughter. It is best simply to rename the intended person: "that Susan must do nothing ..."

**Example 2: The court sanctioned McDonald's for failing to warn its customers about the temperature of the coffee; it had no problem with its manufacturing processes.**

Here, to what "it" refers is unclear: McDonald's or the court?

## 13. MAKE SURE NOUNS/VERBS AND NOUNS/PRONOUNS AGREE

**Incorrect Example 1: The prison <u>warden</u> censors the inmates' mail, and he <u>insist</u> that they read it in the common room.**

*Revised Example 1:* The prison warden censors the inmates' mail, and he <u>insists</u> that they read it in the common room.

**Incorrect Example 2: <u>The Court</u> examined the evidence, and <u>they</u> concluded the evidence was insufficient.**

*Revised Example 2:* The Court examined the evidence, and <u>it</u> concluded the evidence was insufficient.

## 14. AVOID DANGLING MODIFIERS

A dangling modifier is a phrase that does not clearly or sensibly refer to or modify the subject of the sentence.

**Incorrect Example: Taking all factors into consideration, the defendant is likely to prove Officer McFadden violated his Fourth Amendment rights.**

In this example, "taking the factors as into consideration" does not modify the subject, "defendant." Instead, it refers to what the writer or court might do to resolve the issue.

*Revised Example:* Taking all factors into consideration, the Court is likely to conclude that Officer McFadden violated the defendant's Fourth Amendment rights.

# 15. COMMONLY CONFUSED WORDS

## a. AFFECT V. EFFECT

"Affect" is used most often as a verb, as in "her attitude did not affect me." Used as a noun, "affect" refers to a person's demeanor. "Effect" is most often used as a noun, as in "her attitude had no effect on me," and "the price increase had no effect on demand."

## b. IMPLY V. INFER

"Imply" and "infer" are both verbs. "To imply" is to suggest meaning that is not explicitly stated. For example, "When she asked if I needed any assistance, she implied I could not manage on my own." "To infer," on the other hand, is to draw a conclusion from another's statement or action. For example, "she inferred that the speaker thought she was helpless," and "he inferred that he should remain silent." In general, the listener infers what the speaker implies.

## c. IT'S V. ITS

"It's" is a contraction that stands for "it is." Contractions should not be used in legal writing, and you should not have much need for it. On the other hand, "its" is the possessive form of "it." Since corporations, fictitious entities, and courts are referred to as "it," you will use "its" often.

## d. THEIR V. THERE V. THEY'RE

"Their" is a plural possessive pronoun, as in "their feelings" or "their property." "There" means "at that place," as in "put the couch over there." "They're" is a contraction of "they are," and should be avoided in legal writing.

---

*EXERCISES IN GRAMMAR, PUNCTUATION, AND USAGE*

*(Suggested answers appear in Appendix F.)*

*Correct each sentence:*

1. **Looking at each element, the plaintiff will not meet it's burden of proof.**

2. **If the officer's belief is reasonable they are permitted to conduct a brief investigatory stop without a warrant.**

3. **The court must first terminate the parents rights and then it must determine what is in the child's best interest.**

---

4. The frisk, that must be based on a reasonable belief that the suspect is armed and dangerous, must be confined to a weapons search.

5. An employer is not entitled to unilaterally terminate an employee for "blowing the whistle" on his illegal activities.

6. The parties' were unable to agree on contract terms, and thus failed to form an enforceable contract.

7. An employee who can be fired for any reason is considered "at will;" however, they cannot be fired for reporting illegal activities to the appropriate authorities.

8. Starbucks will argue that their coffee beans are not "perishable food products".

9. The Joneses primary complaint was that their neighbors were effecting there ability to enjoy there backyard.

10. Knowledge of falsity can be imputed, constructive, which means the defendant should have known, or actual.

# E. CITATION FORMAT

As a general rule, a legal writer *must cite to legal authority each time she refers to a rule of law or the holding or reasoning of a judicial or agency opinion.* The reason is two-fold: First, legal readers demand proof that the law is as described, and second, they want to know where to find the information in the cited source should they decide to read it for themselves.

This general rule applies to legal scholars and practitioners, but the citation format for scholarly and practical legal writing differs. Both the *ALWD Manual of Citation*[55] and the *Bluebook*[56] are devoted solely to citation format in both kinds of legal writing. This section does not attempt to capture the wealth of information contained in these books, and you will need to become intimately familiar with one or the other. The goal here is to explain the citation process in simple terms and highlight the information most useful to beginning practitioners.

## 1. FULL CITATION FORMS

*The first citation to any authority must be a full citation.* Thereafter, you may use a short cite.[57] If the first, full citation to an authority appears several pages before the next citation to the same source, you may do your reader the favor of citing the authority again in full. The preference in legal writing is to

---

**55.** ALWD CITATION MANUAL: A PROFESSIONAL SYSTEM OF CITATION (3d ed. 2006).

**56.** THE BLUEBOOK: A UNIFORM SYSTEM OF CITATION (Columbia Law Review Ass'n et al. eds, 18th ed. 2005) [hereinafter BLUEBOOK]

**57.** *See infra*, at 292.

cite to the hard copy of the source material; if that is not available, then cite to the electronic version.[58]

## a. CONSTITUTIONS

> ALWD Citation
> Manual, Rule 13;
> Bluebook, Rule 11.

The citation to a current provision of a constitution identifies the document and the corresponding amendment and/or section number:[59]

*Example*: U.S. Const. amend. XIV, § 2.

Note: Most examples in the *Bluebook* use large and small upper case letters for cites to constitutions. Practitioners do not use these; simply use regular upper case and lower case letters as shown above.

## b. STATUTES

> ALWD Citation
> Manual, Rule 14;
> Bluebook, Rule 12.

When possible, cite to the official version of a federal or state code.[60] The citation to a statute contains the name of the code, its location within the code, and a date parenthetical that may contain the publisher but always contains the publication date.

*Example 1*: Ga. Code Ann. § 2–16–1 (2000).

*Example 2*: 28 U.S.C. § 1332.

Both citation manuals set forth in detail the abbreviation forms for federal and state codes.[61] The names of the codes should be copied exactly as they appear.[62]

---

**58.** *See, e.g.*, BLUEBOOK, *supra* note 56, at R. 18, at 151–61. *But see* ALWD CITATION MANUAL, *supra* note 55, at R. 14.5, at 116.

**59.** For state abbreviations, *see* ALWD CITATION MANUAL, *supra* note 55, at app. 3(b), at 454; BLUEBOOK, *supra* note 56, at tbl. T.10, at 342.

**60.** The *ALWD Citation Manual* places a star next to the official code in Appendix 1, and the *Bluebook* identifies the names of the official codes in Table T.1.

**61.** ALWD CITATION MANUAL, *supra* note 55, at app. 1; *Bluebook*, *supra* note 56, at tbl. T.1.

**62.** *See, e.g., ALWD Citation Manual*, *supra* note 55, at app. 1; *Bluebook*, *supra* note 56, at tbl. T.1.

Use two section symbols to indicate multiple consecutive sections but do not put a space between the two symbols. When citing to a supplement, indicate "Supp." in the parenthetical with the publisher (if required) and date.[63]

*Example 3*: Kan. Stat. Ann. §§ 60–212 to –213 (West Supp. 2007).

## c. CASES

> | ALWD Citation |
> | Manual, Rule 12; |
> | Bluebook, Rule 10. |

Citations to cases come in two forms: textual citations and citation sentences. As you might expect, textual citations appear in text. Citation sentences stand alone as separate sentences and end with periods. Many legal writers and readers prefer cites to appear as citation sentences so they do not interrupt the flow of the text. Textual citations are not *wrong*, however, and both citation manuals include them. The only difference in form between a textual citation and citation sentence is the method used to name the case.[64]

A typical case citation contains the name of the case, its reporter location, and a date parenthetical that contains the jurisdiction and the decision year, and any subsequent history of the case. Case names may be underlined or italicized but be consistent.

*Example 1*: *Terry v. Ohio*, 392 U.S. 1 (1968).

The citation indicates that this case can be found in volume 392 of United States Reports beginning at page 1, and it was decided in 1968. Since the court that decided the case is clear from the name of the reporter (U.S.), the date parenthetical need not contain an abbreviation for the court.

*Example 2*: *Hurley v. Brown*, 564 S.E.2d 558 (Ga. Ct. App. 2002).

The citation indicates that this case can be found in volume 564 of the second series of West's Southeastern Regional Reporter, beginning on page 558. The case was decided by the Georgia Court of Appeals in 2002. Since the name of the reporter (Southeastern) does not indicate the court that decided the case, the date parenthetical contains the proper abbreviation for this particular court. Both citation manuals indicate the proper abbreviations for federal and state courts.[65]

---

**63.** ALWD CITATION MANUAL, *supra* note 55, at R. 6.6(b), at 40 & R. 8, at 45; *Bluebook, supra* note 56, at R. 3.1, at 58, & R. 12.3.1, at 104–05.

**64.** *See infra*, at 289.

**65.** ALWD CITATION MANUAL, *supra* note 55, at app. 1; BLUEBOOK, *supra* note 56, at tbl. T.1.

## i) CASE NAMES IN TEXTUAL CITATIONS

In general, both parties should be named by their last or corporate name. You may delete articles and procedural phrases such as "in the matter of."

Case names in textual citations should follow the rule stated above, without using any abbreviations, except for the following words:

and (&)

Association (Assoc.)

Brothers (Bros.)

Company (Co.)

Corporation (Corp.)

Incorporated (Inc.)

Limited (Ltd.)

Number (No.).[66]

*Example*: **In *Jimenez v. Community Asphalt Corp.*, 947 So.2d 532 (Fla. Dist. Ct. App. 2006), the plaintiff sued his employer when the truck he was driving overturned.**

## ii) CASE NAMES IN CITATION SENTENCES

Again, both parties should be named by their last or corporate name. You may delete articles and procedural phrases such as "in the matter of."

Case names in citation sentences may be further abbreviated as indicated in the *ALWD Citation Manual*, Appendix 3, and the *Bluebook*, T.6.

*Example*: **The court held that the employee's appeal could be heard while his intentional misconduct claim remained pending. *Jimenez v. Cmty. Asphalt Corp.*, 947 So.2d 532 (Fla. Dist. Ct. App. 2006).**

# d. BOOKS

| |
|---|
| **ALWD Citation Manual, Rule 22; Bluebook, Rule 15.** |

Book citations include the author's full name, the title, and date parenthetical, including the publisher. If you are citing to a specific page, the page number follows the title.

---

**66.** ALWD CITATION MANUAL, *supra* note 55, at R. 12.2(e)(4), at 68; BLUEBOOK, *supra* note 56, at R. Rule 10.2.1(c), at 82–83.

*Example:* Robin L. West, *Re–Imagining Justice: Progressive Interpretations of Formal Equality, Rights, and the Rule of Law 12* (Ashgate Pub. Co. 2003).

## e. LAW REVIEW ARTICLES

> ALWD Citation
> Manual, Rule 23;
> Bluebook, Rule 16.

Law review citations include the author's full name, the title of the article, the name of the journal, the page number the article begins on, and the date parenthetical. Both citation manuals indicate the proper abbreviations for most journals. *See ALWD Citation Manual,* Appendix 5; *Bluebook,* T.13.

*Example*: Linda L. Berger, *Of Metaphor, Metonymy, and Corporate Money: Rhetorical Choices in Supreme Court Decisions on Campaign Finance Regulations,* 58 Mercer L. Rev. 949 (2007).

## f. RESTATEMENTS

> ALWD Citation
> Manual, Rule 27.1;
> Bluebook, Rule B6.1.3

Citations to Restatements of law include the name of the restatement, the section cited, and a date parenthetical.

*Example*: Restatement (Second) of Torts § 78 (1965).

# 2. PINPOINT CITATIONS

When citing to a case or some form of secondary authority, you are likely to refer to information from a specific page or pages of text. In that instance, you must "pinpoint" the source: Provide the page number where the source material begins and the specific page or pages where you got the information.[67] The two page references are separated by a comma.

*Example 1*: *Terry v. Ohio,* 392 U.S. 1, 17 (1968).

*Example 2*: *Hurley v. Brown,* 564 S.E.2d 558, 589 (Ga. Ct. App. 2002).

---

67. ALWD CITATION MANUAL, *supra* note 55, at R. 5.2, at 33–34; BLUEBOOK, *supra* note 56, at R. B5.1.2, at 7–8.

Both West and Lexis indicate page breaks from the original print sources. In this excerpt from *Terry v. Ohio*, 392 U.S. 1 (1968), on Westlaw, the numbers *18 and *19 indicate where those pages begin in United States Reports. The number **1878 indicates the beginning of that page from another print source, West's Supreme Court Reporter:

---

[13] 🖹 [14] 🖹 The danger in the logic which proceeds upon distinctions between **1878** a 'stop' and an 'arrest,' or 'seizure' of the person, and between a 'frisk' and a 'search' is twofold. It seeks to isolate from constitutional scrutiny the initial stages of the contact between the policeman and the citizen. And by suggesting a rigid all-or-nothing model of justification and regulation under the Amendment, it obscures the utility of limitations upon the scope, as well as the initiation, of police action as a means of constitutional regulation.[FN15] This Court has held in *18* the past that a search which is reasonable at its inception may violate the Fourth Amendment by virtue of its intolerable intensity and scope. Kremen v. United States, 353 U.S. 346, 77 S.Ct. 828, 1L.Ed.2d 876 (1957); *19* Go-Bart Importing Co. v. United States, 282 U.S. 344, 356–358, 51 S.Ct. 153, 158, 75 L.Ed. 374 (1931); see United States v. Di Re, 332 U.S. 581, 586–587, 68 S.Ct. 222, 225, 92 L.Ed. 210 (1948).

---

The same excerpt on Lexis is set forth below. Notice that the Lexis version has a third reference to ***904, a page from a Lexis publication, the Lawyer's Edition:

---

[14] The danger in the logic which proceeds upon distinctions between [**1878] a "stop" and an "arrest," or "seizure" of the person, and between the policeman and the citizen. And by suggesting a rigid all-or-nothing model of justification and regulation under the Amendment, it obscures the utility of limitations upon the scope, as well as the initiation, of police action as a means of constitutional regulation.[15] This Court has held in [*18] the past that [HN7] a search [***904] which is reasonable at its inception may violate the Fourth Amendment by virtue of its intolerable intensity and scope. Kremen v. United States, 353 U.S. (1957); Go-Bart Importing Co. v. [*19] United States, 282 U.S. 344, 356–358 (1931); see United States v. Di Re, 332 U.S. 581, 586–587 (1948).

---

# 3. EXPLANATORY PARENTHETICALS

> **ALWD Citation Manual, Rule 46; Bluebook, Rule B11.**

Explanatory parentheticals give additional information regarding the cited source; they usually come at the end of the citation, followed by a period. They often begin with a present participle, such as "holding," "finding," etc.[68]

---

68. *See supra* at 274 on using parentheticals for conciseness.

*Example*: *See Terry v. Ohio,* 392 U.S. 1, 22 (1968)(holding that an officer's warrantless search may be reasonable where he has reason to believe a suspect is engaged in imminent criminal activity).

# 4. PARALLEL CITATIONS

Parallel citations are citations to the same material (*e.g.,* a statute or case) but in different locations. States used to require citation to their official case reporters and a parallel citation to the corresponding West regional reporter:

*Example: Hurley v. Brown,* 255 Ga. App. 151, 564 S.E.2d 558 (Ga. Ct. App. 2002).

Parallel citations are no longer used in legal memoranda. When filing documents in state courts, check the court's local rules to see if parallel citation is still required. These rules can usually be found on the court's web site. There are no parallel citations for federal cases.

# 5. SHORT CITATION FORMS

## a. NO INTERVENING CITES

> ALWD Citation
> Manual, Rules 12.21,
> 14.6; Bluebook, Rules
> 10.9, 12.9.

Once you have cited a source in full, you may thereafter use a short cite. Where there is no source cited between the first full citation and a second cite to the same source, you may use "*Id.*" to refer to the same section or page. Use "*Id.* at ___," to refer to a different section or page within the same source.

*Example 1:*
First citation: Ga. Code Ann. § 2–16–1 (2000).
Second citation: *Id.* § 2–16–2.

*Example 2:*
First citation: *Hurley v. Brown,* 564 S.E.2d 558 (Ga. Ct. App. 2002).
Second citation: *Id.*

## b. WITH INTERVENING CITES

You may not use "*Id.*" when you cite to a different authority between the first full citation and a second cite to the same source. For statutes, restate the name of the code and give the section to which you are citing. For cases, indicate the last name of the first party, the volume number, the reporter abbreviation, and pinpoint citation.

*Example 1:*

First citation: Ga. Code Ann. § 2–16–1 (2000).

Second Citation: *Hurley v. Brown*, 564 S.E.2d 558 (Ga. Ct. App. 2002).

Third citation: § 2–16–2.

*Example 2:*

First citation: *Hurley v. Brown*, 564 S.E.2d 558 (Ga. Ct. App. 2002).

Second citation: Ga. Code Ann. § 2–16–2 (2000).

Third Citation: *Hurley*, 564 S.E.2d at 559.

# 6. STRING CITATIONS

> **ALWD Citation**
> **Manual, Rules 43.3, 45.4;**
> **Bluebook, Rule 1.4.**

You may string together in one sentence citations that support or contradict your assertions. Both citation manuals require that authorities in a string citation be listed in the following order: constitutions, statutes, treaties, cases (federal then state cases, and for cases from the same court level, most recent cases first). Use semi-colons to connect the citations.

*Example*: U.S. Const. amend. IV; *Terry v. Ohio*, 392 U.S. 1, 22 (1968); *United States v. Mayo*, 361 F.3d 802 (4th Cir. 2004); *United States v. Burton*, 228 F.3d 524 (4th Cir. 2000).

# 7. SIGNALS

> **ALWD Citation**
> **Manual, Rule 44.3;**
> **Bluebook, Rules B4 and**
> **Rule 1.2.**

Signals indicate how the cited authority supports or contradicts your proposition. The use of no signal is the strongest signal; it indicates that the cited authority directly supports your proposition. The rest of the signals and their meanings are listed below. The signals in bold should be used in conjunction with an explanatory parenthetical.

| Support | Useful comparison | Contradiction | Background |
|---|---|---|---|
| *[No signal]* | **Compare ... with** | *Contra* [contrary] | See generally |
| *E.g.,* [for example] | | *But see* | |
| *Accord* [additional case support] | | **But cf.** | |
| *See* [proposition follows from authority] | | | |
| ***See also*** | | | |
| ***Cf.*** [analogous] | | | |

## FIGURE 51

Signals can be combined in string citations, separated by semi-colons, and should appear in the same order listed above, beginning with signals that indicate support for your proposition.[69]

## 8. COMMON CITATION ERRORS

### a. USE REGULAR UPPER AND LOWER CASE LETTERS FOR PRACTITIONERS' DOCUMENTS

The *Bluebook* calls for large and small upper case letters for law review footnotes.[70] Practitioners use regular upper and lower case letters instead.

*Example*: U.S. Const. amend. IV.

*Not*: U.S. CONST. amend. IV.

### b. INSERT A SPACE BETWEEN A § SIGN AND SECTION NUMBER IN A CITATION

When you cite to a section number, insert a space between the section sign(s) and the section or sub-section numbers.[71]

*Example*: Ga. Code Ann. § 2–16–2 (2000).

*Not*: Ga. Code Ann. §2–16–2 (2000).

### c. CITE TO PUBLICATION DATE OF HARD COPY OF CODE

Think of the date in a citation to a statute as its address as opposed to indicating whether it is current. When citing to the preferred hard copy of a statute, include its publication date, NOT the "current as of" date online.

---

**69.** *See* ALWD CITATION MANUAL, *supra* note 55, R. 44.8(a), at 326; BLUEBOOK, *supra* note 56, R. 1.3, at 48.

**70.** *See, e.g.,* BLUEBOOK, *supra* note 56, at R. 15, at 129–37.

**71.** *See* ALWD CITATION MANUAL, *supra* note 55, R. 14.2(d), at 113; BLUEBOOK, *supra* note 56, R. 12.3.1, at 104–05.

## d. WHETHER TO ABBREVIATE U.S. IN CASE NAMES

The ALWD Citation Manual permits you to abbreviate "United States" when it is a named party to a case, but the Bluebook does not.[72]

## e. CITE TO U.S. REPORTS FOR CASES DECIDED BY THE UNITED STATES SUPREME COURT

When possible, cite to the official reporter for United States Supreme Court cases, U.S. Reports, not the Supreme Court Reporter.[73]

## f. INCLUDE JURISDICTION IN DATE PARENTHETICAL WITH A CITE TO REGIONAL REPORTER

When citing to a regional reporter, you must include the proper abbreviation for the court that decided the case since the name of the reporter does not identify the deciding court.[74] The correct abbreviations for the courts' names are in Appendices 1 and 4 of the *ALWD Citation Manual* and Table 1 of the *Bluebook*.

## g. USE THE CORRECT SHORT CITE FOR CASES

Once you have cited a case in full, you may use a short cite that includes just the first party's name, the volume number, the reporter abbreviation, and the pinpoint cite.

*Example*: *Hurley*, 564 S.E.2d at 559.

     *Not*: *Hurley*, at 559.

## h. DO NOT USE ID. AFTER A STRING CITE

You cannot use *id.* after a string cite because the reader is unlikely to know which of the prior sources you mean to cite.

*Example*:

First Citation: *United States v. Mayo*, 361 F.3d 802 (4th Cir. 2004); *United States v. Burton,* 228 F.3d 524 (4th Cir. 2000).

Second citation: *Mayo*, 361 F.3d at 803.

     *Not*: *Id.* at 803.

---

**72.** *Compare* ALWD CITATION MANUAL, *supra* note 55, at R. 12.2(g), at 69, with BLUEBOOK, *supra* note 56, R. B5.1.1, at 7.

**73.** *See* ALWD CITATION MANUAL, *supra* note 55, R. 12.4(c), at 78–79; BLUEBOOK, *supra* note 56, R. B.5.1.3, at 8, & tbl. T.1, at 193.

**74.** *See* ALWD CITATION MANUAL, supra note 55, R.12.6(d), at 85, & R.12.6(e), at 85–86; BLUEBOOK, *supra* note 56, R. 10.4, at 89–90.

### i. SUPRA, INFRA, AND SEE GENERALLY ARE ONLY FOR USE WITH SECONDARY MATERIALS

These signals are used to refer to secondary source materials previously cited but not to primary sources of law. *Supra* and *infra* may also be used to refer to locations within the writer's document.[75]

---

*CITATION EXERCISES FOR PRACTITIONERS*

*(Suggested answers appear in Appendix G.)*

Create the proper citations described below:

1. A 2006 case, Michael Davis versus Larry Crawford, decided by the Missouri Court of Appeals, and reported in volume 215 of the third series of the appropriate regional reporter, beginning at page 214.

2. A second cite to the case in the question above with two intervening cites and to page 215.

3. The case of the United States of America versus Arone McConer, found in volume 530 of the Federal Reporter, third series, on page 484. The case was decided by the United States Circuit Court for the Sixth Circuit in 2008.

4. A law review article written by Martha Minow. It is entitled: "Should Religious Groups Be Exempt from Civil Rights Laws?" and is found in the Boston College Law Review, volume 48, beginning on page 781. The date of the issue was September 2007.

5. A book entitled "Less Safe, Less Free: Why America Is Losing the War on Terror," by David Cole and Jules Lobel. It was published by the New Press in 2007. Cite to a quotation on page 25 of this book. This is the first time this book has been referenced in your text.

6. The seventeenth amendment to the United States Constitution, ratified in 1913. You wish to refer to the second section of the amendment. You found it in a volume of the United States Code Service, published in 1995.

7. The following section of the General Laws of Massachusetts: Chapter 13, section 426. The Massachusetts legislature enacted this statute on October 11, 1969. The copyright date is 1991. The date on the pocket part is 2006, no change in this section.

8. A short cite to the statute in the question above with no intervening cites.

9. A short cite to the statute in Question 7 with intervening cites and to section 428.

---

**75.** *See* ALWD CITATION MANUAL, *supra* note 55, R. 11.4, at 56–59, & R. 44.3, at 324–25; BLUEBOOK, *supra* note 56 R. 4.2, at 66–67, & R. 1.2, at 46–48.

> 10. You assert a proposition that follows from the following two cases: (1) Benjamin Kolmer versus State, reported in volume 977, second series, of the Southern Reporter. The case begins on page 712 and was decided by the Florida District Court of Appeals in 2008, and (2) the United States versus Andrew Sokolow, decided by the United States Supreme Court in 1989 and reported in volume 109 of the Supreme Court Reporter at page 1581 and in volume 490 of United States Reports at page 1.

# F. POLISH

Legal writing needs to do more than sound good. It needs to look good too, and spell checking—the panacea of undergraduate writing—is just the beginning. A legal document that is not polished or professional immeasurably damages the writer's credibility. If you fail to conform to local court rules, the clerk of the court may refuse to accept the document for filing. A writing sample that looks unprofessional will most certainly work against you. A judge who reads a sloppy brief will assume the brief is sloppy in substance as well as form. Creating a polished document means examining the document from a variety of perspectives: the strength of the appeals to logic, emotion, and credibility; the coherence of the organization, including large and small scale concerns; the simplicity of the writing; conformity to the legal reader's expectations; and the accuracy of grammar, punctuation, usage, and citation format.

The following checklists are designed to help legal writers become self-editors. There is a checklist for memoranda and for briefs. The checklists can be modified to suit any type of objective or persuasive legal writing.

## OBJECTIVE WRITING CHECKLIST FOR TRADITIONAL MEMORANDUM

### QUESTION PRESENTED (p. 216)

Includes:

- Controlling authority/jurisdiction
- Legal question
- Significant facts

Asks a question or states issue as declarative sentence

### BRIEF ANSWER (p. 217)

Summarizes the applicable legal rules and analysis in the writer's own words, including WHY or HOW she reached a particular conclusion

May combine rules and analysis to make writing concise (*e.g.*, topic sentence: Paul will be able to prove the first element because ...)

Does not include citations to authority

## STATEMENT OF FACTS (p. 217)

Contains the complete story on which the analysis is based: background, emotional, and legally significant facts. Contains all facts referred to in Discussion section

## DISCUSSION (p. 217)

### Content

Synthesizes all relevant and applicable constitutional, statutory, administrative, and common law

Sets forth an outline for analysis in a roadmap/introductory paragraph and proceeds to analyze each element, requirement, etc. in a deductive manner: from general rule to application of rule to conclusion

Uses case analogies where useful and distinguishes problematic authority

Considers the opponent's best counter-arguments

Reaches an ultimate conclusion on each disputed issue that is consistent with the Brief Answer

### Organization

Large Scale: (p. 218)

- Roadmap/introductory paragraph sets out issues/rules of law to be discussed
- Analysis follows outline established by introduction
- Analysis explains and applies the rules of law using cases, where applicable
- Analysis employs more than one case per issue, where possible

Small scale: (p. 219)

- Paragraphs are a digestible length and limited to one or more related ideas (more than one page is usually difficult to follow)
- Topic sentences signal the subject of the paragraph in a meaningful way
- Sentence structure is not too complicated by stringing a series of clauses together
- Case analogies are effective because they provide enough information about the facts and the holding, and they make an explicit comparison between cases (as opposed to

a simple description of the case that forces the reader to make the comparison herself)

- Reasonable counter-arguments and problematic law/cases are discussed
- Each issue discussed ends with a definitive conclusion that makes the writer's opinion clear

<u>Style and Polish</u>

- Is written in plain English (p. 260)
- The tone of the writing is objective (*i.e.*, even-handed as opposed to argumentative)
- Is clear and concise (p. 263)
- Conforms to legal writing conventions (p. 276)
- Grammar and punctuation are correct (p. 280)
- Spelling and citations are correct (p. 286)

## CONCLUSION

- Summarizes discussion in more detail than Brief Answer
- Contains no citations to authority

## PERSUASIVE WRITING CHECKLIST FOR AN APPELLATE BRIEF

### COVER PAGE (p. 237)

Includes case caption, title of document, and date

### TABLE OF CONTENTS (p. 237)

Includes page references for all parts of brief and all major and minor headings and subheadings

### TABLE OF AUTHORITIES (p. 237)

Sources are listed in alphabetical order and pages on which sources appeal are indicated

### JURISDICTIONAL STATEMENT (p. 237)

Cites basis for court's exercise of subject matter jurisdiction

### STATEMENT OF ISSUES PRESENTED FOR REVIEW (p. 238)

- Contains the controlling rules(s) of law, the precise legal question, and the significant facts, while suggesting the writer's desired outcome
- May be most effective if phrased as a question that should be answered "yes"

## STATEMENT OF THE CASE (p. 238)

Includes the nature of the case, the history of the proceedings, and the disposition below

## STATEMENT OF FACTS (p. 238)

- Tells an interesting, reasonable, and compelling story from your client's point of view
- Stirs the audience's emotion and makes them want to take action in your client's favor (your theory of the case)
- Includes background, emotional, and legally significant facts
- Contains all facts referred to in the Argument section. Page numbers where facts are taken from record are cited (*e.g.*, Transcript, p. 3)

## SUMMARY OF ARGUMENT (p. 239)

- Contains a concise, clear, and accurate statement of the arguments made in the body of the brief without merely repeating the argument headings
- Contains no citations to legal authority

## STANDARD OF REVIEW (p. 239)

- Cites to authority for the level of deference the reviewing court must give to the lower court's decision
- Where the standard of review, the writer is unclear, argues for the applicable standard and why

## ARGUMENT (p. 240)

### Content

- In a roadmap or introductory paragraph, explains the legal context of the case and sets forth the major issues the brief will address (usually the major headings)
- At the same time, paragraph *argues* as to appropriate outcome

*For example, if the major issues are whether the Terry stop and frisk were lawful, this paragraph would explain (1) that the brief was about a Fourth amendment exception to the warrant requirement, (2) that the issues were about the validity of the stop and the frisk, and (3) that both were either lawful or unlawful. One major heading could be devoted to the stop and one to the frisk.*

- Proceeds to deductively argue each issue, element, requirement, etc., including the synthesized rule(s) of law that determine its outcome, the client's affirmative arguments, and those counter-arguments strong enough to warrant a reply

- Where cases are used, the reader is given just enough information about the facts, the holding, and an explicit comparison to prove the point
- Reaches an ultimate conclusion on all issues, which is consistent with the arguments made in the Summary of Argument

Organization (p. 241)

Large scale: (p. 241)

- The headings mirror the questions presented
- The overall theory of the case/argument is discernible from the headings
- The headings include an argument and a reason
- The headings are digestible at a glance
- Transitions between headings are smooth and easy to follow
- The most space is devoted to the most important and complex issues
- The brief is organized by the rules of law or factors that determine the issue

Small scale: (p. 244)

- The brief uses strong, argumentative topic sentences that signal the purpose of each paragraph
- Reasoning proceeds deductively: major premise, minor premise, conclusion
- Case analogies are well-constructed, including the court's holding and reasoning
- Citations make effective use of parentheticals where full textual comparisons are not used or parentheticals provide additional support
- Paragraph and sentence lengths are digestible

Style and Polish (p. 259)

- Is written in plain English (p. 260)
- The brief *argues* as opposed to discusses the law
- Adequately takes opponent's arguments into account
- Rule synthesis and word choice are reasonable so as not to detract from the brief's credibility
- Is clear and concise (p. 263)
- Conforms to legal writing conventions (p. 276)

- Grammar and punctuation are correct (p. 280)
- Spelling and citations are correct (p. 286)

CONCLUSION (p. 241)

States in one sentence the precise relief sought

# G. CUMULATIVE REVISION EXERCISE

The following exercise gives you an opportunity to apply what you have learned about deductive and analogical reasoning, arrangement, and style to a writing sample. Below is an excerpt from a student brief on a *Terry* stop and frisk issue. Only the argument relating to the stop is included here. Review the sample and comment in the text and margins on content, organization, and all aspects of the writer's style.

*REVISION EXERCISE IN CLARITY, CONCISENESS, LEGAL WRITING CONVENTION, GRAMMAR, PUNCTUATION, USAGE, AND CITATION FORMAT*

---

UNITED STATES CIRCUIT COURT OF APPEALS
FOR THE FOURTH CICUIT

---

CRIMINAL CASE NO. CF–0072929

---

UNITED STATES,

Appellant,

v.

PAUL DESMOND,

Appellee,

---

ON APPEAL FROM THE UNITED STATES DISTRICT COURT
FOR THE NORTHERN DISTRICT OF VIRGINIA

---

BRIEF FOR THE APPELLANT

---

## Table of Contents

......

## Table of Authorities

......

<u>Jurisdictional Statement</u>

The Court has jurisdiction of this matter under 18 U.S.C.A. § 3731 ( ).

<u>Statement of Issue Presented for Review</u>

Under the Federal Law did the district court err in holding that Officer Kim did not have reasonable, articulable suspicion to conduct a <u>Terry</u> stop and nevertheless proceeded to conduct an unlawful frisk when: (1) upon seeing the officer the defendant became nervous, put his hands in his pocket, and turned to walk away from the officer, (2) Officer Kim had experience and knowledge of the high crime area where the stop occurred, and (3) the defendant matched the description of a person that had robbed the 7–11 days before, the description being obtained by a face-to-face conversation with a cashier?

. . . . . .

<u>Statement of the Case</u>

The defendant was indicted by a grand jury for Possession with the Intent to Manufacture, Distribute, or Dispense a Controlled Substance. On November 29, 2007, the United States District Court for the Eastern District of Virginia granted a motion for the defendant to suppress the drugs as evidence. The government now appeals.

<u>Statement of Facts</u>

Officer Juan Kim has been employed as a police officer by the City of Alexandria Police Department for over four years. (T. 2) For the past fourteen months, he has worked in the Community Support Division in a pro-active capacity getting to know the local business owners, residents, and children in the high-crime neighborhood of Foxchase. (T. 3), (T. 6)

On the evening of November 11, 2006 around 8:00pm, Office Kim observed Paul Desmond standing in the flickering light of the dark dumpster area on the side of the 7–11 at the corner of Duke and S. Jordan Street. (T. 3) Desmond appeared "disoriented" and "appeared very nervous." (T. 4) Kim observed Desmond "walking in circles" and acting "real fidgety." (T. 4) He was also constantly putting his hands in and out of his pockets and looking into the store. (T. 5) Kim recognized Desmond as fitting the description of a suspect who had recently robbed the 7–11. (T. 6) This description was made by a cashier working at the store. (T. 5–6)

After several minutes observing Desmond, Kim pulled his police cruiser into the parking lot of the 7–11. (T. 7) Upon seeing the Office Kim, Desmond's "body tensed and his eyes ... opened a little wider." (T. 7) He immediately put his hands in his pocket, spun around and headed down Duke St. (T. 7)

Kim decided to follow Desmond down Duke St. in his police cruiser. (T. 8)

1

As he approached Desmond, Kim put on his hazard lights as he pulled to the side of the highway. (T. 22) Kim got out of the car with his weapon by his side and requested that Desmond come over to talk with him. (T. 23, 8) As soon as Desmond started to approach, Kim reholstered his weapon and asked Desmond to remove his hands from his pockets. (T. 24) Desmond complied and inquired about the meaning of the stop. (T. 24—25) Kim explained that he appeared to match the description of a robbery suspect from the 7–11. (T. 25)

Getting a closer look of Desmond, Kim observed that he was sweating, tense, nervous and had a scratch on his face and a lump on his temple. (T. 25) Kim then, concerned for his own safety, asked Desmond for his permission to be searched. (T. 10) Desmond agreed to the search, and complied with Kim's request to place his hands on the hood of the police cruiser. (T. 10, 26) Before touching Desmond, Officer Kim explained to him how the pat down would proceed. (T. 26) Kim then commenced the search, running his hands along the outside of Desmond's clothes until he felt a hard, ridged, three inch lump in the chest pocket. (T. 10–12) Afraid that it might be the butt of a gun or a knife, Desmond removed the object from the pocket. Upon closer inspection, the lump turned out to be an eye dropper and two viles full of PCP. (T. 12) Kim took the drugs from Desmond and placed him under arrest.

### Summary of Argument

The district court failed to consolidate the major elements of why Officer Kim performed a <u>Terry</u> stop of Desmond. The nervous actions, putting hands into his pockets, and aversion of the officer were accompanied by Officer Kim's knowledge and experience of the area. Also, Officer Kim received information about a robber that matched the description of Desmond from a cashier that worked at the 7–11 Desmond where Desmond was stopped. The district court did not properly evaluate these circumstances collectively.

......

### Standard of Review

The issue of whether police had reasonable suspicion necessary to sustain a stop and frisk of a defendant is to be reviewed de novo. <u>US v. Quarles</u>, 330 F.3d 650 (4th Cir. 2003).

......

### Argument

I.  THE TRIAL COURT FAILED TO PROPERLY CONSIDER THE TOTALITY OF CIRCUMSTANCES AND THE PROPER SCOPE OF AN INVESTIGATORY STOP AND FRISK WHEN RULING THAT OFFICER KIM DID NOT HAVE RESONABLE, ARTICULABLE SUSPICION.

In making investigatory stops police officers must be able to point to specific and articulable facts which, taken together with rational inferences from those facts, reasonably warrant that intrusion. Terry v. Ohio, 392 U.S. 1 (U.S. 1968). Reasonable suspicion must consider the totality of the circumstances, for factors which by themselves suggest innocent conduct may amount to reasonable suspicion justifying an investigative stop when taken together. US v. Perkins, 363 F.3d 317 (4th Cir. 2004). The totality of circumstances includes; whether the stop occurred in a high crime area, whether the suspect engaged in evasive behavior or acted nervously, US v. Mayo, 361 F.3d 802 (4th Cir. 2004), information obtained from an informant, Perkins, 363 at 325 and the personal experience of the officer with the particular area. Id. at 322.

### A. The trial court did not properly consider Desmond's conduct prior to the stop, Officer Kim's experience with the area where the stop occurred, and the reliability of the information gained from the 7–11 cashier, in determining the totality of circumstances of reasonable suspicion.

In view of Mayo alone, Desmond's behavior and actions preceding the stop and frisk afforded sufficient reasonable suspicion. The defendant in Mayo upon observing patrolling police officers put his hand in his pocket, turned 180 degrees, and walked away from the officers. Officer Cornett in Mayo believed that the motion of putting the hand into the pocket was to maintain control of a weapon. Mayo, 361 at 804. Upon questioning Mayo, Officer Cornett noted that Mayo's "eyes were extremely wide, his mouth was slightly agape, an it was almost like nothing registered with him. It was almost as if he was in shock." Id. He also observed that Mayo's shirt was "fluttering ... as though he was shaking." Id. In Mayo the court held the officer had reasonable suspicion based on Mayo's actions.

Desmond's interaction with Officer Kim was similar to the interaction with the police officers in Mayo. According to Officer Kim's testimony "when he saw me come into the parking lot, his body tensed, and eyes sort of opened a little bit wider. I think he was very surprised to see me come into the parking lot ... He immediately, you know, put his hands in his pocket again. And he just— he was very nervous. And he turned around, and started walking away." As Desmond walked away "he was walking very fast, and he kept looking back in my direction." The similarities between Mayo and Desmond are nervousness, evasion of the police officers' presence, and putting hands into pockets. The trial court held that these similarities did not amount to reasonable suspicion, since the acts taken individually are innocent. However, in making determination of reasonable suspicion for investigative stop, relevant inquiry is not whether particular conduct is innocent or guilty, but degree of suspicion attached to particular types of non-criminal acts. US v. Sokolow, 490 U.S. 1 (U.S. 1989).

A notable difference between Mayo and Desmond is that a weapon was found on Mayo, where one was not found on Desmond. Because the facts of Mayo are

3

substantially similar to the facts of the current case, it follows that Officer Kim at the time of the stop had the same level of concern for his personal safety as Officer Cornet at the time Mayo was stopped. The trial court improperly applied hindsight bias to the conduct of Officer Kim, since the stop and frisk of Desmond did not produce a weapon. <u>Terry</u>, 392 at 20–22.

The trial court failed to give proper weight to Officer Kim's knowledge and experience of the area in evaluating the totality of circumstances. In <u>Perkins</u> the court concluded the officer's "knowledge and experience reasonably led him to conclude that the situation was potentially dangerous." <u>Perkins</u> 363 at 322. Officer Kim like the officer in <u>Perkins</u> was immediately familiar with the location and prior criminal activity where the stop occurred. Officer Kim stated in his testimony that the 7–11 near to where the stop was made is a "high crime area", and that the store had been robbed prior to the stop of Desmond. Officer Kim was also aware of several larcenies that occurred at the store.

Further, the trial court improperly ignored the information Officer Kim obtained from the 7–11 cashier. Part of the totality of circumstances upon which Officer Kim stopped and frisked Desmond was the information obtained from a 7–11 cashier regarding a robbery that had previously occurred. When an "informant relays information to a law enforcement officer face-to-face, an officer can judge the credibility of the tipster firsthand and thus confirm whether the tip is sufficiently reliable to support reasonable suspicion." <u>Perkins</u>, 363 at 326. The characteristics of the robber provided by the casher matched those of Desmond. The trial court failed to incorporate the information gathered from the cashier into the totality of circumstances used to determine reasonable suspicion.

......

### Conclusion

For the reasons stated above, the grant of the motion to suppress should be reversed.

# APPENDIX A

## ANSWERS TO SHORT EXERCISE ON DISTRIBUTED TERMS

■ ■ ■

*(Exercise appears in Chapter Four on page 117).*

Identify whether the underlined terms in the following premises are distributed or undistributed:

1. Reasonableness is <u>an objective measure</u>.

   Undistributed—predicate term of affirmative proposition. There may be other ways to measure objectivity.

2. <u>The Food and Drug Administration</u> followed its own rulemaking procedures.

   Distributed—proper nouns are distributed.

3. The jury did not have <u>a reasonable doubt</u>.

   Distributed—predicate term of a negative proposition. No reasonable doubt was possessed by the jury.

4. <u>Some parts</u> were defective.

   Undistributed subject term—refers only to some of the parts.

5. Congress delegated <u>some of its authority to a sub-committee on ethics</u>.

   Undistributed—refers specifically just to some, but not all, of its authority.

# APPENDIX B

## SAMPLE TRADITIONAL MEMORANDUM (WITH COMMENTS)

### ■ ■ ■

### Question Presented

Under the Michigan Whistleblowers' Protection Act [(WPA)], did Good Hope Hospital (GHH) commit retaliatory [discharge] when it fired Kathy Knox after she threatened to report MedServe, the blood bank for GHH, to the FDA for distributing allegedly tainted [blood]?

> **Comment:** Controlling law

> **Comment:** Legal question

> **Comment:** Legally significant facts

### Brief Answer

Probably not. First, Knox cannot prove that she was engaged in "protected activity" under the WPA because Knox cannot establish that she was "about to" report the tainted blood since she only made a threat to report but took no other action. Knox would probably be able to prove that she was acting in good faith and was reasonable in believing that MedServe had violated the law due to her workplace observation. The fact that MedServe was a third party instead of her employer would not be an obstacle for the "protected activity" element because of the close connection between MedServe's alleged violations and Knox's employment [setting]. Second, neither party will dispute that GHH fired [Knox]. Lastly,

> **Comment:** Summary of analysis of first element that contains several sub-elements.

> **Comment:** Summary of analysis of second element.

Knox can prove that GHH fired her for her alleged whistleblowing because of the timing of incidents, her work [record] and the pretextual nature of the stated reason for her [discharge].

> **Comment:** Comma needed here with all items in a series. Ch. 9, D.7, p. 282.

> **Comment:** Summary of analysis of third element. Overall, this Brief Answer does a good job of combining the three elements required for a cause of action for retaliatory discharge and the writer's reasons for her conclusions. A statement at the outset that three elements must be proved would have made it easier to follow.

### Statement of Facts

Kathy Knox is a registered nurse who began working at GHH in 1994. She was responsible for retrieving blood from and returning unused blood to MedServe, a blood bank, which leases the space from GHH but runs its own operations. Knox kept track of the blood units she [received], and placed the blood in the refrigerator for surgical use.

> **Comment:** Comma not needed here with a compound verb. See Ch. 9, D.5, p. 281.

In the summer of 2006, Knox began to notice that] the refrigerator was registering a higher temperature than FDA regulations permit. Knox asked the hospital maintenance department to examine the [refrigerator] and they told her it was working properly a few days later. However, she still felt certain was warmer than usual. On June 15, Knox told Mimi Betz, the director of MedServe, about the potential problem with the unused blood Knox was returning to her and suggested that Betz discard it. The next day, when Knox [return] unused blood to MedServe, Betz told her the maintenance department said the refrigerator was fine, and Knox should focus on her own job. On June 20, Knox noticed that one of the "tainted" blood units she had returned to Betz had been given back to her. When she complained, Betz told Knox she was getting tired of Knox's complaints and that she would not "toss perfectly good product" just because Knox imagined there was some problem with it. Knox said, "I care about my patients. If you give me any more bad blood, I am going to the [FDA]". Within

> **Comment:** Strive to be concise: just say "noticed?"

> **Comment:** Comma needed before "and" here because it acts as a coordinating conjunction. See Ch. 9, D.5, p. 281.

> **Comment:** Proofread!

> **Comment:** Improper quotation placement. Should be "... FDA." Ch. 9, D.1, p. 280.

minutes, Betz told Mr. Kleusing, Knox's supervisor, of Knox's threat. One week later, Kleusing fired Knox, claiming he had received complaints from people throughout the hospital that she was difficult to work [with]. When Knox asked Kleusing whether he

> **Comment:** Traditionally, a sentence should not end with a preposition.

was firing her because of her interaction with Betz, Kleusing ignored her question but reminded Knox that she had also been reprimanded once in 2004 for complaints from a particular patient's parents. According to Knox, all the nurses who cared for that patient received complaints, but none of them has been reprimanded or terminated.

Ms. Knox would like to know if she can successfully sue her employer for retaliatory discharge under the Michigan Whistleblowers' [Act].

> **Comment:** Concludes by stating the purpose of the memo (i.e., what the client wants to know).

### Discussion

To establish a prima facie case under the WPA, the plaintiff must show that (1) she was engaged in protected activity as defined by the act, (2) the defendant discharged her, and (3) a causal connection exists between the protected activity and the [discharge]. Chandler v. Dowell Schlumberger Inc.,

> **Comment:** Writer succinctly states the elements required for a retaliatory discharge claim under Michigan law.

572 N.W.2d 210, 212 (Mich. 1998); Terzano v. Wayne Co., 549 N.W.2d 606, 608 (Mich. App. 1996). Neither party should dispute that Knox was discharged. Thus, Knox must satisfy the first and third element to succeed in a claim for retaliatory discharge under the WPA.

The first element requires Knox prove that she was engaged in protected activity because she

> **Comment:** Topic sentence indicates paragraph will discuss first element.

was about to report a violation or suspected violation of law to a public [body]. See Mich. Comp. Laws [§

> **Comment:** There should be a space between the section sign and the section number. See Ch. 9, E.8(b), p. 294.

15].362 (1994); Shallal v. Catholic Soc. Serv. Of Wayne

County, 566 N.W.2d 571, 575 (Mich. [1997]). Knox must first establish that she was "about to" report MedServe's suspected violations to a public body since she did not actually report it. A plaintiff must show that she was "about to" report by clear and convincing [evidence]. Mich. Comp. Laws § 15.363(4) ([1994]). In Shallal, an employee of a social service agency told her boss that she was going to report his misuse of agency funds to the Department of Social Services if he did not "straighten up," and evidence showed that she had discussed reporting her boss with her coworkers and an honorary board member. Shallal, 566 N.W.2d at 573-74. The [Court] held that the employee's express threat to her boss, together with her other acts, was sufficient to conclude that the employee was about to report a suspected violation of the law. Id. at [579]. Similarly, Knox will argue that her statement to Betz that she was going to the FDA if Betz gave her any more unsafe blood evidenced that she was about to report to the [FDA].

GHH will argue that Shallal is distinguishable because in that case, the employee discussed with others her desire to report her boss's conduct before confronting her [boss]. Id. at 576. In contrast, Knox did not have any similar activities to demonstrate her actual intent to report MedServe. Therefore, GHH may argue that the court's holding in Richards v. Sandusky Community Schools, 102 F. Supp. 2d 753 (Mich. 2000), is the applicable rule of law for this [case]. In Richards, the employee contacted a few public bodies but never completed the paperwork for complaints regarding her employer's alleged violations of the law. Id. The court held that this fact, by itself, fell drastically short of the clear and convincing proof

**Comment:** String cite order here is correct; statutes, then cases. See Ch. 9, E.6, p. 293.

**Comment:** Writer explains the first sub-element is that plaintiff was "about to report" but fails to explain what "about to" report means, leaving out a critical part of the syllogism: the major premise. See Ch. 5, B.3(a), p. 164.

**Comment:** Date not needed here for short cite.

**Comment:** Need not capitalize "court" in memoranda. See Ch. 9, C.12, p. 278.

**Comment:** Although the reader can infer what "about to" report means by reading the discussion of Shallal, it would be more effective to articulate a rule up front: That an express threat and some additional activity is sufficient to prove "about to report."

**Comment:** Comparison of Knox to Shallal forms minor premise: that Knox made an express threat. Evidence of additional activity would make the comparison stronger.

**Comment:** The writer anticipates the defendant's counter-argument, see Ch. 6, C.1, p. 195, that the cases are distinguishable because Knox did not engage in any additional activity.

**Comment:** Writer here confuses "rule of law" with the concept of *stare decisis*. The rule of law is the same (*i.e.*, threat + action = "about to" report). The writer really means that *Richards* is more analogous and *Shallal* is distinguishable. For that reason, *Richards* would dictate the outcome in Knox's case.

required by the WPA. Id. Because Knox only made a threat but took no other action, a court will probably find that Knox cannot establish being "about to" report MedServe by clear and convincing [evidence].

Knox must also prove that she was about to report a "suspected violation" to meet the "protected activity" test due to lack of evidence that MedServe did violate the law. See] Melchi v. Burns Int'l Sec. Serv., Inc., 597 F. Supp. 575, 583 (E.D. Mich. 1984). The employee must have been acting in good faith and been subjectively reasonable in the belief that the conduct was a violation of the [law]. Smith v. Gentiva Health Serv. Inc., 296 F. Supp. 2d 758, 762 (E.D. Mich. 2003); Melchi, 597 F. Supp. at 583-84. In Melchi, the court, in light of the pervasive regulation of the nuclear power industry, held that it was reasonable for a security guard to believe that his employer violated the law when he observed destruction and falsification of reports and records by the employer, and he reported in good [faith]. Melchi, 597 F. Supp. at 583-584.

Knox will argue that, like in Melchi, it was reasonable for her to believe that MedServe violated the FDA regulation because she observed that the refrigerator registered a higher temperature than required and she still felt it was warmer than normal after the maintenance told her it worked properly. She was also acting in good faith because she was concerned that the blood was unsafe for her [patients].

GHH may counter that, unlike the security guard in Melchi, who saw his employer destroying reports, Knox only guessed that the refrigerator was not working properly based on her own imagination but

**Comment:** Conclusion on whether Knox was "about to" report. This discussion could have been more concise by combining these two paragraphs and stating from the outset that Knox could not prove "about to" without having done more than threaten to report.

**Comment:** Topic sentence indicates paragraph will discuss the second sub-element of first element. Delete portion after "violation" for conciseness.

**Comment:** This sentence forms the major premise, explaining that an employee suspects a violation where she acts in good faith and with a reasonable belief.

**Comment:** A better discussion of this case would have explained the facts indicating the guard acted in good faith.

**Comment:** The comparison leads to the minor premise: That Knox was reasonable and acted in good faith. The comparison is superficial though, because it does not explain how observing the destruction of reports is like suspecting blood is being stored unsafely. Perhaps the writer could have said that common sense indicators to a trained eye that safety precautions are being violated amount to a reasonable suspicion.

no actual [measurement]. However, GHH's argument will probably fail. In view of the strict regulation of FDA on blood storage, the court is likely to hold that Knox, as a trained nurse with responsibility for blood supply, was reasonable believed in good faith that the blood she returned was unsafe for reuse and MedServe violated the law by redistributing [it].

Because MedServe was not Knox's employer, Knox additionally must prove her would-be reporting of a third party falls under the WPA [protection]. See Terzano, 549 N.W.2d at 610-611. The WPA protects an employee who, while acting in the scope of employment, reports third party violations or suspected violations of the law that directly [affects] the employer's [business]. Id. In Terzano, the court held that the employee was protected under the WPA because his supervisor fired him for reporting to a city electrical inspector violations committed by one of his employer's tenants on the employer's [premise]. Id.

Similarly, MedServe is GHH's tenant and providing blood at the hospital. Knox was acting in her capacity as a nurse when she confronted Betz with a suspected violation of the law related to her employer's [business]. Considering the close connection between the alleged violations and the employment setting, a court is likely to hold that Knox's reporting of MedServe constituted protected activity under the [WPA]. Nevertheless, even though Knox was acting in subjective good faith and her reporting of third party violations would be under protection of the WPA, she cannot prove she was about to report violation of the law by clear and convincing evidence. Thus, the court is likely to hold that Knox cannot establish the first element of her prima facie [case].

**Comment:** The writer anticipates the defendant's counter-argument, see Ch. 6, C.1, p. 195, that the employee in Melchi had actual knowledge of the suspected violation, whereas Knox did not.

**Comment:** Conclusion on requirement of reasonable suspicion and good faith.

**Comment:** Although briefly referred to in the Brief Answer, this requirement comes as a bit of a surprise here. The writer indicated above only that Knox must also prove she was going to report to a public body. It would have been more effective if the writer had incorporated this into her synthesized rule at the outset of this discussion.

**Comment:** Watch noun-verb agreement: "violations . . . affect." See Ch. 9, D.13, p. 284.

**Comment:** Major premise is stated here: Third-party violation must directly affect employer.

**Comment:** Sentence is a bit convoluted but attempts to illustrate the rule stated above. The writer does not include how the tenant's violation, the nature of which is unclear, directly affected the employer.

**Comment:** Comparison to Terzano leads to minor premise: That Betz's violation affected GHH. The comparison is weak though because too much information is missing. How did the third-party action affect the employers in these cases? How are they similar? See Ch. 5, C.2(a), p. 174.

**Comment:** Conclusion on third-party violation. The reader is left to infer what the "close connection" means.

**Comment:** Overall conclusion on first element and all sub-elements (i.e., "about to," "suspected violation," and third-party violation).

To satisfy the element of causation, Knox must present evidence that GHH had "objective notice" of her threat to [report]. [See] Roberson v. Occupational Health Ctr. of America, Inc., 559 N.W.2d 86, 88 (Mich. App. 1997); ("'[A]n employer is entitled to objective notice of a report or a threat to report by the whistleblower.'") (quoting Kaufman & Payton, PC v. Nikkila, 503 N.W.2d 728, 732 (Mich. App. [1993)]). In Roberson, the employee failed to show a causal connection because although she told a manager she was about to report the condition of the building to the Occupational Safety and Health Administration (OSHA), there was no evidence that the employer knew about the employee's filing of a complaint with the OSHA until after she was discharged. Roberson, 559 N.W.2d at [88]. Knox will argue that, unlike in Roberson, Betz directly notified Knox's supervisor Kleusing of Knox's threat of reporting MedServe and Kleusing fired Knox one week [later]. A court will find that GHH had objective notice of Knox's threat to report before she was [terminated].

The causation element also requires Knox show something more than a temporal connection between alleged protected conduct and her [termination]. See West v. Gen. Motors Co., 665 N.W.2d 468, 473 (Mich. App. 2003); Taylor v. Modern Eng'g, Inc., 653 N.W.2d 625, 630 (Mich. App. 2002); Roulston v. Tendercare Inc., 608 N.W.2d 525, 530 (Mich. App. 2000). In Roulston, a nursing home discharged the employee a few hours after knowing she had reported her suspicions of resident abuse to state regulators. The court held that the extent of the supervisor's anger with the employee's protected activity and the employee's average

**Comment:** A reminder that the second element is satisfied and the transition to the third element could be more explicit.

**Comment:** Signals should be underlined or italicized. Pick one and be consistent.

**Comment:** Once *Roberson* quoted *Kaufman* it became the law of that case, and the writer could cite it directly without citing back to *Kaufman.* Helps save space. Here, though, the quote adds nothing that is not stated in the writer's text and could be deleted.

**Comment:** Writer states no synthesized rule or major premise on what "objective notice" means.

**Comment:** Because the writer does not include a major premise, the reader must infer from this discussion that if the employer does not know the employee is going to report a suspected violation, intent to report cannot be the cause of an employee's termination. The question remains, though, as to what form of knowledge constitutes objective notice.

**Comment:** Comparison leads to minor premise that unlike in *Roberson,* GHH knew she intended to report.

**Comment:** Conclusion on the "objective notice" requirement. The analysis would have been stronger if the writer had added that there was evidence that Knox's threat to Betz got back to Kleusing, Knox's supervisor.

**Comment:** This second causation requirement comes as a surprise. The writer should have combined the two requirements up front at the beginning of the discussion of this element.
    The statement of the rule or major premise leaves the reader wondering what more is required

rating performance supported that retaliation, not employee's performance, was a motivating factor in the decision to discharge [her]. Roulston, 608 N.W.2d at 530. Similarly, GHH fired Knox one week after it learned of her threat of reporting MedServe, although Knox had worked at GHH for twelve years. Betz's reaction and statements such as "I am getting tired of this" explain why she immediately expressed her displeasure to [Kleusing]. Thus, the circumstances of this case supported an inference of retaliation.

**Comment:** This is a long and confusing sentence that could be written more directly to improve content and conciseness: "The court held that the supervisor's anger about the employee reporting a violation was a motivating factor in her discharge."
Implication here is that employee's reporting must be a motivating factor in the employer's decision to terminate, but the writer left this inference to the reader. This should have been used to formulate the major premise.

GHH may argue that, in contrast to the employee in Roulston, Knox did not have an unblemished [record]. Knox had been reprimanded once due to complaints from a patient, and GHH received more complaints that she was increasingly difficult to work with. Therefore, GHH fired Knox for a legitimate reason. See Deneau v. Manor Care, Inc., 219 F. Supp. 2d 855, 866 (E.D. Mich. 2002) (holding that the employer fired the employee because of her history of inappropriate behavior, and such reason was legitimate and nondiscriminatory).

**Comment:** Comparison to Roulston leads to minor premise: Kleusing was angry about Knox reporting, which motivated him to fire her.

**Comment:** The writer anticipates the defendant's counter-argument, see Ch. 6, C.1, p. 195, that Knox was fired for cause. Writer could have been more clear on that point.

Knox will counter that this was not the true reason for her [discharge]. None of the nurses who had received complaints in 2004 had been disciplined, let alone terminated for cause. GHH's delay in taking action against Knox in relation to that incident evidences the pretextual nature of its stated reasons for [discharge]. See Melchi, 597 F. Supp. at 584 (holding that the employer's stated reasons for discharge was a pretext for retaliation because of its delay in commencing investigation of the employee's alleged acts). Thus, Knox is likely to prevail on the causation [element].

**Comment:** Once the employer states a valid reason for discharge, the burden shifts back to the employee to prove the stated reason is a pretext. The writer could have made that more clear here.

**Comment:** This is an enthymeme in Aristotelian terms. The writer omits the major premise and combines the minor premise and the conclusion: GHH's delay in sanctioning Knox for the 2004 incident proves the stated reason is a pretext. The major premise, that delay in taking action indicates pretext, is implicit.

**Comment:** Overall conclusion on the third element. It would have been more effective if the writer had included all aspects of the element here: objective notice, temporal connection, and pretext.

## Conclusion

Knox is unlikely to succeed in her whistleblower claim against GHH under Michigan law. Although Knox can probably prove she was reasonable in suspecting that MedServe was violating the law and that this violation directly affected GHH's business, she probably cannot prove she was "about to" report the violation to the FDA. Without more than her stated threat, she cannot prove she was going to report with clear and convincing evidence. There is no question regarding the second element, that GHH discharged Knox. As for the third element, Knox can probably prove that a causal connection exists between her threat to engage in protected activity and her discharge. The reason stated by Kleusing, which related back to an incident years before for which no other nurses were sanctioned, is probably a pretext. However, because Knox cannot prove she was "about to" engage in protected activity, she will not succeed in her [claim].

Comment: Conclusion summarizes the rules of law relating to Knox's claim and the writer's reasons for her conclusions as to each. It is more detailed than the Brief Answer and assumes the writer's familiarity with the analysis in the Discussion.

# APPENDIX C

## SAMPLE APPELLATE BRIEF
## (WITH COMMENTS)

■ ■ ■

UNITED STATES CIRCUIT COURT OF APPEALS
FOR THE FOURTH CIRCUIT

_____

CASE NO. CF-0072929

_____

UNITED STATES,
Appellant,

v.

Paul Desmond,
Appellee.

_____

ON APPEAL FROM THE UNITED STATES
DISTRICT COURT
FOR THE EASTERN DISTRICT OF VIRGINIA
Case No. CF-0072929

_____

BRIEF FOR THE APPELLEE

_____

## TABLE OF CONTENTS

**Comment:** Proofread!

**Comment:** This adverb is unnecessary and takes up space. See Ch.9, C.5, p. 276.

. . . . . . . . . . . . . . . . . . . . . . . . . . . . . . . . . . . . . . . . . . . . . . . . .

## TABLE OF AUTHORITIES

## JURISDICTIONAL STATEMENT

The Court has jurisdiction of this matter under 18 U.S.C. § [3731].

## STATEMENT OF THE ISSUE PRESENTED FOR REVIEW

Under the [Federal Constitution], did Officer Kim violate [Paul's] Fourth Amendment rights by conducting a stop and frisk based on Paul standing in his neighborhood with his hands in his pockets, and did the frisk exceed a lawful scope when Officer Kim manipulated an object in a pocket on Paul's jacket that [would not reasonably hold] a [weapon]?

## STATEMENT OF THE CASE

On November 29, 2007, the United States District Court for the Eastern District of Virginia granted Paul's pretrial motion to suppress this evidence, concluding that the stop and frisk conducted by Officer Kim [was in violation of] Paul's Fourth Amendment rights. (Order 1.) The government appeals this ruling.

## STATEMENT OF THE FACTS

Shortly before 8:00 p.m. on November 11, 2007, Paul Desmond stood by his neighborhood 7-[Eleven] when Officer Juan Kim observed him from a distance of forty or fifty yards across five lanes of traffic and subsequently subjected him to a stop and [frisk]. Officer Kim testified that Paul attracted his attention with his overall "[nervous]" appearance, by putting his hands in his pockets, and because he began walking away when he [approached]. (T. 4-5, 19.) Officer Kim testified that Paul matched the broad description of a robbery suspect because he was a "young black male, tall and thin, wearing dark [clothing]." (T.6.)

After observing Paul, the officer entered the

---

Comment: Cases should be underlined or italicized.

Comment: Year of code?

Comment: United States Consitutition?

Comment: It might be a bit too informal to refer to your client by his first name.

Comment: Since part of the test for the frisk is whether the officer could reasonably believe he would find a weapon, it is begging the question to suggest the officer did not have a reasonable belief because he did not have a reasonable belief. See Ch. 5, B.3(e), p. 169.

Comment: Effectively suggests a question to be answered in the affirmative. See Ch. 8, C.2(b)(i), p. 237. Combines controlling law, legal question, and significant facts. Could probably be stated more persuasively (e.g., "standing alone on a cold night with his hands in his pockets").

Comment: Avoid nominalizations. Just say, "Kim violated ..." See Ch. 9, B.2(h), p. 272.

Comment: Writer needs to be more precise. Did he stand by it? At it? In the parking lot of?

Comment: Statement opens with a favorable and then a sympathetic fact for the defendant (i.e., he was just standing there and was subjected to a stop and frisk). See Ch. 6, B.2(c), p. 190.

Comment: The quotation marks help call the officer's characterization of the defendant's behavior into question.

Comment: The use of passive voice here is confusing. Who did the approaching? See Ch. 9, B.1(e), p. 268.

Comment: The quote here attempts to suggest racial profiling but could detract from the writer's credibility on a very sensitive issue. See Ch. 7, A.2, p. 205. A man matching this description had recently robbed the same 7-Eleven.

parking lot in his cruiser and followed with his hazard lights on as Paul left the lot. He approached Paul with his gun drawn, waved him over, and gave orders to "Stop," and "Come here, let me talk to [you]". T. 8, 23.) Faced with an officer ¬ brandishing a drawn weapon, Paul complied when the officer gave the order a second time to stop. (T. 8.)

Officer Kim told Paul that he matched the description of the suspect in a prior [robbery] and instructed him to place his hands on the hood of the police cruiser so that he could be searched for weapons. (T. 26.) Paul immediately cooperated and repeatedly stated that he was not carrying weapons. (T. 10-12.) After finding no weapons in the pockets where Paul's hands were, Officer Kim [focused] on an object in Paul's smaller, inner shirt chest pocket. Officer Kim manipulated and then removed what turned out to be an eyedropper and two glass vials of phencyclidine. (T. 12.)

## SUMMARY OF ARGUMENT

The motion to suppress the evidence was properly [granted]. The Fourth Amendment of the Constitution guarantees the right to be free from unreasonable searches and [seizures]. When Officer ¬ Juan Kim subjected Paul Desmond to a Terry stop and frisk without reasonable suspicion that Paul was involved in a crime or that [he] was armed, he violated that [right].

For an officer of the law to stop an individual, he must have reasonable, articulable suspicion that criminal activity is afoot. [Furthermore], in order to conduct a search, an officer must have reasonable, articulable suspicion that an individual is armed and stay within [the lawful scope] while conducting the frisk. When Paul stood by his neighborhood 7-Eleven on November 11, 2007, he looked nervous, put his hands in his pockets, and then walked in the opposite direction of Officer Kim. As the district court properly concluded, these facts fall short of reasonable, articulable [suspicion] and Officer Kim exceeded the scope of a lawful search by manipulating an object in a pocket unlikely to contain weapons.

## STANDARD OF REVIEW

The issue before the court is whether the trial court erred in suppressing the evidence. The circuit court reviews the legal conclusions regarding reasonable suspicion for a Terry stop de [novo]. United States v. Arvizu, 534 U.S. 266, 275 (2002).

**Comment:** Improper quotation placement. Should be "... you." See Ch. 9, D.1, p. 280.

**Comment:** The writer has yet to state that the description came from the cashier of the same store.

**Comment:** The use of this word is effective in suggesting Kim was motivated by interest, not fear.

**Comment:** The issue statement characterized the issue as Kim having violated Desmond's Fourth Amendment rights. For parallel construction, the writer might have done the same here, instead of referring to the propriety of granting the motion to suppress.

**Comment:** The rule could be stated more effectively from the defendant's point of view here: "The Constitution requires an officer to have a warrant before he can stop and search unless..."

**Comment:** The multiple "he's" here can get confusing. See Ch. 9, D.12, p. 284.

**Comment:** This paragraph introduces the main argument that is detailed below in the following paragraph. The two paragraphs could probably be combined for conciseness reasons.

**Comment:** Explain a bit what reasonable suspicion means?

**Comment:** What is the lawful scope?

**Comment:** Why? The writer's reason is missing.

**Comment:** Need to use comma after "suspicion," because "and" is a coordinating conjunction here. See Ch. 9, D.5, p. 281.

**Comment:** Latin phrases that have become integrated into the law need not be underlined or italicized. ALWD Man. Rule 1.8; BB Rule 7.

## ARGUMENT

I. THE DISTRICT COURT [PROPERLY GRANTED THE MOTION TO SUPRESS BECAUSE] OFFICER KIM LACKED REASONABLE, ARTICULABLE [SUSPICIAN] TO STOP AND SUBSEQUENTLY FRISK MR. DESMOND AND BECAUSE OFFICER KIM EXCEEDED LAWFUL BOUNDS IN PERFORMING THE FRISK.

> **Comment:** Major heading here incorporates conclusion and reason: stop and frisk were unlawful because Kim had no reasonable, articulable suspicion, and he exceeded the lawful scope of a frisk.

> **Comment:** Proofread!

No reasonable, articulable suspicion existed to justify the search of Mr. Desmond under the Fourth [Amendment]. The Fourth Amendment guarantees the "right of the people to be secure in their persons, houses, papers, and effects, against unreasonable searches and seizures." U.S. Const. amend. IV]. A few well-articulated exceptions exist, one being that when a police officer has reasonable suspicion to believe that criminal activity is [afoot] he may ¬ stop and sometimes frisk an individual. Terry v. Ohio, 392 U.S. 1, 29 (1968). Officer Kim's [stop and frisk of Paul was] conducted without reasonable articulable suspicion and exceeded lawful bounds; thus the evidence discovered was correctly deemed inadmissible by the district court.

> **Comment:** Strong topic sentence argues the overall conclusion: That the search that yielded the evidence was unlawful.

> **Comment:** This sentence frames the issue as a Fourth Amendment issue.

> **Comment:** Use comma to set off introductory phrase. See Ch. 9, D.4, p. 281.

> **Comment:** Noun and verb agree here only if the "stop and frisk" is seen as one event.

A. <u>Officer Kim's Stop of Paul Desmond Was Unlawful Because Officer Kim Lacked Reasonable, Articulable Suspicion of Imminent Criminal [Activity].</u>

> **Comment:** Minor heading sets forth the first of two issues under the major heading: the illegality of the stop.

Officer Kim did not have the necessary [reasonable suspicion of imminent criminal activity based on reasonable, articulable facts] to conduct a Terry stop. Reasonable suspicion requires that an officer stopping an individual must have more than an unparticularized [suspicion] and must articulate facts that led him to believe criminal activity was afoot. Illinois v. Wardlow, 528 U.S. 119, 123-24 (2000[)]. The following can help establish reasonable articulable suspicion: an individual engaging in unusual or nervous behavior indicating ¬ imminent criminal activity, Terry, 392 U.S. at 22-34, matching a description of crime suspects, United States v. Swann, 149 F.3d 271, 274 (4th Cir. 1998), fleeing from officers, Wardlow, 528 U.S. 119-120, and standing in a high crime [area], United States v. Bull, 565 F.2d 869, 871 (4th Cir. 1977). [Office] Kim did not observe Mr. Desmond [in any of these behaviors] and thus lacked reasonable, articulable suspicion.

> **Comment:** Not sure both references to reasonable suspicion are necessary, but topic sentence opens well with argument on behalf of defendant regarding the stop.

> **Comment:** Of what?

> **Comment:** Major premise here is that a stop is justified if the officer has reasonable, articulable suspicion (RAS) of imminent crime.

> **Comment:** Writer highlights here the factors relevant to determining RAS in a totality of the circumstances analysis. See Ch. 5, C.2 (c), p. 176.

> **Comment:** Proofread!

> **Comment:** This phrase seems weak; perhaps say that none of Desmond's behavior added up to RAS in this case? That there was nothing suspicious here?

Mr. Desmond's behavior, though [nervous], did not indicate imminent criminal activity because he merely stood by his neighborhood convenience store. Unusual behavior indicating imminent criminal activity includes an individual appearing to carry something heavy in a pocket, United States v. Mayo, 361 F.3d

> **Comment:** Topic sentence indicates paragraph will argue Desmond's behavior did not suggest criminal activity, but why concede nervousness here?

802, 807-08 (4th Cir. 2004), wearing a heavy jacket on a warm day, Bull, 565 F.2d at 871, or "casing" a store, Terry, 392 U.S. at [22-34]. In contrast, Mr. Desmond carried nothing heavy in his pockets and wore a coat prudently on a fall ¬ evening. Moreover, "casing" is defined as individuals walking by a store approximately a dozen times, staring in the store, and conferring intermittently. Terry, 392 U.S. at 6. Mr. Desmond merely stood outside the store and glanced inside. Thus, Mr. Desmond's behavior fails to provide reasonable, articulable suspicion that he was engaging in criminal activity.

Additionally, Officer Kim relied on a generic description of a suspect who robbed the 7-Eleven several weeks earlier, which falls short of reasonable, articulable [suspicion]. Descriptions of suspects can be used to provide reasonable, articulable suspicion when a crime just occurred, Swann, 149 F.3d at 274; the descriptions include specific clothing, id.; and the description comes from a reliable source, United States v. Brown, 401 F.3d 588, 596 (4th Cir. 2005[)]. In contrast to Swann, though a crime occurred previously at the 7-Eleven, Officer Kim's search and frisk of Mr. Desmond occurred ¬ several weeks later, and he had only a general description of a suspect wearing dark [clothes]. Moreover, the description was so broad it can be compared to an anonymous tip. Anonymous tips from sources untested by the police, when not coupled with a prediction of a suspect's future actions to allow for police surveillance, are insufficient for a Terry stop. Brown, 401 F.3d at 596. Thus, Officer Kim's reliance on the overly broad

**Comment:** This sentence forms the major premise or synthesized rule regarding what constitutes unusual behavior. The writer suggests that nervousness does not lead to reasonable suspicion, but that is not really a fair characterization of the law. If the nervous behavior leads an officer to reasonably believe crime may afoot, that could validate a stop. See Ch. 7, A.2., p. 205, on not exaggerating regarding the law. Here, although the reasoning is logical, the major premise is not credible. A more thorough analysis of nervous behavior in other cases is necessary here.

**Comment:** This topic sentence introduces the argument on the second factor—matching a suspect's description can contribute to RAS—but it does not state the gist of the argument forcefully: that the details known to Kim were not specific enough to make reliance on the description reasonable.

**Comment:** This sentence forms the major premise or sythesized rule on how descriptions can lead to RAS. This rule is formulated using the same technique the writer used for the first factor: stringing together specific details from a few cases. Because it is limited to specific facts, it seems too narrow; it might be better to try to state the synthesized rule more generally and from the defendant's point of view: "A description of a suspect can contribute to RAS but only when the information is detailed and reliable."

**Comment:** Here, the writer applies the rule without explaining how it was applied to Swann. Too much information is missing for the analogy to be effective. See Ch. 5, C.2(a), p. 174. How, specifically, does the timing in Swann compare to the timing in this case and why does that matter?

description falls short of the accepted standards of reasonable [suspicion].

Moreover, an individual going on his way, as Mr. Desmond did, does not necessarily constitute reasonable [suspicion]. [Florida] v. Royer, 460 U.S. 491, 497-98 (1983). [Though] Mr. Desmond initially walked away, analogizing this to the flight in Wardlow is a stretch, because Mr. Desmond did not run and stopped when Officer Kim asked him to [stop].

Thus, Mr. Desmond's movement away from Officer Kim is insufficient to establish reasonable [suspicion].

Finally, the circumstances of the surrounding area where Mr. Desmond stood do not establish reasonable, articulable [suspicion]. Areas that contribute to reasonable suspicion are places such as notorious "crack houses," Minn. v. Dickerson, 508 U.S. 366, 377 (1992), or frequently burglarized shopping centers, Bull, 565 F.2d at 871]. Officer Kim testified the area where Mr. Desmond stood contributed to his suspicion because it is a high crime area, but Mr. Desmond standing by his local convenience store at 8:00 p.m. is hardly comparable to a being at a "crack [house]."

Comment: The paragraph here contains a second syllogism in support of the argument on this factor, but the order of the reasoning is reversed. The minor premise (that the description here was equal to the tip in Brown) is first. The major premise (that tips do not add up to RAS) is second. The logic is still understandable, but the argument is weak, because it is not clear why the description is like the tip. See Ch. 5, C.2(a), p. 174.

Comment: It is not clear from the topic sentence that this paragraph is about flight, the third factor.

Comment: Royer does not speak directly to the Desmond case, so a see signal is needed. ALWD Man. Rule 44.3, BB Rule 1.2.

Comment: There is no major premise here. What is the rule on flight?

Comment: This is the minor premise: Desmond did not flee.

Comment: Conclusion: Desmond's "going on his way" did constitute flight.

Comment: Topic sentence indicates writer has moved to the fourth factor. Here is an example where elegant variation can be confusing. Above, the writer described this factor as "standing in a high crime area," but here, describes it as "the circumstances of the surrounding area." Use consistent phrases to avoid ambiguity. See Ch. 9, B.1(d), p. 267.

Comment: Weak major premise/rule on what areas contribute to RAS. As above, this method of stating the rule is akin to the use of parentheticals without textual explanation. It forces the reader to generalize a rule herself with limited information.

Comment: Writer applies rule to facts without adequately explaining how the rule has been applied in prior cases.

If the [standard] Officer Kim suggests is deemed permissible, then Mr. Desmond could not leave his house without establishing reasonable [suspicion]. Thus, the district court's conclusion that Officer Kim's observations fall short of reasonable suspicion ¬ is in agreement with previous [standards] and should be [upheld].

> **Comment:** level of suspicion? See Ch. 9, B.1(d), p. 267.

> **Comment:** Probably an overstatement. Avoid hyperbole of facts and law. See Ch. 7, A.2, p. 205.

> **Comment:** rulings?

### B. Officer Kim's Frisk of Paul Desmond Was Unlawful Because Officer Kim Lacked Reasonable Articulable Suspicion to Believe Mr. Desmond Was [Armed].

> **Comment:** Overall conclusion that factors present in this case do not constitute RAS to stop.

Officer Kim did not have reasonable, articulable suspicion to stop Mr. Desmond, a prerequisite to conduct a frisk, but even if he [did], he lacked reasonable articulate suspicion to believe that Mr. Desmond was armed and dangerous, which is necessary to conduct a frisk for weapons. Mayo, 361 F.3d at 805; Crittendon, 883 F.2d at 328-29. To have reasonable, articulable suspicion for a frisk, an officer must articulate particular facts that led him to believe a suspect was armed, such as the appearance of something heavy in their pocket, id. at 808, an unnecessary jacket on a warm night, Bull, 565 F.2d at 871, or a weapons holster, Crittendon, 883 F.2d at 329]. Officer Kim was unable to describe any concrete facts that would provide ¬ reasonable, articulable suspicion that Mr. Desmond was armed. Officer Kim contends that he believed Mr. Desmond was armed because he put his hand in his pocket, but an individual must do more than just put his hands in his pocket to satisfy reasonable suspicion. United States v. Burton, 228 F.3d 524, 528 (4th Cir. 2000[)]. In Mayo, reasonable, articulable suspicion was found when an individual's hands in his pockets, coupled with the appearance of something heavy in those pockets, led to a lawful [frisk]. Officer Kim could not identify anything specific with regard to Mr. Desmond's pockets that led him to believe he was [armed], and testified, "It wasn't one particular thing." But in order for a police officer to conduct a frisk he must be able to articulate particular facts that led him to believe an individual was [armed]. Mayo, 361 F.3d at 807-08. Officer Kim was unable to articulate any facts that would lead a reasonable person to suspect that Mr. Desmond was armed ¬ because none existed, rendering the frisk [unreasonable].

> **Comment:** Minor heading sets forth the second issue under the major heading: the illegality of the frisk.

> **Comment:** This introduction to the frisk reminds the court that in order to find the evidence admissible, it must find there was RAS to stop and to frisk. The sentence is long though and could be condensed or broken into two.

> **Comment:** This is the major premise: an officer must have RAS to believe a suspect is armed and dangerous. It contains details of cases that indicate what might contribute to RAS to frisk. Again, a more generalized, synthesized rule would be better here.

> **Comment:** Without textual argument, a signal, or a parenthetical, the extent to which Burton supports this proposition is unknown.

> **Comment:** Cite to holding needed here.

> **Comment:** No comma with a compound verb. See Ch. 9, D.5, p. 281.

> **Comment:** The writer has said this already.

> **Comment:** The writer has said this already too. Implicit comparison leads to minor premise that Desmond did not appear to be armed and conclusion that frisk was unlawful. The problem here is that the argument is essentially unsupported by comparison to case law.

## C. Officer Kim Exceeded The Lawful Scope Of A Frisk Because He Manipulated Mr. Desmond's Pocket Before Removing Its Contents.]

Compounding the unlawfulness of the frisk [itself], the scope of the frisk was unlawful because Officer Kim manipulated the object in Mr. Desmond's pocket before removing its contents. In order to assure an officer's safety, Terry permits the officer to seize items he cannot see only if he reasonably suspects them to be weapons. Crittenden, 883 F.2d at [379]. However, where an officer does not suspect the item is a weapon, he may not slide, squeeze, or manipulate the object to determine if it is contraband.] Id. When Officer Kim conducted the frisk, he immediately determined that no weapons were in the specific pockets Mr. Desmond [touched]. Next, Officer Kim touched an object in an upper shirt pocket, testifying that he proceeded to "[feel] around" and was "trying to get ¬ a better feel for what was in [there]." By manipulating the object in Mr. Desmond's pocket to determine its nature, Officer Kim exceeded the permissible scope of a frisk, and the evidence he recovered was properly deemed inadmissible by the district [court].

## CONCLUSION

For the reasons stated above, the district court's ruling was proper and should be [affirmed].

Respectfully submitted,

_____

March 12, 2008

---

**Comment:** This minor heading indicates the writer's argument that the officer exceeded the permissible scope of a Terry frisk.

**Comment:** Tone here effectively creates feelings of criticism toward the officer's actions.

**Comment:** A synthesized rule here would be helpful. What facts lead an officer to believe that an unseen object is a weapon? Does Crittenden shed light here?

**Comment:** These sentences form a loose, major premise: if an officer reasonably believes an unseen object is a weapon, he may seize it.

**Comment:** Strive to be concise: "he determined Desmond had no weapons in his pants pockets."

**Comment:** This is the minor premise: that Kim did not believe the object in the shirt pocket was a weapon.

**Comment:** Conclusion: Kim unlawfully seized the contents of the pocket because it was not obviously a weapon. Again, the logic works, but the argument is unsupported. The reader needs to know what facts would support an officer seizing an unseen object as a potential weapon. See Ch. 5, C.2(a), p. 174.

**Comment:** Conclusion states in one sentence the precise relief sought.

# APPENDIX D

## SUGGESTED ANSWERS TO EXERCISE IN CLARITY AND CONCISENESS

■ ■ ■

*(Exercise appears in Chapter Nine on page 275.)*

Revise each sentence to be more clear and/or concise.

1. The defendant made a clear and unambiguous indication that he neither agreed nor consented to the aforementioned terms of the proposed contract.

> **Sample answer: The defendant indicated that he did not agree to the proposed terms of the contract.**

2. In its opinion, the United States Court of Appeals for the Ninth Circuit held that, thenceforth, any contract to engage in illegal activity would be null, void, and of no effect whatsoever.

> **Sample answer: A contract to engage in illegal activity is void.**

3. Assuming arguendo that Starbucks produces a perishable food product, Starbucks must be proved that CSP knew its statements were false.

> **Sample answer: Even if Starbucks produces a perishable food product, Starbucks must prove CSP knew its statements were false.**

4. On the night in question, one James Riley stood outside the convenience store hoping to make a connection with his said drug-dealer friend, "Slick."

> **Sample answer: On that night, James Riley stood outside the convenience store hoping to meet his drug-dealer friend, "Slick."**

5. The defendant, Hooper, Hardwick and Homer, Inc. (hereinafter "Hooper"), has engaged, inter alia, in a conspiracy to fix, establish, and maintain the price of new and used truck tires in the city of New York and its metropolitan areas.

> **Sample answer: Hooper, Hardwick and Homer, Inc. ("Hooper"), has engaged, among other things, in a conspiracy to fix new and used**

truck tire prices in the New York metropolitan area.

6. It is beyond question that a citizen is allowed to walk away from a police officer without that fact contributing to reasonable suspicion of imminent criminal activity.

**Sample answer: Walking away from a police officer does not contribute to reasonable suspicion of imminent criminal activity.**

7. In order to succeed, the plaintiff must prove that he gave notice to the seller with regard to the defect within a reasonable period of time.

**Sample answer: The plaintiff must prove he notified the seller about the defect within a reasonable time.**

8. The agency cited the respondent for being in violation of the pertinent regulations set forth herein and determined sua sponte to assess a fine.

**Sample answer: On its own initiative, the agency fined the respondent for violating the pertinent regulations.**

9. In no way did the defendant contribute or add to the confusing nature of the situation, making it highly unlikely that he had anything whatsoever to do with the cause of the accident.

**Sample answer: The defendant contributed neither to the confusion nor the cause of the accident.**

10. In the next section of this memo, I will address the three major defenses that were discussed at the meeting.

**Sample answer: Three major defenses were identified at the meeting.**

# APPENDIX E

## SUGGESTED ANSWERS TO EXERCISE
## IN LEGAL WRITING CONVENTIONS

■ ■ ■

*(Exercise appears in Chapter Nine on page 279.)*

Revise each sentence or excerpt to conform to legal writing convention:

1. I think the Court is unlikely to find for the plaintiff.

> **Suggested answer: The court is unlikely to find for the plaintiff.**

2. Under § 15.2(a) of the statute, the defendant isn't entitled to file an additional brief.

> **Suggested answer: Under section 15.2(a) of the statute, the defendant is not entitled to file an additional brief.**

3. The question becomes, "Did the witness commit perjury?"

> **Suggested answer: The issue is whether the witness committed perjury.**

4. The judgment amount represented damages for medical expenses, out-of-pocket costs and attorney's fees.

> **Suggested answer: The judgment represented damages for medical expenses, out-of-pocket costs, and attorney's fees.**

5. The FAA accused United Airlines of violating safety regulations; they said the mechanics weren't thoroughly checking the planes before each flight.

> **Suggested answer: The FAA accused United Airlines of violating safety regulations. It said the mechanics were not thoroughly checking the planes before each flight.**

6. In Terry, the defendant is casing the outside of a store, and the officer thinks he is about to rob it.

**Suggested answer: In *Terry*, the officer observed the defendant casing the outside of a store and thought he was about to rob it.**

7. My research indicates the officer's belief was reasonable. Firstly, the defendant was seen in a dark alley late at night. Secondly, his behavior was suspicious. Thirdly, he took flight as the officer approached.

**Suggested answer: The officer's belief was reasonable: (1) The defendant was seen in a dark alley late at night, (2) his behavior was suspicious, and (3) he took flight as the officer approached.**

8. Clearly, the officer's belief that the suspect was engaged in imminent criminal activity was entirely reasonable.

**Suggested answer: The officer's belief that the suspect was engaged in imminent criminal activity was reasonable.**

9. In so holding, this Court stated:

In cases such as these, where the totality of the circumstances is the key to the validity of the stop, the court must look at each factor and then make a determination as to whether or not the officer's belief is reasonable.

*Jones*, 87 N.W.2d at 75.

**Suggested answer: The Court has emphasized that the key to the reasonableness inquiry is the "totality of the circumstances." *Jones*, 87 N.W.2d at 75.**

10. We believe that our opponent's position isn't supported by the case law.

**Suggested answer: The opponent's position is not supported by case law.**

# Appendix F

## Suggested Answers to Exercise in Grammar, Punctuation, and Usage

■ ■ ■

*(Exercise appears in Chapter Nine on page 285.)*

Correct each sentence:

1. Looking at each element, the plaintiff will not meet it's burden of proof.

   **Suggested answer: The plaintiff will not meet its burden of proof.**

2. If the officer's belief is reasonable they are permitted to conduct a brief investigatory stop without a warrant.

   **Suggested answer: If the officer's belief is reasonable, he may conduct a brief investigatory stop without a warrant.**

3. The court must first terminate the parents rights and then it must determine what is in the child's best interest.

   **Suggested answer: The court must first terminate the parent's (or parents') rights, and then it must determine what is in the child's best interest.**

4. The frisk, that must be based on a reasonable belief that the suspect is armed and dangerous, must be confined to a weapons search.

   **Suggested answer: The frisk, which must be based on a reasonable belief that the suspect is armed and dangerous, must be confined to a weapons search.**

5. An employer is not entitled to unilaterally terminate an employee for "blowing the whistle" on his illegal activities.

   **Suggested answer: An employer is not entitled to terminate unilaterally an employee for "blowing the whistle" on the employer's illegal activities.**

Note: You could decide here that although the infinitive here is split ("to unilaterally terminate"), the sentence sounds better that way.

6. The parties' were unable to agree on contract terms, and thus failed to form an enforceable contract.

> **Suggested answer: The parties were unable to agree on contract terms and thus failed to form an enforceable contract.**

7. An employee who can be fired for any reason is considered "at will;" however, they cannot be fired for reporting illegal activities to the appropriate authorities.

> **Suggested answer: An employee who can be fired for any reason is considered "at will"; however, she cannot be fired for reporting illegal activities to the appropriate authorities.**

8. Starbucks will argue that their coffee beans are not "perishable food products".

> **Suggested answer: Starbucks will argue that its coffee beans are not "perishable food products."**

9. The Joneses primary complaint was that their neighbor's children were effecting there ability to enjoy there backyard.

> **Suggested answer: The Joneses' primary complaint was that their neighbor's children were affecting their ability to enjoy their backyard.**

10. Knowledge of falsity can be imputed, constructive, which means the defendant should have known, or actual.

> **Suggested answer: Knowledge of falsity can be imputed; constructive, which means the defendant should have known; or actual.**

# APPENDIX G

## SUGGESTED ANSWERS TO CITATION EXERCISE FOR PRACTITIONERS

■ ■ ■

*(Exercise appears in Chapter Nine on page 296.)*

Create the proper citations described below:

1. A 2006 case, Michael Davis versus Larry Crawford, decided by the Missouri Court of Appeals, and reported in volume 215 of the third series of the appropriate regional reporter, beginning at page 214.

> **Answer:** ***Davis v. Crawford,* 215 S.W.3d 214 (Mo. Ct. App. 2006).**

2. A second cite to the case in the question above with two intervening cites and to page 215.

> **Answer:** ***Davis,* 215 S.W.3d at 215.**

3. The case of the United States of America versus Arone McConer, found in volume 530 of the Federal Reporter, third series, on page 484. The case was decided by the United States Circuit Court for the Sixth Circuit in 2008.

> **Answer:** ***United States v. McConer,* 530 F.3d 484 (6th Cir. 2008).**

4. A law review article written by Martha Minow. It is entitled: "Should Religious Groups Be Exempt from Civil Rights Laws?" and is found in the Boston College Law Review, volume 48, beginning on page 781. The date of the issue was September 2007.

> **Answer: Martha Minow,** *Should Religious Groups Be Exempt from Civil Rights Laws?* **48 B.C. L. Rev. 781 (2007).**

5. A book entitled "Less Safe, Less Free: Why America Is Losing the War on Terror," by David Cole and Jules Lobel. It was published by the New Press in 2007. Cite to a quotation on page 25 of this book. This is the first time this book has been referenced in your text.

> **Answer: David Cole & Jules Lobel,** *Less Safe, Less Free: Why America Is Losing the War on Terror* **25 (2007).**

6. The seventeenth amendment to the United States Constitution, ratified in 1913. You wish to refer to the second section of the amendment. You found it in a volume of the United States Code Service, published in 1995.

**Answer: U.S. Const. amend. XVII, § 2.**

7. The following section of the General Laws of Massachusetts: Chapter 13, section 426. The Massachusetts legislature enacted this statute on October 11, 1969. The copyright date is 1991. The date on the pocket part is 2006, no change in this section.

**Answer: Mass. Gen. Laws Ann. ch. 13, § 426 (1991).**

8. A short cite to the statute in the question above with no intervening cites.

**Answer: *Id.***

9. A short cite to the statute in Question 7 with intervening cites and to section 428.

**Answer: Ch. 13, § 428.**

10. You assert a proposition that follows from the following two cases: (1) Benjamin Kolmer versus State, reported in volume 977, second series, of the Southern Reporter. The case begins on page 712 and was decided by the Florida District Court of Appeals in 2008, and (2) the United States versus Andrew Sokolow, decided by the United States Supreme Court in 1989 and reported in volume 109 of the Supreme Court Reporter at page 1581 and in volume 490 of United States Reports at page 1.

**Answer: *See United States v. Sokolow*, 490 U.S. 1 (1989); *Kolmer v. State*, 977 So. 2d 712 (Fla. Dist. Ct. App. 2008).**

# BIBLIOGRAPHY

## Articles

Lama Abu-Odeh, *Post-Colonial Feminism and the Veil: Considering the Differences*, 26 NEW ENG. L. REV. 1527 (1992).

Linda L. Berger, *Applying New Rhetoric to Legal Discourse: The Ebb and Flow of Reader and Writer, Text and Context*, 49 J. LEGAL EDUC. 155 (1999).

Duncan Berry, *Speakable Australian Acts*, 8 INFO. DESIGN J. 48 (1995).

Ann E. Berthoff, *From Problem-Solving to a Theory of Imagination*, 33 C. ENGLISH 636 (1972).

Patricia Bizzell, *Cognition, Convention, and Certainty: What We Need to Know About Writing*, 3 PRE/TEXT 213 (1982).

Guido Calabresi & A. Douglas Melamed, *Property Rules, Liability Rules, and Inalienability: One View of the Cathedral*, 85 HARV. L. REV. 1089 (1972).

Guido Calabresi & Jon T. Hirschoff, *Toward a Test for Strict Liability in Torts*, 81 YALE L.J. 1055 (1972).

Ronald Coase, *The Problem of Social Cost*, 3 LAW & ECON. 1 (1960).

Arthur Corbin, *The Law and the Judges*, 3 YALE REV. 234 (1914).

Ruth B. Cowan, *Women's Rights Through Litigation: An Examination of the American Civil Liberties Union Women's Rights Project, 1971-1976*, 8 COLUM. HUM. RTS. L. REV. 373 (1976).

Kimberlé Crenshaw, *Demarginalizing the Intersection of Race and Sex: A Black Feminist Critique of Antidiscrimination Doctrine, Feminist Theory and Antiracist Politics*, 1989 U. CHI. LEGAL F. 139 (1989).

Clare Dalton, *Where We Stand: Observations on the Situation of Feminist Legal Thought*, 3 BERKELEY WOMEN'S L.J. 1 (1988).

Richard Delgado, *The Imperial Scholar; Reflections on a Review of Civil Rights Literature*, 132 U. PA. L. REV. 561 (1984).

Harold Demsetz, *Toward a Theory of Property Rights*, 57 AM. ECON. ASS'N 347 (1967).

Ronald M. Dworkin, *Is Wealth A Value?*, 9 J. LEGAL STUD. 191 (1980).

Robert C. Ellickson, *Property in Land*, 102 Yale L.J. 1315 (1993).

Lucinda M. Finley, *Transcending Equality Theory: A Way Out of the Maternity and the Workplace Debate*, 86 COLUM. L. REV. 1118 (1986).

Judith D. Fischer, *Bareheaded and Barefaced Counsel: Courts React to Unprofessionalism in Lawyers' Papers*, 31 SUFFOLK U. L. REV. 1 (1997).

Lawrence M. Friedman, *The Law and Society Movement*, 38 STAN. L. REV. 763 (1986).

Jane Kent Gionfriddo, *Thinking Like A Lawyer: The Heuristics of Case Synthesis*, 40 TEX. TECH L. REV. 1 (2007).

Charles J. Goetz & Robert E. Scott, *Enforcing Promises: An Examination of the Basis of Contract*, 89 YALE L.J. 1261 (1980).

Gillian K. Hadfield, *Judicial Competence and the Interpretation of Incomplete Contracts*, 23 J. LEGAL STUD. 159 (1994).

Henry Hansmann, *Condominium and Cooperative Housing: Transactional Efficiency, Tax Subsidies, and Tenure Choice*, 20 J. LEGAL STUD. 25 (1991).

Richard L. Hasen, *The Efficient Duty to Rescue*, 15 INT'L REV. L. & ECON. 141 (1995).

Oliver Wendell Holmes, *The Path of the Law*, 10 HARV. L. REV. 457 (1897).

Joseph C. Hutcheson, Jr., *The Judgment Intuitive: The Function of the 'Hunch' in Judicial Decision*, 14 CORNELL L.Q. 274 (1928-29).

Christine Jolls, Cass R. Sunstein & Richard Thaler, *A Behavioral Approach to Law and Economics*, 50 STAN. L. REV. 1471 (1998).

Duncan Kennedy, *Cost Benefit Analysis of Entitlement Problems*, 33 STAN. L. REV. 387 (1981).

Duncan Kennedy, *A Cultural Pluralist Case for Affirmative Action in Legal Academia*, 1990 DUKE L.J. 705.

Duncan Kennedy, *The Structure of Blackstone's Commentaries*, 28 BUFF. L. REV. 205 (1979).

Randall L. Kennedy, *Racial Critiques of Legal Academia*, 102 HARV. L. REV. 1745 (1989).

Phillip C. Kissam, *Thinking (By Writing) About Legal Writing*, 40 VAND. L. REV. 135 (1987).

Christopher C. Langdell, *Teaching Law as a Science*, 21 AM. L. REV. 123 (1887).

Karl N. Llewellyn, *Remarks on the Theory of Appellate Decision and the Rules or Canons About How Statutes Are to Be Construed*, 3 VAND. L. REV. 395 (1950).

Andrea A. Lunsford, *Cognitive Development and the Basic Writer*, 41 C. ENGLISH 38 (1979).

William Lutz, *Notes Toward a Description of Doublespeak (Revised)*, 13 Q. REV. DOUBLESPEAK 10 (1987).

Mari J. Matsuda, *When the First Quail Calls: Multiple Consciousness as Jurisprudential Method*, 14 WOMEN'S RTS. L. REP. 297 (1992).

Carrie Menkel-Meadow, *Toward Another View of Legal Negotiation: The Structure of Problem Solving*, 31 UCLA L. REV. 754 (1984).

Jenny Morgan, *Feminist Theory as Legal Theory*, 16 MELB. U. L. REV. 743 (1988), *reprinted in* 1 FEMINIST LEGAL THEORY (Frances E. Olsen ed., 1995).

Martha C. Nussbaum, *Flawed Foundations: The Philosophical Critique of (a Particular Type of) Economics*, 64 U. CHI. L. REV. 1197 (1997).

Herman Oliphant, *A Return to Stare Decisis*, 14 ABA J. 71 (1928).

Richard A. Posner, *What Do Judges and Justices Maximize? (The Same Thing Everyone Else Does)*, 3 SUP. CT. ECON. REV. 1 (1993).

Christopher Rideout & Jill Ramsfield, *Legal Writing: A Revised View*, 69 WASH. L. REV. 35 (1994).

Ann C. Scales, *The Emergence of Feminist Jurisprudence: An Essay*, 95 YALE L.J. 1373 (1986).

Louis B. Schwartz, *With Gun and Camera Through Darkest CLS-Land*, 36 STAN. L. REV. 413 (1984).

Steven Shavell, *Criminal Law and the Optimal Use of Nonmonetary Sanctions as a Deterrent*, 85 COLUM. L. REV. 1232 (1985).

Special Issue, *Composition as Art*, 15 C. COMPOSITION & COMM. 1 (1964).

Donald Stewart, *Some History Lessons for Composition Teachers*, 3 RHETORIC REV. 134 (1985).

Cass R. Sunstein, Commentary, *On Analogical Reasoning*, 106 HARV. L. REV. 741 (1993).

Kristen K. Robbins (now Robbins-Tiscione), *The Inside Scoop: What Federal Judges Really Think About the Way Lawyers Write*, 8 J. LEG. WRIT. INST. 257 (2002).

Kristen K. Robbins (now Robbins-Tiscione), *Paradigm Lost: Recapturing Classical Rhetoric to Validate Legal Reasoning*, 27 VT. LAW REV. 483 (2003).

Kristen Konrad Robbins-Tiscione, *From Snail Mail to E-Mail: Traditional Legal Memoranda in the Twenty-First Century*, 58 J. LEGAL EDUC. 32 (2008).

Robin West, *Jurisprudence and Gender*, 55 U. CHI. L. REV. 1 (1988).

Joseph Williams, *On the Maturing of Legal Writers: Two Models of Growth and Development*, 1 J. LEG. WRITING INST. 1 (1991).

## Books & Book Chapters

ANDREW ALTMAN, CRITICAL LEGAL STUDIES: A LIBERAL CRITIQUE 13 (1990).

RUGGERO J. ALDISERT, LOGIC FOR LAWYERS: A GUIDE TO CLEAR LEGAL THINKING (3d ed. 1997).

ALWD CITATION MANUAL: A PROFESSIONAL SYSTEM OF CITATION (3d ed. 2006).

AMERICAN JURISPRUDENCE LEGAL FORMS 2D.

ANTOINE ARNAUD & PIERRE NICOLE, LOGIC, OR THE ART OF THINKING (Jill Vance Buroker ed., 1996).

P. AELIUS ARISTIDES, THE COMPLETE WORKS (Charles A. Behr trans., E.J. Brill 1986).

ARISTOTLE, THE ORGANON (Harold P. Cooke & Hugh Tredennick eds., Harv. Univ. Press 1960).

ARISTOTLE, THE WORKS OF ARISTOTLE (W.D. Ross ed., Clarendon Press 1952).

SAINT AUGUSTINE, CONFESSIONS (Henry Chadwick trans., Oxford Univ. Press 1998).

SAINT AUGUSTINE, DE DOCTRINA CHRISTIANA (R.P.H. Green ed. & trans., Oxford Univ. Press 1995).

GILBERT AUSTIN, CHIRONOMIA (1805).

Author Unknown, AD C. HERENNIUM (RHETORICA AD HERENNIUM) (Harry Caplan trans., Harv. Univ. Press 1954).

FRANCIS BACON, *Book 1 of the Advancement and Proficiency of Learning, in* SELECTED PHILOSOPHICAL WORKS (Rose-Mary Sargent ed., 1999).

FRANCIS BACON, *Idols of the Mind, in* RICHARD HUGHES & P. ALBERT DUHAMEL, RHETORIC: PRINCIPLES AND USAGE (2d ed. 1967).

FRANCIS BACON, THE NEW ORGANON (Lisa Jardine & Michael Silverthorne eds., Cambridge Univ. Press 2000) (1620).

ALEXANDER BAIN, ENGLISH COMPOSITION AND RHETORIC (Scholars' Facsimiles & Reprints 1996) (1871).

CAROL M. BALDWIN, PLAIN LANGUAGE AND THE DOCUMENT REVOLUTION (1999).

DERRICK BELL, RACE, RACISM AND AMERICAN LAW (4th ed. 2000).

JEREMY BENTHAM, THE WORKS OF JEREMY BENTHAM (John Bowring ed., 1843).

JAMES A. BERLIN, RHETORIC AND REALITY: WRITING INSTRUCTION IN AMERICAN COLLEGES 1900-1985 (1987).

SIR WILLIAM BLACKSTONE, BLACKSTONE'S COMMENTARIES ON THE LAWS OF ENGLAND (Cavendish 2001) (1768).

HUGH BLAIR, LECTURES ON RHETORIC AND BELLES LETTRES (1833).

BOETHIUS, DE TOPICIS DIFFERENTIIS (Eleonore Stump ed. & trans., Cornell Univ. Press 2004).

THE BLUEBOOK: A UNIFORM SYSTEM OF CITATION (Columbia Law Review Ass'n et al. eds., 18th ed. 2005).

THOMAS BLOUNT, THE ACADEMY OF ELOQUENCE (R.C. Alston ed., Scolar Press Ltd. 1971) (1654).

KENNETH BURKE, A GRAMMAR OF MOTIVES (1945).

KENNETH BURKE, A RHETORIC OF MOTIVES (1950).

STEVEN J. BURTON, AN INTRODUCTION TO LAW AND LEGAL REASONING (3d ed. 2007).

GEORGE CAMPBELL, A DISSERTATION ON MIRACLES (Gardner Books 2007) (1762).

GEORGE CAMPBELL, PHILOSOPHY OF RHETORIC (Charles Ewer ed., 1823).

MARTHA CHAMALLAS, INTRODUCTION TO FEMINIST LEGAL THEORY (1999).

VEDA R. CHARROW ET AL., CLEAR AND EFFECTIVE LEGAL WRITING (4th ed. 2007).

STUART CHASE, THE POWER OF WORDS (1953).

GEOFFREY CHAUCER, THE CANTERBURY TALES (Jill Mann ed., Penguin Classics 2005).

CICERO, CICERO IN TWENTY-EIGHT VOLUMES (H.M. Hubbell trans., Harv. Univ. Press 1971).

CICERO, DE INVENTIONE (H.M. Hubbell trans., 1968) (c. 87 B.C.).

CICERO, DE ORATORE (E.W. Sutton trans., 1967) (c. 55 B.C.).

CICERO, DIVISIONS OF ORATORY (H. Rackham trans., Harv. Univ. Press 2004).

LANE COOPER, THE RHETORIC OF ARISTOTLE (1932).

EDWARD P.J. CORBETT, CLASSICAL RHETORIC FOR THE MODERN STUDENT (4th ed. 1999).

MARTIN CUTTS, THE PLAIN ENGLISH GUIDE (1995).

RENÉ DESCARTES, DISCOURSE ON METHOD AND THE MEDITATIONS (John Veitch trans., Prometheus Books 1989).

RONALD DWORKIN, LAW'S EMPIRE (1986).

LINDA H. EDWARDS, LEGAL WRITING AND ANALYSIS (2d ed. 2007).

PETER ELBOW, WRITING WITHOUT TEACHERS (2d ed. 1998).

JANET EMIG, THE COMPOSING PROCESS OF TWELFTH GRADERS (1971).

ANN ENQUIST & LAUREL CURRIE OATES, JUST WRITING: GRAMMAR, PUNCTUATION, AND STYLE FOR THE LEGAL WRITER (2d ed. 2005).

ERASMUS, DE DUPLICI COPIA VERBORUM AC RERUM (Craig R. Thompson ed., Univ. of Toronto Press 1978) (1528).

ESSAYS ON CLASSICAL RHETORIC AND MODERN DISCOURSE (Robert J. Connors et al. eds., 1984).

DANIEL FOGARTY, ROOTS FOR A NEW RHETORIC (1959).

JEROME FRANK, LAW AND THE MODERN MIND (1949).

JAMES A. GARDNER, LEGAL ARGUMENT: THE STRUCTURE AND LANGUAGE OF EFFECTIVE ADVOCACY (1993).

BRYAN A. GARNER, LEGAL WRITING IN PLAIN ENGLISH (2001).

BRYAN A. GARNER, THE ELEMENTS OF LEGAL STYLE (2d ed. 2002).

BRYAN A. GARNER, THE REDBOOK: A MANUAL ON LEGAL STYLE (2d ed. 2006).

JOHN F. GENUNG, PRACTICAL ELEMENTS OF RHETORIC (1885).

CAROL GILLIGAN, IN A DIFFERENT VOICE: PSYCHOLOGICAL THEORY AND WOMEN'S DEVELOPMENT (1982).

JAMES L. GOLDEN ET AL., THE RHETORIC OF WESTERN THOUGHT (6th ed. 1997).

JAMES L. GOLDEN & EDWARD P.J. CORBETT, THE RHETORIC OF BLAIR, CAMPBELL, AND WHATLEY (1968).

H.L.A. HART, THE CONCEPT OF LAW (1961).

EKATERINA V. HASKINS, LOGOS AND POWER IN ISOCRATES AND ARISTOTLE (2004).

JOHN HOSKINS, DIRECTIONS FOR SPEECH AND STYLE (Hoyt H. Hudson ed., Princeton Univ. Press 1935).

RICHARD HUGHES & ALBERT DUHAMEL, PRINCIPLES OF RHETORIC (1967).

DAVID HUME, A TREATISE OF HUMAN NATURE (David Fate Norton & Mary J. Norton eds., Oxford Univ. Press 2000).

DAVID HUME, AN ENQUIRY CONCERNING HUMAN UNDERSTANDING (Tom L. Beauchamp ed., Oxford Univ. Press 2000).

ISOCRATES, ISOCRATES (Michael Gagarin ed., David Mirhady & Yun Lee Too trans., U. Texas Press 2000).

DUNCAN KENNEDY, *Legal Education as Training for Hierarchy, in* POLITICS OF LAW: A PROGRESSIVE CRITIQUE (David Kairys ed., 1982).

GEORGE A. KENNEDY, CLASSICAL RHETORIC & ITS CHRISTIAN AND SECULAR TRADITION FROM ANCIENT TO MODERN TIMES (2d ed. 1999).

JAMES L. KINNEAVY, A THEORY OF DISCOURSE (1971).

WILLIAM P. LaPIANA, LOGIC & EXPERIENCE: THE ORIGIN OF MODERN AMERICAN LEGAL EDUCATION (1994).

LAW AND ECONOMICS (Jules Coleman & Jeffrey Lange eds., 1992).

Charles Lawrence III, *The Id, the Ego, and Equal Protection Reckoning with Unconscious Racism, in* CRITICAL RACE THEORY: THE KEY WRITINGS THAT FORMED THE MOVEMENT (Kimberlé Crenshaw et al. eds., 1995).

TERRY LeCLERCQ, GUIDE TO LEGAL WRITING STYLE (3d ed. 2004).

EDWARD H. LEVI, AN INTRODUCTION TO LEGAL REASONING (1949).

KARL N. LLEWELLYN, THE BRAMBLE BUSH: ON OUR LAW AND ITS STUDY (1960).

JOHN LOCKE, AN ESSAY CONCERNING HUMAN UNDERSTANDING (John Yolton ed., Dutton rev. ed. 1964) (1689).

ANDREA A. LUNSFORD & JOHN J. RUSZKIEWICZ, EVERYTHING'S AN ARGUMENT (1999).

CATHERINE A. MacKINNON, FEMINISM UNMODIFIED: DISCOURSES ON LIFE AND LAW (1987).

CATHERINE A. MacKINNON, SEXUAL HARASSMENT OF WORKING WOMEN (1979).

DAVID MELLINKOFF, THE LANGUAGE OF THE LAW (1963).

MARTHA MINOW, MAKING ALL THE DIFFERENCE: INCLUSION, EXCLUSION, AND AMERICAN LAW (1990).

JAMES J. MURPHY, RHETORIC IN THE MIDDLE AGES: A HISTORY OF RHETORICAL THEORY FROM SAINT AUGUSTINE TO THE RENAISSANCE (1974).

JAMES J. MURPHY & RICHARD A. KATULA, A SYNOPTIC HISTORY OF CLASSICAL RHETORIC (3d ed. 2003).

James J. Murphy, *Rhetorical History as a Guide to the Salvation of American Reading and Writing: A Plea for Curricular Courage, in* THE RHETORICAL TRADITION AND MODERN WRITING (James J. Murphy ed., 1982).

RICHARD K. NEUMANN, JR., LEGAL REASONING AND LEGAL WRITING (5th ed. 2005).

THE OXFORD CLASSICAL DICTIONARY (Simon Hornblower & Antony Spawforth eds., 3d ed. 1996).

THE OXFORD COMPACT ENGLISH DICTIONARY (Catherine Soanes ed., 2d ed. 2003).

CHAIM PERELMAN, JUSTICE, LAW, AND ARGUMENT (1980).

CHAIM PERELMAN & LUCIE OLBRECHTS-TYTECA, THE NEW RHETORIC: A TREATISE ON ARGUMENTATION (1958).

CHAIM PERELMAN, THE NEW RHETORIC AND THE HUMANITIES (1979).

CHAIM PERELMAN, THE REALM OF RHETORIC (William Kluback trans., Univ. of Notre Dame Press 1982).

LES PERELMAN, *The Medieval Art of Letter-Writing: Rhetoric as an Institutional Expression, in* TEXTUAL DYNAMICS OF THE PROFESSIONS (CHARLES BAZERMAN & JAMES PARADIS EDS., 1991).

PHILOSOPHICAL WORKS OF DAVID HUME (T.H. Green & T.H. Grose eds., 1964).

A.C. PIGOU, THE ECONOMICS OF WELFARE (4th ed. 1958).

PLATO, COMPLETE WORKS (John M. Cooper ed., Hackett Pub. Co. Inc. 1997).

RICHARD A. POSNER, ECONOMIC ANALYSIS OF LAW (7th ed. 2007).

QUINTILIAN, INSTITUTIO ORATORIO (Donald A. Russell trans. & ed., Harv. Univ. Press 2001).

JILL J. RAMSFIELD, THE LAW AS ARCHITECTURE: BUILDING LEGAL DOCUMENTS (2000).

PETER RAMUS, LOGIKE (1574).

MARY RAY & JILL J. RAMSFIELD, LEGAL WRITING: GETTING IT RIGHT AND GETTING IT WRITTEN (4th ed. 2005).

WAYNE A. REBHORN, RENAISSANCE DEBATES ON RHETORIC (2000).

I.A. RICHARDS & C. K. OGDEN, THE MEANING OF MEANING (1923).

I.A. RICHARDS, THE PHILOSOPHY OF RHETORIC (1936).

CHARLES ROLLIN, THE METHOD OF TEACHING AND STUDYING THE BELLES LETTRES (A. Bettesworth & C. Hitch trans., 1734).

W. D. ROSS, ARISTOTLE'S PRIOR AND POSTERIOR ANALYTICS (Leonardo Taran ed., Garland Publishing, Inc. 1980) (1949).

ANNETTE T. ROTTENBERG, THE STRUCTURE OF ARGUMENT (3d ed. 2000).

KAREN A. SCHRIVER, DYNAMICS IN DOCUMENT DESIGN (1997).

WILLIAM SHAKESPEARE, HAMLET (New Folger ed., Wash. Square Press 2003).

WILLIAM SHAKESPEARE, ROMEO AND JULIET (New Folger ed., Wash. Square Press 2004).

WILLIAM SHAKESPEARE, THE SECOND PART OF KING HENRY VI (New Folger ed., Wash. Square Press 1988).

THOMAS SHERIDAN, A COURSE OF LECTURES ON ELOCUTION (Benjamin Blom, Inc. 1968) (1762).

RICHARD SHERRY, A TREATISE OF SCHEMES AND TROPES (1550).

A SHORT HISTORY OF WRITING INSTRUCTION FROM ANCIENT GREECE TO TWENTIETH-CENTURY AMERICA (James J. Murphy ed., 1990).

DONALD C. STEWART, THE AUTHENTIC VOICE: A PRE-WRITING APPROACH TO STUDENT WRITING (1972).

JONATHAN SWIFT, THE BATTLE OF THE BOOKS (Sir Henry Craik ed., 1912).

JONATHON SWIFT, A PROPOSAL FOR CORRECTING, IMPROVING AND ASCERTAINING THE ENGLISH TONGUE (R.C. Alston ed., Scolar Press 1969) (1712).

JONATHAN SWIFT, GULLIVER'S TRAVELS (The Modern Library 1931).

SELECTED WRITINGS OF FRANCIS BACON (Hugh C. Dick ed., 1955).

ST. JEROME, THE PERPETUAL VIRGINITY OF BLESSED MARY: AGAINST HELVIDIUS (c. 383). http://www.cin.org/users/james/files/helvidiu.htm (last visited April 2, 2008).

TAKIS POULAKOS, SPEAKING FOR THE POLIS (1997).

THOMAS SHERIDAN, A COURSE OF LECTURES ON ELOCUTION (1762, reissued 1968).

WILLIAM STRUNK, JR. & E.B. WHITE, THE ELEMENTS OF STYLE (4th ed. 1999).

LARRY L. TEPLY, LEGAL WRITING ANALYSIS, AND ORAL ARGUMENT (1990).

STEPHEN E. TOULMIN, THE USES OF ARGUMENT (Cambridge Univ. Press updated ed. 2003) (1958).

ROBERTO M. UNGER, KNOWLEDGE & POLITICS (1975).

ROBERTO UNGER, THE CRITICAL LEGAL STUDIES MOVEMENT (1986).

BRIAN VICKERS, IN DEFENCE OF RHETORIC (1988).

GIAMBATTISTA VICO, THE ART OF RHETORIC (Giorgio A. Pinton & Arthur W. Shippee trans. & eds., 1996) (c. 1711-44).

GIAMBATTISTA VICO, THE NEW SCIENCE OF GIAMBATTISTA VICO (Thomas Goddard Bergin & Max Harold Fisch trans., Cornell Univ. Press 3d ed. 1984) (1744).

JOHN WALKER, ELEMENTS OF ELOCUTION (R.C. Alston ed., Scolar Press 1969) (1781).

JOHN WARD, A SYSTEM OF ORATORY (1759).

RICHARD M. WEAVER, LANGUAGE IS SERMONIC (Richard L. Johannesen, Rennard Strickland & Ralph T. Eubanks eds., 1970).

RICHARD WEAVER, THE ETHICS OF RHETORIC (1953).

WEST'S LEGAL FORMS.

RICHARD WHATELY, ELEMENTS OF RHETORIC (Douglas Ehninger ed., 1963).

JOSEPH WILLIAMS, STYLE: LESSONS IN CLARITY AND GRACE (9th ed. 2006).

THOMAS WILSON, THE ART OF RHETORIC (Peter Medine ed., Penn. State Univ. Press 1994) (1560).

THE WRITING TEACHER'S SOURCEBOOK (Gary Tate & Edward P.J. Corbett eds., 2d ed. 1988).

• Robert J. Connors, *The Rise and Fall of the Modes of Discourse*, 32 C. COMPOSITION & COMM. 444 (1981).

• Linda Flower & John R. Hayes, *The Cognition of Discovery: Defining a Rhetorical Problem*, 31 C. COMPOSITION & COMM. 21 (1980).

• Sondra Perl, *Understanding Composing*, 31 C. COMPOSITION & COMM. 363 (1980).

• Nancy Sommers, *Revision Strategies of Student Writers and Experienced Adult Writers*, 31 C. COMPOSITION & COMM. 378 (1980).

THE WRITING TEACHER'S SOURCEBOOK (Gary Tate, Edward P.J. Corbett & Nancy Myers eds., 3d ed. 1994).

- JAMES A. BERLIN, CONTEMPORARY COMPOSITION: THE MAJOR PEDAGOGICAL THEORIES,

THE WRITING TEACHERS' SOURCEBOOK (Edward P.J. Corbett, Nancy Myers & Gary Tate eds., 4th ed. 2000).

- James Berlin, *Rhetoric and Ideology in the Writing Class*
- Lisa Ede & Andrea Lunsford, *Audience Address/Audience Invoked: The Role of Audience in Composition Theory and Pedagogy*
- James A. Reither, *Writing and Knowing: Toward Redefining the Writing Process*

RICHARD WYDICK, PLAIN ENGLISH FOR LAWYERS (5th ed. 2005).

RICHARD YOUNG, PARADIGMS AND PROBLEMS: SOME NEEDED RESEARCH IN RHETORICAL INVENTION, RESEARCH ON COMPOSING: POINTS OF VIEW OF DEPARTURE (Charles R. Cooper & Lee Odell eds., 1978).

Richard E. Young & Alton L. Becker, *Toward a Modern Theory of Rhetoric*, reprinted in CONTEMPORARY RHETORIC: A CONCEPTUAL BACKGROUND WITH READINGS (W. Ross Winterowd ed., 1975).

## Cases & Briefs

Brief of Appellants, Brown v. Board of Educ., No. 1, 347 U.S. 483 (1955), 1952 WL 82041.

Califano v. Goldfarb, 430 U.S. 199 (1977).

Clinton v. Jones, 520 U.S. 681 (1997).

Brief of Petitioner, Clinton v. Jones, No. 95-1853, 520 U.S. 681 (1997), 1996 WL 448096.

Brief of Respondent, Clinton v. Jones, No. 95-1853, 520 U.S. 681 (1997), 1996 WL 509501.

Dawson v. Cal. Dep't of Corr., No. C 05-2253, 2006 WL 2067078 (N.D. Cal. July 25, 2006).

F.D.I.C. v. Maxxam, Inc., 523 F.3d 566 (5th Cir. 2008).

Frontiero v. Richardson, 411 U.S. 677 (1973).

Glassalum Engineering Corp. v. 392208 Ontario Ltd., 487 So. 2d 87 (Fla. Dist. Ct. App. 1986).

Gosnell v. Rentokil, Inc., 175 F.R.D. 508 (N.D. Ill. 1997).

Henderson v. State, 445 So. 2d 1364 (Miss. 1984).

*In re* Hawkins, 502 N.W.2d 770 (Minn. 1993).

Matter of Generes, 69 F.3d 821 (7th Cir. 1995).

Reed v. Reed, 401 U.S. 71 (1971).

Brief of Appellants, Roe v. Wade, No. 70-18, 410 U.S. 113 (1973), 1971 WL 128054.

Smith v. United Transp. Union Local No. 81, 594 F. Supp. 96 (S.D. Cal. 1984).

Schneckloth v. Bustamonte, 412 U.S. 218 (1973).

Wallace v. Mercantile County Bank, 514 F. Supp. 2d 776 (D. Md. 2007).


## Statutes, Orders, Rules & Model Laws

ARIZ. SUP. CT. R.

Center for Professional Responsibility of the American Bar Association, Dates of Adoption of the Model Rules of Professional Conduct by State, http://www. abanet.org/cpr/mrpc/alpha_states.html (last visited October 15, 2008).

Exec. Order No. 12,044, 3 C.F.R. 152 (1978).

Exec. Order No. 12,174, 3 C.F.R. 462 (1980).

FED. R. APP. P.

FED. R. CIV. P.

MD. CT. R.

MODEL RULES OF PROF'L CONDUCT (2008), *available at* http://www.abanet.org/cpr/ mrpc/home.html.

TEX. CIV. PRAC. & REM. CODE ANN. " 96.001-.004 (2007).

TEX. R. APP. P.


## Other

ABRAHAM LINCOLN, The Gettysburg Address (November 19, 1863), *available at* http://showcase.netins.net/web/creative/lincoln/speeches/gettysburg.htm.

ARNOBIUS, AGAINST THE HEATHEN (c. 303), http://www.newadvent.org/fathers/06311. htm (last visited Aug. 25, 2008).

GIDEON O. BURTON, SILVA RHETORICAE, http://humanities.byu.edu/rhetoric/Silva. htm (last visited May 18, 2008).

Independent Counsel's Report to Congress on the Investigation of President Clinton (Sept. 9, 1998), *available at* http:// thomas.loc.gov/icreport/.

MARTIN LUTHER KING, JR., *I Have A Dream* (Aug. 28, 1963), *in* RIPPLES OF HOPE: GREAT AMERICAN CIVIL RIGHTS SPEECHES (Josh Gottheimer ed., 2003).

THOMAS J. KINNEY, THE COMMON TOPICS (2003-04), http://www.u.arizona. edu/?tkinney/pdf/handouts/commontopics.pdf

MICHAEL QUINION, *World Wide Words* (April 25, 2008), http://www.worldwidewords. org/qa/qa-ona1.htm.

# FIGURES INDEX

# Names and Subject Index

CASES:

†